Communism on Tomorrow Street

Communism on Tomorrow Street

Mass Housing and
Everyday Life after Stalin

Steven E. Harris

Woodrow Wilson Center Press
Washington, D.C.

The Johns Hopkins University Press
Baltimore

EDITORIAL OFFICES

Woodrow Wilson Center Press
One Woodrow Wilson Plaza
1300 Pennsylvania Avenue, N.W.
Washington, D.C. 20004-3027
Telephone: 202-691-4029
www.wilsoncenter.org

ORDER FROM

The Johns Hopkins University Press
Hampden Station
P.O. Box 50370
Baltimore, Maryland 21211
Telephone: 1-800-537-5487
www.press.jhu.edu/books/

Library of Congress Cataloging-in-Publication Data

Harris, Steven E. (Steven Emmett)
    Communism on tomorrow street : Mass housing and everyday life after
Stalin / Steven E. Harris.
        pages ; cm
    Includes bibliographical references and index.
    ISBN 978-1-4214-0566-7 (hardcover : alkaline paper)
    1. Housing—Soviet Union—History.   2. Public housing—Soviet
Union—History.   3. Housing policy—Soviet Union.   4. Communism
and architecture—Soviet Union.   I. Title.
    HD7345.A3H33   2012
    363.5′85094709045—dc23   2012007460

Wilson Center

The Woodrow Wilson International Center for Scholars is the national, living US memorial honoring President Woodrow Wilson. In providing an essential link between the worlds of ideas and public policy, the Center addresses current and emerging challenges confronting the United States and the world. The Center promotes policy-relevant research and dialogue to increase understanding and enhance the capabilities and knowledge of leaders, citizens, and institutions worldwide. Created by an act of Congress in 1968, the Center is a nonpartisan institution headquartered in Washington, D.C., and supported by both public and private funds.

Conclusions or opinions expressed in Center publications and programs are those of the authors and speakers and do not necessarily reflect the views of the Center staff, fellows, trustees, advisory groups, or any individuals or organizations that provide financial support to the Center.

The Center is the publisher of *The Wilson Quarterly* and home of Woodrow Wilson Center Press and *dialogue* television and radio. For more information about the Center's activities and publications, please visit us on the Web at www.wilsoncenter.org.

To Ginochka, Henry Francis, and Emmett Alexey
and our life together on Tomorrow Street

Contents

Tables and Figures

Figures

Acknowledgments

Because I took substantially longer to write a book about Soviet mass housing than it took Khrushchev to build it, I benefited from the help of many people along the way. My initial interest in Soviet housing and everyday life arose from my experience of living in a communal apartment (*kommunalka*) in Saint Petersburg when I taught English at School No. 157 in the mid-1990s. Like most Westerners, the extraordinariness of the *kommunalka* helped maintain Russia's exotic Soviet otherness for me at a time when Russians only seemed to want to forget the Soviet past and become a normal Western country. Little did I know then that the housing in which most Petersburgers lived—single-family apartments in the mass housing that encircled their city—was also a Soviet story whose ordinariness as a way of life obfuscated its extraordinary role in shaping Soviet history after Stalin.

When I began graduate school at the University of Chicago in 1996, I initially stuck to the exotic for my M.A. thesis and focused on the communal apartment at the very start of the Soviet experiment. When it came time to choose a dissertation topic, Sheila Fitzpatrick, my adviser and mentor, suggested that I examine what happened in the Soviet housing picture under Khrushchev. At first I was skeptical of venturing so far into the later decades of Soviet history and especially beyond the 1920s, the era that had caught my imagination as an undergraduate student in Donald Raleigh's courses at the University of North Carolina, Chapel Hill. Moreover, like much of the Soviet field, most Russian history graduate students at Chicago were immersed in dissecting the Stalin period; the Khrushchev era and beyond were still terra incognita for most of us. Ultimately, my move from the communal apartment to a separate apartment (*khrushchevka*), and from the Stalin era to the Khrushchev period, came at exactly the right time in the flow of Soviet historiography. In choosing to study the *khrushchevka*, I was thus fortunate enough to be part of an emerging wave of graduate students and scholars who wanted to know what became of Soviet life after Stalin.

The first life of this book was thus a Ph.D. dissertation in history, which I researched in the archives of Moscow and Saint Petersburg, and wrote in the city of Chicago. I thank Sheila Fitzpatrick for teaching me the craft of history and for encouraging me to venture into the Khrushchev period. I also thank the other members of my Ph.D. committee—Ronald Suny, Michael Geyer, and the late Richard Hellie—for their invaluable advice on this book's first draft. As a graduate student at Chicago, I benefited greatly from the intellectually vibrant community of Russian history graduate students. The legendary Russian Studies Workshop—where graduate students and outside scholars presented their works in progress—was a critical part of our training. It was there, as first-year graduate students, where we saw what went into the research and writing of Soviet history, and where we later presented our own dissertation chapters after months or in some cases years in the archives.

Among my fellow graduate students at Chicago, I especially thank Stephen Bittner for blazing the trail into the Khrushchev period with his study of the social and intellectual life of the Arbat. His book on Khrushchev's thaw has had an enormous influence on my own work, and his sharp feedback on my entire book has made it better. I thank Charles Hachten, whose expertise on Soviet property relations and law improved my understanding of these topics. Jonathan Bone, Chris Burton, Michael David, Matthew Lenoe, Steven Richmond, Joshua Sanborn, and Alison Smith, who were all completing their dissertations when I arrived in Chicago, proved to be indispensable unofficial older mentors. I am also indebted to Kiril Tomoff, with whom I shared an excellent separate apartment on my first research trip to Moscow in 1998, for helping me navigate Russian archives and libraries and their many strange rituals.

At Chicago, I also benefited from the European History Workshop and its graduate students, who challenged me to think more broadly and theoretically about my work on Soviet housing. I thank in particular Dana Simmons, whose Ph.D. dissertation on "Minimal Frenchmen" has shaped my understanding of the pan-European origins of the *khrushchevka*'s design. I also thank Stephen Sawyer, who was the first to encourage me to think about how Soviet urban dwellers' move to the separate apartment could help us rethink the thaw by paying closer attention to its social dynamics outside high politics and high culture.

Like most Russian history graduate students from Chicago and elsewhere, I became an unapologetic "archive rat," who dove headlong into the recently opened archives of the former Soviet Union. For a total of almost two years, I lived in Moscow and Saint Petersburg, and immersed myself in the rich archival holdings of state, party, and arts and literature archives, as well as the two cities' libraries. Local scholars and the expatriate group of foreign graduate students provided a vibrant intellectual community and indispensable help in finding new sources and thinking about one's project in a new way. Back in the United States, I benefited from the critical feedback that many scholars provided on my work at many conferences and workshops. I thank in particular Heather DeHaan, Miriam Dobson, John Farrell, Juliane Fürst, Andrew Jenks, Polly Jones, Sharon Kowalsky, Ann Livschiz, Kristin Roth-Ey, Shawn Salmon, Paul Stronski, Il'ia Utekhin, Vadim Volkov, Amir Weiner, and Elena Zubkova for their help with my project and for many great conversations about Soviet history and the *khrushchevka*.

In addition to the scholars who were beginning to do archival research on the Khrushchev period (many of whom are listed above), I have greatly benefited over the years from those who shared my interests in housing and architecture, domestic life and mass consumption, and urbanization in state socialist regimes. I am especially indebted to Greg Castillo for his critical feedback on my entire book. His work on domestic design in the United States, East and West Germany, and the Soviet Union has greatly advanced our understanding of the transnational dimensions of mass housing and consumption. I also thank Daria Bocharnikova, Ekaterina Gerasimova, Stephen Lovell, Julia Obertreis, Karl Qualls, Susan Reid, and Christine Varga-Harris for their scholarship and feedback on my project. In its latter stages, I benefited additionally from György Péteri's work on transnational exchanges during the Cold War. I thank him for encouraging me to expand a conference paper about Soviet architects' contacts with their Western counterparts, the result of which was my short book *Two Lessons in Modernism: What the* Architectural Review *and America's Mass Media*

Taught Soviet Architects about the West. Although the content of this work does not appear in the present book, its focus on transnational history helped me sharpen my analysis of the *khrushchevka*'s pan-European origins.

The second life of my book has taken place primarily in Washington, where I relocated in 2003 for what I thought would be just one year on a Kennan Research Scholarship. The Kennan Institute and the Woodrow Wilson International Center for Scholars provided a stimulating environment and excellent research resources for beginning the long task of transforming my lengthy dissertation into a manuscript. Blair Ruble, the director of the Kennan Institute, whose own work on Soviet housing and urban history has shaped how many of us understand these topics, has been a valued mentor. I also thank my research assistant at the Kennan Institute, William Clark, for his indispensable help in tracking down and researching sources at the Library of Congress, and for our many conversations about conspiracy theories.

I am indebted to many individuals at the Woodrow Wilson Center Press and the John Hopkins University Press for their work in transforming my manuscript into a book. I especially thank Joe Brinley, the director of the Woodrow Wilson Center Press, for his guidance and encouragement on completing my manuscript since I was a research scholar at the Kennan Institute. I also thank MacKenzie Cotters and Cherie Worth of the Woodrow Wilson Center Press and Christina Cheakalos and Karen Willmes of the Johns Hopkins University Press for their work on this project. In addition, I am indebted to Melody Wilson for her work editing my manuscript and answering my many questions over email, and to Alfred Imhoff for his thorough copyediting of the manuscript. Throughout this book, I use the transliteration system of the Library of Congress for all Russian words rendered in English. All translations are my own, unless otherwise noted, and any mistakes are likewise my own.

Fortunately for me, my year at the Kennan Institute coincided with the inaugural year of a new Russian history workshop hosted by Georgetown University. The Russian History Seminar of Washington has become a premier venue for Russian historians presenting their works in progress. I thank Eric Lohr for organizing this group and Catherine Evtuhov, David Goldfrank, and the late Richard Stites for hosting it over the years. I am also indebted to Michael David-Fox, another member of our Washington *kruzhok*, for his critical feedback on various aspects (and chapters) of my book. Soon after arriving at the Kennan Institute, Michael encouraged me to write a book review, which ultimately turned into my review essay "In Search of 'Ordinary' Russia: Everyday Life in the NEP, the Thaw, and the Communal Apartment," which was published in *Kritika: Explorations in Russian and Eurasian History*. This essay and Michael's feedback helped me think more critically about how the differences between communal and separate apartments have shaped scholars' approach to Soviet housing and everyday life, including my own, as noted at the beginning of these acknowledgments. Working on this review essay also focused my attention on scholars' study of "ordinary people" in Soviet history and what we mean by invoking this admittedly amorphous category.

After my year at the Kennan Institute, I was fortunate to be hired as a postdoctoral teaching fellow in Western civilization at George Mason University. During my two years at George Mason, I benefited from a new community of historians and scholars, and gained invaluable experience teaching undergraduate students. I thank the Russian historians there—Steven Barnes and Rex Wade—and my fellow postdoctoral colleagues—Charles Lipp, Timur Pollack-Lagushenko, Matthew Romaniello, Matthew Specter, and Allan Tulchin—for our excellent conversations between classes and their feedback on my project. I also thank Mills Kelly for running the Western Civilization Program at George Mason and for his support in preparing for the job market. His insightful suggestion that Khrushchev's regime faced a crisis of rising expectations that grew out of the mass housing program became an enduring theme in my book.

While I was at George Mason University, I also worked on two related articles. I thank Rex Wade for inviting me to write an essay on mass housing and generational conflict for a special edition of *The Soviet and Post-Soviet Review*. The result was my article "'We Too Want to Live in Normal Apartments': Soviet Mass Housing and the Marginalization of the Elderly under Khrushchev and Brezhnev." I also thank Lewis Siegelbaum for inviting me to contribute my essay "'I Know All the Secrets of My Neighbors': The Quest for Privacy in the Era of the Separate Apartment" to the volume *Borders of Socialism: Private Spheres of Soviet Russia*. I thank both Rex and Lewis for their critical feedback on early drafts of these projects. Although neither of my two essays appears in this book, each helped me develop some of its key themes. The first one allowed me to explore more fully how urban residents perceived and shaped the waiting list for housing as a register of social hierarchies, and the second one focused my attention on the ways that urban residents turned to, instead of away from, the Soviet state to secure the autonomy and greater privacy promised by mass housing.

After two years at George Mason University, I was fortunate to be hired in 2006 as an assistant professor of history at the University of Mary Washington, where I presently teach courses in Russian and European history, as well as conspiracy theories. I thank my colleagues in the Department of History and American Studies—Nabil Al-Tikriti, Porter Blakemore, Sue Fernsebner, Claudine Ferrell, Jeff McClurken, Krystyn Moon, Bruce O'Brien, Allyson Poska, and Jess Rigelhaupt—for their support and encouragement as I completed my book. I also thank my students for their patience in listening to my many tales of living in a communal apartment and lectures on mass housing.

Over the years, the personnel at many archives and libraries in the United States and Russia provided indispensable aid as I researched my topic. As a graduate student, the University of Chicago's Regenstein Library provided an incredible collection of primary and secondary sources that allowed me to begin my dissertation research. I thank the Slavic bibliographer June Farris for helping me locate sources in the library's rich collection on many occasions and for helping me understand how Russian-language sources are organized in American libraries. I am indebted to the archivists and staffs of the many archives I used in Moscow and Saint Petersburg for helping me locate valuable materials and allowing me to bivouac for months at a time in their reading rooms. I thank the librarians and staff of Moscow's Russian State Library (or "Leninka") and the State Public Historical Library (or "Istorichka") as they are affectionately known. I also thank the librarians and staff of the National Library of Saint Petersburg (or "Publichka") for its warm atmosphere and the most democratic system of reading rooms, and the Academy of Sciences Library, also in Saint Petersburg. In Washington, I am fortunate to claim the Library of Congress as my neighborhood, municipal library. The librarians and staff of the European Reading Room have helped me on countless occasions to track down sources and find new ones, and even survive the earthquake of 2011 with good humor.

This book was also made possible by generous funding from several sources. Funding from the University of Chicago allowed me to undertake my graduate studies and provided additional research grants for travel to Russia. Research fellowships from the U.S. Information

Agency and the Fulbright-Hays Program allowed me to conduct extensive research in Russia, and a fellowship from the Social Sciences Research Council made it possible to complete my dissertation. A Research Scholarship from the Kennan Institute made it possible to begin revising my dissertation into a manuscript. A Faculty Development Grant and Jepson Fellowship from the University of Mary Washington, and a Bernadotte Schmitt Grant from the American Historical Association allowed me to complete the final stages of research and writing.

During the year I spent teaching English in Saint Petersburg and on several return trips, many Petersburgers opened their homes to me and extended their friendship to a young American curious about their country and way of life. Igor Persianov, a fellow teacher at School No. 157, deserves special thanks for finding me a room in my first *kommunalka* on Vasilievskii Island. I thank my dear friend Alexander Vlasov for helping me enjoy and make sense of that experience and of much else from the Soviet past that remains in Russia's post-Soviet existence. I thank Alexander and his *kruzhok* of archaeology enthusiasts for taking me along to Uglich on two archaeological digs and for many other adventures. I also thank Elena Lagutina and Andrei Pochinkov for endless evenings and conversations spent in the kitchen of their unusually long communal apartment off Nevskii Prospekt and for letting me rent a room in that apartment (the last of its kind in a building whose apartments have all gone "separate").

Thanks to these friends and many more local residents of Russia's Northern Capital, Saint Petersburg has remained my home away from home in Russia. I thank John Bailyn and Wallace Sherlock for organizing the "Petro-Teach" program that originally brought me to the city and allowed me to teach English to so many wonderful and intelligent students at School No. 157 in the Smolny district. If I had not stumbled across a flyer advertising their program during my last year at the University of North Carolina (back in the days when flyers were the main way one found out about such things), I might never have gone to Russia to begin with or have simply ended up in Moscow. I am also greatly indebted to the encouragement and instruction I received as an undergraduate from Donald Raleigh at North Carolina. Don's electrifying courses in Soviet history got me interested in the field late in my undergraduate career and convinced me that being a historian was a worthwhile pursuit. His enthusiasm for the study and teaching of all things Soviet and Russian has been an inspiration, and his encouragement over the years has helped me finish this book.

I thank my late father, Emmett Harris, and my mother, Pierrette Harris, for all their love, support, and patience over the many years that I have devoted to studying Russia, going there, and working on this project. I also thank my mother-in-law, Sharon Faranda, for her encouragement and enthusiasm. Luckily for me, my wonderful and loving older sister, Anne, was already at the University of Chicago when I got there, completing her Ph.D. in art history. Anne and her husband Mac, who was also finishing his Ph.D. in art history at the university, helped me navigate the waters of graduate school and thrive in its rigorous intellectual environment. I dearly value our "Chicago years" together, which we divided between our neighborhood on the Near North Side of this great American city and the University of Chicago in Hyde Park, with incredible modern art and architecture in between. I thank them both for listening to me talk endlessly about Soviet housing over the years and for their indispensable feedback at each stage of writing this book. Their three children, Oliver, Iris, and Eleanor, have made our lives since Chicago even more fun. I love being your uncle! Now get to work on your dissertations.

Beginning with my year at the Kennan Institute, I was fortunate to find a new community of friends and fellow scholars in my new home, Washington. I especially thank Margaret Paxson and Charles King for our many conversations about Soviet history and how to write a book about it. Their many insights and support have made this a better book, and their friendship has made living in Washington more enjoyable than I ever imagined. I also thank Nida Gelazis for her feedback on my project and for introducing all of us to Lithuanian *kugelis*. To the members of "Tashi station"—Fred Jacob, Kevin "Kevstar" Morse, and Prophet Dan Steinberg—I extend my deep gratitude for teaching me the ways of American popular culture and for helping me find the love of my life, your fellow Tashi comrade, Regina Faranda.

I thank my wife, Gina, for making it possible for me to finish a project I should have completed long before we met. When we went on our first date, she asked me where my book was. Here it is! I share her devotion to the first duty and the respect she has for ordinary Russians who say what they think and do what they want. And now I share in the *vospitanie* of our wonderful young sons, Henry and Emmett, who were born in Washington. I dedicate this book to Gina, Henry, Emmett and our life together on Tomorrow Street.

Communism on Tomorrow Street

Introduction:
Moving to the Separate Apartment

The year 1956 was a tumultuous one for the Soviet Union. In February, its new leader, Nikita Khrushchev, stunned the party faithful at the Twentieth Communist Party Congress with a stinging denunciation of Joseph Stalin's crimes. Khrushchev's "Secret Speech" was a dramatic moment in turning the page on Stalin's bloody regime, encouraging a thaw in state-society relations, and reviving the country's quest for communism. But by year's end, Khrushchev was meting out his own brutal repression to Hungarians for daring to declare that they would define their own course and even reject the Warsaw Pact.

Below the surface of these well-known events, daily transformations were taking place in the Soviet Union, whereby ordinary citizens tested the waters of Khrushchev's thaw, unsure of where the new limits lay, but determined to make the most of Soviet life after Stalin. Though lacking the political spotlight of the "Secret Speech" or the geopolitical drama of the Hungarian Revolution, ordinary Soviet citizens' words and actions could be dramatic in their own right and can tell us as much, if not more, about what this post-Stalinist existence and Khrushchev's reforms were all about. The present study examines the reform in which most citizens were eager to participate: Khrushchev's campaign to resolve the "housing question" (*zhilishchnyi vopros*) by moving people out of overcrowded communal housing and into single-family, separate apartments. As I argue in this book, moving to the separate apartment was the way most ordinary people experienced and shaped Khrushchev's thaw.

1

To begin our investigation, let us start with a forgotten story of revolt in 1956, far removed from the streets of Budapest but right under
Khrushchev's nose in Moscow. In December 1956, the Ministry of Internal Affairs (Ministerstvo Vnutrennikh Del, MVD) informed the
Communist Party's Central Committee that 131 workers, joined by
their families, had squatted under cover of night in twenty apartments
in a new building. The laborers were all employed by the state in housing construction, with some working for a construction firm and others
at a factory producing reinforced concrete.[1] They were workers at
the forefront of new housing construction and prefabrication technologies that produced the ubiquitous five-story apartment blocks of the
Khrushchev era (figure I.1). The single-family apartments in these
buildings would later become known as *khrushchevki* (singular: *khrushchevka*), a nickname that mocked their diminutive stature and forever
linked them to Khrushchev. But for these workers desperate for better housing, the *khrushchevka*, or "the separate apartment" (*otdel'naia
kvartira*), as it was commonly and officially called, was as much theirs
as it was the state's or Khrushchev's, and no less desirable for its paltry
dimensions.

The previous living conditions of these workers and their families—
a dormitory in which three to four families were crammed into individual rooms 28 to 32 square meters in size—made even the smallest
khrushchevka seem like a luxury. The new building's proximity to their
present dwelling just one street away suggested how frustrating it must
have been to live in their incredibly overcrowded dormitory, while
building new housing. (Whether the laborers had worked on the building they took over was unclear, and how the families planned to divvy
up twenty apartments among what appeared to be 131 households was
also uncertain.) The squatters' action suggested a subversive Marxist
interpretation of exploited workers taking back the fruits of their labor
through collective action. In their dormitory and through their work,
the workers and their families had constituted a community where they
shared the same grievances and trusted one another enough to plan the
takeover of a building and face the repercussions together. Their strategy, as far as the MVD account indicated, was to hold out until the
local authorities caved in and allowed them to have their new homes.[2]

The district prosecutor at first ordered the police to evict the squatters. Whether the police tried to use force was unclear, but whatever
they did evidently failed. Subsequently, local party and soviet (munici-

Figure I.1. A Khrushchev-Era Apartment Building in Contemporary Saint Petersburg, October 2010.

Source: Photographed by the author.

pal) officials tried negotiating with the squatters to get them back to their dormitory. But the squatters held fast to their demands that the authorities issue them housing permits and turn on the building's water and gas. For three days already they had barricaded themselves in the building and created a human barrier at its entrance with pregnant women in front, followed by women and children, and men in the back. Their dramatic display of civil disobedience and the powerful symbolism evoked in its gendered organization came through even in the dry MVD report chronicling their revolt. The most physically vulnerable members of the community held its greatest power and were practically daring the police of one of the most violent and murderous regimes in world history to violate their power by force. The squatters gambled that the authorities would take pity on people who needed good housing. Insofar as avoiding physical removal was concerned, their strategy had thus far worked. Even the MVD wanted nothing to do with these squatters and referred the Moscow police to the city procuracy for help in evicting them if all else failed. By the third day of the squatters' action, the police had evidently chosen not to use force and were hoping that the more civil approach of negotiation or simply leaving the squatters in the dark without water would eventually work.[3]

The MVD report does not tell us what ultimately happened to the squatters. Yet this two-page snapshot of these workers' lives raises questions that this book seeks to answer about where ordinary people and Khrushchev's attempts to adequately house them fit in the Soviet experiment after Stalin. As the squatters' story suggests, mass housing was not something that the "state" created for "society," as if one was entirely separate from the other. These workers were agents of the state as builders of housing, but they were also members of families and together formed a community that was willing to take dramatic action to get better housing. How does such a blurring of the lines between state and society help us rethink who made the separate apartment under Khrushchev and who could claim it to be theirs? What roles did ordinary citizens play in this campaign to modernize urban life and continue the project of creating a classless society? What kind of post-Stalinist subject did the new social spaces of mass housing and its official discourses produce in conjunction with what ordinary people said and did in their everyday lives?

In December 1956, Khrushchev's moves to overcome the "excesses" of Stalin's terror state were hardly permanent, as the events in Budapest made clear. The unpredictable nature of this post-Stalinist existence raises other questions about the Moscow squatters' actions. In their desperate, last-ditch attempt to ameliorate their living conditions, the squatters risked provoking the wrath of the world's most powerful totalitarian regime. What convinced these people that this was a wise decision and that they were entitled to their own, single-family apartments? The MVD, evidently paralyzed by the power that pregnant women wielded, preferred negotiation over violence to resolve the situation. What did such an uncharacteristically restrained response by the Soviet Union's organ of internal police suggest had happened to the state's willingness to use violence and terror since Stalin's death? What, if anything, did mass housing have to do with the Soviet state's decision to curtail its use of mass violence and terror under Khrushchev?

In addressing these questions, this book demonstrates how the state *and* its citizens made a distinctly Soviet version of mass housing that forever changed the country and what its people expected to gain from socialism. At the center of this study is the story of ordinary urban dwellers and their move from communal apartments, barracks, and dormitories to separate apartments. I use residents' mass, internal migration out of the housing that they had been forced to share with others and into their own private apartments as a frame for exploring the Soviet Union's broader move out of the Stalin era and into the Khrushchev period. When the members of a family left their communal apartment (*kommunal'naia kvartira* or *kommunalka*) for a separate apartment, they left behind the Stalinist past as embodied in their previous housing for a new and empty apartment, a clean slate mirroring the uncharted reformism and "thaw" of the Khrushchev era. After architects and urban planners had done their work, these ordinary residents set about building communism on "Tomorrow Street"—as portrayed in Yuri Pimenov's famous painting (see below)—by inhabiting the empty and sometimes incompletely built spaces of mass housing. Moving to the separate apartment is an ideal metaphor for exploring the transition from Stalinism to the Khrushchev era; but unlike most metaphors, it was experienced by millions of people annually. From 1953 to 1970, the Soviet government and its citizens in both cities and the countryside constructed 38,284,000 apartments and individually built homes, which permitted 140,900,000 individuals to acquire newly built housing.[4]

This book contributes to a growing body of scholarship that examines the critical roles that mass housing and consumption played in the post-Stalinist reinvention of the Soviet Union and other state socialist regimes such as East Germany and Czechoslovakia.[5] Blair Ruble's earlier study remains the most succinct account of Khrushchev's mass housing campaign, the design of the *khrushchevka*, and its limitations in meeting Soviet citizens' needs.[6] Scholars have subsequently explored the mass housing campaign through analyses of specific topics of the overall project, such as property relations and gender.[7] Turning our attention to architectural history, Stephen Bittner has examined how mass housing intersected with the high cultural politics of the thaw and debates over the architectural legacies of the Soviet and pre-Soviet past.[8] Examining the prescriptions for consumer behaviors and domestic tastes in official discourses on mass housing, scholars have interpreted the *khrushchevka* as a central site in the Khrushchev regime's project to fulfill the revolutionary goals of creating a New Soviet Man and Woman.[9] In a series of important articles, Susan Reid has studied several different topics, such as the intersection of gender and Cold War politics, the scientific discourses that informed mass housing, and urban residents' comments at furniture exhibitions.[10]

Building upon this scholarship, the present study seeks to provide the most comprehensive and integrated historical analysis of the design, distribution, and consumption of Soviet mass housing and ordinary people's experience of moving to the separate apartment. Scholars of Soviet social history have paid the greatest attention to such groups as workers, the intelligentsia, peasants, the family, women, and nationalities. This book shifts our attention to the ordinary residents of mass housing and the separate apartment as a new social group that began to take shape under Khrushchev in a newly built environment on the outskirts of the Soviet cityscape. Like the couple and their neighbors in Pimenov's iconic painting of the period, *Wedding on Tomorrow Street* (1962), shown as figure I.2, urban dwellers entered their new neighborhoods and apartments full of anticipation about a new way of life that awaited them. As Pimenov's painting suggests, Communism on Tomorrow Street was a work in progress, whose final steps ordinary residents would need to take on their own. In adapting the title of his painting for the title of this book, I point to my exploration of how ordinary people's expectations for the future and their lived experience intersected in mass housing with the regime's own hopes of reviving the communist project after Stalin. To explain how this occurred and why it mattered, this book examines the history of Soviet mass housing in three historical contexts: the international "housing question" that originated in the pan-European housing reform movement of the nineteenth century; the goals and legacies of the Russian Revolution; and the "thaw" in state-society relations after Stalin.

The Housing Question

Far from being a uniquely Soviet experience under Khrushchev, mass housing transformed cities around the world in the second half of the twentieth century, from Chicago and Moscow to Brasilia and Islamabad. As a major project of the modern welfare state, it provided millions of urban dwellers with single-family apartments designed according to standardized plans in high-density, multistory buildings. Its minimalist

Figure I.2. *Wedding on Tomorrow Street*, by Yuri Pimenov, 1962.

aesthetics and prefabricated materials promised a postwar urban existence permeated by scientific planning and synthetic materials. Countries around the world built mass housing to sustain or attain modernization and to at last resolve the "housing question" of the nineteenth century.

After World War II, mass housing emerged as a universal form of habitation that met the needs of the masses in vastly different contexts, including postwar reconstruction in Europe and the building of a new capital in Brazil. It existed across political and socioeconomic systems, from capitalist liberal democracies to socialist one-party states and the postcolonial developing world. Mass housing was thus a global phenomenon that created the foundations of a common urban existence across borders, while still allowing states an opportunity to emphasize their fundamental ideological differences. One of these states was the Soviet Union, which emerged in the second half of the twentieth century as a superpower on the world stage after more than thirty years of revolution, wars, and brutal dictatorship.

The Soviet system of housing that Khrushchev inherited from Stalin was one particular, if extreme, outcome of the pan-European housing reform movement and its adherents' search for a definitive solution to the housing question. European social reformers and governments since the nineteenth century had positioned the housing question as a subset of the overall "social question," both of which crystallized during and after World War I when state intervention in social and economic spheres such as housing massively expanded. Whereas other combatant states retreated from such interventions after the war, the new Soviet state remained firmly entrenched, driven by its Marxist-Leninist ideology to create a classless society and facing few obstacles from a decimated civil society.[11]

The Soviet Union subsequently failed to resolve the housing question during the New Economic Policy (NEP) and under Stalin. But the NEP and the Stalin era were not merely periods in which housing conditions worsened, only to be suddenly set on an entirely new course by Khrushchev's team of reformers. Instead, Khrushchev's regime built the mass housing campaign upon the economic, architectural, and legal frameworks of a housing sector forged since 1917, particularly under Stalin before the war.[12] What was new about Khrushchev's approach in contrast to Stalin's were massive investments of material, financial, and labor resources, and a renewed commitment to finally resolve the housing question.

But Khrushchev's mass housing campaign was not only a Soviet story of reform after Stalin. Equally important to explaining how it ultimately shaped ordinary residents' everyday lives were its origins in the ideas of the nineteenth-century pan-European housing reform movement, especially norms for minimum living space, whose adaptation by the Bolsheviks and long-term impact on the design and distribution of the *khrushchevka* remain little understood by historians. In its broadest historical context, mass housing under Khrushchev was the realization of the Bolsheviks' original plans for housing, whereby the workers' state would eliminate once and for all the pan-European housing question of industrializing societies by providing all citizens with adequate and healthy habitation on an egalitarian basis. As this book seeks to show, the ordinary resident of mass housing who lived in the *khrushchevka* was the social product of an enormous state experiment in building housing that had its origins in nineteenth-century housing reform ideas and their particular evolution in the Soviet context.

Mass Housing and the Russian Revolution

As those Moscow workers who squatted in a new apartment building in 1956 showed, mass housing's appearance in the Soviet cityscape could trigger desperate actions among residents eager to immediately improve their living conditions. It seemed that everyone wanted to get more out of this project and to do it more quickly than was humanly possible.

Instead of definitively resolving the housing question, I argue in this book, Khrushchev's regime touched off a crisis of rising expectations that affected all major actors. Under Khrushchev, the leadership's expectations of what mass housing could do stoked its broader utopian plans for building communism and beating the capitalist West in the competition over living standards. In 1957, Khrushchev's regime boldly announced that all housing shortages would be eradicated within ten to twelve years.[13] This deadline set a powerful precedent for Khrushchev's better-known declaration in 1961 that Soviet society would build communism by 1980.[14] Local soviet officials and factory managers believed that waiting lists for living space would finally be cleared and that labor turnover would be reduced once factories had satisfied their workers' housing needs. The architects of mass housing saw it as an unprecedented opportunity to expand their power to reshape the everyday lives of an entire society through the rational organization of space. The members of the cultural intelligentsia who were charged with explaining to urban dwellers the proper ways of living in a separate apartment believed that they could at last rid society of its philistine tendencies and raise the "culturedness" (*kul'turnost'*) of all Soviet citizens.[15] Meanwhile, the urban dwellers languishing in communal apartments and dormitories put incredible pressure on Khrushchev's regime to fulfill its goal of putting all Soviet families in separate apartments. But once they got there, these residents found themselves writing new petitions about construction and design defects, while others searched stores in vain for new furniture and household goods.

What did people—from the top leaders to the ordinary urban dweller—do when their expectations continued to rise in the face of a reality that never seemed to catch up? The answer to this question focuses our attention on how the Khrushchev period differed from the Stalin era and the violent legacy of the Soviet Union's origins in the Russian Revolution. In the face of an important campaign's shortcomings and failures, state and society under Khrushchev did not engage in mass terror. This was unusual in a country where waging war on society had been the government's modus operandi and executing scapegoats was the norm when things did not go as planned. After the Russian Revolution of October 1917, the Bolsheviks used Marxist ideology to sanction the mass murder of their perceived enemies and the violent destruction of the old ways of life to achieve their revolutionary aims: an industrialized and classless society free of exploitation and enjoying material plenty. Khrushchev's regime, scholars have shown, saw itself reviving and advancing, rather than abandoning, these aims of the Russian Revolution and used mass housing to bring them about.[16] As will be shown in this book, Khrushchev's regime embarked on the mass housing campaign to finish two incomplete projects of the Russian Revolution—resolving the housing question and constructing communism—but without mass violence and terror.

Although historians have examined the intersection of housing, terror, and coercion from the Russian Revolution to Stalin's years in power, they have yet to explore the connection between mass housing and the Khrushchev regime's abandonment of terror and mass violence.[17] This book argues that the two were closely related and mutually reinforcing. As a campaign that mobilized human, financial, and material resources to fulfill a state objective, mass housing was nothing new. Under Stalin, the state mobilized society and its resources for collectivization, rapid industrialization, and war. But unlike these past campaigns, Khrushchev's mass housing program was the first major campaign in Soviet history that did not result in the widespread destruction of human life.

In choosing the separate apartment, state and society were choosing a different set of political and social relations than those of the Russian Revolution and Stalinist past. Under Khrushchev, the architects, constructors, municipal government functionaries, and local party members who were responsible for shortcomings in housing still risked public reprimands and demotions, but they were not labeled enemies of the people or executed. Instead of relying on neighbors denouncing each other as enemies of the people, the state under Khrushchev used nonviolent "social organizations" to have citizens bring each other into line.[18] By taking warring neighbors out of communal apartments and putting them into single-family apartments, Khrushchev's regime reinforced its turn away from terror in everyday life. In short, when the Soviet state provided an individual and his or her family with their own toilet, it was making an investment in the civil order of a new society whose members would be trained to use their new private spaces responsibly and to police one another in the public spaces of the mass housing community.

Mass housing's role in fulfilling the Russian Revolution by civil means was further reflected in one of its most understated, but revealing, features: the broad consensus between state and society on the superiority of the single-family, separate apartment and their shared distaste for communal housing. How did this consensus emerge? When and why did state and society "choose" the separate apartment over the alternatives? These questions draw our attention to the origins of the separate apartment, the very existence of which in the Soviet Union should strike us as an ideological anomaly. After all, what was a single-family apartment with the trappings of bourgeois family life—privacy, traditional gender roles, new consumer goods, and aspects of private ownership— doing in a socialist country in the first place?

Under the Tsarist regime, workers languished in overcrowded tenements and factory barracks while the single-family apartments of the bourgeoisie and aristocracy stood out as symbols of class inequalities and exploitation. In the wake of the October Revolution, the Bolsheviks and their fellow travelers waged war on the family, private property, and traditional life as pillars of the Tsarist order. The family would soon "wither away," once collectivist living arrangements had laid the foundations for socialism in everyday life. From the perspective of these early Bolshevik visions, the separate apartment was not the solution but the problem. But by the mid-1950s, Khrushchev's regime presented mass housing and the separate apartment as the long-awaited fulfillment of the Bolsheviks' revolutionary aims to resolve the housing question and create a classless society.

As I argue in this book, the consensus on making the separate apartment a mass phenomenon in Soviet life began to take shape under Stalin before the war. Stalin's and Khrushchev's regimes contributed different elements to this consensus, which reflected the cultural values and social priorities of each. The Stalinist regime marginalized radical architectural theories on collectivist living and rehabilitated the single-family apartment as a "cultured" form of urban housing that reflected Stalinism's profamily values and social stratification. Stalin's regime made separate apartments available only to the elites in the party-state hierarchy, industry, and the cultural intelligentsia, while the rest of society made do in communal apartments, barracks, and dormitories. By the time Khrushchev came to power, the single-family apartment had thus already emerged as the ideal, if extremely scarce, form of urban housing. What made Khrushchev's approach different was his decision to make the separate apartment a mass phenomenon. Through the mass housing campaign, his regime distributed separate apartments to the one social group—the family—that cut across all other social divisions. This reflected and advanced the populism of his social agenda like no other reform. For the first time in Soviet history, the state was taking significant steps to improve the housing conditions of most urban dwellers and fulfill the egalitarian promise of the Russian Revolution.

The Separate Apartment and the Thaw

In the early 1950s, the Soviet Union's housing crisis intersected with the political turmoil brought about by the country's search for new leadership and new directions after Stalin's death. Khrushchev ultimately emerged as the country's new leader and spearheaded fundamental reforms to the socialist system until his removal from power in 1964. Both contemporary observers and scholars have described the period after Stalin as a "thaw" in state-society relations, during which the Communist Party curtailed the worst excesses of Stalinism and allowed for greater freedoms in social and cultural life.[19] Whereas historical periods typically acquire their labels after the fact, the origins of the term "thaw" were situated at the very beginning of this era, when the Soviet writer Ilya Ehrenburg wrote his 1954 novella *The Thaw* (*Ottepel'*).

Ehrenburg's tale, set in a provincial town far from the high politics of Moscow, examines the lives of several couples in the local Soviet intelligentsia that undergo turbulent changes in their love lives, family relationships, and careers in the transitory period between a harsh winter's closing weeks and the dawn of a liberating spring. The novella's main point is that there is more to life than meeting production quotas or enduring loveless marriages. People have personal needs and desires, which must also be fulfilled alongside work to achieve one's full potential as a human being. Removed from its mid-twentieth-century Soviet context, Ehrenburg's novella is a modern tale of urban professionals anywhere in the world attempting to achieve a balance between their private and professional lives with enough spare time on their hands to contemplate the meaning of the choices they face. But in its post-Stalinist context, the novella also captured the sense of the new opportunities and changes that people enjoyed as the deep freeze of Stalinism gave way to an uncertain but invigorating set of alternatives for what lay in the future.[20]

In the wake of Ehrenburg's novella, images of ice melting after years of deep freeze became the choice metaphor for repairing the injustices of the Stalin years and describing positive change under Khrushchev. The 1961 film *Clear Skies* (*Chistoe nebo*) depicted a river breaking out of its freeze as the sign that the political reforms of a new day would allow the hero (a fighter pilot previously disgraced for having been a prisoner of war) to become whole again in his personal life and regain his Communist Party membership. In a similar fashion, mass housing would allow families, individuals, and apartments to become whole again following the violence of the Stalin years, which had torn apart people's lives and homes. The fragmented world of communal apartments was subdivided between warring neighbors and reflected the upheavals of life under Stalin. In theory, the move to a fully integrated, family apartment in a well-designed neighborhood would repair that fragmented existence and resolve any tension between public and private life.

Although Ehrenburg made only vague references in his novella to dramatic changes in high politics following Stalin's death, the dilapidated state of industrial workers' housing emerges in his story as a central sign of the Stalinist state's neglect of people's everyday material lives and the positive improvements that must come once the thaw begins.[21] The factory director Ivan Zhuravlev's decision to endlessly postpone the construction of new housing for his workers in favor of production ultimately ruins him. When an unexpected storm destroys their makeshift habitats, he is called to Moscow to answer for his misplaced priorities and loses his job. As spring arrives, the company town at last sees the construction of workers' new housing.

The industrial workers who are the beneficiaries of such change and their role in the novella suggest that not all members of this community are meant to experience the thaw in the same way. The representatives of the Soviet intelligentsia at the center of Ehrenburg's story—teachers, painters, engineers, and students—grapple with the weighty issues of love, art, and death in a changing world and exercise their agency by making life-changing decisions at critical moments. In contrast, ordinary workers are faceless, passive characters on the margins of the novella, who are to be pitied for their dire living conditions and fate at the hands of nature's arbitrariness and a neglectful boss but who are properly grateful once construction gets going.

Scholars, inspired in part by Ehrenburg's story, have used the "thaw" as an organizing concept to examine the new and unpredictable ways that people—namely, the cultural intelligentsia—could talk and act after Stalin's death. In this sense, the thaw represents a mentalité, made possible but also delimited by the top leadership through such actions as Khrushchev's "Secret Speech," the dismantling of the Gulag, and the rehabilitation of those repressed under Stalin.[22] For other scholars, the thaw represented a relaxation of controls within the state apparatus, which enterprising members of the cultural intelligentsia exploited to reshape education and popular tastes in matters ranging from clothing to home décor. Still others use the thaw to describe the emergence of the Soviet Union's foreign policy of peaceful coexistence with the West and its greater openness to cultural contacts with the outside world.[23]

In addition to the thaw, scholars have employed the concept of "de-Stalinization" to describe the reforms of the Khrushchev era. Although the "thaw" and "de-Stalinization" are sometimes used interchangeably, meaningful distinctions exist. Scholars tend to prefer de-Stalinization when examining policies that effected systemic changes, primarily in the Communist Party, the police state, and the economy.[24] They use de-Stalinization to describe how the power vacuum created by Stalin's death and the dismantling of his personality cult reshaped all spheres of life, from public opinion to the Soviet citizen's sense of self.[25] Although some scholars have examined the institutional and economic history of mass housing as examples of de-Stalinization,[26] others have seen it as part of the thaw when studying such topics as architectural and cultural history.[27]

The range of social actors who appear in scholars' traditional treatment of the thaw has often reflected the subtle distinctions between the Soviet intelligentsia and ordinary workers that Ehrenburg included in his story. Although scholars have tended to imply that the thaw touched most Soviet citizens, as Ehrenburg does, their evidence has mostly been drawn from the intersection of high politics and high culture. From Khrushchev's "Secret Speech" to Alexander Solzhenitsyn's novel *One Day in the Life of Ivan Denisovich*, the thaw's chief agents were Communist Party leaders, who managed and occasionally reversed it, and the members of the cultural intelligentsia who exploited it to nurture their liberal values, supposedly on behalf of the rest of society.[28] Scholars often assume that the cultural intelligentsia's words and actions captured the thaw's essence and shaped how most Soviet citizens experienced it.[29] In a rather self-serving gesture, it is a novella within Ehrenburg's own novella and the local Soviet intelligentsia's various reactions to it that get his story going. How else could Soviet citizens possibly begin to think and act differently than by reading and discussing a novel?

Including social groups outside the cultural intelligentsia in the thaw narrative has proven difficult for scholars. While the cultural intelligentsia enjoyed the thaw, ordinary people, like the passive workers in the background of Ehrenburg's novella, got "reforms," including new consumer items, better housing, and tourism.[30] Some scholars have examined ordinary people in the context of the thaw, but mainly where their actions intersected with key moments of its traditional narrative, such as popular reactions to the "Secret Speech" and Solzhenitsyn's book.[31] Casting a wider net, others have explored how the cultural logic of the thaw—a schizophrenic approach to liberalization, punctuated by contradictions and reversals—shaped and reflected the discourses of social policies such as mass housing, through which ordinary people left their mark on the thaw by further legitimizing demands for better living standards.[32]

Further complicating the picture, a few historians have shown that people did not always react as expected according to traditional thaw narratives. Rather than celebrating the dismantling of the Gulag, a move that seemingly embodied the thaw, some citizens criticized prisoners' releases and did so in the Stalinist discourse of rooting out "enemies of the people."[33] And some readers of children's literature not only refused to heap praise on writers for exploring new themes but sometimes challenged their authority to set moral standards and proper taste.[34]

This latter dynamic—the unpredictable things that ordinary people said and did, especially to the consternation of members of the cultural intelligentsia—represents a major understudied aspect of the thaw and features prominently in this book. City dwellers' words and actions reveal a different field of tensions within the thaw from the conventional narratives of society (i.e., the cultural intelligentsia) struggling with the state (Communist Party ideologues) over the limits of the permissible (in high culture). As we will see, ordinary residents who were willing to challenge the authority of the architects, furniture designers, and local housing officials involved with mass housing exhibited what scholars have identified as the thaw's chief dynamics but reserved for the cultural intelligentsia: iconoclasm, calls for change, attacking founding myths, scorning past accomplishments, and recalibrating existing discourses for new aims.[35] By living in a separate apartment and critiquing mass housing, urban dwellers transformed the thaw from an elite into a popular experience.

The mass housing campaign encompassed all layers of society, from the top leaders who devised it to the urban residents who moved into separate apartments. Everyone had a housing question to resolve in the Soviet Union, including those, like the Moscow construction workers discussed above, who built separate apartments for a living. Recognizing the range of actors and what they could decide in this campaign complicates our conventional understanding of how this state and its society organized themselves. The evidence presented in this book makes it difficult to say that the "state" imposed or gave "society" the separate apartment with little input from the latter, as traditional models of Soviet totalitarianism or the welfare state would suggest. Government functionaries with their own housing questions to resolve benefited as much from mass housing as the ordinary people it was intended to help, who themselves were required to invest incredible amounts of time, labor, and financial resources to improve their living conditions.[36]

A survey of the many actors involved in the mass housing campaign who appear in the pages of this book illustrates the mass participation it elicited. Those directly involved in the campaign included the architects, construction workers, civil engineers, and factory workers in the building supplies industries who designed and constructed the housing, and the local municipal officials and factory managers who were in charge of its distribution. The campaign depended upon an army of bureaucrats who worked for various ministries and institutions in charge of mass housing's planning, financing, and statistical accounting. A new line of furniture designed specifically for new housing required an additional contingent of designers, planners, manufacturers, furniture store personnel, and managers of furniture exhibitions. Bureaucrats at the Party Control Commission, the State Control Commission, and the All-Union Central Council of Professional Unions provided much-needed oversight on the campaign. Writers and artists represented mass housing and shaped the meanings of the separate apartment in literature and art. Journalists from both national and local newspapers chronicled the campaign's successes and failures. Writers for magazines and homemaking advice pamphlets explained the new aesthetic principles and rational way of life of separate apartments. All these workers, bureaucrats, and professionals not only worked in some fashion to make mass housing possible but were also urban residents with their own housing question to resolve.

Urban dwellers in occupations completely unrelated to housing likewise participated in ways that went far beyond receiving a separate apartment from the state. In the "people's construction" campaign, industrial workers volunteered for overtime work on their factory's housing projects in exchange for a separate apartment. Members of housing construction cooperatives helped finance the construction of their housing. With the aid of state loans, people continued to build single-family homes in midsized cities and towns. Urban dwellers participated directly in the distribution of housing by initiating legal (and not so legal) living space exchanges, and shaped the meaning of the waiting list for living space by lobbying municipal officials in writing and in person. Once in their new apartments, residents invited friends and family over for a housewarming party (*novosel'e*) to celebrate their new way of life. They joined neighborhood "social organizations," patrolled their own streets, and attended house committee meetings. They visited furniture and apartment exhibitions, where they shared their impressions of the *khrushchevka* and its household objects with architects and furniture designers in comment books. Their complaints in letters to architectural congresses and at residential meetings even influenced design changes in the next generation of separate apartments. And with an eye on life in the West, they flocked to the American Exhibition in Moscow in 1959 to see how their capitalist counterparts lived while Khrushchev and Nixon sparred in the kitchen.

As these interactions illustrate, the ordinary residents of mass housing actively engaged state actors in shaping the separate apartment and its meanings. They exercised their agency within official discourses and institutions that ultimately remained under the control of the Communist Party's Central Committee and its top leadership. Khrushchev's regime exercised the sole authority to start the mass housing campaign and to determine the contours of its most important features, such as the amount of housing built and the rules for its distribution. Through its total control of the mass media, the party defined the permissible representations of mass housing. Propaganda heralding the campaign's goals and achievements delimited the discourses that people used in residential meetings and letters of complaint. Advice literature on homemaking established norms for domestic and consumer behavior meant to guide residents (especially housewives) in their new everyday lives. Yet the moment we begin to identify the persons who wrote the content of housing propaganda, we find ourselves once more dealing with individuals far removed from the top leadership with their own housing question to resolve. Such persons worked for the state within its rules, but they were also urban residents in search of a separate apartment with a vested interest in making mass housing work.

Finally, several paragraphs are in order to explain my use of the terms "ordinary people" and "ordinary residents" when describing the main characters of this story—the millions of Soviet citizens who moved into separate apartments under Khrushchev's regime. I use "ordinary" first and foremost to capture the common experiences of mass housing residents that cut across social lines. The experience of moving to a separate apartment and settling into everyday life in new microdistricts on the outskirts of town was becoming a rather ordinary thing for Soviet citizens from almost all walks of life. In this sense, the "ordinary residents" of mass housing were people who lived through and shaped a common experience repeated in cities throughout the Soviet Union. I do not mean to suggest, however, that these residents were an undifferentiated whole. Quite the contrary; throughout this book, I try to identify as much as possible who such residents were in terms of age, gender, profession, and personal history, and how their individual backgrounds and social identities intersected with their experiences as "ordinary residents" of mass housing.

Thinking about who belonged to the ranks of "ordinary people" and how Khrushchev's mass housing shaped them as a group also allows us to both question and clarify social differences that run deep in twentieth-century Russian history. Although Ehrenburg's novella suggests a sharp distinction between the Soviet intelligentsia and ordinary people, this book shows that members of the intelligentsia could be ordinary residents as well in search of their own separate apartments. Throughout the book, I adopt the broader, official definition of the intelligentsia, which not only included members of the remaining pre-revolutionary Russian intelligentsia and the cultural elite but also members of the Communist Party and those who had received a technical or higher education and moved up the ranks of society as engineers, administrators, educators, lawyers, doctors, agronomists, and so on.[37] Many of these members of the "Soviet intelligentsia," as this broader category is known to historians and as they are called throughout this book, joined industrial workers in making the move to the separate apartment and becoming the "ordinary residents" of mass housing estates.

A useful distinction between these "ordinary residents" and the intelligentsia does exist, however, when I discuss the relationship between residents of the *khrushchevka* and its makers—namely, mass housing architects, furniture designers, and homemaking advice specialists. In this case, I use the term "cultural intelligentsia"—which included writers, artists, composers, and filmmakers among others—to denote the subset of the Soviet intelligentsia whose job it was to advance the cultural edification of the masses.[38] Concerned as they were with redefining ordinary people's everyday lives and cultural habits, mass housing architects, furniture designers, and homemaking advice specialists belonged to the cultural intelligentsia. As this book shows, their authority to reshape everyday life came under attack by ordinary residents of mass housing, some of whom were members of the broader Soviet intelligentsia.

I also use "ordinary" to contrast mass housing residents with the more well-known actors of the thaw, to whom historians have normally assigned the greatest agency. Unlike politicians or writers who were famous in their time and left lengthy paper trails in print media and the archives, most of the people in this story left only fleeting traces of their existence in statistical sourcebooks, letters of complaint, comment books at exhibitions, or residential meetings that somebody thought worthwhile to record. These residents of mass housing are thus "ordinary" to the historian in the sense of having fallen largely out of the historical record and not belonging to the ranks of individuals who were well known at the time. The intent of the present study is to identify experiences that were common or ordinary to millions of mass housing residents, and to restore their proper place in Soviet life after Stalin.

But as Yanni Kotsonis points out in a recent historiographical essay, the historian of "ordinary people" should not only attempt to recoup their fleeting traces in a noble effort to restore their voice and agency for their own sake. The historian must also explain what was extraordinary about the words and actions of these people who have typically slipped through the cracks of the historical record and receded into the faceless whole of the masses.[39] I hope this book achieves this by demonstrating how ordinary residents anticipated and enacted aspects of the thaw that we have traditionally attributed to Khrushchev, the Communist Party, and well-published members of the cultural intelligentsia.

Another way I reveal what was extraordinary about mass housing residents' everyday lives is to contrast their experiences with what came before the Khrushchev era. As Sheila Fitzpatrick has shown, everyday life under Stalin was anything but ordinary with respect to what Soviet citizens thought to be normal and predictable. Whether one experienced social mobility up the ranks of Soviet society or was cast down to the lowest depths of the Gulag in a nightmare of false accusations and terrifying repression, there was something inherently extraordinary about life under Stalin.[40] In the Khrushchev era, people's lives became decidedly less turbulent and less violent, and more settled and more normal, which in itself was an extraordinary thing. The move to the single-family separate apartment embodied this incredible change from the Stalin era to the Khrushchev era. The ordinariness and normality that its way of life represented were something that Soviet citizens had come to crave under Stalin and demanded once he was dead. The fact that the Soviet leaders under Khrushchev, normally accustomed to waging war on society, agreed with this craving and thus tried to make the separate apartment available to everyone was an extraordinary moment in Soviet history.

Plan of the Book and an Overview of Primary Sources

As with any human-made object that enjoyed a social life worth studying, a history of the *khrushchevka* requires us to examine its production, circulation, and consumption and show how each was related to the other. This book is organized accordingly.

Part I, which consists of chapters 1 and 2, focuses on the making of the separate apartment, with particular attention to its design. Chapter 1 traces the origins of the *khrushchevka*'s layout and dimensions to the quest for minimum living space standards in the nineteenth-century pan-European housing reform movement. I demonstrate how the Bolsheviks' peculiar adaptation of these minimum standards created a fundamental contradiction between the principles of socialist housing distribution based in square meters of living space per person and the ideal of single-family occupancy once it was resurrected in the Stalinist 1930s. Chapter 2 examines how the architects of mass housing resolved this contradiction, which had led to the communalization of apartments, and in so doing laid the foundations for the *khrushchevka*'s design. The chapter also traces the dramatic expansion of mass housing construction under Khrushchev and architects' failed attempts to reform the principles of design in response to residents' growing needs and desires. These first two chapters together provide an original explanation of the *khrushchevka*'s design origins that allows us to better understand what urban dwellers said and did about the apartment's problems.

In part II, which comprises chapter 3 and 4, we turn our attention to the allocation of housing and its role in reorganizing Soviet society after Stalin. In a case study of Leningrad, chapter 3 reveals the problems that Khrushchev's regime faced implementing its vision of the egalitarian social order that mass housing promised to deliver. In response and in resistance to that vision, urban dwellers and municipal officials put forth various notions of socially differentiated access to housing based on who a person had become in Soviet society and what he or she had contributed or suffered under Stalin. In doing so, they reshaped the very meaning of the waiting list for living space and politicized it as a register of existing social hierarchies precisely at the time that Khrushchev's regime hoped to empty it of its political meaning and bring the housing question to a final resolution. In chapter 4, I examine how the regime's egalitarian visions were further complicated by two opportunities that it gave urban dwellers to gain fast-track access to the separate apartment outside the system of waiting lists for state housing. The first was "people's construction" in the middle to late 1950s, which enabled factory laborers to work extra hours on their enterprises' housing in exchange for a separate apartment. Its rhetoric of volunteerism and mutual help presaged a communist way of life in which workers could pursue their self-interest not at the exploitation of others but within communities whose members both worked and lived together. The second opportunity was the housing construction cooperative, which appropriated the rhetoric of people's construction, displaced it as the fast-track method for obtaining a separate apartment, and served urban professionals and cultural elites instead of workers. By shutting down people's construction and opting for the cooperative, the regime quietly signaled that class still mattered in a society that was theoretically about to make the final transition to communism.[41]

Having considered the separate apartment's making and distribution in parts I and II, we turn in part III (chapters 5 through 7) to what residents said and did when they moved into their new apartments and neighborhoods. Chapter 5 examines how the discourse on the "communist way of life" incorporated separate apartments as a critical link in the idealized mass housing communities of the communist future. It then explores how residents went about creating community in new neighborhoods that suffered design and structural deficiencies. Despite these shortcomings, residents' efforts often bolstered rhetoric on the communist way of life that called upon urban dwellers to take an active role in running their communities. In chapter 6, I venture into the *khrushchevka* and its material world of new furniture and household objects as further signs of what the communist way of life promised in theory and delivered in practice. Chapter 7 concludes by examining the politics of complaint that emerged as residents of the *khrushchevka* confronted architects, furniture designers, and housing officials about the shortcomings of mass housing and furniture. In their complaints, urban residents brought discussions back to the unresolved design issues addressed in chapters 1 and 2. They insisted that the housing question was far from over and that some were willing to invoke Stalin-era tactics of coercion and public denunciation to force architects and housing officials to fix design flaws and construction defects.

The present study is based on extensive research in archival and published sources. From top Communist Party archives to local newspapers, the primary sources used in this study allow for an original analysis that connects the *khrushchevka*'s design origins and its allocation to Soviet citizens' everyday lives and their own participation in its making. Original research in central state, party, and economics archives elucidates the leadership's role in shaping little-understood phases of the mass housing campaign, such as a failed reform of the waiting lists for state housing and high-level discussions about class that stalled the re-creation of cooperative housing for urban professionals and cultural elites. The roles that the campaign's architects, furniture designers, and taste arbiters played in shaping the *khrushchevka* and their dialogue with ordinary residents are revealed through original research in the art and literature archives of both Moscow and Saint Petersburg, as well as extensive research in published sources such as architectural journals, homemaking advice pamphlets, and newspapers. New research in Saint Petersburg's local archives shifts our attention away from the leadership and Moscow to ordinary people's roles in shaping the move to the separate apartment, the meaning of the waiting list, and the creation of mass housing communities. With a prerevolutionary housing stock that primarily consisted of communal apartments created in the wake of the Russian Revolution, Leningrad provides an ideal setting for examining how urban dwellers relocated from the overcrowded *kommunalka* to the single-family separate apartment. To begin our investigation, let us first turn to the nineteenth-century origins of the housing question that Soviet citizens in the mid–twentieth century were far from convinced had been answered to their liking.

Part I

Making the Separate Apartment

Chapter 1

The Soviet Path to Minimum Living Space and the Single-Family Apartment

In a letter to the Third All-Union Congress of Architects in 1961, three faculty members of the Polytechnic Institute in Gor'kii lamented the shrinking dimensions of mass housing. "The existing standardized models of small-sized apartments can't in any way satisfy people in the present, let alone the future," the men huffed. "It isn't normal when you can't put a coat closet in an entranceway, when people have to drag in their furniture through the balcony and, we're sorry to say, carry out a coffin almost vertically, when a member of the family who's just bathed has to run out of the tub so another in dire need can use the space for another purpose." Such compact spaces did more than inconvenience those eager to use the toilet, bury the dead, or furnish their apartment. It even threatened class privileges. Small apartments lacked the extra workspace needed by writers and artists—"that is, those who fulfill, think over, and form the greater part of their creative work at home."[1] For members of the Soviet intelligentsia, to whom the Bolsheviks had provided extra living space soon after the Russian Revolution, Khrushchev's separate apartment must have seemed like a cruel joke.[2] Citizens of other social backgrounds, who were busy accumulating furniture and new consumer items, also found the separate apartment's small dimensions to be a major drawback. Upon moving to the separate apartment, many residents asked the same question: Why did apartments have to be so small?

The minimalist dimensions of the "small-sized apartment" (*malo-metrazhnaia kvartira*) were indelible features of Khrushchev's mass housing campaign. The *khrushchevka* had low ceilings, narrow corridors and doorways, a compact kitchen, and one to three small rooms. Spaces common in the prerevolutionary apartments of the bourgeoisie and aristocracy had been erased. These included the service entrance to the kitchen, the back stairwell, the vestibule between the inner and outer entrance doors, and the adjoining, larger foyer. The toilet and bath, which had occupied separate units in the past, were combined in the same space; and kitchens were condensed. Upon entering a *khru-shchevka*, a resident stepped not into an entranceway but immediately into the corridor that led to the kitchen, rooms, and bathroom. In some apartments, residents had to walk through a pass-through room to access another room that lacked access to the corridor. Rooms served two or three functions instead of one. A main room was a dining and sitting room during the day, but someone's bedroom at night. A new line of minimalist furniture lacking all ornamentation was designed to conform to these spaces. Small tables, chairs, stools, sinks, stoves, and cabinets were squeezed into the compact kitchen; couches folded out into beds, and bookcases featured foldout desks. The separate apartment not only shrunk space but also the objects that went in it. According to one post-Soviet joke, the *khrushchevka* was so small that a toddler's portable potty had its handle on the inside rather than the outside.[3]

Scholars have provided several explanations for the *khrushchevka*'s small size and why it mattered. Echoing Khrushchev's exhortations to architects and constructors, some have argued that the separate apartment's minimalist dimensions were a function of cost. The leadership committed unprecedented, but not limitless, resources to mass housing. Industrial and military needs remained greater priorities that were never eclipsed by housing and consumer needs. Separate apartments had to be cheap if the regime's ambitious goal of fully resolving the housing question in ten to twelve years after 1957 was to be met. Operating under such budget and time constraints, the regime chose prefabricated panel housing based on a few standardized models. Lowering ceilings, simplifying layouts, slashing an apartment's floor space, and reducing the number of rooms were key elements of keeping costs down. Khrushchev's personal involvement in architectural affairs and his previous experience in managing housing construction played no small role in shaping housing policies toward cheaper and more efficient construction.[4]

Other scholars have argued that ideology played a critical role in making apartments smaller and more efficient. Inspired by the constructivist aesthetics of the 1920s, architects and furniture designers under Khrushchev remade the Soviet home into a scientifically and rationally organized space to complete the transformation of all residents into the New Soviet Man and New Soviet Woman. Throughout the new apartment, unnecessary ornamentation and excess spaces were purged in the name of scientific management and efficiency. Nowhere was this better seen than the kitchen, which architects designed as a laboratory of industrial efficiency and rational organization. The kitchen was even a site of Cold War ideological conflict in which the Soviet housewife's mastery of rational living and restrained consumerism would prove the superiority of socialism over the grotesque excesses of irrational capitalist consumption. The "austere consumerism" that characterized separate apartments and consumer items under Khrushchev were not simply a matter of necessity dictated by budget constraints or, pace János Kornai, by the inevitable shortages of a planned economy.[5] Such austerity was instead an ideologically inspired choice made primarily by members of the cultural intelligentsia. In designing the *khrushchevka* and telling residents how to use it, architects, furniture designers, and taste arbiters revitalized the Russian intelligentsia's historical and self-appointed struggle (from both its prerevolutionary and early Soviet past) to rid society of lowbrow, petit bourgeois values and define the proper tastes and consumer behaviors of a modern, socialist society.[6]

To be sure, not all architects were excited by the design aesthetic of new housing. In explaining why smaller apartments and lower cost went hand in hand, some scholars have examined what this meant for architects working in the supposedly more liberal atmosphere of Khrushchev's thaw. The architectural principle that embodied the regime's obsession with low costs and small apartments was known as *tipovoe proektirovanie*, or "standard-design construction from prefabricated parts." As Stephen Bittner argues, Khrushchev's regime imposed *tipovoe proektirovanie* on an architectural profession that was initially skeptical if not resistant to the limitations it placed on architects' creative work. It effectively banned their previous tendency, nurtured under Stalin, to design costly individual works frequently based on a neoclassical style and full of ornamentation. In the early years of the mass housing campaign, architects' role was subordinated to that of construction firms that produced reinforced concrete panels and assembled them on site in identical five-story buildings. *Tipovoe proektirovanie* limited rather than expanded many architects' impact on mass housing architecture and, by extension, millions of Soviet citizens' everyday lives.[7]

Taken together, these factors provide an incomplete and sometimes contradictory explanation for the *khrushchevka*'s design origins. Because *tipovoe proektirovanie* could have been applied to larger apartments, its adoption alone does not explain why apartments had to be so small and how their internal layouts were planned. Cost constraints required cheaper building methods and standardization, but their effect on an apartment's internal layout was less clear because, as we shall see below, apartments with less living space were actually more expensive to construct. The role of ideology is similarly less certain. Cost constraints and *tipovoe proektirovanie* imposed conditions on architects that an ideology of "austere consumerism" seemed to justify rather than guide. Scholars are right in arguing that the design elements of mass housing under Khrushchev were rooted in the ideological and aesthetic visions of the Soviet home that constructivist architects had promoted in the 1920s. The problem, as this chapter and the next show, is that the work architects did under Stalin in the 1930s, when constructivism was officially banned, ultimately had a greater impact on the *khrushchevka*'s design.

In the first two chapters of this book, I present an alternative explanation for the design origins of the *khrushchevka* that focuses on the intersection of housing design and distribution. In this chapter, I lay the groundwork for this explanation by showing how the Soviet Union developed from 1917 through the late 1930s two critical pillars of the *khrushchevka*'s design: minimum living space norms and the principle of single-family occupancy. In explaining why the *khrushchevka* was so small, scholars have largely overlooked how these two attributes were related and ultimately conflicted with one another.[8] Understanding when and how the Soviet Union developed these two pillars is critical to comprehending the difficulties that Soviet architects faced in designing a separate apartment for the general population. The main challenge, as this chapter demonstrates, was that minimum living space norms shaped the distribution of housing in such a way that made single-family occupancy almost impossible to achieve in practice. Architects' solutions and how they embedded them in the design of the *khrushchevka* will be the subject of chapter 2.

In explaining the Soviet Union's path to minimum living space and single-family occupancy, I situate the *khrushchevka*'s design origins in the broader pan-European history of the "housing question" and the search for the minimum dwelling unit. This chapter is the first to trace the origins of the *khrushchevka*'s design from the pan-European history of housing reform through the Russian Revolution and Stalin period. By demonstrating how the Soviet Union borrowed and transformed pan-European ideas on minimum living space and single-family occupancy, I show that the *khrushchevka* had a shared past with Western approaches to resolving the housing question and building mass housing, but with certain significant divergences. There were, as I argue in these first two chapters, different paths to mass housing in the twentieth century.

The key to understanding where the *khrushchevka*'s design was situated in relation to Western approaches to mass housing was nineteenth-century European reformers' search for minimum living standards—including food, wages, and housing—which served as the basis for the Bolsheviks' own approach to determining their citizens' minimum needs.[9] Once adopted in the Soviet context, however, these ideas on minimum living standards operated in ways that had not been intended by their reformist authors and early Bolshevik proponents, but that served the needs of the Soviet state as it struggled to deal with massive housing shortages, especially under Stalin. The Stalinist regime's decision to simultaneously embrace single-family occupancy, after earlier attempts to let the family wither away in collectivist housing, further complicated the design picture and was a critical step in the direction of the *khrushchevka*. To begin unpacking its design origins, we first turn to the evolution of the pan-European housing question out of which the Soviet Union carved its own path to minimum living space.

The International Housing Question

European social reformers in the nineteenth century, including those in Tsarist Russia, identified the housing question as a major part of the overall "social question" of industrializing societies. They legitimized, but failed to expand as desired, the state's role in improving the living conditions of the urban working poor. Despite having what they believed to be the necessary scientific and architectural knowledge to fully resolve the housing question, advocates of reform were constantly deprived of the machinery of the modern state. Even World War I, which served as a powerful catalyst for state intervention in society, left the pillars of private building and free market relations intact in most countries and did not lead to long-lasting housing programs that would place construction, distribution, and maintenance in the hands of the state. The Bolsheviks, in contrast, were determined not to suffer such shortcomings in housing reform and went well beyond the limited role that European governments and Tsarist Russia had afforded the state in resolving the housing question.

The major European housing reform movements of the nineteenth century developed in England, France, and Germany. Social reformers in Tsarist Russia and the United States also worked on the housing question and drew upon the ideas and experiences of their Western European counterparts. Similar to efforts aimed at resolving the social question, the answers proposed to the housing question developed within an international community of reformers.[10] International meetings became a mainstay of the movement after the first international congress on inexpensive dwellings held in Paris in 1889.[11] The scale of state intervention was a contentious question of housing reform raised at such meetings.[12] Social reformers generally sought greater state intervention, ranging from building codes and rent control to financial incentives for private builders and municipalities to build working-class housing. In opposition to this agenda stood private builders and landowners, who advocated market solutions to the housing crisis and limited government involvement.[13] Housing policies, where they existed, were implemented exclusively within individual states. This disjuncture between the international origins of the housing question and the national implementation of reform became more pronounced when World War I elevated housing to one of many national concerns upon which a state's survival depended.[14] After the war, housing policies remained national in scope, while their ideas continued to develop in an international context.

Most housing reformers were middle-class professionals such as hygienists, public health advocates, economists, architects, urban planners, and engineers, who saw the deficiencies of the built environment as the main culprits behind poor living conditions and social ills. Their strategy called for a scientific approach applied universally by the state through a regulatory regime of building standards, health codes, and sanitation inspections. For these reformers, accumulating data on housing conditions was a prerequisite for state intervention. In England, the secretary of the Poor Law Commissioners, Edwin Chadwick, produced the 1842 "Report on the Sanitary Condition of the Labouring Population," which was an early government examination of poor housing's impact on the health of urban and rural dwellers.[15] Social reformers outside government conducted their own studies. In 1901, Dutch socialists in the Amsterdam Labor League published an account of poor housing conditions, which they hoped would convince public opinion of the need for state involvement.[16]

Government censuses provided an additional source of data. In Moscow, censuses in 1882 and 1912 produced a wealth of information, including density, types of housing structures, categories of ownership, household structure, and amenities. Russia's first national census in 1897 provided additional information on such issues as density and household structure.[17] To transform such data into tangible policies, reformers lobbied for legislation creating regulatory regimes. In France, from 1850 to 1902 the government used the Melun Law to allow health inspections of housing by state bodies such as the Commissions on Unhealthful Dwellings.[18] In England, the Common Lodging Housing Acts (1851–53) similarly established a regulatory regime whereby "lodging-houses were now required to be registered and inspected; minimum standards of space, cleanliness and ventilation were laid down, basement bedrooms forbidden and unmarrieds of the opposite sex separated."[19]

Despite such legislation, reformers were frustrated with the small scale of state intervention, which failed to match their scientific recommendations. In Germany, one such reformer among health professionals was Max von Pettenkofer (1818–1901). Based in Munich, Pettenkofer pioneered hygiene as an academic discipline and public policy tool. His work on cholera identified poor housing as one of the factors spreading such diseases. As we shall see below, his suggestions for minimum space norms to prevent disease shaped housing reform in nineteenth-century Europe and even the Soviet state's approach. In his lifetime, however, he was frustrated by the state's inability or unwillingness to do all that it could. He lamented this situation in an 1873 lecture to the Verein für Volksbildung (Society for Public Education) of Munich: "The civil power or police authority is, as a rule, well disposed and perfectly willing to carry out whatever medical science places conveniently into its hands for execution, but in regard to police regulations on housing we still have a long way to go."[20]

Although Pettenkofer's theories on cholera were ultimately shown to be wrong, public health advocates still admired him in the mid–twentieth century for having helped legitimize their work in a sphere that included state intervention. In his glowing assessment of Pettenkofer's impact on hygiene and public health, Henry Sigerist wrote in the United States in 1941 that "this new science called for new men, for a new type of men, equally well trained in medicine and science, conscious of social problems, well versed in questions of public administration, indefatigable crusaders for health who at times must proceed with the smoothness of the diplomat and at times with the ruthlessness of the dictator."[21] Such comments reflected the frustration that reformers had long felt when facing the intransigence of free market advocates and the reluctance of governments to intervene in housing.

Pettenkofer's impact reached far beyond Munich and into Tsarist Russia, illustrating again the international context in which the housing question evolved. One of his students was Friedrich Erismann, who was originally from Switzerland and advanced the cause of public health in Russia, where he served as Moscow University's chair of hygiene.[22] Russian physicians produced their own studies on public health conditions and worked through the *zemstva* (locally elected government councils) to promote reform.[23] Advocates of housing reform in Russia published studies that compared their housing conditions and policies with those in the West.[24] Russian architects learned about housing design and construction techniques in the United States through their trade publications *Zodchii* (*Architect*) and *Nedelia stroitelia* (*Builder's Weekly*). The enormous scale and construction technology of American architecture struck Russian architects as positive developments. They also read about American advancements in prefabricated architecture and standardized parts.[25] As these examples indicate, Russian hygienists, social reformers, and architects were active participants in the international community of housing reform well before 1917, and their work contributed to an international body of knowledge about the housing question upon which the Bolsheviks later drew in devising their own set of answers.

Although many social reformers focused on fixing the built environment of the working classes, others concentrated on fixing the morals and behaviors of inhabitants through housing. A leader in this camp was Frédéric Le Play in France, whose movement sought to transform working-class tenants through the inculcation of bourgeois norms and values. For reformers like Le Play, regulating health conditions or providing salubrious and less crowded housing was not enough. He believed that workers should live in housing that also improved them as members of society. The model he advocated was the single-family home with its own garden located outside the city center. In addition to benefits to physical health, the individual home would provide a stable family life and privacy to protect its inhabitants from crime and the temptations of the city. The obligation of paying off a mortgage would encourage thrift among workers, who would now have a long-term stake in the economic well-being of the country.[26]

As Ann-Louise Shapiro argues, reformers hoped this transformative project would effect social reconciliation between the propertied and working classes: "Through home ownership, the worker reentered the mainstream of social life, transformed from an uprooted nomad into a settled petty proprietor. The social question was to be solved, then, by causing the working class to disappear into the bourgeoisie."[27] Reformers like Le Play used housing to transform people's morals and behaviors, alongside approaches that focused more narrowly on fixing the built environment to prevent diseases. But as historians have argued, even recommendations based purely on disease prevention could impose normative values upon working-class tenants.[28] As we shall see in this chapter and later ones, the Soviet Union combined both approaches in its strategy on housing.

Lacking the power of the future Soviet state, nineteenth-century social reformers worked through the institutions of civil society, such as charitable organizations, model building societies, and scientific associations. They used such associations to sway public opinion in favor of greater state involvement in the housing question. In late-nineteenth-century Germany, the Verein für öffentliche Gesundheitspflege (Society for Public Hygiene)—whose members included architects, doctors, sanitation specialists, and local government officials—helped secure regulatory restrictions on the number of people concentrated in a single area.[29] In England, charitable organizations, such as the Society for Improving the Condition of the Labouring Classes, built housing for workers that served as models of salubrious dwellings.[30] Philanthropic groups and industrialists worked along similar lines as Le Play to build housing for needy workers with an eye toward changing their behaviors and sense of self. In France, the industrialist Jean Dollfus constructed a *cité ouvrière* (factory housing settlement) in 1853 for his workers at Mulhouse, which provided garden homes financed through fifteen-year mortgages. His project became a model for social reformers who wished to use housing as a tool to inculcate in working-class individuals the bourgeois ideals of strong family life, temperance, and thriftiness.[31] In England, factory housing dated as far back as the 1830s. Industrialists saw it as a way to maintain a healthy workforce and encourage social conciliation, thereby overcoming the conflicts in modern life between labor and capital, and man and machine. Like Le Play, English industrialists saw factory housing, examples of which were based on the designs of middle-class homes, as new habitats to engender healthy bourgeois morals and behaviors among workers.[32]

To what degree did nineteenth-century social reform succeed at drawing the state into a more active role in resolving the housing question? In several countries, social reformers did much to raise public awareness of housing deficiencies, define minimum standards of housing for the urban working classes, secure government regulation through building standards and health inspections, and even encourage the state to assist in the financing and construction of some housing. By the end of the nineteenth century, France and England began moving toward comprehensive nationwide policies to regulate housing and build more dwellings specifically for workers. In England, the government made its first tangible steps in the direction of council housing (i.e., housing built and maintained by local municipalities) through the Housing of the Working Classes Acts of 1890 and 1900.[33] In 1894, France instituted legislation designed to stimulate the construction of inexpensive housing for workers through various financial incentives for private builders.[34] In 1902, it replaced the Melun Law of 1850 with a nationwide regulatory regime that expanded the powers of municipal authorities, instituted universal health standards, and subjected everyone's housing to its oversight.[35] In the same year, the Netherlands issued a Housing Act, which was the country's first nationwide legislation making available state assistance for housing construction by local government and independent housing societies.[36]

Although the housing reform movement succeeded in raising awareness and establishing regulatory legislation, the amount of new housing built specifically for workers by private builders, charitable groups, and local government was negligible before World War I.[37] The regulatory regimes raised health standards and reformed building codes, but had the unintended consequence of making new housing construction more expensive, which hindered growth.[38] Social reformers' calls for expanding the state's role in resolving the housing question repeatedly ran up against opposition from private builders and those who advocated a free market path to meeting housing needs. In Germany, additional opposition to national legislation came from municipal governments and the German states, which saw in reforms encroachments on their autonomy.[39] Until World War I, states generally stayed out of constructing, distributing, and maintaining urban housing, preferring a limited involvement through building regulations, health inspections, and attracting more capital to the construction industry.[40]

The housing reform movement of the nineteenth century was not without its critics. In late-nineteenth-century England, a government study found that workers took the tenements built by model societies to be "a sort of prison: They look upon themselves as being watched."[41] In France, some social reformers and socialists criticized the *cité ouvrière* for making workers dependent upon their employers, thereby putting them at a disadvantage in labor negotiations.[42] Meanwhile, socialists rejected reformers' goals of social reconciliation and highlighted instead the class tensions that pitted working-class tenants against bourgeois landlords. Socialists still seeking accommodation with the existing order sought greater state intervention in ways that were meant to punish landlords and reward tenants, such as rent control and expropriating private property, as well as state-built housing.[43]

More radical socialists, following Friedrich Engels's scathing critique of housing reform in *The Housing Question* (1872), saw all efforts, bourgeois or socialist, to resolve the housing crisis within the existing order as futile at best or buttressing capitalism at worst. Like all subsets of the overall social question, Marxists believed that the housing question could only be resolved after the social revolution.[44] Engels's essay and his earlier book, *The Condition of the Working Class in England* (1844), powerfully shaped the body of knowledge and assumptions that the Bolsheviks had about urban housing in industrializing countries and the deficiencies of reform. Public health officials and architects in late Tsarist Russia also left the Bolsheviks with substantial knowledge about the housing question in Russia and the West. What made Engels's essay different, of course, was the Marxist framework in which he interpreted the same data on urban housing.

In their earliest statements on housing, the Bolsheviks combined the knowledge of social reformers and Marxist ideology to frame their approach. Their first party program, issued at the Second Congress of the Russian Social-Democratic Labor Party in 1903 (where the party split into its Bolshevik and Menshevik factions), called for local authorities to join with workers in overseeing the sanitary conditions of factory housing, as well as its regulation and payment of rent. Echoing social reformers' critiques of the *cité ouvrière*, the party program declared the goal of its proposals to be "the protection of hired workers from entrepreneurs' interference in their lives and activities as private persons and citizens." Such proposals were not ends in themselves, as was true for some social reformers. Instead, they were set within the program's broader goals of shielding "the working class from physical and moral degeneration" and furthering "its ability to wage the struggle for liberation." The program called for the "inviolability of the person and dwelling," which would appear to call for securing a person's privacy from the prying eyes of the state or moralizing employers. Yet this, too, was not an end in itself, but part of the Bolsheviks' Marxist vision for overthrowing the Tsarist regime and advancing Russia's capitalist development with a democratic republic and Constitution, all in anticipation of the eventual social revolution.[45]

In *State and Revolution* (1917), Lenin further interpreted Engels's *The Housing Question* to explain what the Bolsheviks were supposed to do with housing in the midst of revolution. As stated previously, Engels argued that socialist and bourgeois reformers were mistaken to believe that they could resolve the social question by solving the housing question first. In the long run, the social revolution would create the circumstances for the complete resolution of the housing question. Engels pointed out that one such circumstance was "abolishing the antithesis between town and country," one of the main divisions in the human condition that only got worse under capitalism and could only be solved under socialism. In the initial stages of the social revolution, the proletariat would take short-term measures to address the housing crisis "by expropriating a part of the luxury dwellings belonging to the propertied classes and by quartering workers in the remaining part."[46] Lenin concurred and emphasized that the proletarian state would undertake such expropriations and the redistribution of housing.[47] Engels predicted that after the revolution, the proletariat would most likely continue to collect some form of rent on housing, "at least in a transitional period."[48] Lenin saw in this another responsibility for the proletarian state. He added, however, that the complete elimination of rent would coincide with the "withering away of the state."[49]

The Bolsheviks' social revolution and approach to housing set them apart from social reformers eager to work within the established order. Nevertheless, the Bolsheviks' reliance on the state, albeit a proletarian one, to produce their desired ends owed much to what nineteenth-century social reform had done to legitimize the state's role in solving social questions. According to Marxism, the expansion of state control over the economy and society was supposed to happen as capitalism approached its final death throes. Such an expansion occurred in part because of social reformers' efforts to enlist the state in achieving their goals. To the Bolsheviks, social reformers' failure to resolve the housing question did not mean that the expansion of state control over housing had been wrong, but that it had simply not gone far enough and only served to bolster the established order and the interests of the ruling classes.

The Impact of World War I

State involvement in the housing question changed dramatically during and after World War I in European states where the housing reform movement had been active. In recent years, historians have broadened our understanding of the war beyond its military and diplomatic aspects to address its profound impact on life in the twentieth century, from the home front to artistic and popular culture.[50] States mobilized their societies' human, material, cultural, and financial resources to pursue total war and also resolve domestic social problems on an unprecedented scale. As a result, World War I was an enormous advancement in the development of the twentieth century's welfare state.[51] Along similar lines, scholars of Russia have moved beyond debates about the war's role in causing the Revolution to examine how it led to the fundamental transformations of states and societies that marked the true beginning of the twentieth century.[52]

For some historians, greater state intervention was part of "an unwritten social contract," whereby governments compensated their citizens for participation in the war with welfare measures and social reform.[53] Others emphasize the state's role in coordinating efforts by employers, labor organizations, and professionals (including urban planners and architects) to secure social conciliation within the established order, resolve social problems that impeded the war effort, undertake postwar reconstruction, and advance a country's ability to succeed in the postwar global economy.[54] States were less concerned with compensating their citizens, according to this line of argument, than using the opportunities created by the war to expand, as Stephen Kotkin describes it, "a field of social activity for the state."[55] The combatant states of World War I were now more willing to pursue social engineering to accomplish domestic aims as they would the organization of armies to pursue a war. In Kotkin's analysis of Magnitogorsk under Stalin, housing was one of many fields the Soviet state entered in order to transform society on a scale never attempted by other combatant states after World War I.

Although no state ever went as far as the Soviet Union, some initially pursued notable interventions in their housing sectors. Whether it was a matter of expanding social welfare, compensating citizens for service, boosting economic competitiveness, social engineering, or a combination of all of these agendas, combatant states intervened during and after World War I on an unprecedented scale in their housing sectors to face the economic and social demands of total war. Rent restrictions, the construction of state housing, and the extension of regulatory standards were among the most prevalent forms of state involvement in housing, whose supporters spanned the political spectrum. Austria, for example, instituted rent restrictions during the war in 1917. Social Democrats, who came to power in the city of Vienna in 1919, expanded upon this by controlling rents, carrying out housing requisitions, and mounting a municipal housing construction program specifically geared toward the city's working-class housing.[56] In Russia, the Tsarist regime instituted rent control measures during the war as well. The Provisional Government, which came to power after the February Revolution of 1917, advanced state intervention in municipal affairs with a June 1917 decree whereby city governments were to assume greater responsibilities in urban planning, municipal management, and improving basic city services.[57]

The unintended consequence of rent control measures that outlasted the war in countries like England and France was to draw the state even further into the housing question. Rent control gave private builders even less incentive to build cheaper housing for workers, thereby putting more pressure on governments to build and manage such housing themselves.[58] Council housing—one of the pillars of England's twentieth-century welfare state—saw its first serious expansion after World War I, when the government massively expanded funding for local governments to build housing and financial incentives for private builders to construct dwellings for low-income residents. Overall, from 1919 to 1939, municipalities built 1.1 million dwellings, while private builders constructed 2.4 million houses independently and an additional 430,000 with state aid.[59] Germany similarly entered into public housing construction, which the state had largely avoided before World War I.[60] State housing construction in Berlin counted for 61 percent of new housing from 1924 to 1928, while private builders constructed 35 percent, and individual property owners 4 percent.[61] In Amsterdam, the City Council authorized its first housing construction project in 1914. Over the course of the war and until 1922, the city and housing societies using state resources built most of Amsterdam's new housing.[62]

Beyond housing construction, states presided over the creation of institutions and initiatives that brought together government bureaucracies, employers, labor organizations, and urban planning experts. These public-private relationships in housing and urban planning constituted a chief pillar in the expansion of what some historians term a "parastatal complex." According to this model, states during the war extended their control over spheres such as housing by drawing private associations and individuals into "professionalized, institutionalized domains or publics" focused on particular matters of public welfare.[63]

In France, the government sought to coordinate public and private efforts in urban planning soon after the war by creating the Commission supérieure d'aménagement, d'embellissement et d'extension des villes (High Commission for the Planning, Beautification, and Growth of Cities) in 1919. Members of this government commission included urban specialists drawn from private associations geared toward resolving public problems such as the Société française des architectes-urbanistes (French Society of Architects and Urban Planners) and the Conseil supérieur des beaux arts (High Council of the Fine Arts). In the 1920s in the United States, the Department of Commerce received suggestions on urban planning devised by the American Institute of Planners and the National Association of Real Estate Developers. The Better Homes for America Movement and the Architects' Small House Bureau produced model designs, while the Building Code Committee of the Commerce Department established minimum space standards in coordination with private builders.[64]

Resistance to having governments assume greater responsibility in housing stunted or rolled back efforts to mount comprehensive state building programs that would have encompassed the construction, distribution, and maintenance of housing. The same "parastatal complex" that allowed states to extend their influence over housing also supported private property and free market relations in housing. One of the underlying assumptions informing state intervention in several countries was that such efforts would allow the free market to predominate once more after the war in the construction, allocation, and maintenance of urban housing.[65] The U.S. government was perhaps the most eager to extricate itself from the nation's housing construction picture. Federal efforts to construct public housing during the war for workers in war services industries produced only 16,000 homes throughout the country. Soon after the war, Congress abandoned calls to expand this into a broader program for federal public housing.[66]

In sum, state intervention in housing during and after World War I increased in most combatant states in ways that left the fundamental pillars of private property and civil society intact. States expanded upon the nineteenth century's regulatory regimes in the areas of minimum living standards, the adoption of standardized models and construction materials, and the promotion of modern building technologies such as prefabricated housing.[67] Governments even built some state housing to increase the urban housing stock for low-income residents but did not supplant the private building sector. To Marxist theoreticians and Bolshevik revolutionaries, these policies were half-measures that would never fully resolve the housing question and only delay the social revolution.

Bolshevik Approaches to Housing

War, revolution, and Bolshevik ideology combined in Russia to produce long-term outcomes in state formation and control over housing that were different from those of other European countries. Historians who examine the impact of World War I on the formation of the Soviet state have shown how the Bolsheviks adopted and took to extreme ends certain state practices—terror, surveillance, the requisitioning of food, and the expropriation of private property—that were initially developed under the Tsarist regime and the Provisional Government, and employed in other combatant states to meet the demands of total war. Although most states curtailed these practices after the war, the Bolsheviks pursued them after 1917 and through the Civil War, and made them into fundamental features of the Soviet system.[68] As the writer Denis de Rougemont succinctly put it in 1951, "Out of total war emerged the first totalitarian régime—Lenin's—which soon served as an inspiration to Mussolini and to Hitler. Their régimes gave us totalitarianism as a specific and clearly definable phenomenon, which is the establishment of the idea of a permanent state of war in the human mind and in international relations. This is the vicious circle in which twentieth-century Europe has been locked up."[69]

The Bolsheviks' approach to housing is a revealing example of World War I's impact on the Soviet state's formation and intervention in social life. Yet historians who have examined Soviet state formation in the pan-European context of World War I and across the 1917 divide have overlooked the housing question in this story. On matters of everyday material life, food requisitions feature much more prominently in their studies.[70] In contrast, scholars of Soviet housing typically begin their story in 1917 and pay little attention to the broader pan-European context, World War I, and late Tsarist policies to explain the Bolshevik approach to the housing question that included the abolishment of private property, mass expropriations of private apartments, state ownership of the housing stock, the creation of the communal apartment, the rationing of living space in square meters, and the use of housing as a mechanism of social control.[71] Whereas most scholars argue that these outcomes were uniquely Soviet, the present analysis locates their origins in the pan-European housing reform movement and how World War I and the Bolshevik Revolution transformed its underlying principles into a Soviet answer to the housing question.

Housing reform in Tsarist Russia had followed similar trends in Europe and the United States up to World War I, which spurred the Tsarist regime and Provisional Government to extend state control over housing and social life as in other combatant states. The war also contributed to worsening conditions in urban housing in Russia and elsewhere. Although the war had similar effects on housing and state intervention in Russia and other countries, the Russian revolutions of 1917 introduced a qualitatively different element beginning with mass expropriations and the redistribution of private property. With comparatively minor exceptions, such requisitions did not occur in other combatant states.[72] In Russia, the first expropriations were carried out after the February Revolution of 1917, as crowds destroyed buildings and symbols of the Old Regime and expropriated the housing of Tsarist elites and officials.[73] After the October Revolution, urban workers and local revolutionary authorities continued expropriations and targeted the apartments of the middle classes.[74] Revolution in Russia breached the walls of private property on a scale unseen elsewhere. The Bolsheviks—who were driven by Marxist ideology to eliminate private property, resolve the housing question, and create a classless society— sought to make this breach permanent. Their main strategy for achieving these ends, however, had roots in both the history of the pan-European housing reform movement and the expansion of states' social interventions during World War I.

Upon taking power, the Bolsheviks wasted no time dismantling institutions of private property and extending state control over housing. Their famous "Decree on Land," issued on their second day in power, abolished and redistributed private property in land.[75] They followed with a moratorium on rent that continued efforts begun by the Tsarist regime and mirrored similar decrees in other combatant states for temporarily assisting those in need and those whom the state needed to fight the war.[76] Illustrating how the Bolsheviks picked up where the Provisional Government left off on this issue, the decree used a law of August 5, 1917, as the basis for determining the level of rents that still had to be paid.[77] Soon thereafter, the Bolsheviks issued a decree allowing municipal authorities to confiscate unused housing, relocate people in need of space, and begin establishing a regime of control over the housing stock that far outstripped what other combatant states were doing.[78] In August 1918, the Bolsheviks extended their attack on private property with their decree, "On the Abolition of the Right to Immovable Private Property in Cities," which allowed local authorities in cities with 10,000 or more people to expropriate all buildings as they saw fit.[79] Through these measures, the Bolsheviks created a legal regime sanctioning the nationalization of the country's urban housing stock. World War I had not even ended for most combatant states, and the Bolsheviks had already outstripped them by extending the formal trappings of state control over housing.

In pursuing these measures, the Bolsheviks were also attempting to rein in a chaotic situation. They sought to end spontaneous expropriations by revolutionary mobs and local authorities, and halt further de-struction of the housing stock in the face of mass deurbanization and the collapse of municipal government. Like other combatant states, the Bolsheviks were responding to circumstances. This did not signal a retreat from the revolutionary project in housing; nor did it shake the Bolsheviks' conviction that private property had to be wiped out. Some historians have argued that Bolshevik ideology on housing was "rather weak" and suggested few details apart from the forcible relocation of urban workers into the housing of the ruling classes. With no apparent plan, according to this view, the Bolsheviks and their local authorities spent more time responding to circumstances than implementing ideas.[80] Others have argued that circumstances arising from war and revolution were always overshadowed by the Bolsheviks' intention to extend control over housing as a means of social control and labor discipline, but devoid of any larger vision of creating a new society.[81] Both interpretations miss the larger point: Bolshevik ideology played a crucial role in shaping their response to circumstances, created in no small part by a Marxist inspired assault on private property, and in laying the groundwork for a total transformation of housing and society that extended far beyond the narrow goal of social control.

Historians of the Soviet Union's earliest housing policies have ne-glected to consider how the Bolsheviks' worldview on housing—from recognizing that there was a "housing question" to the state's role in resolving it—crystallized in war and revolution as the most extreme version of nineteenth-century pan-European housing reform. Far from impeding reform ideas or reducing them to the aim of social control, war and revolution opened a space for the Bolsheviks to pursue what many social reformers in the nineteenth century had desired: a total resolution of the housing question. In articulating this goal, the Bolshe-viks were not providing a cynical justification for ending private prop-erty and using housing to control people for its own sake. They acted on what their own ideology told them: that they alone could accom-plish the goal of definitively resolving the housing question, which would serve as a major pillar of the new social order.

Rather than being "weak," Bolshevik ideology on housing would be better described as revolutionary, infinitely expansive, and ultimately tied to the broader project of creating a new society. The Second Program of the Communist Party, issued in March 1919, reflected how the Bolsheviks' approach to housing had evolved through war and revolution since their first party program. Nikolai Bukharin and Evgenii Preobrazhenskii's popular explanation of the new Party Program in *The ABC of Communism* divided their chapter titled "The Communists' Program on the Housing Question" into a section on "The Housing Question in Capitalist Society" and another on "The Housing Question in the Proletarian State."[82] This separation of the world into two camps illustrated a fundamental assumption made by the Bolsheviks that shaped their answers to the housing question and Khrushchev's mass housing campaign forty years later. The October Revolution had created a rupture in historical time between the capitalist society of the past and the future socialist society. As a building block of that future society, the Soviet answer to the housing question would be fundamentally different from the half-measures seen under capitalism.

Bukharin and Preobrazhenskii drew heavily upon the knowledge of the prewar housing reform movement, as refracted through a Marxist lens. Their footnotes dutifully cited Engels's *The Housing Question* and four other works on housing, including *The Housing Question in the West and in Russia* by V. Sviatlovskii, the author of other studies on Russian housing at the turn of the century.[83] The Bolshevik authors explained that housing under capitalism was a source of exploitation and class difference. Poor housing conditions in England, Brussels, and Budapest led to lower life expectancy for workers as compared with the bourgeoisie. Workers paid rent to "capitalist house owners" at levels that represented a substantially greater percentage of their wages than what bourgeois tenants paid. Whereas workers inhabited overcrowded housing on the outskirts of town, the bourgeoisie enjoyed spacious dwellings in garden districts with clean streets. Bukharin and Preobrazhenskii concluded, "Nowhere are the privileges of the bourgeoisie more evident than in housing."[84]

The housing question in the proletarian state, they explained, was being resolved in a radically different way by nationalizing the bourgeoisie's apartments, relocating workers to these dwellings, and placing a moratorium on rent. The Communist Party's main task now was to establish a viable "housing economy" that protected nationalized housing from deterioration. As the authors admitted, local authorities' excessive measures led to the expropriation of small houses, which nobody could maintain and thus fell into disrepair. Without new construction, local soviets had begun to fulfill what became one of their chief functions: "the fair distribution of all citizens in all houses." Directly handling housing distribution was a major endeavor that other

European states had avoided, but which the Bolsheviks eagerly undertook to start answering the housing question. Local soviets redistributed empty apartments according to a "definite plan." They determined the number of houses that remained in large cities and their "capacity" for housing people. They forced people who had "a number of rooms that exceeds the norm" to take on more residents.[85] During the next three decades, these mechanisms evolved into permanent features of the Soviet housing system: distribution according to a plan; gathering statistical data on housing and its density; and using norms to redistribute space.

The Bolsheviks were not interested in nationalizing private property and redistributing housing just for the sake of social control. According to the new Party Program, they intended to use these tools of "soviet power" to fulfill what amounted to the goals of nineteenth-century housing reform: "the improvement of the housing conditions of the toiling masses; the elimination of overcrowding and the unsanitary state of old districts; the elimination of unfit housing and the reconstruction of old housing." To be sure, the Bolsheviks sought to go beyond these goals by building new housing for the new society of the communist future. The best form of housing for this society was still unclear, but Bukharin and Preobrazhenskii suggested two categories: "fully equipped large houses with gardens, common dining facilities and so on, or well-appointed small workers' houses." Different options were on the table, and it was the new proletarian state's responsibility to figure out which ones would be built for the future communist society.[86] Far from being "weak," the Bolshevik approach sanctioned an infinite expansion of state responsibilities from fixing the problems of today to building the housing of tomorrow. Allocating housing was one of the most important of these responsibilities and, as I argue in this chapter and the next, it would shape in unexpected ways the design of mass housing under Khrushchev. Let us now consider in greater detail how Soviet housing allocation evolved in the context of the housing question we have established thus far.

The Quest for Minimal Living Space

The Soviet system of distributing housing was significantly different from a free market or social market approach. But its basic concepts, such as living space (*zhilaia ploshchad'*) and the sanitary norm (*sanitar-*

naia norma), originated in ideas about minimum living standards in the nineteenth-century housing reform movement. The circuitous path these ideas took from pan-European housing reform through their early Soviet adaptation to shaping the *khrushchevka*'s design starts with a smelly French jail in the mid–nineteenth century. In 1843, the historian Dana Simmons explains, France's Interior Ministry tasked its scientists to discover the minimum amount of airflow a prisoner would need to avoid asphyxiating on the smell of his own excrement. They suggested that a prisoner needed a minimum of 10 cubic meters of airflow hourly, which in the summer would be elevated to 12 cubic meters. Such recommendations shaped the work of public health experts, who set about finding minimum living standards for the laboring classes but soon switched from minimum amounts of airflow to minimum amounts of space. By 1848, the prefect of Paris decreed that inexpensive apartments rented by workers, the so-called *garnis*, had to provide a minimum of 14 cubic meters of space per person. His counterparts in London had already established similar regulations that entitled an adult to a minimum of 8.5 cubic meters and a child to 4.2 cubic meters.[87]

The search for smaller spaces was motivated by several factors, starting with cost. In the prison, government officials wanted to give inmates just enough air to live. But their wish to isolate prisoners individually spoke to a broader concern for social control. As Simmons explains, the prison "cell offered both hermetic protection from outside influences and a perfectly regulated environment."[88] Outside the prison and in the city, particularly after the Revolution of 1848, public health professionals and municipal officials hoped to stem overcrowding, which they believed led to infectious diseases, immoral behavior, and social disorder among urban workers.[89] In late Imperial Russia, health professionals and reformers adopted a similar approach, which included studies on the existing dimensions and densities of housing, their social effects, and recommendations for minimum standards. Their studies drew extensively upon the work and policies of their Western European counterparts.[90]

Max von Pettenkofer, whose role in shaping the housing question we have already seen, was particularly influential. Echoing French prison reformers, Pettenkofer developed minimum standards of cubic space based on the airflow one individual required while asleep.[91] As we saw above, Pettenkofer was among those nineteenth-century hygienists and medical professionals in Russia and Europe who were frustrated by governments and private property interests unwilling to allow them free rein in housing. Regulating public spaces like prisons and boulevards was one thing, but dictating the living standards of rental properties proved more difficult. The Parisian authorities in 1848 and again in 1883 were simply unable to translate the prefect's 14-cubic-meter minimum into reality for the city's workers.[92] In England, however, the Public Health Act of 1891 instituted minimum norms for rental housing. A room, which could double as a bedroom, had to have at least 400 cubic feet of space for each adult in it, whereas a bedroom had to have a minimum of 300 cubic feet per adult; half these amounts were deemed sufficient for children.[93] In addition to cubic space, reformers developed other minimum standards and sought to regulate the use of space along gender and generational lines. The proposed Prussian Housing Bill of 1904 featured minimum norms for kitchens and toilets and mandated "the provision of separate rooms for children over the age of ten or unmarried lodgers of different sexes."[94]

The Bolshevik regime appropriated and surged ahead of these earlier policies with its own version of minimum living space soon after the October Revolution. Thus far, I have used the term "living space" without further qualification to mean housing in general. A more precise definition is now required to clarify to which parts of housing the term pertained in Soviet usage. The term "living space" (*zhilaia ploshchad'*) represented only the floor space in an apartment's rooms. The floor space in kitchens, corridors, bathrooms, toilets, and other auxiliary units fell into a separate category known as "auxiliary space" (*vspomogatel'naia* or *podsobnaia ploshchad'*). The sum of the two categories—living and auxiliary space—was known as "overall space" or "useful space" (*obshchaia* or *poleznaia ploshchad'*).[95] Census takers and local soviet authorities throughout the Soviet period used the amount of square meters of living space per person to assess one's quality of housing, determine needs, and allocate space. Their definition and application of the spatial category "living space" evolved from the nineteenth-century pan-European housing reform movement into a fundamental pillar of the Soviet answer to the housing question in the twentieth century. Throughout this book, it is important to keep in mind the particular spatial categories to which our sources refer in order to understand what was being reported in statistics (e.g., overall space or living space) and what parts of an apartment architects and residents were discussing.

In July 1919, the People's Commissariat of Health established a minimum norm of 8.25 square meters of living space per person in temporary housing regulations. Reflecting the outlook of nineteenth-century European hygienists, the norm functioned originally as a minimum in three dimensions. "The height of living quarters must be no less than 2.50 meters (3.5 *arshina*) and the floor space no less than 8.25 square meters (1.8 square *sazheni*) per person."[96] Echoing England's late-nineteenth-century regulations, adults were to have a minimum of 30 cubic meters, while children under 14 were entitled to a minimum of 20 cubic meters. Together, the square meter minimum and cubic meter minimum constituted norms that were "minimal and fundamental from the sanitary-hygienic point of view." The regulations included other "minimal requirements" in housing, reflecting similar attempts by European governments to legislate minimum standards in amenities. A dwelling had to have at least one room and a kitchen. Living quarters had to be dry, enjoy sufficient natural light, have access to fresh air, and come with toilets. Where residents of more than one apartment shared the same toilets, a minimum of one "seat" (*ochko*) for every 10 to 15 people was mandatory, as well as separate toilets for men and women. No mention was made of bathrooms for washing, presumably on the assumption that people went to public baths.[97]

Among the Commissariat of Health's "minimal requirements," the two-dimensional measure of living space was the only one that provided a common basis for assessing needs. It soon became apparent that height, auxiliary spaces, and amenities were simply too varied to incorporate into a standard measure for distribution. In defining needs, the Soviet state soon abandoned a measure based on three dimensions and several "minimal requirements," and settled instead on only living space in square meters. In May 1920, the Soviet of Ministers ordered local authorities to use the Health Commissariat's July 1919 regulations as their guide in devising "living space norms."[98] In June 1921, it set 8.25 square meters per person as the only universal minimum norm to resettle space from expropriated private apartments.[99] The norm eventually became known as the "housing-sanitary norm" (*zhilishchno-sanitarnaia norma*),[100] the "sanitary norm" (*sanitarnaia norma*),[101] or simply the "housing norm" (*zhilishchnaia norma*).[102]

Extreme shortages further transformed the Soviet implementation of minimum living space by reducing what people actually had to levels far below 8.25 square meters. The average amount of living space per person in cities throughout the Soviet Union was measured at 6.45 square meters in 1923 and fell to 4.09 by 1940.[103] Although the 8.25-square-meter norm was originally intended as a minimum, it immediately functioned in practice as a maximum. A family with more than 8.25 square meters had the extra space (*izlishki*) taken away and redistributed to others.[104] National legislation referred to the maximum limit as "established norms," thereby acknowledging that no universal standard existed and that maximum norms were locally defined.[105] Local authorities were allowed and even expected to distribute housing well under the sanitary norm according to the average amount of space per individual in their locality.[106] Consequently, though the sanitary norm provided the maximum limit, the actual amount of space one received corresponded to locally determined norms of living space per person.[107] Despite the extreme shortages that undermined the original intention of the sanitary norm, the state kept it as the fundamental measure of housing needs over the entire course of Soviet history. The norm retained its original meaning as a universal, minimum living standard only in the ideal sense of a level to which the state would raise all citizens.[108] In the Russian Republic, it was raised only twice: to 9 square meters in 1929, and to 12 square meters in 1983.[109]

Although Pettenkofer and other nineteenth-century hygienists may have approved of the Bolshevik state's involvement in public health, they would not have recognized what became of their concept of minimum living standards. As the Soviet hygienist Aleksandr Marzeev readily illustrated in explaining the provenance of the sanitary norm, what Soviet citizens got in 1919 was a simplified version of Pettenkofer's calculations, which had focused primarily on air quality as the criterion for housing sanitation and on cubic space for his recommendations. Marzeev used these calculations to demonstrate how Pettenkofer had first concluded that one person needed 75 cubic meters of space. If the air was properly ventilated, however, Pettenkofer recommended that a person would only need 25 to 30 cubic meters of space. Marzeev added to Pettenkofer's minimum level of cubic space a ceiling height of 3 meters. The result, Marzeev explained, was that "hygienic living space for one person must be equal to 8.25 to 9 square meters." According to Marzeev, this was how the Soviet Union had developed the sanitary norm, or what he called the "minimal hygienic norm of living space."[110]

Marzeev thus implied that policymakers in 1919 had looked directly at Pettenkofer's calculations as a guide for formulating the sanitary norm. I have found no evidence from 1919 or later years to support such a direct link to Pettenkofer. Marzeev's text, *Kommunal'naia gigiena (Public Health)*, was published in 1951, which was one of the worst years in the late Stalin period to credit a Western individual for such a fundamental feature of Soviet life. Because his sourcebook was meant for public health specialists, Marzeev's reference was likely too obscure to attract much attention. Speaking to that audience, he may have simply used Pettenkofer's calculations to ground a long-standing principle of Soviet housing in an established authority on public hygiene. At the very least, Marzeev's explanation indicated that even after World War II, Soviet housing specialists had not forgotten that the Soviet Union's sanitary norm had emerged from a pan-European quest for minimum living space standards, which a German specialist had done much to shape. Marzeev's account also indicated that Soviet policymakers had begun adapting minimum living standards as soon as they had adopted them in 1919.

As Marzeev indicated, the Soviet conversion of Pettenkofer's calculations was based on the assumption that the height of a room would remain at three meters. Although this assumption may have applied to the prerevolutionary housing stock, it did not correspond to separate apartments subsequently built in the Soviet Union. As discussed above, the 1919 regulations mandated a minimum height of only 2.5 meters. Though some separate apartments under Stalin retained a height of 2.7 meters, separate apartments under Khrushchev dropped to 2.5 meters and even 2.2 meters.[111] In deciding that two dimensions were enough for determining citizens' needs, the Soviet state simplified and reduced from the start its sanitary norm and Pettenkofer's emphasis on air circulation. As long as ceiling heights stayed below three meters, the 9-square-meter norm fell short of his recommendations. Beginning in 1919, therefore, Soviet housing regulations had already significantly altered the concept of minimum living standards. This adaptation set the Soviet case in housing apart from its counterparts in the West and would have tremendous consequences for the distribution and design of mass housing in the 1950s and 1960s.

Absent from Marzeev's account was the impact that Soviet minimum living space standards had on the West. The Soviet version of minimum living space inspired and even got ahead of Western architects who pursued the cause of minimum standards after World War I. The 1929 founding conference of modernist architects' premier international body, the International Congress for Modern Architecture (CIAM), was devoted to "Housing for a Subsistence Minimum." CIAM's attempt to establish a universal minimum by soliciting data on housing from conference participants fell flat but was pursued again by Karel Teige in his monumental treatise *The Minimum Dwelling* (1932). Teige urged architects to develop an entirely new and technologically advanced minimal dwelling out of the real-life conditions of urban workers whose housing, however presently awful, had already negated the family and presaged collectivist living alternatives. He argued against basing minimum living standards on purely physiological criteria that produced not a new kind of housing but just a shrunken version of the bourgeois family apartment. This was precisely the problem associated with Le Corbusier's own quest for the minimal dwelling. In 1933, Le Corbusier proposed a model for minimal housing called "The Biological Unit: The Cell of 14 m2 per Occupant." He claimed to draw his norm from past municipal regulations and, echoing his Soviet counterparts, he reduced nineteenth-century minimum standards from three dimensions to simply two. But the "Biological Unit" itself was actually a section of his 1929 *salon d'automne* design for a family apartment. As Simmons argues, modernist architects' search for the minimal dwelling relied more heavily on the past than their ideology of breaking from it would suggest.[112]

Soviet practice exhibited a similar tendency to shrink the traditional, family apartment through minimum standards instead of creating something entirely new, as Teige hoped. Nevertheless, Soviet minimum norms still shaped distribution and the categories of domestic space in novel ways. From 1919 to the end of the Soviet period, residents received state housing in square meters of living space per individual, irrespective of auxiliary spaces and their amenities. This fragmented domestic space into living space (*zhilaia ploshchad'*) and auxiliary space (*vspomogatel'naia* or *podsobnaia ploshchad'*). The rental agreement extended to citizens "the right to use living quarters [*zhiloe pomeshchenie*]" and "the right to use living space," but not the right to a kitchen, bathroom, toilet, or corridor. These were explicitly excluded from the rental agreement.[113] A citizen paid rent only on living space without regard to auxiliary spaces.[114] Article 44 of the Soviet Constitution of 1977 did finally grant Soviet citizens "a right to housing [*zhilishche*]." Yet it only further defined this as "well-built housing," while living space remained the only unit guaranteed by distribution.[115] In measuring needs and distributing housing in square meters of living space, the Soviet Union set itself apart from Western practices, for which "apartments" and "rooms" still mattered in determining needs and allocating housing. As one of the first scholars of Soviet housing, Timothy Sosnovy, noted in 1959, "The USSR is the only country in the world where housing is measured in square meters of living space per person rather than in terms of apartments or number of occupants per room."[116]

In the Soviet context, living space and the sanitary norm were radically reinterpreted and transformed to serve other ends never before conceived by European social reformers. In the 1920s and 1930s, the quantitative measure of living space became intertwined with the ideological program of replacing the family through the socialization of everyday life and the collective, which informed early Bolshevik ideas on recreating society.[117] Counting and distributing housing in square meters of living space denied the very spatial units—the apartment and its rooms—through which a single family and its social practices were represented spatially. By reducing housing to the quantitative category of living space, the state imposed the collectivist values of equality, economy, and mutual responsibility upon each individual who had the same amount of space. This was especially true in localities like Magnitogorsk, where collectivist ideology and extreme shortages gave living space such meanings.[118]

In reality, the practice of basing housing on living space fell far short of collectivist ideals. Communal apartments, barracks, and dormitories were overcrowded, and their material conditions deteriorated. Such housing devolved into spaces of mutual antagonism and distrust. When the state sought to bolster the family in the 1930s, a reasonable outcome of this ideological reversal would have been a return to thinking about housing in terms of apartments and rooms.[119] Yet the Stalinist state did not relinquish the concept of living space, for three main reasons. First, a quantitative measure allowed for maximum use of available space under extreme shortages at a time when industrialization took priority over new housing construction. Second, by ensuring communal distribution, living space helped turn the home into a site of social surveillance, a central concern of the Stalinist state. Third, once local soviets and factory managers controlled housing through the mechanism of living space, they were unlikely to give it up. In sum, measuring housing in square meters of living space facilitated the transformation of a minimum norm into a state mechanism for expropriating and distributing housing.[120]

By the 1930s, the Soviet application of living space and the sanitary norm produced results that nineteenth-century social reformers had hardly intended. The Soviet state's use of these tools made sense as long as most housing remained communal but would pose major problems in design if the government ever decided that apartments intended for single-family occupancy were preferable. This was, of course, precisely what Khrushchev's regime did in the mass housing campaign. But before we can get to the *khrushchevka* to see our long-awaited Soviet answer to the nineteenth century's housing question, we must first consider more closely how the Soviet Union rejected single-family apartments in the 1920s only to fall in love with them all over again under Stalin. The separate apartments built under Stalin, though few and far between, are a critical link in our story that ties nineteenth-century housing reform and minimum living space standards to the *khrushchevka*.

The Death and Resurrection of the Single-Family Apartment

On ideological grounds alone, the separate apartment was a strange fit for a socialist country on its way to communism. Housing that privileged privacy, the family, traditional gender roles, and the accumulation of new consumer goods was not the intended outcome of the October Revolution in the home. After 1917, the Bolsheviks declared war on these bastions of the bourgeois social order with the intent of solving the housing question for the laboring classes that languished in basements and tenement buildings.[121] For the propertied classes, the immediate result of the Revolution was the transformation of their homes into communal apartments. Workers expropriated and moved into the single-family apartments of the bourgeoisie and aristocracy under the banner of class war in an often violent and traumatic process for the previous inhabitants who stayed.[122]

The communal apartment was a shock to different inhabitants for different reasons. For the prerevolutionary bourgeoisie and aristocracy, it represented a loss of property, an invasion of privacy, and a leveling of social differences. Living communally in cramped quarters with uninvited strangers from the lower orders was indeed a new experience for the affluent urban classes of Tsarist Russia. The revolution in the propertied classes' homes extended into the 1920s as local authorities and Soviet law took over from revolutionary mobs in redistributing their apartments to other people. Former owners tried to beat local officials to the punch by bringing in friends and relatives to live with them. They sought on their own terms the "condensing" (*uplotnenie*) of their apartments into communal apartments.[123] For the laboring classes, living communally was not so new. Their prerevolutionary barracks and tenement buildings had given them a taste of cramped living conditions.[124] What was new for them was living with former members of the bourgeoisie and aristocracy, and using the unfamiliar amenities of their opulently designed homes.[125]

In the long run, redistributing existing apartments was not enough for Bolshevik revolutionaries and their fellow travelers intent on creating a new way of life. New forms of housing would need to be built in order to truly remake society and create a New Soviet Man and Woman. Unfortunately, Karl Marx and Friedrich Engels had given little indication about the form housing would take under communism. Engels himself had eschewed responsibility for mapping out a complete solution in his 1872 treatise *The Housing Question*: "To speculate as to how a future society would organise the distribution of food and dwellings leads directly to *utopia*" (emphasis in the original).[126] In the Marxist worldview, only those who lived after the overthrow of capitalism could make such decisions. Under communism, people would no longer be forced to accept whatever housing capitalism produced as tools of class oppression, but would instead create housing out of their own ideas as people finally in control of their social organization.[127] In revolutionary Russia, this task fell primarily to visionary architects and other members of the radical intelligentsia, for whom the total transformation of everyday life had been a central goal before 1917 and which the Bolshevik Revolution had now made possible.[128]

Revolutionary activists took the lead during the heady days of "war communism" in the Civil War (1918–21) by creating "house communes" (*doma-kommuny*) out of prerevolutionary dwellings. In the 1920s, architects and urban planners improved upon these early experiments with designs for new "house communes."[129] The Union of Contemporary Architects (Ob"edinenie Sovremennykh Arkhitektorov, OSA) was the epicenter of collectivist living designs, where visionaries such as Mikhail

Barshch and Moisei Ginzburg planned the cities and housing of the future.[130] In house communes, residents would have small rooms primarily for sleeping, while cooking, eating, child rearing, and leisure would be socialized in rationally designed communal spaces such as dining facilities, nurseries, and clubs. The "housing question" and the "women question" intersected in these designs. Women would be the chief beneficiaries of collectivist housing, which would free them from household labor and childrearing so they could join the workforce in constructing socialism.[131] Activists in the Communist Party's Zhenotdel (Women's Department) likewise pressed for these radical improvements in women's living and working conditions. Calls for the communalization of domestic work and the enhancement of women's everyday lives fell under the rubric of "the socialization of everyday life."[132] Whether in theory (the *dom-kommuna*) or in practice (the communal apartment), all roads appeared to be heading toward collectivist housing of one form or another in the 1920s.

Rapid industrialization during the First Five-Year Plan (1928–32) significantly altered the context in which architects and others sought to resolve the housing question. The construction of new dwellings fell far behind the demands of urbanization as resources were poured into industrialization. The industrialization drive reinforced the communalization of the housing stock and the construction of communal housing such as barracks and dormitories. In industrializing towns like Magnitogorsk, communal housing was declared to be socialist; it was concrete evidence that the Revolution continued not only in the factory but also in the home. The resemblance of such conditions to prerevolutionary workers' housing and the fact that barracks and dormitories hardly lived up to the rational designs of the *dom-kommuna* mattered very little. In Magnitogorsk, barracks and dormitories were socialist by virtue of being represented as such and existing in a socialist state.[133]

The work of avant-garde architects and urban planners culminated during the broader "cultural revolution" of the late 1920s and early 1930s when leftist Communists and radical visionaries claimed the banner of class war to storm the barricades of the bourgeois intelligentsia in the name of creating a truly proletarian culture.[134] Debates raged between "urbanists," who foresaw new, rationally planned socialist cities, and "disurbanists," who wanted to resolve the urban/rural divide by dismantling cities and evenly redistributing their human and material resources.[135] With its focus on meeting the needs of rapid industrialization, the Stalinist state lost patience with avant-garde architects and urban planners, whose designs were either too expensive or too impractical. Along with other radical Communists and visionaries, the architects of the *dom-kommuna* and their allies in the Zhenotdel were marginalized as the Stalinist party-state brought the "cultural revolution" to an end in the early 1930s. The Zhenotdel was abolished in January 1930. Its duties were dispersed among other Communist Party organizations, and its focus on the "socialization of everyday life" was abandoned in favor of elevating women individually.[136] The party next turned its attention to radical architects and urban planning theorists. In May 1930, the party's Central Committee issued the decree "Concerning Work on the Reconstruction of Everyday Life," which rejected projects for collectivist living and revolutionary town planning.[137] The decree also initiated the Stalinization of the architectural profession, which eventually brought all architectural groups under central state control in the early 1930s.[138]

Although the Communist Party cited costs and lack of resources in its May 1930 decree as reasons for rejecting the visionaries' plans, it also worried about the political risks of indulging the purveyors of a cultural revolution run amok. In planning the complete communalization of everyday life—including "eating, housing, and the upbringing of children, while separating them from their parents, obliterating everyday family relations, preventing the individual preparation of food by administrative fiat"—architects and urban visionaries had gotten ahead of themselves and created instead "harmful, utopian undertakings." The antifamily collectivism that informed utopian scheming risked "severely discrediting the very idea of the socialist reconstruction of everyday life." The party condemned such excesses as vain attempts to leap directly into socialism before industrialization had created the requisite material foundations. It still declared its support for the reconstruction of everyday life, as well as communal facilities such as cafeterias, public baths, and laundries. But for now, the party announced a more tempered approach to reconstructing the everyday without specifying what it would look like.[139]

In May 1930, the party said little about what kind of housing was preferable other than the promise to build "separate residential houses for toilers."[140] The family's withering away seemed off the table, but exactly what would these houses look like? The answer became clearer in the next few years as the single-family apartment reemerged in the architectural void left vacant by the party's condemnation of collectivist housing. Central and local government policies soon mandated the construction of single-family apartments in which the kitchen, bathroom, and toilet were reintegrated with rooms to form a single living unit.[141] The shift to single-family occupancy reflected the Stalinist state's broader rehabilitation of the family in rhetoric and policies such as the banning of abortion and limits on divorce.[142] These changes did not mean that Stalin's regime intended to make separate apartments available to all citizens. For most people, new housing came in the form of barracks and dormitories, and also apartments intended for communal distribution. Only those lucky enough to be in the elite— party-state officials, specialists, and elites in the cultural intelligentsia —had a chance to receive the few spacious separate apartments that architects built under Stalin.[143] Even in Magnitogorsk, specialists and elite officials lived in single-family homes previously inhabited by foreign engineers.[144]

In addition to being a reward for elites, the Stalin-era separate apartment served a broader social function: buttressing the regime's attempts to talk about and justify social differences under socialism. The separate apartment emerged in Stalinist discourse as an ideal domestic setting not yet attainable by all, in which a person acquired *kul'turnost'*, the process of becoming a more cultured individual in taste, behavior, and personal hygiene.[145] In the postwar years, the separate apartment remained an item of extreme shortage and privilege where the Stalinist elite could cultivate its "middle-class" values.[146]

In their journals and meetings of the 1930s, architects dutifully advocated single-family apartments and repudiated collectivist designs. The architect Roman Khiger, a member of the now-defunct OSA,[147] explained that architects had previously reduced or eliminated the kitchen, bathroom, and toilet in a crude attempt to lay the foundations for "the socialist reconstruction of everyday life." These spaces were now heading back into apartments. The task of the architect was "to provide each living unit with the possibility of having the maximum comforts in everyday conditions, and the more these comforts will be individualized in the sense of their use, the higher will be the quality of socialist housing."[148] Interpreting the Communist Party's "unmask[ing] of the theory of 'deurbanization' and the 'socialization of everyday life,'" the architect P. Blokhin explained, "from this moment, the separate apartment with a kitchen, bath or shower, and all the necessary amenities holds a firm place in design."[149] Single-family apartments were now safely "socialist"; it was the architect's job to make them the cutting-edge of housing design.

Many architects seized the moment by designing elite single-family apartments in expensive and ornately decorated buildings that embodied the neoclassical and neo-Renaissance style of Stalinist architecture. To provide an architectural form for the privileges of the new elite, architects referenced nineteenth- and early-twentieth-century bourgeois and aristocratic homes in prerevolutionary Russia and the West. Domestic space in elite apartments was organized into public, private, and service spheres, which had been typical of European bourgeois apartments in the late nineteenth century.[150] The architect G. Simonov explained in 1936, "The apartment is meant for the family; from this we must consider the apartment not as the sum of separate, isolated rooms but proceed from the specialization of spaces, with a separation into important spaces and second-tier spaces." Simonov drew on the English cottage as a model. "In the English cottage, a small room, connected to the kitchen, is usually placed downstairs; on the second floor are the bedrooms, bathroom and toilet. Recently we've generally used the same principle but combined on one plane."[151] Split-level apartments were rare but not unheard of in elite 1930s housing as illustrated by I. Zholtovskii's apartment house on Mokhovaia Street in Moscow.[152]

The architect A. Mikhailov justified the newfound reliance on "the Renaissance and classical heritage" by arguing that these styles "clearly reflect the diversity of a person's relationship to society and nature." In this context, "diversity" was coded language for class differences. Mikhailov's model domestic setting was a "typical noble country estate." He admired how its public and intimate spaces were spatially interconnected. "Buildings of 'public' [*obshchestvennoe*] use are always at the center of [an estate's] composition. Of course, these aren't like the public buildings we have now, like a club and other buildings. But, in any event you see where the guests congregated in the center of a hall. Buildings with intimate spaces were adjoined to these halls and all this was done so that rooms were closely integrated with one another."[153]

Relating his observations to contemporary apartments, Mikhailov addressed "the relationship between outward-facing architecture and that of the intimate sphere." He explained that "the country estate always appears before a visitor with its front side." Transposed to a present-day apartment under socialism, this space became the room for receiving members of elite Soviet society. "If there's a Komsomol member in the family, they'll need a room designated and designed for his meetings with comrades."[154] The function Mikhailov assigned to this sitting room echoed its place in the nineteenth-century bourgeois home where, as Jürgen Habermas tells us, "the line between private and public sphere extended right through the home" and "the family room became a reception room in which private people gather to form a public."[155] Similar to the nineteenth-century bourgeoisie, the Soviet public for which Mikhailov wanted his colleagues to build was not all of society but an elite minority that included engineering-technical personnel and Stakhanovites. As for the intimate sphere, the country estate included it as an organic space closely related to nature, where "you'll see a terrace, a flight of stairs with vegetation, water, and fountains nearby. This is where the second part, the intimate one, already stands out."[156]

As Mikhailov readily acknowledged, this spatial division between public and private spaces was rooted in the country estate of an aristocrat. Adopting such a model and referencing its source would have been anathema to the Bolsheviks and radical architects in the wake of the Revolution, when their solution to the housing question entailed expropriations of private property and making a clean break from the past. How times had changed. The recreation of a family-oriented, spatially differentiated model for apartments was now thoroughly socialist. Mikhailov explained that "socialist culture" was evolving in such a way that people's demands, family relations, and relationship to nature were becoming more diverse. Architects would need to design the built environment to meet these changes and "recognize the diverse and growing demands that the person of socialist society now asks of our socialist architecture."[157]

Even the spaces that connected the public, service, and intimate spheres of the elite Soviet home were growing increasingly complex. According to one architect, the front entrance should lead to the living room, while an inner corridor should connect the largest room with a bedroom and yet another corridor should connect the kitchen to the dining room.[158] The architect P. Blokhin praised recent designs that included a "service corridor, uniting the kitchen, sanitary unit [i.e., combined bathroom and toilet] and pantry." The front part of the apartment was designed as an entrance space with direct access only to rooms.[159]

Karo Alabian, an architect who pursued the Stalinization of the profession and its turn toward traditional styles, included the studied division of public and private spaces in a three-room apartment (figure 1.1).[160] The front of the apartment included its main service area, the kitchen, as well as its public spaces for receiving guests, the drawing room and a dining niche. The conspicuous grand piano in the drawing room marked this apartment as the home of a cultured member of the creative intelligentsia. Its public portion was accessed through its main entrance and its adjoining foyer, which served as a transitional buffer space announcing the intimate sphere, which began with a small corridor, off which were located two bedrooms and a combined bathroom and toilet.[161]

The division of domestic space into public and private spaces was upheld as late as 1954 in the collection *Interior of a Residential House*. Its authors noted that "the bathroom and toilet adjoining the bedrooms belong to the back of the apartment and form with them its 'intimate' part, which is not directly connected to its front entranceway."[162] This arrangement required two separate plumbing systems, a luxury that would not survive Khrushchev's mass housing campaign.

In addition to promoting a division of public, private, and service spaces in the apartment, architects included spaces with singular functions that echoed the prerevolutionary apartments of the bourgeoisie and aristocracy. In his praise of I. Zholtovskii's apartment house on Mokhovaia Street in Moscow, an architect noted that he "proceeded from the fundamental prerequisite that one family will occupy every apartment and that each room will have a special designation: a bedroom, a dining room, an office and so on."[163] Having trained and practiced as an architect before the Russian Revolution, Zholtovskii was a direct link to prerevolutionary architectural practices.[164] Other architects advocated similar spaces that harked back to the prerevolutionary era. Simonov advocated bay windows and elaborate open-air balconies. He saw a dining room and an office as distinct spaces, separated by a removable divider, curtains, or double doors so the two could become one larger room.[165]

Without a hint of irony, architects also included space for a domestic in the elite apartments of the world's first workers' state. Zholtovskii's building on Mokhovaia Street contained spaces meant for servants.[166] In 1934, the architect of a new apartment building for engineering-technical personnel in Moscow was chastised for leaving out servants'

Figure 1.1. Plan for a three-room apartment (architect, K. Alabian). The units of the apartment are listed below the blueprint: (1) entranceway, 3.95 square meters; (2) foyer, 5.45 square meters; (3) living room, 20.5 square meters; (4) dining niche, 6 square meters; (5) kitchen, 4.9 square meters; (6) bedroom, 16.25 square meters; (7) corridor, 5.45 square meters; (8) bathroom and toilet, 4 square meters; (9) bedroom, 16.25 square meers.

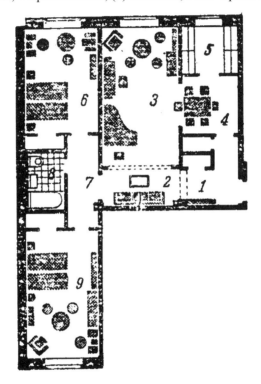

1. Трехкомнатная квартира

1—передняя—3,95 м² 2—фойе—5,45 м²
3—жилая комната—20,5 м² 4 — столо-
вая-ниша- 6,0 м² 5—кухня – 4,9 м² 6—
спальня—16,25 м² 7—коридор—5,45 м²
8 – ванная-уборная—4,0 м² 9—спаль·
ня – 16,25 м²

Source: Iu. Shass, "Malometrazhnaia kvartira," *Arkhitektura SSSR*, no. 5 (1940): 12.

quarters.[167] In a novel application of minimum living standards hark-
ing back to concerns about air flow in our cramped French prison cell
in 1843, the architect P. Aleshin argued that servants were entitled to
even more space than the sanitary norm: "The maximum size of a
room for a domestic is set at 9 square meters. That's nonsense. If there
aren't any cracks or ventilation in such a room, the domestic will suf-
focate, and in a 6-meter room all the more. There's a limit for a residential room, 12 square meters, below which it's not permitted to go."[168]

According to Aleshin, bigger apartments were better and smaller
apartments were a big mistake. He mocked the minimalist designs of
the disgraced avant-garde with an epithet usually reserved for rem-
nants of the prerevolutionary past: "Apartments with few rooms are a
holdover from the past [*perezhitok*]." In contrast, larger apartments
were in demand. "Take the latest law on abortion," he explained. "We
find a lot of demand for apartments intended for four to five children."[169]
For this architect, the state's profamily policies and decision to make
abortion illegal served as convenient justifications for larger apartments. Never mind that the state had no intention or means to make
spacious apartments available to all.

In addition to their own quarters, servants required service entrances
and back stairwells to access the kitchen, separating them from family
members' movement in and out of the apartment (figure 1.2). Simonov
explained that a back stairwell was justified as a safety feature in case
of fires, but feared its expense.[170] Aleshin advocated a compromise
whereby the back stairwell would be eliminated and the back entrance
would be moved to the main stairwell as a separate entrance to the
apartment's housekeeping spaces. His proposal preserved the division
of space between the intimate sphere and service spaces with a particular emphasis on motion: "If we have one staircase, then it's necessary
to draw all movement related to servicing the apartment to this staircase, isolating it from the entrance hall. Movement related to servicing
the apartment must have an independent exit but not through the front
entrance area."[171]

To justify such features, architects only had to look to contemporary European designs as a model. Drawing upon what they saw on a
tour of European cities in 1936, a team of twelve Leningrad housing
construction and municipal officials asserted that the back entrance
and stairwell had fallen out of favor in contemporary European housing and that Soviet apartments should adopt the new model with both

Figure 1.2. Floor plan of a Stalin-era single-family apartment (architect, K. Dzhus). The apartment's spacious interior included three rooms and a dining room, two balconies, a back entrance off the kitchen, and a separated toilet and bathroom.

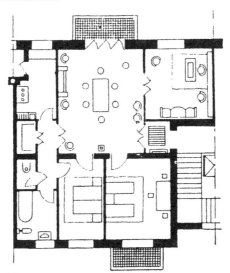

Квартира в 4 комнаты. План

Арх. К. И. Джус

Logement de 4 pièces. Plan

Arch. K. I. Djoʟs

Source: K. Dzhus, "Planirovka kvartiry v novykh zhilykh domakh," *Arkhitektura SSSR,* no. 9 (1936): 12.

the main entrance and the service entrance leading into an apartment from the same stairwell. The Leningraders' tour took them through several European cities—including Stockholm, Paris, Lille, London, and Leeds—to research Western urban planning and housing construction. (When they stopped in Berlin, the Nazi authorities denied them the opportunity to see much of the city and its housing.) In their report to Lazar' Kaganovich, the Politburo member who played a pivotal role in the Stalinization of architecture and its embrace of monumentalism,[172] the Leningraders made several other recommendations for elite apartments.[173]

These recommendations included technological gadgets such as automatic doors in a building's main entrance and automatic lights in

common spaces. Apartments should also include such modern amenities as bathtubs and showers, as well as built-in closets.[174] The Leningrad
officials were particularly fond of the two- to three-room apartments
they had seen in Sweden, which included kitchens and baths, as well as
sufficiently tall ceilings of 2.7 to 2.8 meters. Although Sweden built
both residential and nonresidential buildings equally well, England
and France invested too much in the latter and skimped on housing,
which "they build cheaply and badly in pursuit of cutting costs." This
was a reference to the austere designs of modernist architecture that
the Stalinist regime had only recently condemned at home. Commenting
on a set of nine-story apartment buildings (whose location was not
noted), the Leningraders lamented that the "architecture recalls ours
of the period 1926–30. That means mainly four- to five-story buildings
based on a rectangular plan." The smooth surfaces of the buildings'
facades and their balconies' solid appearance were further evidence of
their close resemblance to the architecture of the avant-garde.[175] But
whereas a building's outer architecture could no longer hint at such
aesthetics, the interior design of apartments allowed for more flexibility and borrowing from modernist designs.

As always, the kitchen was the site of modern domestic innovation
and Stalin's elites could not do without one. After having been threatened with near extinction by some *dom-kommuna* architects, the single-
family kitchen was back. The Leningrad officials' recommendations
suggested that they had seen models inspired by the compact and technologically advanced designs of the legendary Frankfurt Kitchen.[176]
They called for a kitchen with "the maximum comforts (a washing
area, electrical or gas stove, electrical refrigerator, kitchen table, and
wall cupboards for various necessities) so that all of a kitchen's equipment becomes an integral part of an apartment, and not the resident's
property."[177] This last point reflected the kitchen's compact and rational design, but may have also provided ideological cover. A Soviet
elite's apartment might be based on Western capitalist designs, but it
would not engender residents with the proprietary habits of their
Western bourgeois counterparts. Like other attributes of Stalinist architecture and urban planning, such as monumentalism and neoclassicism, the kitchen and the single-family apartment were socialist because of their presence in a socialist country that had already deposed
capitalism through the Russian Revolution.[178]

By this logic, whatever was designed or built in the Soviet Union was automatically socialist, regardless of its historical origins, and whatever existed in the West was hopelessly capitalist. Foreshadowing the rhetorical claims of Cold War duels over domestic space and standards of living, the Leningrad officials dutifully reported to Kaganovich that European cities devoted their resources to improving the bourgeoisie's central neighborhoods, while the working class languished in substandard housing on the periphery.[179] The European worker typically inhabited "a house made out of plywood with a paltry amount of living space, overcrowded with poor inhabitants." The touring officials even took pleasure in pointing out the irony in the names of certain districts such as "Belle Ville" in Paris, where workers lived in squalor. Perhaps Kaganovich recognized the greater irony that these officials might as well have been describing the living conditions of Soviet workers in contrast to those of Stalin's new elite. Perhaps not. After all, according to the cultural logic of Stalinist architecture, there was nothing bourgeois about separate apartments and neoclassicism once they were adopted in the Soviet Union.

Another characteristic of prerevolutionary and Western housing that was magically cleansed of its bourgeois connotations was the architect's attention to an individual client's needs. Architects building for Stalin's new elite advocated a closer relationship between design and residents. Apartments should reflect tenants' social differences and meet the needs of different social groups. The architect O. Vutke explained in 1936 that under present conditions, whereby people received goods as a reward for their labor, some housing was specifically designed for specialists, while Stakhonovites and other "decorated persons" received priority in distribution. Vutke associated attempts to reduce the number of apartment designs and "search for a single, principal planning resolution" with misguided efforts at social leveling. Differences in design would continue under communism, he argued, because people would have different needs.[180] Blokhin repeated much the same in 1937, explaining that better-quality housing was reserved for certain social groups: "In reality, houses of a better type are intended to be settled by the distinguished people of our country, Stakhonovites, great scientists, persons standing out in the arts, and other citizens, for whom Soviet power displays special care regarding the arrangement of their everyday lives."[181]

Such architects were concerned that modern design techniques—standardization and quantitative space measurements—made it impossible for architects to know and meet tenants' needs. Simonov identified "ignorance of the person, for whom we build," as the main cause of "the defects of our modern living unit."[182] Mikhailov argued that "in the quest for residential architecture, it's always necessary to consider which kind of housing is needed for satisfying the needs of, let's say, engineering-technical personnel, Stakhonovites, and so on."[183] The architect I. Vainshtein explained that "in planning a residential building we have no idea who will live in the future apartments and for whom we build. We only plan abstract 'units.'" According to Vainshtein, the solution—to have architects become acquainted with future tenants—was a chief example of their "care for the person."[184] Through "contact with future residents," architects would tailor apartments to tenants' professional needs. "Why must we make all apartments in a new building the same height?" Vainshtein wondered. "Why, for example, must an artist live in the same apartment as the commercial director of a factory? Indeed an artist needs to draw his paintings, he needs more light, a room of greater height. Why, let's say, must the violinist Oistrakh live in the same apartment as the pilot Vodop'ianov?"[185] Such calls for diversity in apartment designs illustrate again how closely the rehabilitation of single-family occupancy and separate apartments in the 1930s was related (and restricted) to the rise of a new elite under Stalin and the justifications that made their privileges palatable.

Conclusion

As the immediate discussion above has shown, the resurrection of the single-family apartment in the 1930s reflected the social and cultural values of Stalinism. In place of the egalitarianism and collectivist lifestyle that informed the *dom-kommuna* housing projects of the 1920s, the Stalin-era separate apartment embraced the family and class differences, now euphemistically known as "diversity" in a socialist society. Having been marked for extinction in Marxist theory and the early days of the Russian Revolution as a vestige of the bourgeois order, the single-family apartment returned on the heels of political transformations in the late 1920s and early 1930s. As Stalin's regime poured resources into industrialization, it rejected the avant-garde and Zhenotdel's projects for the immediate transformation of social life as premature, politically risky, and too costly. Stepping into the void, the single-family apartment provided the ideal domestic setting for a slower path to social transformation and the propagation of *kul'turnost'*. Though only available to Stalin's new elite, the single-family apartment and the civilized lifestyle it represented were ideals to which all could aspire and eventually acquire under communism.

The single-family apartment's return was not only inspired by internal transformations specific to Stalinism. Like the norms for minimum living space that the Bolsheviks had earlier adopted and adapted from the pan-European housing reform movement, the single-family occupancy of apartments was an international standard, albeit of modern urban bourgeois life, that Stalin's regime was eager to borrow and harness for its own purposes as it looked forward to building a socialist version of modernity. Soviet housing experts were sent abroad to figure out how best to design and build such apartments, while architects at home turned to housing layouts and architectural styles from the European and Russian past for aesthetic inspiration in designing facades and balancing the public, private, and service spaces of elite urban apartments. Stalin's regime broke many economic and cultural ties with the West, including links to the international style in architecture, as it embarked upon its autarkic version of industrialization. Yet as the historian Yves Cohen reminds us, severing such ties did not prevent the regime from continuing to borrow ideas and objects from the West, retooling them to fit Soviet conditions, and repackaging them as socialist.[186] Norms for minimum living space and the modernist aesthetics of CIAM were not the only architectural trends the West had to offer. The single-family bourgeois apartment was another.

As this chapter has shown, the Soviet Union obtained and retooled two elements—norms for minimum living space and single-family occupancy—into two critical pillars of its housing system at two very different times in its prewar history. Whereas the Bolsheviks adopted the first in the wake of the October Revolution and through the 1920s, Stalin's regime rehabilitated the second in the 1930s. Both elements had their origins in different aspects of the pan-European housing reform movement. Public hygiene specialists such as Max von Pettenkofer developed minimum living space norms to improve the health and housing conditions of the urban working poor. Single-family occupancy was the requisite living arrangement that reformers such as Frédéric Le

Play promoted to transmit proper bourgeois values and behaviors to workers and their families. Once inside the Soviet Union, both elements were adapted to Soviet conditions and acquired new functions to serve Soviet goals. Minimum living space norms and single-family occupancy also interacted in ways that neither nineteenth-century housing reformers nor Soviet policymakers intended, namely, by putting the distribution of housing in tension with design. We now turn to this issue in the next chapter and to the problems it posed for architects committed to extending the separate apartment to the general population. Explaining how architects solved the unforeseen tensions between minimum living space norms and single-family occupancy will help us answer the question that began this chapter and frustrated so many ordinary urban dwellers: Why did the *khrushchevka* have to be so small?

Chapter 2

Khrushchevka: The Soviet Answer
to the Housing Question

At first glance, the distribution of housing had little influence on design because it followed rather than preceded the architect's job. But in the case of the *khrushchevka*, the process was in a certain sense reversed. The basic problem had to do with the inherent contradiction between design and distribution, the outline of which we began to see in chapter 1. In theory, a separate apartment by design was supposed to be settled by an individual family. In practice, under the rules of housing distribution, an apartment was parceled out to individuals (not families) in square meters of living space, which only included the floor space of rooms but not auxiliary spaces such as kitchens and corridors. If it had too much living space, any apartment could be settled communally regardless of its architect's intent. In chapter 1, we saw how architects who embraced single-family occupancy under Stalin designed separate apartments for elites. In this chapter, I examine how a different set of architects, who were mainly from the marginalized avant-garde of the 1920s, resolved the unintended communal distribution of apartments. In doing so, these architects skillfully leveraged the conditions of socialist housing distribution to pursue their enduring dream of creating a minimal dwelling unit for the mass urban resident in an era when their constructivist aesthetics and the international style were officially banned. Their design formula became the template for the *khrushchevka* but left future architects in the 1950s and 1960s with an ambiguous legacy of architectural choices and limitations.

The architects' solution to the communalization of separate apartments was the drastic reduction in living space to such a level that local officials would be unable to settle apartments with more than one family. This solution, I argue, was the fundamental reason separate apartments under Khrushchev were so small. The problem of communal distribution and the architects' solution constituted the fundamentally Soviet aspects of the separate apartment's design that distinguished it from prerevolutionary and Western models of single-family apartments. This chapter demonstrates how architects made the solution to communal distribution a founding design principle of the *khrushchevka*. It shows how this solution's repercussions shaped the other factors to which scholars have pointed—such as costs, aesthetics, and ideology, which were discussed in chapter 1—to explain its small dimensions and compact layout. My explanation provides a novel way of thinking about the evolution of the *khrushchevka*'s design that will help us make sense of residents' reactions and complaints, which will be examined in later chapters of this book.

Avant-Garde Architects Strike Back

With the Stalinization of their profession and crackdown on dissenters, the avant-garde architects of the *dom-kommuna* were forbidden from questioning the wisdom of single-family housing, much less pointing out its bourgeois origins or offering alternative designs based on collectivist living. Yet the constructivist architects who continued to work under Stalin, such as Mikhail Barshch and Moisei Ginzburg, were not entirely powerless to criticize the new line in architecture that provided single-family apartments for elites, while leaving the majority of urban dwellers in barracks, dormitories, and communal apartments. Nor were they entirely incapable of promoting the principles and aesthetics of their previous work, such as scientific management and minimalism. Under the cultural logic of Stalinism, as best illustrated in the discourse on *kul'turnost'* (culturedness), the privileges of the Soviet intelligentsia would in theory be available to all once communism was built.[1] This enabled former members of the Union of Contemporary Architects (Ob"edinenie Sovremennykh Arkhitektorov, OSA) and other like-minded architects to argue that because all citizens would eventually enjoy single-family apartments, current designs would need to be simplified and made less expensive to achieve this goal. With this explanation, they made recommendations that echoed many of the architectural principles they had espoused in the 1920s.

The logic of *kul'turnost'* was not the only factor that gave avant-garde architects an opening to critique palatial apartments and continue promoting their officially disgraced ideas. Another crucial factor was the reality that awaited any separate apartment once it was released to local authorities for distribution. An apartment that was too large for just one family was allocated communally to as many families as local authorities could place in it. As will be recalled, an apartment was deemed too large once its living space per family member exceeded local norms. In the face of extreme shortages that lowered local distribution norms well below the sanitary norm of 9 square meters per person, local authorities could little afford to let just one family occupy one apartment. A prerevolutionary single-family apartment that had survived intact the mass expropriations of private property soon after the October Revolution eventually underwent communalization for these reasons.

Such a fate did not only await prerevolutionary single-family apartments. It also threatened to turn any single-family apartment built after 1917 into a communal apartment. Architects of the former avant-garde relished every opportunity to point out this troubling contradiction between the design of an apartment intended for one family and its allocation to two or more families. If the Soviet Union truly intended to make single-family occupancy an ideal to which all citizens could aspire, not just the elites, then apartments would need to be built their way: small and economical. By appropriating official discourses of prosperity and "culturedness" for all citizens in the future, distancing themselves from the *dom-kommuna*, and offering a solution to communal distribution, the architects of the defunct avant-garde kept alive their vision of minimum living space. In doing so, they laid the design groundwork for the Khrushchev-era separate apartment.

In a 1936 article, "The Minimal Living Unit," the architect A. Urban dutifully urged his colleagues to reject "the extremes—the kilometers of corridors in the 'house communes' of recent years and all attempts to put several small families into 5- to 6-room apartments of the old type." They should design instead the "minimal apartment," intended "for the bachelor and the person with a small family," and make it "a completely independent organism."[2] At a 1936 meeting of architects, G. Vol'fenzon argued that large apartments "in the majority of cases are settled not with one family but with several families. As a result, the architect's entire intention comes to nothing." In backing Vol'fenzon, another architect noted that "an apartment intended for one family should be settled with only one family."[3] By 1939, even P. Blokhin, who as we saw in chapter 1 had praised spacious apartments for elites, threw in his lot for smaller apartments. Along with A. Zal'tsman, Blokhin criticized apartments with excessive living space because "an apartment had to be settled with two or several families." This undercut the architect's design work: "An apartment which is not intended for one family loses the quality of a thought-out and functionally complete organism and turns into a mechanical aggregate of rooms."[4] Their allusion to "mechanism" was a clever appropriation of an epithet that opponents of OSA had thrown at it in the late 1920s.[5] Blokhin and Zal'tsman reworked the term to criticize architects who thoughtlessly designed large apartments that automatically became communal upon distribution.

The elite apartments described in chapter 1 were also fair game for such communalization.[6] Commenting on the servant's space in elite apartments, the architect Simonov explained at a 1936 housing architecture meeting that her niche could be used as extra kitchen space in the event that an apartment was distributed communally.[7] In addition to luxurious apartments intended solely for elites, architects under Stalin built large but less ornate apartments, the communalization of which was highly likely. As one architect lamented at a 1937 meeting, it was taken for granted that two to three families would end up in apartments designed with six rooms.[8] In 1940, Iu. Shass criticized "the 'noninterference' of architects in questions concerning the settlement and use of residential buildings." In a scathing comparison to exploitative prerevolutionary housing, he blasted the communal settlement of apartments as the continuation of "an ugly tradition," which had more to do with "the 'shrunken' type of apartments of former for-profit tenement houses" than "a modern type of apartment."[9] Soviet apartments had not advanced beyond housing in which members of the working classes rented rooms, parts of rooms, or simply cots.

Census data and local studies backed up the architects' assertions that large separate apartments were becoming communal. According to a Moscow study reported in 1940, 70 to 90 percent of people moving into newly constructed apartment buildings only received rooms in apartments. The architects L. Gel'berg and B. Plessein drew the obvious conclusion: "The fundamental cause of the settlement of apartments by room is, in our opinion, their great living space, the consequence of designers' incomplete consideration of the real conditions of settlement."[10] "Real conditions" referred to massive shortages and to settling housing by living space well under the sanitary norm. Fifteen years later, policymakers in Moscow understood the problem in much the same way. Communal living, which was already the norm for many urban residents at the time of the 1926 census, had grown more severe for two reasons: The average amount of space per person dropped, while new apartments remained too large, averaging approximately 40 square meters of living space, or 2.6 rooms per apartment and 16 square meters per room. Consequently, "newly built buildings were settled with a few families per apartment."[11]

During World War II, the widespread destruction of urban housing and deepening shortages enabled architects to continue pressing their case against unintended communal settlement. A. Zal'tsman explained in 1943 that because architects could not tell whether their apartments would be settled by single families or communally, their design work was reduced to making "an apartment for all circumstances." Instead of designing apartments that would serve both kinds of settlement patterns, he urged architects simply to design some apartments for communal settlement and others for single families.[12] Moisei Ginzburg argued for adopting standard designs of single-family housing and the industrialization of construction to rebuild in the wake of massive wartime destruction. For Ginzburg, the war exposed more than ever the deficiencies of past practices and constant changes in architectural agendas, along with architects' fundamental inability to realize their intentions in housing: "In the majority of cases the living units we designed were not used as we intended; for example, a single-family apartment was settled with many families, a hotel turned into a dormitory, planned amenities were not realized, and so on."[13] In 1944, Blokhin made a similar point when he warned against an "excess in apartments' floor space, which subsequently led to settling a few families in individual apartments."[14]

Keeping the Separate Apartment Separate

What was the architects' solution to unplanned communal distribution? Beginning in the 1930s, several architects promoted the reduction in the number of rooms and amount of living space to levels below the sanitary norm as the starting point of any apartment design that would ensure single-family occupancy.[15] Because the architects knew that they had no say in drawing up the rules on distribution or their execution, their only tool for keeping apartments separate was design. As Gel'berg and Plessein explained, "Obviously, in order to settle housing as apartments and to make this a mass reality, we need to have a type of individual apartment with lower average living space."[16] An apartment needed to be small enough so that local authorities could settle only one family in it according to distribution norms. Such a solution stood in sharp contrast to spacious elite apartments where rooms were assigned singular functions. It pointed to minimalist living designs, which the authors justified by arguing that all they were really doing was trying to make single-family occupancy universal. Surely this was an unimpeachable goal for a country that was building communism, at which time everyone would enjoy the cultured lifestyle presently available only to elites. As Mikhail Barshch, a former member of OSA, implausibly asserted in 1937, "In our housing construction we strive to provide every family with a good, individual, isolated dwelling." Preoccupied as it was with industrialization and political terror, the Stalinist state was doing nothing of the kind. Nonetheless, invoking this goal served such architects as Barshch well as a way to keep working on minimal apartment designs and criticize larger ones.[17] The government's own call for designing smaller apartments with fewer rooms in a 1934 decree provided an additional boost to architects in search of the minimal apartment.[18]

Barshch, who was forever an OSA member at heart, declared that a large, communalized apartment "cannot be seen as rational" and drew attention to its inefficient use of space. "Almost 40 percent of the common space in an apartment settled with a few families becomes, as it were, 'alienated.'" The solution was a smaller apartment that ensured single-family occupancy so that one family could make full use of the amenities and auxiliary spaces that modern housing afforded. For now, a single-family of four should get an apartment with overall floor space (i.e., both auxiliary and living space) of 40 to 60 square meters. Lest anyone think such dimensions were too small, Barshch reassured potential critics that such apartments would go to two- to three-person families once living space norms were raised.[19] Blokhin similarly argued in favor of reducing the number of rooms in apartments to ensure single-family occupancy. In a dig at the architects of elite apartments, he lamented the "facadism" (*fasadnichestvo*) that had gripped many architects since the Communist Party's condemnation of collectivist living projects and their reluctance to build for the broader population. In making his case, he seized upon the government's call in 1934 cited above "to build apartments with 2, 3, and 4 rooms designated for the individual settlement of one family."[20]

During the war, Blokhin continued to push for reducing apartment sizes to ensure that they remained separate. He recommended apartments with 18 to 30 square meters of living space for families of three to five people: "Practice has shown that settling apartments with individual families is realistically possible only when the design is calculated on a 6-meter norm." Although 6 square meters of living space per person fell well below the sanitary norm, anything higher "inevitably leads to settling apartments with a few families."[21] Similarly, Zal'tsman foresaw in the midst of the war a "minimal living space norm" of 6 to 9 square meters per person but believed it could go even lower so that "small-sized apartments" could be reduced to 26 to 30 square meters of living space, with individual rooms at 11 or 12 square meters. In one of the clearest admissions that such apartments were not meant for elites, Zal'tsman argued that these smaller apartments would satisfy "the average family in our country" and recommended that they become "the normal type for mass housing construction after the war." In contrast, elites would continue to enjoy what he termed "higher-quality apartments" that included more floor space, more rooms, space for a domestic, and higher ceilings.[22]

The architects in favor of minimum dwellings were hopeful that reducing living space would cut down on communalization and become the anchor of future designs. As Blokhin explained, "The estimated living space norm turns out to be one of the most important, initial moments in the design of residential buildings."[23] Under distribution rules and extreme shortages, a drastic reduction in living space was the only way to keep an apartment separate. The architects, some of whom had worked in OSA in the 1920s, exploited these conditions to bring minimalist designs and aesthetics back into architectural discussion. We should remember that these conditions were real and not merely part of a rhetorical strategy that the architects used to maintain a disgraced style and its principles. No matter what aesthetic the architects ultimately chose to employ and whatever ideology they wished to project onto the design of the Soviet home, an apartment's living space and number of rooms would need to be reduced in order to keep it separate. It was not the constructivist aesthetic and its ideology of rational, minimalist living space that ultimately forced apartments under Khrushchev to be small. Rather, it was the rules and practices of distribution dating back to minimum living space standards established in 1919 that restricted how big a single-family apartment could be.

Distribution shrunk not only a separate apartment's living space but also kitchens, corridors, and bathrooms. The link here revolved around the unintended consequences that reducing living space had on the cost of building an apartment. Although cutting living space ensured single-family occupancy, it raised the cost of construction, which architects most often represented as the cost of producing 1 square meter of living space in one apartment or section of a building (figure 2.1).[24] The more infrastructure a building had in relation to its living space, the greater the cost would be of producing 1 square meter of living space. As will be recalled, living space only referred to rooms; the remaining spaces—kitchen, corridor, bathroom, and toilet—were auxiliary spaces (*podsobnaia* or *vspomogatel'naia ploshchad'*), and the sum of living and auxiliary spaces was overall or useful space (*obshchaia* or *poleznaia ploshchad'*). Because housing was distributed in units of living space and not whole apartments, it made sense to use the cost of producing 1 square meter of living space (as opposed to overall space) as a benchmark for estimating how much it would cost to resolve housing shortages. However, construction costs also included plumbing, electrical lines, radiators, and other infrastructure. So the cost of producing 1 meter of living space also had to reflect the costs of these items.

The cost of infrastructure was factored in as follows. Because most of a building's infrastructure was located in the auxiliary spaces of apartments, architects used the proportion of living to auxiliary space as a shorthand measure of cost. By this measure, buildings with higher yields of living space in proportion to auxiliary and non–apartment building spaces would produce 1 square meter of living space more cheaply. In other words, more and bigger rooms combined with fewer unnecessary auxiliary spaces and smaller kitchens, bathrooms, and corridors meant cheaper buildings. In contrast, the lower the yield of living space was in proportion to auxiliary spaces, the higher the cost of constructing 1 square meter of living space would be. In this case, fewer and smaller rooms combined with kitchens, bathrooms, toilets,

Figure 2.1. Section plan for small apartments in 1939. The information at the right provides an immediate summary of the section's vital statistics for quick comparison with other plans: The living space and overall space of each apartment are given to calculate its K_1; the cubic space and total living space of each section are provided to calculate its K_2.

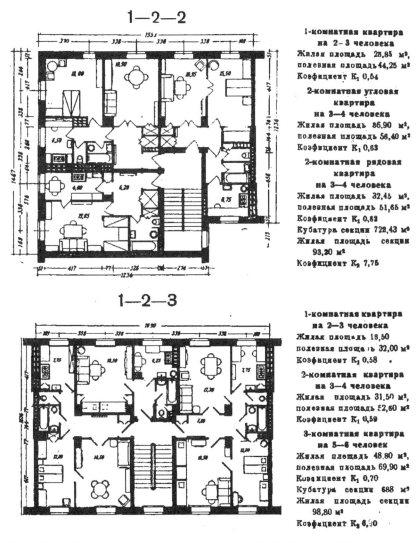

Source: P. Blokhin and A. Zal'tsman, "O tipovykh proektakh zhilykh sektsii dlia massovogo stroitel'stva 1939 goda," *Arkhitektura SSSR*, no. 2 (1939).

and corridors meant more expensive housing. When the architects in search of the minimum dwelling set about lowering the amount of living space to prevent communalization, therefore, they found themselves in this latter situation. All things being equal, reducing living space did not make apartments cheaper to build; it made them more expensive.

Architects used various coefficients relating living space to auxiliary and non–apartment building spaces as shorthand tools for estimating and comparing the cost of 1 square meter of living space across designs.[25] The most widely used was K_1, the coefficient of living space to overall space in an apartment. A three-room apartment with 48.8 square meters of living space and 69.9 square meters of overall space yielded a K_1 of 0.7; see the bottom section layout in figure 2.1. By keeping this coefficient as high as possible, architects could be reasonably confident that their designs were cost-effective. But as living space was reduced to ensure single-family occupancy, it became harder to maintain cost-effectiveness as represented by K_1. Apartments with less living space in the same section layout shown in figure 2.1 were comparatively more expensive to build; a two-room apartment yielded a K_1 of 0.59, and a one-room apartment yielded a K_1 of 0.58.[26]

A second indicator, K_2, was the coefficient of overall cubic space to living space in a section or building. By including the spaces outside apartments, such as stairwells and floor landings, and ceiling heights in a building, this coefficient gave architects a more accurate indication of cost than was possible with the K_1 coefficient.[27] The second section above contained 688 cubic meters and 98.8 square meters of living space, yielding a K_2 of 6.9.[28] Architects strove to produce designs with lower K_2 levels because this meant that more living space was produced in relation to overall cubic space and its infrastructure. As the architects who favored the minimum dwelling unit turned to smaller apartment designs with less living space, it became increasingly difficult to keep this coefficient low.

Using these coefficients shaped design by encouraging architects to build apartments with more living space in proportion to auxiliary units in order to keep costs down. This contributed in the Stalin period to the design of larger apartments that became communal upon distribution but were cheaper than smaller apartments. The architects of elite apartments were thus able to justify their work and warn against a return to minimalist designs. Simonov declared bluntly that "the smaller an apartment's floor space, the more expensive it is."[29]

Champions of the minimal apartment conceded the point. Barshch grudgingly noted that larger apartments with two or three families were simply cheaper to construct than apartments intended for single-family occupancy.[30] Roman Khiger, the former OSA member we met in chapter 1, succinctly captured the problem in 1933: "One-room units are less economical since their service spaces [i.e., auxiliary spaces] cover a small amount of living space with excessively high overhead costs, while four-room units yield too much floor space and are inconvenient precisely on this count since it is almost always necessary in practice to settle this space with 2 to 3 families."[31]

The architect Nikolai Bylinkin similarly explained in 1938 that "as a rule, a three- to four-room apartment has been treated like an apartment for two families. This has occurred for economic reasons, since the cost of 1 square meter of living space in a three-room apartment is 10 percent less expensive, and in a four-room apartment 15 percent less expensive, than the cost of 1 square meter in a two-room apartment."[32] Architects in search of the minimum dwelling unit for all Soviet families thus faced the following dilemma: If they made apartments with less living space to ensure single-family occupancy, they increased the estimated costs of construction. The solution to this increase in cost, as it turned out, dovetailed perfectly with the avant-garde architects' visions for smaller apartments.

To resolve the cost issue, the architects drastically reduced the size and infrastructure of auxiliary spaces. As the architect A. Ol' explained in 1937, two two-room apartments were 24 percent more expensive than two three-room apartments, but the former were preferable because they ensured single-family occupancy. To offset the increase in cost, he urged architects to develop designs that were "more rational and economical," and suggested that the entranceway be made part of living space, that the bathroom and toilet be combined into one unit, and that smaller bathtubs that only allowed one to sit replace longer ones.[33] As living space dropped to resolve the distribution question, the dimensions of auxiliary spaces dropped and their layouts were simplified to keep down the cost of 1 square meter of living space.[34] Bathrooms and toilets were combined in the same space. "Pass-through" rooms were included, not only to prevent communal distribution but also to eliminate corridors.[35] Kitchens and entrances were reduced in size.[36] Such measures ensured that the coefficient of cubic space to living space would be lower in separate apartments than communal ones, thereby proving their cost-effectiveness.[37]

The design principles of the minimal apartment, which were developed by architects under Stalin but were applied on a mass scale only under Khrushchev, represented a double reduction of space justified for vastly different reasons. To ensure that apartments were distributed to individual families, the architects reduced living space; but to offset the consequent increase in cost estimates, they minimized auxiliary spaces and simplified layouts.[38] When scholars assume that Khrushchev's regime constructed small apartments because they were cheaper to build, they are only right insofar as shrinking kitchens, corridors, and bathrooms were concerned. Most of an apartment, its living space, was reduced because of the distribution question, a necessity that actually increased construction cost estimates. Under socialist conditions of housing distribution, the separate apartment simply could not exist as a single-family dwelling unless its living space was reduced.

The standard designs of the *khrushchevka* realized the architects' efforts to make the larger apartments of the Stalin era fit socialist conditions of distribution and reduce construction costs. The standard floor plan for three types of apartment buildings, which is shown in figure 2.2, featured the simplified layouts, smaller number of rooms, and decreased dimensions typical of the *khrushchevka*. This miniature version of the single-family apartment, which was arrived at by shrinking the dimensions of large Stalin-era apartments (compare with figures 1.1 and 1.2 in chapter 1), was precisely the approach to the minimal living unit that Karel Teige had warned modernist architects against in the early 1930s.

As the plan illustrates, architects under Khrushchev demonstrated the cost-effectiveness of their designs by recording the space coefficients that served as barometers of costs. Their floor plans showed how architects altered the arrangement of domestic space characteristic of pre-revolutionary and Stalin-era elite apartments. With the transition to the *khrushchevka*, the organization of domestic space into intimate, public, and service spheres was largely erased. Spaces with unique functions (e.g., dining room, living room, office, bedroom) were no longer mentioned by name on floor plans or assigned to separate rooms. Each function could now be arranged in any room, which usually played

Figure 2.2. Floor plan for a four-apartment section in mass housing built under Khrushchev. The section featured three two-room apartments and one three-room apartment. The caption indicates that the design was intended for standardized models 1-510, 1-511, and 1-515, which included lengthwise load-bearing walls.

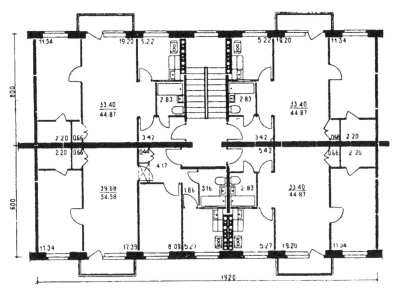

Секция 2-2-2-3, применяемая в действующих типовых проектах домов серий 1-510, 1-511 и 1-515 (с продольными несущими стенами)

Source: K. Metel'skii, "Predlozheniia proektirovshchikov MITEPa," *Arkhitektura SSSR*, no. 6 (1962): 13.

host to two or more functions. Auxiliary spaces were shrunken to keep cost estimates in line. Bathrooms and toilets were placed next to kitchens to economize an apartment's infrastructure, thereby tearing right through the balance between the intimate sphere and the public sphere of an apartment. As explained above, designs included pass-through rooms and less living space to ensure single-family occupancy. The outcome was the Soviet version of the minimal dwelling in which spatial dimensions and arrangements had been shaped by distribution norms.

At the December 1954 All-Union Conference of Constructors, P. Blokhin, the same architect who had promoted smaller apartments in the 1930s, reiterated yet again how apartments had to shed living space in order to remain separate. To settle small families into separate apartments, he explained, more one-room apartments with 18 to 22 square meters of living space and more two-room apartments with 25 to 28 square meters of living space would have to be built. However, he noted the subsequent cost increases this caused: "Repeated studies, carried out by the Institute of Housing Architecture of the Academy of Architecture USSR, show that the less living space there is in an apartment, the more expensive is the construction cost of each square meter of living space in this apartment." Much as he and others had previously pointed out in the 1930s, he added that "this is understandable, [because] the less overall living space there is in an apartment, the more auxiliary space there is in the apartment in proportion to living space." His solution to the cost question, unsurprisingly, was to decrease auxiliary space. To do this, the bathroom and toilet could be combined into one space. He suggested that the dimensions of the kitchen and entranceway be reduced. In addition, "corridors, passages, and other communicative spaces" could be entirely removed. By "other communicative spaces," he may have had in mind the vestibule and the small passageway connecting a kitchen to a larger room. He suggested that movement between rooms in a smaller apartment without corridors could be achieved with pass-through rooms.[39]

Architects such as Blokhin justified these changes on the grounds that one family living alone could easily adapt to such reductions in auxiliary spaces and alterations to apartment layout. He explained that "these methods of reducing auxiliary spaces need to be recognized as permissible, if one pays attention to the fact that the question centers on an apartment of little living space, intended for settlement by a small family."[40] The architect L. Karlik followed a similar logic in 1959. The combined bathroom and toilet was acceptable because 90 percent of these apartments were designed for families of up to four persons. Presumably, Karlik reasoned that four persons in one family could endure the inconveniences of this space-saver that precluded one's use of the sink or bath when someone else used the toilet. Kitchens in these designs were very small, reduced to 4.5 square meters in three- and four-room apartments and 4.2 square meters in one- and two-room apartments. Karlik justified these smaller spaces by noting that "residents of these apartments will be undertaking housekeeping work to a limited extent."[41]

Whereas Blokhin and Karlik explained the logic behind smaller apartments to an audience of their peers, others spoke about it more publicly in the pages of major newspapers. For example, an official at Gosstroi of the USSR (the State Committee on Construction, the main state agency overseeing mass housing construction) explained in *Izvestiia* in December 1956, "One of our designers' mistakes is creating apartments, which it's known are destined for two-three families. Such an apartment in theory is meant for one family, but they settle there, as a rule, a few families, since its floor space is indeed large." His solution was one long familiar to architects since the Stalin era: "[S]mall apartments designated for one family." To keep apartments separate and make them cheaper so more people could receive them, they would need to become smaller in overall floor space and more compact and simplified in design. He added that "every designer and constructor must firmly remember that if residential buildings will be 20 percent cheaper, then 20 percent more families will receive separate apartments."[42]

By the late 1950s and early 1960s, the living space in separate apartments had indeed been reduced enough to ensure a substantial increase in single-family occupancy. Studies by Gosstroi USSR showed that throughout the Soviet Union, single-family occupancy was achieved in 91 to 92 percent of newly built apartments for the years 1959 to 1962, and had grown to 95.3 percent by 1963.[43] *Arkhitektura SSSR* reported in 1966 that single-family occupancy was achieved in 90 percent of new apartments.[44] While reporting a 95 percent rate for 1968, a 1973 source continued to express concern for communal settlement of new housing. By then, the Soviet government and its architects seem to have accepted that there would always be some communal settlement of new apartments.[45]

The Stalinist Origins of the *Khrushchevka*

The reemergence of the separate apartment under Stalin brings into sharper focus what was and was not new about Khrushchev's mass housing campaign. Khrushchev's regime did not reintroduce single-family occupancy as an ideal into Soviet life. As this and the previous chapter demonstrate, that was a contribution of the Stalin era. The separate apartment reemerged in the stratified social structure under Stalinism as a legitimate form of socialist housing but not its exclusive form. Although some elites moved into spacious, single-family apartments that managed to remain separate after their distribution, most people lived in communal forms of housing.

The innovation of Khrushchev's regime was its determination to make the separate apartment accessible to all social groups. By virtue of its mass production, the separate apartment would be accessible to the one social group, the family, that transcended all social and national groups throughout the Soviet Union. From Khrushchev's perspective, what made the separate apartment under Stalin unsocialist and potentially bourgeois was not single-family occupancy, as some Bolsheviks and their fellow travelers surmised after 1917, but rather that so few people had access to this way of life. Underlying this unsocialist outcome were the design "excesses" of Stalinist architects and their resistance to industrialized construction methods. At the All-Union Conference of Constructors in December 1954 that promoted the regime's move toward mass housing, Khrushchev forcefully condemned Stalin's architects for wasting resources and preventing more people from obtaining separate apartments.[46]

The origins of the *khrushchevka*'s internal arrangement shed new light on how different elements of the Soviet past ultimately shaped Khrushchev's mass housing campaign. Historians have demonstrated how the architects in favor of mass housing under Khrushchev looked back to the constructivist tradition of the 1920s to refine their designs, plan major urban renewal projects such as Novyi Arbat in Moscow, and articulate the separate apartment's ideological role in combating "petit bourgeois" mentalities and consumer habits. Such influence was manifested in the minimalist outer architecture of mass housing, the rational planning of new housing ensembles, and advice pamphlets on living in new apartments.[47] As this chapter argues, however, it was the work that the architects in search of the Soviet minimum dwelling did in the 1930s on making the separate apartment fit the realities of shortages and housing distribution that shaped the fundamental principles of the *khrushchevka*'s internal design.

For most scholars, the Stalin era's only influence on the *khrushchevka*'s design was that it produced a particular kind of separate apartment—expensive, intended for elites, and plagued by petit bourgeois tastes—that was ultimately rejected under Khrushchev. This view echoes the criticism of the Stalinist architectural legacy that Khrushchev personally endorsed. But as the new party line in architecture, such representations of the Stalin period neglected to recognize the critical advancements that some architects had made on separate apartment design under Stalin in the 1930s that shaped the *khrushchevka*. Khrushchev's new line on architecture similarly obfuscated the differences of opinion that had existed among architects under Stalin about what form the separate apartment should take. In contrast to the Khrushchev period—when architects were compelled to design only standardized, small apartments—the Stalin era afforded architects greater latitude to debate the merits of apartments based on different designs, materials, and construction methods. This did not mean the Stalin period was more liberal than Khrushchev's regime. Rather, it was a reflection of the ideological stances each regime had taken on which layers of society were entitled to a separate apartment. The diversity of architectural opinion under Stalin reflected the "diversity" of a stratified social structure for which architects built different kinds of apartments— luxurious ones for elites, large ones for communal living for most people, and small, single-family apartments for all in the future. In contrast, the singular focus on mass housing under Khrushchev reflected the regime's egalitarian ideology of providing "a separate apartment to every family" as quickly and efficiently as possible.[48]

Architects' work in the Stalin era, especially before the war, had a greater effect on the *khrushchevka* than scholars have previously appreciated. Insofar as designing the interior layout of apartments was concerned, mass housing architects under Khrushchev paid less attention to 1920s collectivist living projects and more attention to what former OSA members and others had subsequently developed in the 1930s and 1940s. There were notable exceptions, such as Natan Osterman's House of the New Way of Life, in which apartments that lacked kitchens and included collectivized facilities recalled the *dom-kommuna*.[49] But for the majority of mass housing built under Khrushchev, the kitchen was an integral part of the Soviet home and the internal layout of apartments was shaped by the principles and compromises that architects had worked out under Stalin. The architects who developed the fundamental design principles of the minimal apartment under Stalin were essentially coming to terms with both the ideological turn toward the family and the "real conditions" of housing distribution and shortages. Working within the limits imposed by these factors, over which they had absolutely no control, the former OSA architects and their allies produced the basic architectural parameters of a separate apartment for the masses that would remain separate but also cheap. This was the architectural blueprint for separate apartments that mass housing architects under Khrushchev inherited from their Stalin-era colleagues and transformed into the *khrushchevka*.

At the heart of the Soviet architect's problems was a tool—quantifiable, minimum living standards—which was supposed to have enabled architects to solve the housing question and design a new way of life rather than restrict what they could do with domestic space. As Dana Simmons argues, "the notion of the 'ration,' a physiological minimum norm, had a profound and largely unrecognized influence on the development of modern architecture." The results indicated greater continuity between nineteenth-century housing reform and twentieth-century mass housing than modernist architects, who were hoping for a break from the past, were prepared to admit. Simmons concludes that "minimal architecture represented historical continuity more than rupture. By accepting static, physiological norms as the basis for the minimum dwelling, architects and planners inserted themselves into a tradition that went back to the prison experiments of the 1840s."[50] The internal design of the *khrushchevka* shared similar origins in the pan-European search for a minimum standard of living space.

Although the *khrushchevka*'s design principles were established before World War II, the war's impact and the Stalinist state's early postwar efforts at housing reconstruction shaped other aspects of Khrushchev's mass housing campaign. In addition to enduring worsening housing shortages in the 1920s and 1930s, ordinary urban dwellers suffered through even more created during World War II. According to official published accounts, one half of all housing in the 1,710 cities and towns falling under occupation or damaged was destroyed during the war.[51] One source lists this amount of destroyed housing as 1,209,000 houses,[52] while another represented it as 70 million square meters of living space. Note that this latter number only referred to floor space in rooms; a more complete estimate including auxiliary space would yield approximately 96 million square meters of overall housing space.[53] The country lost one-third of its entire housing and left 25 million people homeless.[54] Despite having taken control of housing with all the tools of nineteenth-century housing reform, the Soviet state was further away from resolving the housing question in 1945 than the Bolsheviks had been in 1917.

Because of the war, Stalin's regime was more willing to seek advice from allies and depend on ordinary families and rural builders to reconstruct the housing stock (table 2.1) alongside state housing. The profound pressure that the war placed on the Soviet government to allow and even encourage citizens to rebuild and construct their own housing continued to be felt years later in such episodes as the people's construction campaign of the middle to late 1950s (see chapter 4), as well as the very design of low-cost housing for individual constructors, the single-family home. The Stalinist state found itself drawn to this model not only for practical, wartime needs but also through the friendly advice of American architects concerning prefabrication technology. Soviet architects learned much from their American counterparts about the prefabricated construction of free-standing homes through such contacts as the March 1945 exhibition, "Rapid Construction in the USA," presented at the House of Architects in Moscow. As Richard Anderson argues, what Soviet architects learned through such contacts served as a critical bridge between their own work on prefabrication technology before the war and Khrushchev's mass housing campaign. According to Anderson, despite its association with American practice during the war, the single-family home survived the emergence of the Cold War conflict and remained an important pillar in the Stalinist state's postwar efforts to rebuild.[55]

The Soviet state's reliance on individually constructed homes is further illustrated by a closer examination of the official data available on wartime housing construction. The claim that 102.5 million square meters of overall space was either reconstructed or newly built during the war (table 2.1) is significantly higher than one would expect, given the widespread destruction of Soviet cities during the war. Indeed, given this number and my estimate above that 96 million square meters of overall space was destroyed during the war, the Soviet Union would have exited the war with a net gain of 6.5 million square meters of overall space. This hardly seems plausible. Determining what was meant by reconstructed housing in the wartime construction data may help elucidate this question. A minimalist definition of reconstruction (e.g., fixing damaged housing so that it can serve as a shelter) would have allowed for more housing to be counted toward wartime reconstruction efforts. In any event, the data show that collective farms, collective farmers, the rural intelligentsia, and the individual housing sector accounted for the majority of newly built or reconstructed housing from 1941 to 1950, and continued to outpace state housing construction until 1961.[56] This suggests that most new or reconstructed housing from

Table 2.1. Construction of Housing in the Soviet Union, 1917–65 (millions of square meters of overall space)

Years	Housing Built by State and Cooperative Enterprises and Organizations, and Housing Cooperatives	Housing Built by Workers and White-Collar Employees at Their Expense and with State Credit (i.e., Individual Housing)	Housing Built by Collective Farms, Collective Farmers, and Rural Intelligentsia	Total Housing Constructed
1918–28	23.7	27.5	151.8	203
1929–32	32.6	7.6	16.7	56.9
1933–37	37.2	7.1	23	67.3
1938–41	34.4	10.8	36.4	81.6
1941–46	41.3	13.6	47.6	102.5
1946–50	72.4	44.7	83.8	200.9
1951–55	113	65.1	62.4	240.5
1956–60	224	113.8	136.3	474.1
1961–65	300.4	94	96.2	490.6

Source: Narodnoe khoziaistvo SSSR v 1967 g. (Moscow: Statistika, 1968), 675. As explained in this source, the data for the years 1941 to 1950 represent both housing that was newly built and housing that was reconstructed.

the beginning of World War II until the early 1960s came in the form of individual houses.

Projections for postwar reconstruction further emphasized the state's reliance on citizens to rebuild. In the first postwar Five-Year Plan (1946–50), the target for state-constructed housing, including new housing and reconstructed housing, was set at 72.4 million square meters of living space. Of this amount, state enterprises, institutions, and other workplaces were to produce 65 million square meters, while local soviets were supposed to build 7.4 million square meters. The target for local soviets was significantly lower in comparison with the individual housing sector, from which the state hoped to gain 12 million square meters of living space (again, including both new and reconstructed housing). As an additional method of increasing the housing stock, the first postwar five-year plan proposed the construction of buildings with one to two apartments that people could purchase.[57] The officially reported outcomes of this five-year plan give us as much a general sense of what was actually built as they reveal the sleight of hand that accompanied Soviet housing statistics. The state had hoped to produce a total of 72.4 million square meters of living space, and the official outcome was, amazingly enough, 72.4 million square meters (table 2.1). This would seem to confirm that the state had indeed fulfilled the plan, until one notes that this outcome was reported in overall space, whereas the target number had been set in living space. It is possible, but unlikely, that a simple clerical error explains why one category of space was used for the target and another for the outcome.

When one translates the target of 72.4 million square meters of living space into overall space (based on the conversion I used above to calculate wartime losses), one arrives at approximately 99 million square meters of overall space. The officially reported outcome, 72.4 million square meters of overall space, now appears far short of the plan's target. Because the targets and reported outcomes did not differentiate between reconstructed and newly constructed housing, it is difficult to discern how much was newly built or merely reconstructed. Add to this the fact that the target and outcome numbers not only just happened to be the same but were reported in different units, and what we have here is a rather clumsy case of incredibly massaged housing statistics.

As this example shows, official statistics made sources of state housing look more productive than they really were. The same may have held true for individual housing construction. Instead of producing a target of 12 million square meters of living space (or 16 million square meters of overall space), individual constructors produced 44.7 million square meters of overall space under the first Five-Year Plan after the war. If this outcome was as implausible as those reported for the state, the evidence for artificially inflating it is less easily discernible because the target and outcome numbers, reported in different units, were not suspiciously identical. At the very least, the data suggest that Stalin's regime did not hide the fact that individual housing constructors were doing a better job of rebuilding after the war than state organizations. But however much individual constructors, collective farmers, and the rural intelligentsia actually built, the state's encouragement of these sectors did not come at the expense of the housing system it had forged before the war. In larger cities like Leningrad and Moscow, housing remained a public good that was built, distributed, and managed by either local soviets or the workplace. Cooperatives, with extremely minor exceptions (which will be examined in chapter 4), remained on the dust heap of failed 1920s experiments. Shortages were extreme and most urban dwellers continued to live in barracks, dormitories, and communal apartments, as they had before the war. In the midst of this bleak picture, and despite its reliance on individual citizens to rebuild, Stalin's regime never relinquished the notion that only the state could ultimately resolve the housing question. On this critical point, which had its roots in nineteenth-century housing reform, Khrushchev's regime dutifully continued where its predecessor left off.

As historians have shown, the lines of continuity on housing between the Stalin and Khrushchev eras went deeper and contradict the image of a break with the past that Khrushchev's regime projected. It was precisely during the war's last stages and Stalin's last years in power that elements within the regime were already discussing and cobbling together the policies and rationales that would later constitute Khrushchev's mass housing campaign. The Stalinist leadership became increasingly aware of the dire need to tackle the country's housing crisis in a more systematic and sustained fashion than had been possible during the chaos of war and the early years of reconstruction. Better housing conditions in the long term would allow the state to rely less on force and more on material incentives to secure the acquiescence, if not the sincere loyalty, of the people. Responding to the regime's call for more housing, certain architects developed and promoted anew uniform and simplified apartment designs to be constructed more cheaply out of reinforced concrete and on a mass scale through prefabrication technology. They discussed plans for microdistricts, which were an urban planning program for well-designed neighborhoods that served residents' needs and promoted communal values, and that would become a standard feature of Khrushchev's mass housing. The criticism of "excesses" by spendthrift architects who designed ornamental buildings for elites was already heard in the early 1950s and would later become one of Khrushchev's favorite causes. In Stalin's last years, the state established new bureaucracies, such as the Ministry of Urban Construction and the State Committee on Construction Affairs, to integrate standardized designs into construction practice. Economic ministries at the center and local actors in the state's building industry already began to reform the worst inefficiencies of the planned economy in order to rationalize and consolidate the industry, improve its workers' qualifications, and reorganize financing.[58]

From increased construction to better economic planning, several elements of Khrushchev's mass housing campaign were thus already emerging and even interacting in the last stages of the war and the postwar years of Stalin's rule. But as the historian Mark Smith demonstrates, what was absent in the postwar years before Stalin's death was a concerted effort to bring these changes and suggested reforms together into a coherent campaign and tie it to a larger ideological vision beyond reconstruction and recovery. Having a leader with some personal experience in housing construction and urban affairs would also help to fully commit the Communist Party to such a program.[59] As historians have shown in other spheres of Soviet life, such as education reform, Stalin's death removed the greatest obstacle for reformers eager to translate their ideas into reality.[60] Stepping into the leadership void, Khrushchev gave direction to many of their ideas and molded them into reforms that have long been associated with his attempts to de-Stalinize state and society. More than any other reform, it was mass housing to which Khrushchev devoted particular attention and resources, elevating it to the level of a campaign reminiscent of the industrialization drive and willing to stake his regime's legitimacy on at last resolving the housing question of the nineteenth century.

Millions of New Apartments

The design successes of the *khrushchevka* were bolstered by the massive increase in construction that Khrushchev's regime made possible over the course of the 1950s and 1960s. Factories churned out prefabricated parts and reinforced concrete, while building cranes dotted the Soviet cityscape as construction crews put apartments together piece by piece. Along with new housing pushing the boundaries of cities outward came a deluge of statistics informing Soviet citizens and the outside world that the USSR was finally resolving its housing question. Contemporary chronicles of the mass housing campaign, such as the 1958 book *Millions of New Apartments*, inundated readers with statistics ranging from square meters built and the number of people getting new housing to the amount of labor and finances pumped into the campaign.[61] Newspapers likewise offered a steady diet of reporting on the massive quantities of new housing built at breakneck speed by virtue of the industry's modernization and industrialization.[62] Similar to their use in the industrialization drive under Stalin,[63] this constant stream of quantitative data was a critical aspect of constructing mass housing as an overwhelmingly successful campaign of overfulfilled plans that demonstrated the state's "care for the person" as it built Communism on Tomorrow Street. But unlike the Stalinist industrialization drive and its focus on heavy industry, the numbers touting Khrushchev's mass housing campaign bolstered promises about improving people's living conditions and access to consumer goods and furniture. As we will see later in this book, the quantitative claims of the campaign risked, along with other propaganda, raising urban dwellers' expectations that their housing question would be quickly resolved.

The proliferating quantitative data on housing construction were not only about "constructing" the *khrushchevka* as a propagandistic abstraction meant to elicit excitement about the regime's ability to end housing shortages. The housing statistics, even when massaged as we saw above, actually referred to a concrete reality. Massive numbers of five-story buildings really were being constructed and were changing the face of the Soviet cityscape. To be sure, keeping an eye out for embellishments of the data is important in researching not only published statistics but also those found in archives. Where we can be confident of their accuracy, the statistics can tell us much about the trajectory of the campaign's output and who built it.[64] Although a careful reading and comparison with other sources can help us spot outright embellishments, the manner in which statistics were massaged or merely presented provides clues about what the regime sought to hide, what it valued, how it measured success, and whose contributions it wished to highlight in shaping the meanings of the mass housing campaign.

For example, in addition to reporting housing built in square meters of overall or living space, Khrushchev's regime reported the number of apartments constructed with comprehensive data going back as far as 1950. This qualitative unit of measurement echoed the broader move to the separate apartment, whereby families enjoyed a fully integrated and private home rather than square meters in a communal apartment. Its data (table 2.2) represented well the surge in housing construction under Khrushchev. After modest growth in the early 1950s, construction made its first jump in 1957, peaked in 1959, moderately declined for the next several years, and leveled out at an annual output of approximately 2.2 million apartments.

Statisticians used a rather broad definition of "apartment" in order to include in their data all housing built in both cities and the countryside. By "apartment," they meant any "detached unit" (*obosoblennoe pomeshchenie*) in a building.[65] Therefore, whatever detached houses in-

Table 2.2. Annual Construction of Apartments in the Soviet Union, 1950–70

Year	Number of Apartments	Year	Number of Apartments
1950	1,073,000	1961	2,435,000
1951	972,000	1962	2,383,000
1952	972,000	1963	2,322,000
1953	1,245,000	1964	2,184,000
1954	1,351,000	1965	2,227,000
1955	1,512,000	1966	2,291,000
1956	1,548,000	1967	2,312,000
1957	2,060,000	1968	2,233,000
1958	2,382,000	1969	2,231,000
1959	2,711,000	1970	2,266,000
1960	2,591,000		

Note: The sourcebooks do not provide data for 1951 and 1952. These were estimated here as follows. The 1974 sourcebook reports that the Five-Year Plan for 1951–55 produced 6,052,000 apartments. The 1959 sourcebook reported annual production for each year from 1953 to 1959. Therefore, subtracting its output numbers for 1953, 1954, and 1955 from 6,052,000 yields the output for 1951 and 1952 combined: 1,944,000 apartments. The average of this amount is 972,000, which is used here as an estimate for 1951 and 1952. This may be a low estimate for what was constructed during these two years because the data for each year from 1956 to 1959 in the 1959 sourcebook were somewhat higher than what later editions reported (e.g., the 1965 sourcebook) by approximately 100,000 to 300,000 apartments per year. If the 1959 sourcebook's data for the years 1953 to 1955 were also inflated in comparison with what was later reported, then their share of the 6,052,000 apartments is less than presented here, and the years 1951 and 1952 likely yielded a greater amount than 972,000 apartments annually.

Sources: Narodnoe khoziaistvo SSSR v 1959 godu (Moscow: Gosstatizdat TsSU SSSR, 1960), 568. This source is hereafter cited as *Nkh SSSR*, followed by the year reported: *Nkh SSSR v 1960 godu*, 205; *Nkh SSSR v 1965 g.*, 611; *Nkh SSSR v 1974 g.*, 581.

dividual constructors or peasants built were included as "apartments." Because they made no distinction between a communal and a separate apartment, each counted as one "apartment" in their data. Eliding this critical difference that mattered so much to both ordinary residents and the regime suggests that a decision was made not to advertise the fact that somewhere on the order of 5 to 10 percent of newly built city apartments still ended up being distributed communally under Khrushchev. As illustrated above, such information did appear in specialized published sources, but including it in aggregate statistics would have publicized the regime's failure to entirely eliminate the communalization of new apartments, thereby undercutting the mass housing campaign's goal of allowing all families their own apartments.

In statistical sourcebooks, the more traditional representation of construction in square meters of overall space revealed much about the sources of new housing and how they changed over time (table 2.3). A cursory glance at these data suggests a neat division between "state" and "society," yet a closer reading of each category indicates much overlap. State housing included housing built by "state and cooperative enterprises and organizations," but also "housing cooperatives."

As will be explained in detail in chapter 4, housing cooperatives in the 1920s and 1930s were financed in part by citizens, as were those created after 1958. Individual constructors, whom one might think of as "society" building separately from the "state," actually benefited from government loans to build their housing. Although collective farmers and the rural intelligentsia were listed as building their own homes, collective farms—a state institution—were also included in that category. As is shown throughout this book, during Khrushchev's mass housing campaign it was often difficult to determine where the state ended and society began. Though this reflected the regime's own vision of moving toward communism, where people would increasingly take over responsibilities from the state, it was also part of the practical organization and financing of mass housing.

According to table 2.3, state organizations did not start building the majority of new housing until sometime in the late 1950s. By 1961, the state was building most new housing and continued to steadily expand its contribution through the late 1960s. Nonetheless, Khrushchev's regime continued to depend on Soviet citizens to build their own homes, as evidenced by what individual constructors built, as well as collective farmers and the rural intelligentsia. The individual housing sector,

Table 2.3. *Annual Construction of Housing in the Soviet Union, 1951–70 (millions of square meters of overall space)*

Years	Housing Built by State and Cooperative Enterprises and Organizations, and Housing Cooperatives	Housing Built by Workers and White-Collar Employees at Their Expense and with State Credit (i.e., Individual Housing)	Housing Built by Collective Farms, Collective Farmers, and Rural Intelligentsia[1]	Total Housing Constructed
1951	20.3	7.3	12.5	48
1952	20	7.4	12.5	48
1953	23.2	7.6	12.5	48
1954	24.5	8.1	12.5	48
1955	25	8.4	12.5	48
1956	29.5	11.5	27.3	94.8
1957	38.5	13.5	27.3	94.8
1958	46.7	24.5	27.3	94.8
1959	53.5	27.2	27.3	94.8
1960	55.8	27	27.3	94.8
1961	56.6	23.6	22.5	102.7
1962	59.8	20.7	19.5	100
1963	61.9	17.4	18.3	97.6
1964	58.9	16.2	17.6	92.7
1965	63.1	16.1	18.3	97.6
1966	65.9	15.9	20.3	102.1
1967	68.7	15.6	20.2	104.5
1968	69.3	14.2	18.6	102.1
1969	72	14.1	17.7	103.8
1970	76.6	13	16.4	106

Sources: *Narodnoe khoziaistvo SSSR v 1960 godu* (Moscow: Gosstatizdat TsSU SSSR, 1961), 611. This source is hereafter cited as *Nkh SSSR*, followed by the year reported: *Nkh SSSR v 1961 godu*, 613; *Nkh SSSR v 1962 godu*, 498; *Nkh SSSR v 1965 g.*, 609; *Nkh SSSR v 1967 g.*, 675; *Nkh SSSR v 1974 g.*, 579.

[1] For the years 1951–1960, the data for housing constructed by collective farms, collective farmers, and the rural intelligentsia were reported only in the aggregate covering two sets of years, 1951–1955 and 1956–1960. Based on this data, I have calculated the annual average for each of these years. Likewise, the data for total housing constructed in the same years is based on the annual average reported in the sourcebooks for the two sets of years, 1951–1955 and 1956–1960.

labeled in statistics as "housing built by workers and white-collar employees at their own expense and with state credits," followed a very different path during the Khrushchev years in comparison with state and cooperative construction, as is shown in table 2.4. After a phenomenal surge in 1958, individual housing construction peaked in 1959 and then fell steadily through the 1960s. As we will see in chapter 4, the surge in individual construction in 1958 is best explained by the supposition that statisticians likely added data from "people's construction" to the individual construction category without explicitly acknowl-

Table 2.4. Annual Construction of State Housing and Individual Housing in the Soviet Union, 1918–70 (millions of square meters of overall space)

Year	Housing Built by State and Cooperative Enterprises and Organizations, and Housing Cooperatives	Housing Built by Workers and White-Collar Employees at Their Expense and with State Credit (i.e., Individual Housing)	Total
1951	20.3	7.3	27.6
1952	20	7.4	27.4
1953	23.2	7.6	30.8
1954	24.5	8.1	32.6
1955	25	8.4	33.4
1956	29.5	11.5	41
1957	38.5	13.5	52
1958	46.7	24.5	71.2
1959	53.5	27.2	80.7
1960	55.8	27	82.8
1961	56.6	23.6	80.2
1962	59.8	20.7	80.5
1963	61.9	17.4	79.3
1964	58.9	16.2	75.1
1965	63.1	16.1	79.2
1966	65.9	15.9	81.8
1967	68.7	15.6	84.3
1968	69.3	14.2	83.5
1969	72	14.1	86.1
1970	76.6	13	89.6

Note: Because the data for collective farms, collective farmers, and the rural intelligentsia were not reported in square meters of overall space on an annual basis until 1961, this table only compares the two categories for which such annual data are available from 1951 through 1970.

Sources: Narodnoe khoziaistvo SSSR v 1960 godu (Moscow: Gosstatizdat TsSU SSSR, 1961), 611. This source is hereafter cited as *Nkh SSSR*, followed by the year reported: *Nkh SSSR v 1961 godu*, 613; *Nkh SSSR v 1962 godu*, 498; *Nkh SSSR v 1965 g.*, 609; *Nkh SSSR v 1967 g.*, 675; *Nkh SSSR v 1974 g.*, 579.

edging this. (Through people's construction, industrial laborers worked extra hours on their factory's housing construction projects in exchange for a separate apartment in that housing.)

In turn, the rapid decrease in individual housing construction statistics in the early 1960s can be partly explained by the demise of people's construction after 1959. Similar to individual housing construction, people's construction was a labor-intensive building method that fell far short of the regime's desire to modernize the industry and produce prefabricated apartments on a mass scale. As Khrushchev's regime expanded modern building methods, it sought to phase out less standardized and industrialized modes of construction. Yet as table 2.4 shows, the regime continued to rely on individual families to contribute to the expansion of the housing stock.

When it came to reporting how many Soviet citizens received apartments, the regime's statistics continued to gloss over the issue of whether they received single-family or communal dwellings. Instead of representing the number of families who received separate apartments—a logical step given the purpose of the campaign—official statistics showed the number of individuals receiving new and old housing (table 2.5).

Such reporting hid the number of separate apartments that continued to be settled communally, although other published sources (see above) exposed this reality. Conversely, the data revealed a normally overlooked aspect of the mass housing campaign: Whereas most people received newly built housing, many others continued to receive space in old buildings, which in cities most likely meant rooms in communal apartments, until the *khrushchevki* began to be recycled in the distribution system. The data thus exposed a more complicated picture of the mass housing campaign, during which Soviet citizens not only migrated to new separate apartments but also continued to move from one communal apartment to another.

In Search of Design Alternatives

For the architects who designed the Khrushchev-era separate apartment, their product was a stunning success on many levels. The state had at last devoted the resources that enabled them to transform their blueprints into reality, as evidenced by the surge in housing construction. Their designs ensured that most new apartments were settled with

Table 2.5. *Number of Persons Receiving Living Space in the Soviet Union Annually, 1950–70*

Year	Number of Persons Receiving Living Space or Building Their Own Apartments in Newly Built Houses	Number of Persons Receiving or Increasing Living Space in Previously Built Houses	Total Number of Persons Receiving Living Space or Building Their Own Apartments
1950	4,000,000	1,300,000	5,300,000
1951	4,100,000	1,400,000	5,500,000
1952	4,000,000	1,400,000	5,400,000
1953	4,400,000	1,700,000	6,100,000
1954	4,700,000	1,800,000	6,500,000
1955	5,300,000	1,800,000	7,100,000
1956	5,700,000	2,100,000	7,800,000
1957	7,600,000	2,500,000	10,100,000
1958	8,800,000	2,700,000	11,500,000
1959	10,000,000	2,600,000	12,600,000
1960	9,600,000	2,400,000	12,000,000
1961	9,000,000	2,300,000	11,300,000
1962	8,800,000	2,400,000	11,200,000
1963	8,600,000	2,400,000	11,000,000
1964	8,100,000	2,200,000	10,300,000
1965	8,200,000	2,600,000	10,800,000
1966	8,500,000	2,400,000	10,900,000
1967	8,600,000	2,500,000	11,100,000
1968	8,300,000	2,500,000	10,800,000
1969	8,300,000	2,600,000	10,900,000
1970	8,400,000	2,800,000	11,200,000

Sources: Narodnoe khoziaistvo SSSR v 1967 godu (Moscow: Statistika, 1968), 681. This source is hereafter cited as *Nkh SSSR*, followed by the year reported: *Nkh SSSR v 1974 g.*, 585.

single families rather than communally. Although many architects remained focused on simply getting families into separate apartments that remained separate, others grew increasingly frustrated with the limitations that their own efforts at doing so had imposed on designing domestic space.

The state never reformed the distribution system to solve the problem of communal distribution entirely, but architects and housing officials in the late 1950s and 1960s proposed reforms for measuring and categorizing apartment spaces in order to work greater flexibility into design and make apartments bigger. In devising alternative methods of computing construction costs, such architects drew logical conclusions from the separate apartment's increasing prominence in Soviet life. They argued that a conceptual switch had occurred in thinking about housing—from the quantitative approach of square meters and the generic notion of living space to a qualitative approach that recognized different domestic spaces and, most important, the apartment itself as a whole, indivisible unit, identified with the family. If statistics on housing construction could acknowledge the existence of apartments, why could not the systems of distribution, spatial categorization, and costs assessments do so as well?

One proposal sought to replace the conventional way of computing the cost of 1 square meter of living space with "the cost of settling in one person," that took into account family size so that auxiliary spaces and infrastructure could meet all family members' needs.[66] In another proposal, housing would feature two kinds of spatial categories. The first was "standardized spaces," which would be designed to match family size and age structure. These standardized spaces included rooms, bedrooms, a bathroom and a toilet, a kitchen, storage space, and closets. Outside an apartment, they included a room for baby carriages, storage spaces, a laundry, shower rooms, and garbage space. The second category, "transitional space," would account for all the spaces that connected the standardized spaces. These included an entranceway, corridors and subcorridors, and stairs within a single apartment. Outside an apartment, they included corridors, stairwells, passageways, galleries, and elevators. The estimated cost would be based on the proportion of transitional to standardized space. By keeping this ratio low, the idea was to heavily reduce the size of transitional space without affecting the sizes of kitchens, bathrooms, and toilets, which had become quite small.[67]

Although these and other proposals never materialized, mass housing architects were not alone in seeking reform.[68] As early as 1956,
Vladimir Kucherenko, the head of Gosstroi USSR from 1955 to 1961,[69]
urged that "living space" be replaced by "apartment" as the unit of
construction.[70] But "apartment" never became the unit of cost measurement or distribution, and "living space" remained the link tying design
to distribution. Decreasing all auxiliary spaces, a formula that had
been invented by architects twenty years earlier, remained the best way
to keep apartments cheap.

Mass housing architects debated such questions in meetings and in
their professional journal, *Arkhitektura SSSR*; but on occasion, their
discussions spilled over into the mass media. In a telling incident in the
pages of *Izvestiia* in March 1960, several architects argued in a series of
articles about how to make an apartment that was economical, well
designed, and would remain separate upon distribution. Some argued
that the methods of estimating cost led directly to irrational designs
and that reform was necessary to make apartments people would like.
Others rejected such criticism as a reckless affront to their professional
and cultural authority, and maintained that their achievements in answering the demands of the mass housing campaign overshadowed any
shortcomings. By bringing their debate into the pages of *Izvestiia*, these
architects helped politicize problems many residents were already facing in their new homes and made the solutions a question of continuing
or forestalling reform. In casting doubt on architects' cultural authority, this debate continued what Khrushchev had already started at the
December 1954 All-Union Conference of Constructors, where he ridi-
culed architects for producing costly, individual designs instead of em-
bracing cheaper mass housing. Having already devoted themselves to
this new direction, the architects engaged in the present debate in
Izvestiia were now advancing the wider discussion on mass housing by
addressing the relative merits of the quantitative and qualitative measurements of success.

One such architect, N. Narin'iani, along with an engineer, B. Dmitriev,
delivered the first salvo of this public exchange with their article "Under
the Yoke of the Coefficient." They argued that architects had made
single-family occupancy and lower construction costs central priorities
overshadowing all other issues. In describing one design, they exclaimed, "What a narrow entrance-way in the apartment! There's no
place to hang a coat rack in it. And look at the kitchen. One can't turn

around and there isn't any room for a refrigerator or a washing machine." New consumer items were crowding out residents, reducing their control over domestic space. "There isn't a corridor in this apartment at all, therefore such things as coats, skis, a bicycle, and so forth have to be stored in a room. The room ceases to belong to a person." The critics also decried "pass-through" rooms, which were difficult to use as bedrooms.

Rather than lament residents' acquisitive tendencies, as did the arbiters of domestic taste,[71] Narin'iani and Dmitriev accepted them as normal phenomena to be accommodated. In their estimation, apartment designs failed to meet consumers' growing needs. Part of the solution was to recognize that the principles underlying present designs were anachronistic. The first was the categorization of domestic space into living space and auxiliary space; the second was the cost indicators that rested on this division. Together, they produced small auxiliary spaces. The critics explained that this system had worked well for communal apartments, in which auxiliary spaces were underutilized, but were poorly suited for the separate apartment, which afforded a family exclusive use over auxiliary spaces. Narin'iani and Dmitriev suggested that architects abandon cost indicators based on the proportion of living space to auxiliary space or the cubic space of an apartment building, and adopt an approach predicated on an apartment's "overall space." Architects could then develop "rational apartment plans" and distribute the same amount of space among living and auxiliary units according to a family's needs, instead of a cost indicator.[72] By reconceptualizing the apartment as a whole unit in which its layout was no longer shaped by cost indicators, the critics were trying to bring design into line with the mass housing campaign's organizing principle of single-family occupancy.

Narin'iani and Dmitriev's statement quickly provoked a negative reaction. Within two weeks, forty-two engineers and architects, led by V. Lagutenko, wrote an angry response in *Izvestiia* titled "In the Captivity of Abstractions." In their opinion, architects had achieved the main goal of the mass housing campaign, single-family occupancy, through adjustments in design. Working within the structural limitations that bound design to distribution and cost indicators, they had made access to single-family apartments available to millions. If apartments suffered minor design shortcomings, this was a small price to pay for having moved people from communal apartments to separate apartments that actually remained separate. This task was challenging enough, and Lagutenko and his coauthors took credit for its long-term social benefits: "In giving every family a separate apartment, we provide better conditions for the upbringing of children and the rest and work of adults." By questioning the design formula that ensured single-family occupancy, Narin'iani and Dmitriev were undermining architects and engineers' sense of accomplishment in improving people's everyday lives.[73]

Lagutenko and his colleagues were particularly offended by Narin'iani and Dmitriev's suggestion that "today's apartments are planned by thoughtless designers with little experience, who view residents' demands and comforts disdainfully." In their defense, they cited a recent study of fifty thousand apartments in forty-two cities in which residents of single-family apartments "expressed great satisfaction." They asserted that many people would gladly take a separate apartment with smaller dimensions over a communal apartment. They insisted that new designs were of sound quality, met residents' daily needs, and provided ample space for consumer items.[74] Ultimately, these architects and engineers wanted to be judged according to utilitarian criteria: enabling the greatest number of people to attain a separate apartment by producing less expensive designs that ensured single-family occupancy.

Within two weeks, *Izvestiia* published a third piece on the debate. In his article "What's This Argument About?" the architect M. Orlov backed Narin'iani and Dmitriev's criticisms and chastised Lagutenko and his colleagues for resisting change. All architects, Orlov explained, were working toward the same goal: "the creation of a more rational and economical apartment design that is comfortable for people and intended for one family." In critiquing the continued application of cost indicators and demonstrating how they led to irrational layouts, Narin'iani and Dmitriev had merely identified a major problem preventing the realization of a common goal. Echoing Narin'iani and Dmitriev, Orlov explained that the cost indicators, which favored a high yield of living space and a low yield of auxiliary spaces, "were born at a time when we designed apartments that were settled by the room and all the auxiliary spaces of an apartment and its equipment were used communally." Because people in communal apartments made more use of living space than auxiliary space, Orlov argued, it mattered little that architects increased living space and lowered auxiliary space in apartments destined to become communal. "But when we switched over to the new design principles of an apartment meant for one family, we needed to change our approach to auxiliary space," he concluded. "Homemakers can now use this space alone however they please." Continuing to use the cost indicators was no longer rational because they resulted in unnecessarily reduced auxiliary spaces, which families now hoped to use more than they had in communal apartments.[75]

The deeper problem of cost indicators was that they were only an approximate measure. If an architect, in search of better coefficients on paper, merely reassigned square meters from auxiliary space to living space, or vice versa, but used the same amount of building materials and infrastructure, construction costs were not actually lowered. This led Nar'iniani and Dmitriev to describe cost indicators as "artificial." Such indicators also made design innovations nearly impossible. To drive the point home, Orlov drew upon one of Lagutenko's own designs. Although the apartment had the same overall floor space as a currently used prototype, Lagutenko had designed its layout and auxiliary spaces to make the apartment more comfortable: The bathroom and toilet were now separated, and the kitchen had its own entrance off the hallway. However, these innovations increased auxiliary space relative to living space, resulting in unfavorable cost estimates. As long as the system of cost indicators remained unchanged, architects would be unable to redesign apartments with more spacious auxiliary spaces and more flexible layouts.[76] Figure 2.3 illustrates the kind of improvements that Orlov, Narin'iani, and Dmitriev advocated.

Orlov also took Lagutenko and his colleagues to task for overreacting to Nar'iniani and Dmitriev's criticisms. The very "tone" of their response "could only elicit bewilderment." Criticism had hit the raw nerve of architects' professional and cultural authority. Orlov concluded that they must accept that design was an evolving project demanding constant innovation. At the crux of the matter was the question of what success meant in mass housing and who could define it. Lagutenko and his colleagues subscribed to a utilitarian and quantitative definition. In calling for fresh approaches, Nar'iniani, Dmitriev, and Orlov were backing an expanding definition of success that validated and drew upon residents' rising expectations for a better-quality Soviet home under Khrushchev. As we will see in later chapters, residents wanted more spacious auxiliary units, better layouts, and higher construction quality, and they were very eager to communicate their desires to architects.

Figure 2.3. Revised floor plan for a four-apartment section. In this proposed revision to the section floor plan of figure 2.2, architects eliminated pass-through rooms (except in the three-room unit, bottom left), separated bathrooms and toilets, and increased (slightly) the dimensions of corridors and kitchens. The caption stressed that these proposed alterations were done using the same amount of overall space in each apartment in the original section. Although this point was meant to illustrate the improvements architects were making, it also highlighted the overall limitations they faced.

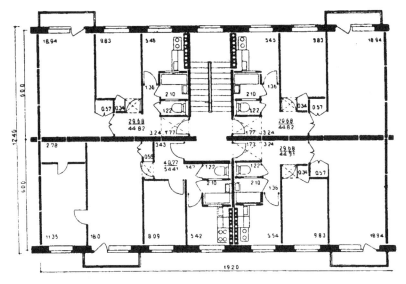

Та же секция. Предлагаемые улучшения планировки квартир
с сохранением их прежних общих площадей

Source: Metel'skii, "Predlozheniia proektirovshchikov MITEPa," 13.

Conclusion

In the 1960s and beyond, the Soviet government continued to rely on architects' design work to ensure that apartments remain separate. Once most new apartments were small enough to fit only one family and remain separate, the main goal had been reached. The Soviet leadership never reformed the underlying principles that tied design and cost to the distribution of housing. This was a fateful decision for the internal layout of separate apartments and the architect's role in designing mass housing. By refusing to reform the distribution side of the equation, the state constricted what architects could do with the space of a separate apartment, forcing them to concentrate on mundane technical questions and minor design adjustments. Mass housing architects were incapable of developing an articulate and novel vision of the separate apartment's spatial organization and had to settle for a shrunken version of the Stalin-era separate apartment. In 1932, Karel Teige had warned modernist architects against taking such a path. The Soviet experience demonstrated how decisions meant to solve one problem—communal distribution—produced unintended consequences that pushed architects precisely in the direction that Teige had feared.

The communal distribution of housing was itself a result of decisions the Soviet government made in its earliest years to implement minimum living space norms under conditions of extreme shortages. The Soviet state's unprecedented intervention in the housing question (and all "questions" for that matter) would seem to have fulfilled the desires of some nineteenth-century reformers eager to have the state force through their ostensibly scientific ideas. Yet the Soviet state's intervention had unintended consequences that diverged from (some, like Henry Sigerist, might have said "realized") the goals of nineteenth-century reformers and twentieth-century modernist architects alike. Such intervention allowed minimum living space norms to acquire functions unforeseen by nineteenth-century reformers. With total control over distribution, the Soviet state used minimum norms as maximum cutoffs in ways that restricted what architects could design, rather than liberate them to create a new way of life out of ideas alone. Although the architects of the disgraced avant-garde pounced on these circumstances in the 1930s to continue advancing their visions for a Soviet minimum dwelling unit, others in the 1950s expressed misgivings about the results and searched for more flexible alternatives.

As these first two chapters have shown, the *khrushchevka*'s design history was rooted in the Soviet Union's adoption and adaptation of ideas in the pan-European housing reform movement of the nineteenth century, which it then tried to align with another pan-European ideal of urban everyday life resurrected under Stalin: the single-family occupancy of apartments. For architects of mass housing, the *khrushchevka* was the logical solution to the ensuing tensions between minimum living space norms, a socialist system of housing distribution, and single-family occupancy. The *khrushchevka* was the Soviet Union's ultimate answer to a nineteenth-century housing question that had become plagued by unforeseen obstacles of the Soviet Union's own making. In its outer shell—its modernist aesthetics and embrace of single-family occupancy—the *khrushchevka* resembled similar mass housing programs for public housing in the West. But on the inside, the underlying principles that drove and delimited its design revealed a more complicated and uniquely Soviet path to the minimum dwelling unit. In this history of the *khrushchevka*, I have thus far examined how its production, insofar as design was concerned, was deeply imbedded in the principles of socialist housing distribution. We now turn to the allocation of the *khrushchevka* and how its circulation gave the new Soviet leadership under Khrushchev and its citizenry the chance to reorder society after Stalinism.

Part II

Distributing Housing,
Reordering Society

Chapter 3

The Waiting List

In its July 1957 housing decree, the Soviet leadership confidently declared that mass housing would eradicate shortages in ten to twelve years. From Khrushchev to the ordinary urban dweller, all sides agreed that this was a good thing, but such declarations also raised citizens' expectations of moving into separate apartments sooner rather than later. In response, the leadership scrambled to revamp housing distribution according to the socialist ideals of equality, rational organization, and legality that constituted the Khrushchev regime's broader vision of reforming Soviet governance after Stalin. Ordinary citizens projected their hopes and anxieties about improving their living conditions onto the state's system of housing distribution and turned its chief mechanism, the waiting list for living space, into a politically charged tool precisely at the time when Khrushchev's regime hoped to depoliticize it. In doing so, ordinary people shaped not only the allocation of housing but also its meaning by basing their claims on what they had suffered or contributed under Stalin. The distribution of separate apartments—which was never just about housing—provides us with a unique window onto the ways ordinary citizens and local officials envisioned and shaped the social order that Khrushchev's regime was trying to prepare for communism.

Upon taking power in 1917, the Bolsheviks had sought to allocate housing on a rational and universal basis in a socialist economy designed to eliminate material inequalities. As discussed in chapter 1, they based distribution on what they presented as scientifically determined health standards of minimum living space. Census takers accumulated the data necessary for determining citizens' needs and setting construction targets. Supplanting a market economy, local officials were supposed to apply this knowledge in distributing living space. In practice, distribution devolved into an inefficient system that bred severe shortages and inequalities. Instead of a well-coordinated system, ministries and local soviets competed fiercely over scarce living space. Minimum space norms became maximum limits of progressively smaller units that undermined their original public health intentions. Instead of egalitarian distribution, people's relative importance to the state trumped need based on health standards and family composition. And when they did not get what they wanted, citizens inundated party and state institutions with petitions. Informal practices, including patronage and bribes, further undermined the rules of distribution, turning it into a highly personalized endeavor.

With mass housing, Khrushchev's regime sought a fresh start. Its leaders believed that prevailing practices in distribution undermined urban planning and improvements in living conditions. The massive building effort alone was not enough to solve these problems; distribution had to be reformed. The new leadership's strategy rested on two key proposals, which are examined in the first section of this chapter. First, local soviets were to be placed exclusively in charge of distributing state housing, thereby eliminating the institutional conflicts that had arisen between local soviets and enterprises. Second, the rules local soviets used for managing allocation were to be based on objective measurements of need. Exceptions to the rules and the discretionary authority of local officials were to be curtailed. Strict oversight over all stages of distribution would ensure its integrity. These proposals reflected the Khrushchev regime's broader visions for reforming governance after Stalin and putting the country back on its path to communism.

Unlike Stalin's repressive methods for dealing with economic shortcomings, Khrushchev's regime chose not to handle problems in the housing economy through mass arrests or parading scapegoats before angry mobs at purge hearings. Through a reform of housing distribution, Khrushchev's leadership sought to reinstate the scientific and legal bases of socialism and to achieve the ultimate goal of communism, whereby goods would be allocated according to need. In short, Khrushchev's regime used housing distribution as a nonviolent means to continue the project of reordering the Soviet social body in preparation for the final jump to communism.

As this chapter demonstrates, the regime's well-intentioned reforms and the magnitude of mass housing construction threw the Stalinist system of distribution into a deep state of flux, only to reproduce that system's most fundamental features before Khrushchev's ouster in 1964. Scholars have explored the distribution reforms as a story of institutional conflict in which the interests of enterprise managers and industrial ministers won out over the beleaguered municipal soviet.[1] More recently, Stephen Bittner has examined how the Khrushchev regime's distribution reforms bolstered the role of local soviets in the everyday lives of Muscovites and promoted, but ultimately failed to fully implement, its egalitarian values.[2] Shifting our attention away from the distribution reforms, Christine Varga-Harris has shown through citizens' petitions for housing how ordinary people identified entitlements as a critical element in notions of Soviet citizenship and a recharged social contract between state and society.[3] Some social groups, such as the elderly, interpreted their inability to obtain a separate apartment as social marginalization by government officials and fellow citizens, who refused to recognize their suffering and sacrifices under Stalin. In doing so, pensioners contributed to the construction of the waiting list as a politically charged register of where one stood in Soviet society.[4] Less well understood is how pressure from ordinary urban dwellers and their competing definitions of equality and social justice intersected with local authorities' attempts to overhaul housing allocation in the face of so much new living space. The role of the waiting list as a focal point for constructing social identities and stratification in a period of intense change likewise remains largely unexamined. How state officials and ordinary citizens under Khrushchev used the waiting list in the ongoing project of weeding out socially suspect elements from the Soviet social body is unknown to historians.[5]

This chapter explores these questions in Leningrad when the city revamped housing allocation to absorb a rapidly expanding stock from the mid-1950s to the early 1960s. In comparison with Moscow, as studied by Bittner, distribution reform in Leningrad proved to be much more politically charged and led to an unintended crisis in which thousands of residents were summarily dismissed from waiting lists. In pursuing its reform, the Leningrad city soviet held closed-door meetings to instruct district soviet officials on how to allocate housing and revamp the city's waiting lists. The archived stenographic records of these meetings, examined here for the first time, provide us with a unique, behind-the-scenes account of distribution practices and debates that were kept out of the mass press. Indeed, one of the most remarkable aspects of this story is how little residents knew about the constant adjustments that city authorities made to distribution and their plans to pull off a major overhaul that disrupted many people's lives.

Because residents were unaware of the city's plans, they did not have any direct input on the reform. Yet district soviet deputies spoke on their constituents' behalf at meetings with city bosses and leveraged what residents said to them in challenging city leaders' decisions. The acrimony between city officials and district deputies revolved around issues ranging from the size of waiting lists to deputies' discretionary authority in allowing people onto lists. The status of "native Leningraders" (*korennye leningradtsy*) was particularly divisive. Despite the city soviet's reluctance to recognize native Leningraders as a separate entitlement category, district deputies lobbied on behalf of citizens who believed that their long-term residence entitled them to better housing before others. This intensely emotional issue, which was deeply embedded in the symbolism and sacrifices of the city, served as a stunning example of how residents and district deputies could politicize the waiting list in ways that the city soviet and Khrushchev's regime hoped to avoid.

The native Leningrader issue and the closed-door meetings in which it was debated elucidate the broader complexities of relations between "state" and "society" under Khrushchev. District deputies, who were also residents with their own housing questions, came to view the people they placed on their waiting lists as a constituency whose housing claims they had an obligation to protect before the city soviet. In their petitions and face-to-face meetings with deputies, residents invested the waiting list with a social significance that deputies leveraged in shaping distribution reform. Urban dwellers and district soviet officials subscribed to a sense of social justice that was rooted not in universal notions of citizenship and equal rights based on quantitative need, as Khrushchev's regime desired, but rather in a moral economy based on social differences and participation in Soviet historical experiences such as industrialization and the war. Another critical Stalinist experience was citizenship itself, which produced what Golfo Alexopoulos calls a "hierarchy of states of civic belonging" in which citizens enjoyed different rights and obligations.[6] Residents and district officials in

Leningrad acted on and preserved that Stalinist legacy in ways we have only begun to understand. They espoused notions of equality whereby individuals had an equal right to what they were due not according to universal standards of need quantified in square meters of living space but according to the persons they and their family members had become in a hierarchical relationship to others.

All Housing to the Soviets

The top leadership and local officials began pushing serious reform of housing distribution soon after Stalin's death in 1953. In this new and uncertain political context, policymakers traced long-standing problems in distribution to a major housing law from 1937 that divided state housing between local soviets and the workplace. Their solution was to shift the balance of power to local soviets. The push for reform culminated in a 1958 draft for a unionwide law that would have put local soviets in charge of all state housing distribution. Advocates of reform were locked in an institutional conflict with industrial ministries and factory managers who jealously guarded their housing stocks as patrimonies for their employees and workers. Behind this bureaucratic struggle lay a broader fight over Stalinist social values and alternative visions of Soviet society and governance. Arguments in favor of the unionwide reform and evidence of rampant dysfunction shaped the context for what transpired in Leningrad, but so did the lack of direction from the top leadership. The 1958 draft decree was never issued and ended up in the Communist Party's archive. Although the government remained formally committed to transferring housing to local soviets, it was left up to local authorities to decide whether and how to do this.[7]

Stalin had been dead barely a month before two Moscow city leaders lobbied his would-be successors, Georgii Malenkov and Nikita Khrushchev, for an overhaul of housing distribution. Mikhail Iasnov, the city soviet chairman, and Nikolai Mikhailov, a secretary in the city party committee, argued that the present system impeded the city's ten-year urban renewal plan (1951–61) and efforts to eliminate shortages. Under the plan, enterprises would produce 7 million square meters of living space and the city soviet would produce 3 million square meters, which Iasnov and Mikhailov claimed were enough to eradicate the city's housing crisis in just a few years. Yet enterprises distributed what they built for their own needs, making it impossible for the city to provide housing to those who really needed it, such as the 392,000 people living in barracks and irreparable housing. Instead of building housing where the plan mandated, enterprises built on vacant plots, where they avoided the legal obligation to find housing for residents whose buildings they would need to destroy.[8]

Iasnov and Mikhailov's proposal envisioned municipal governance predicated on serving the needs of all Muscovites above the fractured interests of industrial ministries. They spoke out against inequalities in the city's housing distribution. Ministries and enterprises built and kept most of the city's housing and allocated it to their labor forces above living space norms. Meanwhile, most Muscovites depended on the soviets for their dwellings. The 32,000 families (or 128,000 people) currently on soviet waiting lists averaged less than 2 square meters per person. In contrast, one particular ministry was building enough housing to provide its 17,000-member workforce in Moscow with 18 square meters of living space per individual. A class issue was evident in the two officials' criticism of current practices. Ministries allocated their housing mainly to administrative employees, leaving other workers to get their housing from district soviets. Ministries and enterprises also gave too much housing to newcomers who arrived in Moscow to work for them. The new arrivals effectively jumped ahead of "native Muscovites" (*korennye Moskvichi*) who had already been waiting years for housing. This unpopular state of affairs provoked "a multitude of justifiable complaints and censures" from Muscovites. By favoring native Muscovites and contrasting them to recent arrivals, Iasnov and Mikhailov suggested that not all people should have an equal claim to the city's housing. Social identity based on long-term residence in one place could be a weapon in the local politics of housing distribution.[9]

In a memorandum to Malenkov and the union-level Council of Ministers in December 1953, Khrushchev threw his weight behind Iasnov and Mikhailov's idea that the Moscow soviet should run all housing distribution in the city. He stressed that enterprises' current methods of distributing housing impeded the city's urban renewal and made it impossible to improve the living conditions of those in greatest need. Having the Moscow city soviet manage all distribution could fix these problems in one fell swoop. Such reasoning reflected the populism that informed Khrushchev's support for mass housing generally, as well as his trademark search for the quick and total solution. Khrushchev pushed for a "centralization of living space allocation in the city of Moscow."[10] Centralizing authority over the lives of so many spoke to a vision of governance not normally associated with the thaw or egalitarianism.[11] But for a technocrat like Khrushchev, only the centralization of power could bring about the de-Stalinization of a dysfunctional housing economy rife with inequalities that bore little relationship to the plan and remained divided among industrial fiefdoms warring over scarce resources.

The difficulties of implementing Khrushchev's vision for a more centralized and egalitarian distribution of housing became evident when the government in Moscow told Leningrad's city leaders in July 1955 to tighten their oversight over enterprises' housing distribution and ensure that those who needed housing got it. The government's definition of need cut three ways that revealed the underlying tensions of distribution reform. Need could be based on the poor state of a family's housing conditions alone, such as "dilapidated houses and barracks, earmarked for removal." But the government also defined need with regard to entitlement groups, which identified persons in relation to what they or their family members had done for the Soviet Union. Leningrad was to assign priority to "invalids of the Fatherland war, families of dead soldiers, and those demobilized from the Soviet Army, who are in need of housing." In addition, the Leningrad city soviet was "to set aside living space for workers of enterprises and organizations and to provide for other necessities." In other words, the city soviet still had an obligation to help enterprises allocate housing to continue meeting their labor needs.[12]

In support of such directives, conflicting as they were, the government had gathered ample evidence to back the centralization of allocation under local soviets everywhere. In September 1954, for example, it zeroed in on people's housing needs in eight oblasts and the city of Stalingrad. As a sign of shifting priorities since Stalin's death, Moscow forced ministries and local enterprises to fork over 25 million rubles to build new housing for those occupying "spaces unsuitable for housing."[13] Such housing included "mud huts" as well as "sheds, corridors, storerooms, bathhouses, kitchens, bathrooms, attics, train cars, dilapidated barracks, spaces that used to be toilets, and various temporary dwellings made from old materials after the end of the Great Patriotic War." Many of the people forced to live in such conditions included

phans."[14] Need was thus not only based on the amount and condition
of living quarters but also on the sacrifices and vulnerabilities of the
persons involved.

By the end of 1955, the government found that its intervention from
the previous September had not yielded the intended results. The power
of local officials to make distribution decisions as they saw fit was cited
as a chief reason for failing to get housing to those who needed it.
Local officials did obstruct distribution plans, but how much is unclear;
they were likely singled out as convenient scapegoats for Moscow's
problems. In any event, curtailing their power became a major cause
of distribution reform that added discipline to Khrushchev's vision of
centralized governance. A case in point was Kalinin, where "oblast and
city soviet officials in many cases allocated living space by individual
instructions and furthermore ignored the waiting lists and people in
extreme need of living space."[15] In Lipetsk, "managers of highly placed
organizations normally distribute space . . . by verbal instructions and
likewise city housing administrators [do so] arbitrarily."[16] Local soviets
did a poor job of maintaining waiting lists and in some localities even
lost them.[17]

The central authorities in Moscow intervened in these oblasts to set
straight their housing distribution. To local authorities, such interventions by Moscow and its sprawling ministries were the real problem. So
explained Leningrad's oblast party chief, Ivan Spiridonov, and the
city soviet chair, Nikolai Smirnov, to the Central Committee as it
mulled over the unionwide proposal to shift housing distribution to
local soviets in 1958. They explained that the city had drawn up distribution plans based on projected targets for newly built housing, but
that over the course of the year, local enterprise chiefs appealed directly to Moscow to force the city to deliver additional allotments outside the plan. Enterprises had gone over the heads of city authorities,
no doubt angering Spiridonov and Smirnov. Behind this institutional
conflict in the command economy lay deeper problems about transparency and people's faith in the housing system that again touched on
issues of governance in a time of political flux. The city's housing allocation plans were made public through collective labor contracts that
indicated the amount of housing to be distributed at a particular workplace. In addition, local soviets posted the names of people who would

receive housing. Consequently, manipulations from above triggered shortfalls in distribution and "dissatisfaction among working people who are deprived of the living space earmarked for them by the plan."[18] Transparency was fine until it was time to distribute blame for misallocations. In a period when local soviets were becoming more responsive to residents' needs, the opinion of their loudest constituents mattered for making the case that local soviets needed more control over housing.

But city and district soviets could just as easily blame their constituents for disrupting distribution by taking advantage of loopholes. Working people were not only innocent victims in the game of allocating housing, but also influential agents playing the system to meet their needs. A case in point was people's ability to hold onto space they were supposed to vacate when relocating to new mass housing. Local soviets expected to redistribute old housing to others in need, thereby clearing waiting lists. They soon found, however, that some residents retained control over such space. The underlying issue was article 27 of the 1937 housing decree, by which a resident and his family could not keep "extra housing space," defined as space that exceeded maximum living space limits and came "in the form of isolated rooms." Whereas workplaces could redistribute such space with complete disregard for a resident's wishes, residents of local soviet housing were allowed three months to locate anyone they chose to live in the freed-up space.[19]

In March 1954, the Moscow oblast soviet complained that this grace period allowed residents to redistribute excess space to people who had never registered on a soviet list. Such a complaint illustrated how ordinary residents could pull off some line jumping of their own, all within the letter of the law. According to the Moscow oblast soviet, such a practice was the linchpin of an underground and at times lucrative housing market.[20] The Ministry of the Communal Economy backed up the oblast's complaints by lobbying the government to close the grace period.[21] For local soviets and their backers, reform meant restricting the little autonomy residents enjoyed in redistributing space. Local soviets continued to voice similar complaints about vacated space and even illegal squatting to the Central Committee when it considered the 1958 draft decree to give local soviets control over all waiting lists.[22] Housing exchanges provided residents with even more opportunities to manipulate distribution, including the illegal purchase and sale of state housing.[23] But as the government discovered, local bureaucrats ma-

nipulated exchanges as well; in their case, to legitimize housing allocation to people outside the line.[24] In the visions of better governance
implied in these investigations and accusations, ordinary residents, enterprises, and local soviets would all lose advantages in shaping housing distribution.

After several years of chronicling major problems, the Central Committee in 1958 gathered input from city soviets and jurists in preparation for the unionwide decree to reform housing distribution.[25] The
proposed decree, "On the Further Improvement in the Distribution of
State Living Space," was never passed, but its provisions merit analysis
as a reflection of where housing distribution reform stood and how
Leningrad's attempts fit into such efforts. The central goal of the reform, as originally outlined by Iasnov and Mikhailov, was to give local
soviets authority over allocating all state housing.

The draft decree fell well short of the mark and presented an ambiguous picture of where true power lay. On the one hand, it declared
that all existing and future state housing in ministries and enterprises
(i.e., workplace housing) was to be placed under local soviet authority.
It even listed the entitlement groups that stood to improve their living
conditions first: "war invalids and the families of war dead; demobilized officers, those serving extra time in the Soviet Army, and the families of active duty personnel; families with many children; leading
workers of production; citizens who live in barracks, dilapidated houses,
and other premises unfit for habitation; workers, employees, and
young specialists who have been transferred or sent to work in other
locations." On the other hand, the decree made no mention of giving
local soviets control over workplace waiting lists and combining them
with their own. Instead, it announced that whatever housing ministries
and other workplaces built "gets distributed first to the workers and
employees in these organizations who need living space." Workplaces
would thus still be able to put the needs of their workforce ahead of a
city's general population. As the decree's later provisions suggested,
the local soviet's "authority" over workplace housing amounted to administrative tasks, including issuing housing permits and publicly dis-
playing the lists of people scheduled to get housing.[26]

The proposed decree would have done little to centralize authority
over housing allocation as originally envisioned by Khrushchev. But in
a revealing move that responded to local authorities' long-standing
complaints, it proposed a crackdown on the tactics ordinary citizens

used to manipulate the system. The decree would have mandated that a court could evict citizens from their new housing if they refused to give up their vacated space. Local soviets would still have to respect people's right to settle others into extra space within a three-month period, but they could ask a court to evict a person from state housing if he owned a house as personal property. Those who left town could only retain their housing if mandated by law, and any relatives who could not go with them would be forced to give up any extra space or relocate elsewhere. Local soviets would now have to approve any subletting of state housing.[27]

The failure to pass the proposed decree, even in its watered down state, suggested that Khrushchev and his allies lacked the political wherewithal to implement a reform that would cut, however modestly, into ministries and enterprises' power to distribute their housing. The transfer of housing to local soviets stalled as a vaguely stated goal, thereby underlining the lack of direction from the top on how to proceed. But such uncertainty also opened opportunities for local officials and ordinary citizens to reshape housing distribution themselves. We now turn to the case of Leningrad to see how this city undertook an overhaul of its housing distribution.

Who Got Housing in Leningrad's Moscow District in 1955?

As a window onto Leningrad's housing distribution before this overhaul, let us examine the Moscow district of the city in 1955, an area that would soon see tremendous mass housing construction. The district began 1955 with 1,809 families on its waiting list and ended it with 1,830. The list was broken down in two ways that illustrated central tensions in distribution. The first represented the years people were placed on the list, reproduced as table 3.1; the second reported people by entitlement category or method by which they had been placed on the list, reproduced as table 3.2. Table 3.1 said almost nothing about a person other than the time he had invested waiting; it reduced the district soviet's role to automatically removing people off the list once their number came up in line. Table 3.2 recognized people according to entitlement categories and suggested the discretionary authority local authorities had in placing such people on lists.[28] As we shall see, city

Table 3.1. Moscow District Waiting List in 1955, by Year of Admittance

Year of Admittance to Waiting List	Number of Families
1945	103
1946	349
1947	146
1948	178
1949	94
1950	78
1951	81
1952	132
1953	134
1954	209
1955	337
	Total 1,841

Source: Tsentral'nyi gosudarstvennyi arkhiv Sankt-Peterburga (Central State Archive of Saint Petersburg), f. 103, op. 5, d. 330, l. 66. The report does not explain the discrepancy between the total amount, 1,841, calculated here by adding up the data reported annually, and 1,830, indicated earlier in the report.

officials, district deputies, and residents advocated the principles of table 3.1 when critiquing or shaping the behavior of others; they preferred the principles of table 3.2 when protecting their own interests.

This snapshot of the Moscow district's waiting list tells us that those on it the longest had been admitted in 1945, indicating that the soviet had wiped the slate clean at the end of the war.[29] People were thus waiting for up to ten years to improve their living conditions, which was a

Table 3.2. Moscow District Waiting List in 1955, by Entitlement Group

Entitlement Groups and Other Persons on Waiting List	Number of Families
Invalids of the Fatherland War	60
Those serving in the military and families of war dead	617
Other citizens	443
By decision of the People's Court	58
By sanction of the procurator	16
Army officers by Government Order 100	86
Army officers by Government Order 75	84
The demobilized	462
The rehabilitated	4
Total	1,830

Source: Tsentral'nyi gosudarstvennyi arkhiv Sankt-Peterburga (Central State Archive of Saint Petersburg), f. 103, op. 5, d. 330, l. 66.

trend urban dwellers would experience well into the mass housing campaign. Although it is impossible to tell how many people in each year on the list had already gotten off, table 3.1 suggests that the soviet took on different numbers of people every year. We can only speculate about the factors that accounted for such fluctuations. The greatest number of people remaining on the list had been admitted in 1946, which could be explained by an influx of residents returning to the city after the war. From 1947 to 1951, the district soviet admitted fewer people to the list, perhaps deciding that it could not add more until more housing was available. Beginning in 1952, the soviet appeared to have added more people every year through 1955, suggesting that new housing construction spurred it to take on more residents.[30]

Table 3.2 sheds more light on the people the district took onto its list and the range of party-state officials involved in shaping it. Most people belonged to entitlement groups that privileged World War II veterans, the families of dead soldiers, and active duty personnel. The only other clearly indentified entitlement group included persons who had been repressed under Stalin and recently rehabilitated. Although the Soviet government created entitlement categories,[31] city and district soviets, local courts, and the procuracy ultimately decided who got on waiting lists. The large and murky category "other citizens" in table 3.2 suggests that local officials exercised much discretion in allowing people onto lists without having to provide any reasons.[32] Tightening such authority became a major point of contention in reforming distribution.

As we saw in chapter 1, combatant states had created entitlement categories related to military service in World War I, and the new Bolshevik regime had followed suit. Judging by the Moscow district's data, such entitlement categories had expanded after World War II. Although this underscored the war's impact on constructing hierarchies of need in housing, inclusion in such categories was hardly a sign of elite status. Responsibility for these people had fallen to local soviets, which barely controlled a quarter of the state housing stock in the mid-1950s.[33] Local soviets did not allocate housing to the Soviet Union's real elites in the party-state apparatus and the members of the cultural intelligentsia who looked toward the Communist Party, their workplace, or patrons for solutions to their housing questions. Instead, local soviets served those in the general population who were unable to get housing from their workplace. This did not mean that securing a spot on a soviet waiting list was meaningless, even if the wait took years. A soviet waiting list was a register of social differentiation that meant much to ordinary people, who helped construct its social and political meanings in ways Khrushchev's regime was eager to avoid.

Getting onto a waiting list was only half the struggle; getting off the list and into better housing was the next challenge. First came years of waiting, during which proactive residents continued to petition the authorities to quicken the process. A family was taken off the waiting list when it received housing, but this did not necessarily mean that it obtained it from the local soviet. The Moscow district soviet explained that it provided 123 families with housing in 1955. The soviet removed an additional 193 people from its roll because they received housing from their place of work.[34] This underscored how the workplace allocated most state housing and suggested that different family members stood in different lines to improve their household's chances.

As indicated above, the district soviet did not distribute all housing by going through the list in the order people had gotten onto it. Of the 123 people the Moscow district provided with housing, 93 received it "in order of the line" (*v poriadke ocheredi*) and 30 "by jumping the line" (*vne ocheredi*). The soviet's way of documenting distribution obfuscated who these people were and when they had gotten onto the waiting list. It listed the 123 people only by their entitlement group (table 3.3) and not by the year they were placed on the list. In contrast, it was impossible to tell which entitlement groups the 93 people belonged to. Presumably most of the 30 people had jumped to the head of the line

Table 3.3. Distribution of Housing in the Moscow District in 1955

Entitlement Groups and Other Persons Receiving Housing	Number of Families	Amount of Housing Received	
		Number of Rooms	Square Meters of Living Space
Invalids of the Fatherland War	19	20	328
Families of war dead	37	39	617
The demobilized	15	18	277
Army officers by Government Order 100	13	15	295
Army officers by Government Order 75	17	17	340
By decision of the People's Court	6	6	63
By sanction of the procurator	2	2	27
Other people (second line)	14	17	234
Total	123	134	2,181

Source: Tsentral'nyi gosudarstvennyi arkhiv Sankt-Peterburga (Central State Archive of Saint Petersburg), f. 103, op. 5, d. 330, ll. 66–67.

because of their entitlement category. Yet 14 "other people" got housing from a "second line."[35] Were they part of this group of 30? What was this second line?

By hiding information from superiors, not to mention the public, the district soviet's internal report reflected a lack of transparency that reformers wished to eliminate. For soviet officials who wanted to retain some autonomy in distributing housing, these obfuscations were critical tools. Having a supply of housing for unforeseen events was also necessary to maintain discretionary authority. The soviet allocated space to people who faced emergency situations and were thus "not on the list." In 1955, it distributed thirty rooms to families living in buildings that required major repairs, were unsafe, or were slated for demolition. Other families were removed from public establishments, which they had used for housing such as schools and public kitchens. The Moscow soviet also set aside nineteen rooms for its housing administration's office space.[36]

As the allocation of "rooms" suggests, the soviet distributed housing in communal, not single-family, apartments. Table 3.3 shows that almost all families received one room. The soviet's supply included sixteen rooms that the people's court ordered vacated, fifty-nine vacated rooms, and nine rooms made available after renovations.[37] More than half the housing the soviet distributed was newly built: twenty-six rooms in housing the city soviet had recently constructed and seventy-three rooms in newly built housing that workplaces were obligated to give to the local soviet. Consequently, the Moscow district distributed old and new housing one room at a time, and converted new apartments into communal ones upon distribution. As we have already seen, the communalization of new apartments under Stalin was a regular phenomenon that was never entirely eliminated under Khrushchev. In 1955, the Moscow district gave no indication that it would change this practice. Working with distribution norms rooted in the Commissariat of Health's 1919 regulations on minimum living space (see chapter 1), this local soviet continued to see housing as rooms and square meters, not single-family apartments.

Our snapshot of the Moscow district's housing in 1955 sheds light on the pressures district officials faced and the tools they would leverage when they met with higher-ups from the city soviet over the next several years to iron out distribution reforms behind closed doors. District officials did not have enough housing to meet their constituents' needs and could barely make a dent in their waiting lists over one year. They relied on a hodgepodge of recycled and new housing from various sources and allocated it by the room, not as whole apartments. Creating entitlement categories was out of their hands and other authorities, such as the courts, could force them to distribute housing to particular persons or groups. Nonetheless, district officials enjoyed much leeway in deciding who actually got onto waiting lists as members of entitlement categories and when they got off. They operated as the gatekeepers to better housing between desperate constituents and a new regime determined to centralize housing governance. Nowhere was this better illustrated than in the case of the native Leningrader. Although this social group did not have its own official category of entitlement, district officials lobbied on native Leningraders' behalf and simultaneously exploited them to preserve their discretionary authority in distributing housing.

Native Leningraders

Citing the government's July 1955 orders discussed above, Leningrad's city soviet tightened control over distribution with new rules in August 1956. It vowed to crack down on housing personnel for "settling living space without housing permits and hiding vacated living space." It extended control over enterprises' vacated space by mandating that they redistribute it to employees presently on a local soviet's waiting list. Henceforth, the police could only issue a residency permit (*propiska*), which allowed a person to live in the city, if an individual produced a city soviet housing permit. Because this applied to all state housing, the idea was to force enterprises to pass their allocation decisions through the city's soviets.[38]

Most important, the city soviet established four methods for getting onto a soviet waiting list that reflected once again the tensions between definitions of need based on housing conditions versus those based on who a person was and what he or she had done. According to the first method, a person had to meet each of the following three preconditions: she had been a resident of the city in soviet housing for at least five years before the start of the war (i.e., since at least June 1936); her housing had been destroyed for war-related reasons; and she had been living most recently in the city before January 1, 1956. These preconditions favored the long-term resident or "native Leningrader" (*korennoi* or *iskonnyi leningradets*) but expected her to have already returned to the city. The second method took people who had housing deemed "unfit for habitation" *and* a housing permit from the city or district soviet. Because city and district soviets would only begin issuing permits for workplace housing in August 1956, people who had settled into workplace housing beforehand were excluded from this method. The third method for getting onto a list defined need according to the amount of living space one had. A person and his family with "less than 3 square meters per resident" in soviet housing could be admitted to a soviet waiting list.[39]

Each of the first three methods discriminated against residents of workplace housing. This latest salvo in the institutional struggle between soviets and the workplace soon intersected with politically charged debates over local social identities revolving around who belonged in the city and who should be excluded. Native Leningraders felt they were entitled to better housing and a spot on a soviet waiting list by virtue of their attachment to the city, regardless of the institution that issued their present housing. Unlike enterprises that looked after their workforce alone, soviets were supposed to serve the needs of all. With the new instructions, the city soviet ran afoul of this ideal and acted more like a workplace by restricting access to soviet waiting lists. With the fourth method for getting onto a soviet waiting list, the city eased its restrictions, but only slightly by allowing onto lists people "demobilized from the Soviet Army, who lost living space in the city of Leningrad in connection with entering the Army."[40] Among long-term residents in workplace housing, only demobilized soldiers could get onto a soviet list.

The immediate effect of the August 1956 decree was a surge in the number of people on soviet waiting lists. By January 1, 1957, 19,000 families had gotten onto lists, instead of the projected 12,000 to 13,000, pushing the overall number from 30,000 to 49,000. During the next several years, A. I. Sokolov, the city soviet's deputy chairman and point man on housing distribution, urged his district deputies to expand lists more gradually and dampen people's expectations. At a January 1957 meeting, Sokolov warned district deputies, "Don't promise anybody that we'll clear the lists in two or three years." The amount they could allocate was increasing from year to year, "but not so much that we'll satisfy everyone waiting in line." He claimed that Leningrad had followed Moscow's lead of having local soviets take onto their waiting lists people with less than 3 square meters of living space per person because of complaints Leningraders had sent to the Central Committee and the Council of Ministers. In response, Sokolov wanted district soviets to give their constituents a reality check: "We started putting people on the list, but that doesn't mean today we took them on and tomorrow give out the housing." What the soviets gave out by putting people on waiting lists were reasonable expectations. Once people got on a list, "then they'll have hope, even if it takes 10 years, they'll get [housing]." Thankfully, Sokolov noted, people on lists no longer wrote letters of complaint. But they would have to wait: "We created prospects, admitted them to the list, but they will receive the space in the order of the line."[41]

In order not to erode the psychological assurance of such prospects, Sokolov strongly argued for limiting the number of people soviets took onto their lists. He categorically rejected suggestions that people in workplace housing who had lived in the city before the war be taken on soviet lists. "Let their ministry take care of them. We'll have to meet their needs later, without a doubt, but not now." People living in the individual housing sector were not to be admitted onto waiting lists either unless they had lost their homes on account of the war. His stated reason for excluding these and others was lack of sufficient housing.[42] At stake behind Sokolov's reasoning were the waiting list's political importance and ability to temporarily absorb people's rising expectations for better housing. With ten years on a waiting list, they still had hope; anything longer was presumed to be intolerable.

District soviet officials resisted Sokolov's conservative stance, particularly regarding native Leningraders. They argued that a person's status as a native Leningrader transcended the bifurcation of housing between soviets and the workplace. The Moscow district official, Korsukov, described native Leningraders as victims of circumstance who deserved more from their city. He drew a composite sketch of "a child, who during the war lost his father, mother, was placed in a children's home, lived somewhere, returned fourteen years old, ended up in a handicraft trade school, he's drawn to Leningrad and he thinks of himself as a Leningrader. They return, live in dormitories after finishing a trade school. Admit them to the line or not?" Answering his own question, Korsukov recommended that they take such orphans onto their lists. Bending somewhat to this pressure, Sokolov conceded that orphans should receive housing directly upon leaving orphanages, but only "small rooms," while those who lived in dormitories would remain there and be placed on soviet waiting lists for better housing. Korsukov also provided a more general definition of the native Leningrader as a person who had suffered and fought during the war, specifically in the city. "Many think of themselves as patriots of Leningrad because here they were born, lived, fought in the blockade and we don't put them [on a waiting list] because they lived in workplace housing before the war and by now these houses are gone." In Korsukov's view, such people had slipped through the cracks. To resolve their situation, he suggested that those "who lived [in the city] before the war and lost space during the war, as Leningraders, should be put on the line."[43]

In contrast, Korsukov treated rehabilitated persons quite differently. Finding their increase in number burdensome, he was annoyed that rehabilitated persons actively pursued all avenues to get housing in Leningrad: "There's a large group of rehabilitated persons who were freed in the years 1945–46, they live in other cities, now they've heard they can come to Leningrad, they come, show 1945 documents, but they've been living for ten years where they served time and now they demand to be taken onto the line, and many of them apply for this while not presently registered in Leningrad." Korsukov did not entertain the possibility that a rehabilitated person could be a native Leningrader.[44] In fact, rehabilitated persons on his own district's waiting lists had lived in the city before being repressed and probably considered themselves native Leningraders. According to a report on housing distribution in the Moscow district for 1957, prior residence in the district was a condition for rehabilitated persons' admission to its waiting lists. There were eleven rehabilitated persons and their families on the district's waiting list at the beginning of the year, forty-six more were admitted over the course of the year, and thirty-three received housing off the list during the year.[45]

Although Korsukov depicted rehabilitated persons as opportunists, he nevertheless expressed some doubt about rejecting them.[46] His ambivalence echoed worries that others in Soviet society expressed as the Gulag was dismantled and political prisoners came home.[47] The contrast he drew between the rehabilitated and native Leningraders suggested that there was still something illegitimate about the former's claim to housing in the city and, by extension, to being a member of

Soviet society. The waiting list, especially in this era of mass housing construction, could be an effective, nonviolent tool for local bureaucrats like Korsukov to have their say in reordering Soviet society and weeding out its undesirable elements.

Sokolov played a similar game. In response to Korsukov, Sokolov pushed an unwritten hierarchy whereby rehabilitated persons could return. Rehabilitated persons who had left their place of incarceration and were now living somewhere else were not to be taken onto a waiting list. Those who still lived where they had been imprisoned could be taken on, but district soviets had to tell them not to come to Leningrad until they were about to receive housing. Exceptions could be made, however, for leading members of the Soviet intelligentsia. Sokolov explained: "But one needs to take into account that if he was a professor, was chair of a department in an institute, now he's rehabilitated, but we're going to tell him, live there in Vologda, but he's a prominent scholar. One needs to examine every case separately." Sokolov's comments revealed that, in the order of things, it was simply too incongruous to let a respected professor languish in a provincial town instead of returning home to Leningrad, where his skills and status belonged. In contrast, people "exiled as members of nationalities" should always be denied access to the city's waiting lists. This was quite an incredible statement for Sokolov to make, considering how blatantly he was rejecting the Khrushchev regime's release of such prisoners from the Gulag. Yet it again echoed Soviet citizens' anxieties about the return to their communities of Gulag prisoners who had been repressed as members of particular ethnic groups or for participation in anti-Soviet nationalist groups during and after World War II.[48] Coaching his colleagues on how to respond to such people, Sokolov said, "You can write: They wrongly exiled you, you're free, rehabilitated, but we can't do anything. You're set up now, live there. They received housing in exile, so let them live and work there."[49]

In short, Sokolov wanted to cherry-pick the rehabilitated persons the city needed while leaving out those he deemed undesirable. As a reflection of the kind of society in which Sokolov wanted to live, his recommendations foresaw a Leningrad free of entire nationalities that Stalin had repressed and sent off to the Gulag. If city and district officials followed his demand to "examine every case separately," policing the waiting list would be a highly effective way of keeping excised members of society out and letting those they wanted back in.

District officials continued to press Sokolov on native Leningraders by contrasting them to another social group deemed unworthy of equal access to housing: recent arrivals who had come to work in the city. An official from the Kurortnyi district, Shmitko, complained that "citizen Leningraders" with slightly more than 3 square meters of living space could not get on a waiting list, whereas recent arrivals got on a list if they fell under this cut off. He suggested that persons with less than 3 square meters needed to have lived in the city for at least five years in order to get onto a waiting list.[50] Shmitko sought to protect native Leningraders from what he saw as an unjust leveling of their rights to housing with those of recent arrivals. An objective definition of need based on square meters (the third method of getting onto a list in the August 1956 regulations) thus collided with a definition of right based on social identity and a hierarchical view of citizenship. As such discussions over housing revealed, there were "citizen Leningraders," and then there were others like recent arrivals and rehabilitated members of particular nationalities.

The social identities in question—native Leningrader, newcomer, rehabilitated person, exiled nationalities—were not only labels that city and district officials used to describe actual social groups but also reflections of the type of person, with their values and economic worth, that these officials wanted to either include or exclude from Leningrad and society more broadly. The native Leningrader was an innocent victim of circumstances who followed the rules and deserved better. He was someone in need of help, and his dependence on a local soviet official was crucial to the latter's sense of self and righteous indignation at outsiders who abused the system or higher-ups who curtailed his discretionary authority with new regulations. Unlike exiled nationalities or rehabilitated persons, the native Leningrader did not threaten to expose by his mere presence in town the injustices that had gone into creating Soviet society. In contrast, as the embodiment of those who abused the Soviet system, the recent arrival was a devious manipulator, who had circumvented the power of the local soviet official and had poached housing on his territory, instead of waiting patiently like the meek and well-deserving native Leningrader. In reality, some native Leningraders were likely just as manipulative, while some recent arrivals likely tried to play by the rules. But in this politicized tug-of-war over distribution between city and district officials, perceptions mattered more than reality.

In decrying recent arrivals, district officials revealed the opprobrium they faced from city residents for not stopping them. "There's a definite loophole here," the Petrograd district official Dorogin observed, "and it's very bad, people justly reproach us for it, that a person came to Leningrad alone, then his wife and kids came, space got small, less than 3 meters per person, and we take them onto the line." Dorogin derided such calculated schemes: "A person came alone in 1950, got a job that came with housing, then it turns out he's an invalid, in eight months his wife arrived with a child, then two daughters, in 1953 the son-in-law arrived, then the daughter with a grandson, and the living space ends up less than 3 square meters per person and we take them onto the line." Recent arrivals manipulated the system in other ways. "Comrade Dorogin is right," another district official explained. "We have a lot of space unfit for habitation that people who came in 1955 have settled in, or they became courtyard cleaners, then brought the relatives in from the village." Such families then forced local soviets to provide them better housing.[51]

Pushing the issue further, Shmitko lobbied against the rule that prevented soviets from taking native Leningraders onto waiting lists just because they lived in workplace housing. The logical endpoint of his proposal led Shmitko to observe that "in the near future, perhaps in one or two years, we will take onto the list all those who live in local soviet housing and workplace housing, because distribution will be conducted through local soviets."[52] Getting onto a soviet waiting list would then no longer depend on whether a resident already lived in local soviet or workplace housing. Shmitko's comment was the first in these meetings to hint at the union-level reform for handing housing distribution to local soviets. As Moscow's city leaders Iasnov and Mikhailov had done in 1953, Shmitko linked the reform to a more just outcome for a city's native residents.

People's petitions for better housing supported Shmitko's suggested concessions for native Leningraders and, I would argue, shaped how he and others lobbied Sokolov. For example, a surgeon, Galina Sobetskaia, wrote to Voroshilov in March 1954 about her difficulties finding adequate housing for herself and her son. Relocated to Ulianovsk oblast during the war, they had returned to Leningrad in 1951, but her attempts to get onto a waiting list had failed. Temporary living arrangements with her sister and then an acquaintance had not worked out, and she could not afford to rent a room privately. "Is it possible,"

Sobetskaia asked, "that I, a Soviet doctor, do not deserve for 23 years of my work 10 meters of living space in my native city?" In addition to having paid her dues as a doctor, Sobetskaia appealed to her status as a native Leningrader to claim her entitlement to better housing. She had been born and educated in the city. Apart from her surviving sister, all that she had in Leningrad were "the graves of those people dear to me—my father, mother, a daughter, dead in the blockade in 1942." Sobetskaia, who had previously had housing in Leningrad, identified with the city and felt clearly wronged that she might not be able to stay on account of her housing dilemma: "And why must I leave my native city and in old age start again to set up a new life somewhere in a strange place?"[53] Instead of asking Voroshilov for housing up front, she asked him to have her put on a waiting list. Sokolov's own comments recounted above about the psychological value of the waiting list echoed her reasoning on this point. "I ask you now," she wrote, "to allow as an exception for me to be placed in line, so that I can have some kind of hope to receive space at some point."[54]

According to such petitions, a typical native Leningrader had lived in the city before the war, was likely born there, and had contributed to the city's struggle for survival in the war, usually by remaining in the city during the blockade. As Georgii Ekgardt explained in a letter to Khrushchev in 1956, "I think of Leningrad as my motherland, because here's where I got an education, spent most of my life, and where my kids were born and raised."[55] Native Leningraders claimed that their long-term residence in the city entitled them to better housing, especially a separate apartment. They further defined that entitlement in relationship to others and implicitly rejected the Khrushchev regime's attempts to make housing an item to which all citizens should have equal access based on quantitative measurements of need alone.

In 1959, 39 residents living in apartment building No. 47 on the Black River Embankment in the northern part of Leningrad decried the injustice that had arisen when newcomers to the city got separate apartments ahead of native Leningraders. In a letter to the city soviet, they proposed that in the course of repairing their prerevolutionary building, which still suffered damage from wartime bombing, the city should transform their communal apartments back into single-family apartments. These dwellers saw in the architecture of their prerevolutionary building an alternative way of life far superior to their cramped communal apartments. Their building was perfectly suited for such a transformation back to separate apartments, they wrote, because most apartments had four rooms, as well as a front and back entrance. Their request was entirely reasonable. After all, the Soviet leadership itself wanted "every family to have a separate apartment." Moreover, the residents of this building deserved separate apartments. Most were "native dwellers of the city, have lived in this house for 20 to 40 years, living through all the misfortunes of the war together with the hero-city." But alas, it was not native Leningraders who benefited first: "When it comes to improving people's lives through housing in the current state of affairs, those who enjoy privileged conditions ahead of others are people who've been in our city five to ten years, almost all of them receive separate apartments."[56] Their sentiment was shared three years later in 1962 by a pensioner who lamented that native Leningraders "have spent their entire lives in Leningrad, endured the oppressive blockade, poured their lives into their work, and now that they need some peace and quiet, they can't get it." But those who had come to Leningrad once the war was over "have all the separate apartments."[57]

Whereas one's status as a native Leningrader was beyond reproach, being a rehabilitated person could be a problem worth omitting from a petition. Sobetskaia, for example, failed to mention that she had been exiled from Leningrad in 1938, banned from large urban areas in 1942, and had this restriction dropped in 1948. In her letter, she termed her exile from Leningrad as time "on the periphery."[58] Yet in contrast to Sobetskaia, other rehabilitated persons played up their status to explain why they were entitled to housing.[59] Even those related to repressed persons did not hide such associations. One woman, writing to the city party committee in 1962, based her petition for an extra room partly on the grounds that she had lost it because of the wrongful repression of her husband in 1937 and that she was entitled to the room now that her husband had been posthumously rehabilitated.[60]

Other native Leningraders identified the division of state housing between local soviets and the workplace as the cause of their problems. Writing to the city newspaper, *Smena*, in mid-1955, a twenty-eight-year-old war veteran and native of the city, R. S. Rakhmetulin, petitioned for a place on the city soviet's waiting list. Having been demobilized and back in the city since 1951, Rakhmetulin was informed in 1952 that he had not come back early enough upon demobilization to be admitted to the Smol'nyi district soviet's waiting list. He could not get onto the list for the additional reason that he had previously lived in workplace housing. He was employed at a mechanical factory, and he had been unable to obtain housing through his place of work despite, or perhaps on account of, his demands for a room without waiting in line. He asserted that his factory's distribution was "in extreme disorder, since someone receives [space] by jumping the line, but those in need go to the back of the plan and onto the list for a vacated room, but rooms never get vacated." He wrote that he presently shared a 32-square-meter room with eleven people from two families, but did not indicate whether he had obtained this space from his factory or by renting privately.[61]

Rakhmetulin saw himself as unfairly excluded from both systems of distribution. Whereas the local soviet refused him a place in line by adhering too closely to the rules, alleged corruption at his factory prevented people in need, such as himself, from receiving housing. He laid out the reasons that he felt legitimated his demand to be placed on a waiting list. First and foremost, he needed a separate room in order to bring his family that had been split up by the war back together. Whereas he had been evacuated from the city in 1941 and had begun fighting in the army in 1944, his seventy-three-year-old father and sixty-seven-year-old mother had been evacuated in 1942 to Kuibyshev oblast. His parents had not returned to the city immediately following the war on account of his father's poor health. So he now wanted to bring them back to the city, but explained that he could not do so as long as he was sharing a room with two other families. By receiving better housing, he could better care for his parents, who "until now await the day when it will be possible to live in a united family, moreover here, in Leningrad." In short, his family deserved to be together and live in better housing because they were native Leningraders. Four years of enduring his present intolerable housing arrangement had entitled him at the very least to "the most paltry everyday amenities to which a Soviet person has a right."[62]

Blueprint for Reform

While residents staked their claims to waiting lists, Sokolov and the city soviet tightened their control over workplace housing. One of their targets was people's construction. This was the system by which factory workers received separate apartments in exchange for working extra hours on their enterprise's housing construction. As we will see in chapter 4, this was a convenient way for factory administrators to build housing for their workers without having to give any of it to the local soviet because it was registered as personal instead of state property.

At a September 1958 meeting, Sokolov chastised district officials for letting enterprises pass their new housing off as people's construction to avoid giving local soviets their share of the new space.[63] "What's this people's construction," Sokolov wanted to know, "when 21,700 [rubles] of state money were invested? Workers worked, but how? During work time, and when you say it's for the enterprise, for the factory [labor] committee, what kind of people's construction is this?"[64] His hostility toward people's construction drew a sharp contrast to the media campaign, examined in the next chapter, that touted workers' initiatives and self-interest in building their housing as the foundation for new economic relations. In opposing people's construction, Sokolov and the Leningrad city soviet were likely bolstered by recent, high-level discussions in Moscow on the 1958 housing reform described above.[65]

During the next several months, competing claims over workplace housing intensified. At a March 1959 meeting, Sokolov told enterprise representatives that the city soviet was taking more of some workplace housing because it had handled the financing. Enterprise representatives were livid. Because some of this housing had been built as people's construction, Sokolov's move would anger their workforce. One representative lobbied Sokolov to let his workplace keep 1,700 square meters of a building reserved for its workers in exchange for their work on it. He warned: "Considering that the collective participated in this affair and they all know about it, we think the principle which was established [exchange of housing for labor] should be preserved. You won't gain a lot from this, but we'll have lots of unpleasantries."[66]

By the end of 1959, the city soviet moved to unify the workplace and soviet waiting lists under the latter's control. Its report on distribution for 1959 announced, "Beginning in 1961, the distribution of all living space being built in the city of Leningrad will be carried out through the executive committees of the district soviets." The reform would be implemented by "[creating] a single line of citizens who need improvement in their housing conditions." The city soviet justified this "Proposal for 1961" by repeating familiar accusations. Enterprises distributed housing unequally among their workforce, giving disproportionally more to engineering-technical workers and white-collar employees than to workers. Enterprises allocated housing to individuals who already had enough, instead of those who did not, and largely ignored entitlement groups such as the rehabilitated and demobilized officers. In contrast, local soviets distributed housing proportionally among working people and attended to the needs of entitlement groups; they instituted greater transparency by making waiting lists public.[67]

The city soviet's plan to unify the lists preserved some differences between workplace and soviet lists, largely to the disadvantage of residents waiting on the former. The plan also underscored the importance of the waiting list as a register of social differences based on one's wartime experiences and status as native Leningrader, but suggested that this aspect of waiting lists would be phased out after they were unified. According to the plan, people on workplace lists would be integrated into the unified waiting lists through two channels. Those living in the city since before the war would be inserted "parallel to the existing line in the district." This presumably meant that their place on the unified waiting list would be determined by the date when they had originally been placed on their workplace list and would be roughly the same as the place of residents from local soviet lists who had gotten onto those lists at about the same time. In contrast, those on workplace lists who had arrived in Leningrad after the war would be sent to the back of the line for the year they had arrived in the city. This meant that if someone on a workplace list arrived in 1947, she would be placed at the end of the unified list for that year, behind all residents who had originally been taken on the local soviet list in 1947.[68]

The plan for unifying the lists thus favored residents originally on local soviet lists, but also provided distinctions that favored native Leningraders on workplace lists who had endured the blockade or at least had proof of residence in the city before the war started. After the lists were combined, however, the criteria for getting onto a waiting list in the future would not favor native Leningraders or recognize people's wartime experiences. Residents would be required to show they had been living in Leningrad since only before January 1, 1956. Having met this criteria, they could get onto the list if they also lacked living space or lived in housing unfit for habitation or had less than 3 square meters of living space per family member.[69]

To further centralize distribution, the city soviet turned next to reining in district officials' discretionary authority through objective criteria for admitting people onto waiting lists and, more worrisome still for these officials, yearly distribution targets for entitlement groups. Having taken on too many people since the August 1956 rules went into effect, district officials now worried about those people already on their lists. They had built up a waiting list constituency and were now primarily interested in protecting them. By unifying the waiting lists and tightening control over discretionary authority, the city soviet's reform made it increasingly difficult for district officials to meet the needs of their increasingly impatient constituents.

Sokolov informed the district soviets about the impending reform as early as March 1960, at a meeting on distribution for the year. The city soviet had an overall supply of 624,000 square meters of living space to distribute. Most of it was already earmarked for specific groups or organizations. For example, to fulfill government decrees targeting certain enterprises and to give enterprises their share in housing they helped build, the city soviet had to allocate 102,000 square meters to these enterprises. In contrast, the district soviets were allocated only 73,000 square meters just for people who had gotten on a soviet waiting list in 1956. Sokolov admitted that this was less than satisfactory, given how many people they had taken on in 1956, but he told his deputies that "there's no other way."[70]

Sokolov's announcement provoked an outcry from district officials. Keenly interested in avoiding blame for this move, the official from the Moscow district, Miagkov, urged the city soviet to publicize the year's distribution plan "so that [citizens] don't come to the district soviets and ask such questions which we can't answer." He added, "In reality people are forming the opinion that we're swindlers, take bribes and so on, this proves to be an absolute insult."[71] District officials had been too candid in communicating distribution forecasts to residents, illustrating once more how the mass housing campaign was raising expectations for a quick resolution of everyone's housing question. What was now at stake was the distribution of blame. The representative of the Sverdlovsk district, Popov, blasted Sokolov for making the decision about the year's housing distribution behind district officials' backs and expecting them to take the fall for it:

Look at what you've done for the distribution of living space in 1960. For four months you kept this question a secret. The chairmen of the [district soviet] executive committees knew absolutely nothing about the plan for housing distribution in the city until today, but indeed we're the ones standing, as they say, on the front line, we stand face to face with people who declare to us every day that they're sick of paying 300 rubles for a corner [i.e., renting housing privately].[72]

Popov explained that district officials had told people there would be as much housing distributed in 1960 as there had been the year before. He complained that similar shortfalls had appeared without their knowledge in housing earmarked for people with active tuberculosis. Popov's criticisms grew so intense that Sokolov finally interjected, "Why are you going into hysterics?" "I'm not going into hysterics," Popov shot back, "but I ask . . . [*sic*] I ask you to consult with us, but you called us together at the moment when this question has already been decided." Sokolov insisted that the city soviet wanted the district officials' "remarks and suggestions," but let it be known that the plan was now set and blamed them for not coming forth earlier with their problems. "You didn't talk with us about this question, but you can't decide anything five minutes before the Red Arrow's [a train to Moscow] departure."[73]

While recognizing the difficult situation district officials faced, the Kalinin district representative, Belov, warned against publicizing the distribution plan. He cautioned that the presence of foreigners in the city precluded announcing it in the press. Sokolov agreed with Belov and explained that making the distribution plan public would be an embarrassment. He noted with some sarcasm that in principle "we would be happy, it would be very good, were we able to explain things to toilers through the press, but . . . many foreigners come here, and we're going to write about how many people we have who live without space? This isn't permissible." For all its control over the mass media, even the Soviet state faced limitations imposed by the gaze of foreign eyes on what it could tell its population. As Belov contended, people nonetheless had to be informed in some manner. Sokolov advised his colleagues to rely solely on "oral explanation" and avoid putting anything in writing. In addition to "oral consultations," district officials were to rely on another traditional mechanism of communication with the people, their written petitions. Making communication between district officials and individuals more direct and discreet were the only changes Sokolov would allow.[74]

This discussion vividly illustrated the difference between the theory and practice of distribution reform. According to its proposal, the city was committed to greater transparency and objective assessments of people's housing needs. But instead of pushing for transparency, Sokolov asked his colleagues to fall back on personal consultations and citizens' petitions. These were the very practices that encouraged district officials to use their discretionary authority and make exceptions to the rule. As Belov's and Sokolov's comments suggested, the presence of foreigners in the city influenced them to rely on more traditional and personalized, but also atomizing, means of communication. These practices made it possible to diffuse potential public anger over the distribution plan by turning what was essentially a citywide problem into thousands of individual cases. For Sokolov and the city soviet, these communicative strategies had the additional, political advantage of shifting blame onto district soviets.

Beyond the problem of communicating the distribution plan to the public, district officials charged that the shortfall in housing for soviets would exacerbate inequalities. Belov complained that this was unacceptable, given how long the waiting lists had become: "We have 4,000 families, few of them diverged from the instructions, and we will give [housing] to only 200 families this year. So what's the outlook here?"[75] He charged that enterprises benefited from personal connections in getting the housing they needed: "How do individual departments receive [housing]—it's clear to everyone, by sometimes making use of personal contacts with comrades at the Soviet of Ministers. The directors travel there and so there's your result." Belov argued that an enterprise's economic importance did not justify better access to housing:

> Here we have a plastics scientific-research institute. In comparison with other enterprises and institutes, this is a comparatively small institute, but it is now of great significance and therefore the institute's director goes to Moscow and they give his workers apartments. And only because this is chemistry. They exploit exactly this and find themselves in a considerably better position than other city enterprises. Well this, I believe, is wrong.[76]

District officials such as Belov were not angry over inequalities and the leverage enterprises enjoyed as such. Instead, they worried that the unification of the waiting lists would lessen, rather than augment, their own leverage and leave them shouldering constituents' discontent when things went badly. At a November 1960 meeting, the purpose of which was to discuss the draft decree on the waiting list reform, Sokolov explained that people who had gotten onto soviet or workplace lists as exceptions to previous rules would be sent to the back of the unified lists. He claimed that 20 percent of people presently on district waiting lists had gotten on as exceptions. Particularly egregious examples included Vasileostrovskii district, where 60 percent of the waiting list was made up of exceptions, and Oktiabr'skii district, where 40 percent were exceptions. Sokolov announced that exceptions on both workplace and soviet lists would be placed on the unified lists as if they had just gotten onto a list in 1961, thereby significantly extending their wait. Belov vigorously protested this move and argued that district soviets had made reasonable exceptions that should be allowed to stand in the unified lists. To make his case an issue of social justice, rather than just saving face before constituents, he invoked the fate of native Leningraders: "We made exceptions only in special cases, that is, regarding the sick and invalids who found themselves in difficult housing conditions. These citizens are native Leningraders and have a privileged right to better housing conditions."[77]

Popov voiced similar objections. District officials had made slight exceptions for getting onto lists for "those people who had 3 to 5 centimeters per person more than 3 square meters." In contrast, workplaces such as the Kirov and Baltiiskii factories had made much more liberal exceptions, taking onto their lists "people who have 6 meters and perhaps more." To right such wrongs, district officials did not advocate egalitarian distribution. In a telling comment, Popov concluded that "it would be wrong to place these people on an equal footing." In addition to arguing that the district soviets' exceptions had been "justified," Popov warned, as he had done before, that the city soviet's latest move would turn residents against district officials because it overturned promises they had already made: "If we put them [people allowed onto soviet lists as exceptions] at the end of the line, that is on the 1961 line, these citizens won't let us work, they'll flood every place with complaints and petitions." What was at stake here was the credibility of a district official's word in the eyes of his constituents who could make his life difficult if the promises he made were broken. In Popov's view, minor exceptions made by district officials should remain untouched, while minor exceptions made at workplaces should be resituated on the unified lists at the end of the year they were originally made and behind all the people who had been on the soviet's list in that year. Popov defined these minor workplace exceptions as cases in which people with no more than 4.5 square meters of living space per person had gotten onto workplace lists.[78]

As for workplace exceptions that exceeded 4.5 square meters, Popov said that they should simply be thrown off the unified lists and that workplaces, not soviets, should be forced to remove these people: "Otherwise things will turn out in such a way that a factory that took a citizen onto a list is good, but when this question fell to soviet power, then they [local soviets] take the citizen off the line, and people start to think that soviet power is bad." Sokolov responded in defense of enterprises and their own reputations in the eyes of their workers: "So the management of a factory must say [to its workers], considering that we're transferring the line over to the executive committee [of the district soviet] you have to be kicked off the line?" Popov shot back, "That means we have to be the bad ones?"[79] In this political fight for control over housing, allocating blame for the repercussions of reform was as important as allocating the housing itself.

Belov and Popov not only worried about losing face before their residents; they also feared losing their discretionary authority in distribution. The new rules would severely reduce their autonomy by imposing objective criteria for getting people onto lists and forcing soviets to allocate housing only in order of the line. Another district official, Samoilov, flatly declared, "I think it necessary to reject this standard formulation, strictly by way of the line." As an alternative, he pointed to the Kiev district soviet in Moscow that had drawn up distribution plans for 1960 and 1961, but did not simply work mechanically through its overall waiting list. Instead, it earmarked 40 percent of the housing for people according to the year when they got their place in line, which in this case was 1954. The other 60 percent was broken down by specific categories of residents such as war invalids, people with tuberculosis, and the mentally ill. In the distribution plan, these categories appeared as separate lists.[80]

As in the case of the Moscow district in Leningrad described above, this was essentially how Leningrad soviets had devised their yearly distribution plans. With the unified list reform, the city soviet wanted to centralize its authority over distribution and prevent district soviets from drawing up separate distribution lists. In response to Samoilov, Sokolov reiterated that the district soviets were to implement orders from the city soviet without modifications. If district officials believed that an instruction was flawed, they were to consult the city soviet before making changes. Sokolov then accused the district soviets of misappropriating housing intended for entitlement groups: "You said don't put limits, then we allocated living space for people with tuberculosis, but you give it out to other citizens. I'll give you examples and will report on the fact that of 40,000 [square meters] for people with tuberculosis, you didn't give out a great amount."[81] Sokolov was not against distribution quotas for certain groups. He simply wanted the city soviet to control such quotas and have district soviets implement them without modifications.

Samoilov did not give up so easily, and he asked that a separate distribution category be established for people who were in extreme need of housing. Sokolov dismissed this as another attempt to protect district soviets' ability to grant exceptions: "I strove all the time to exclude from the instructions [of the draft decree] a point on exceptions. Now you're trying to get 'those in dire need' written in—this will be those very same exceptions." And Sokolov argued that people would easily exploit this category: "But, tell me, what person out of 5,000 people in need won't try his luck to write a petition and say that he is 'in dire need'—they'll all do this and then you try to verify—is he in fact 'in dire need' or not."[82]

Sokolov repeatedly emphasized that district soviets had to distribute housing by order of the queue (*v poriadke ocheredi*) to ensure that the most needy got their housing. Because waiting lists would grow to 180,000 families with the reform, it would be impossible for district soviets to take into consideration all the details of a family's housing conditions in order to determine that its need was legitimate. As Sokolov put it, "Today one person has it more difficult, tomorrow another has it more difficult, but another has it easier: One person has a newborn, another has a death in the family. Who's going to sort this out?" Sokolov insisted that applying objective standards was the best way of determining need. "How do we figure this out? He who has up to 3 square meters per person has a difficult situation, he who has more than 3 square meters, he has an easier situation." Objective standards also had to be applied when a person was taken off the list and received housing. Sokolov concluded, "When we will have the method implemented, namely 'in order of the line,' it'll be easier for us to sort things out in all these cases. Therefore it's necessary to allocate space strictly by the line, but if we give [space] not to the first, but to the 300th, then in will come the complaints."[83]

Sokolov bluntly rejected the idea of loosening the line principle and reordering previous exceptions by district officials in the new combined lists to favor them over workplace exceptions. Nevertheless, even he admitted that completely objective standards could not be applied all the time. Toward the end of the November 1960 meeting, a district official laid out a typical scenario by which a native Leningrader who had gotten onto a waiting list as a minor exception would suffer under the proposed reform. The resident, who had lived in Leningrad since 1935, got onto a waiting list in 1956 with 3.1 square meters of living space per person, but would now be sent to the back of the line. Another person, living in the city since 1955, had gotten onto a waiting list in that same year. In comparing these two people, the district official questioned whether allowing the second person such a "privileged footing" was right. Sokolov responded by saying that making an exception for the first person was permissible in this case, but qualified this in a revealing way. "In principle we'll agree on this, but take into account that primary producers in factories must likewise be the first in line to be provided with housing."[84]

At the November 1960 meeting, it became clear that Sokolov and the city soviet were shaping the reform to eliminate some deviations from the rules while preserving others. Instead of putting this in writing, Sokolov merely emphasized the kinds of exceptions that had to be understood. For example, he addressed the issue of workplace exceptions whereby people had gotten onto waiting lists while already living in space in excess of 7 square meters. According to the new rules, such people would be sent to the back of the line, but not in all cases. As Sokolov explained, "But here another thing needs to be taken into account: He's an old producer, worked in the given enterprise for 45 years, lives on the fifth floor, he has difficulty getting up [the stairs]." Flagging such cases would be done outside the new rules, and the person would receive space outside the line. Sokolov continued, "According to the instructions of the oblast union soviet, he has a privileged right, it's necessary to improve the housing conditions of such citizens, [while] not placing him on the line, since this is absolutely not required. Is this clear to you?" "Clear," someone answered.[85]

Other district officials were not satisfied, and Samoilov returned to this question, complaining about people who had gotten onto workplace waiting lists with space in excess of 7 square meters. In such cases, Sokolov advised his colleagues to think about the person involved and to determine need based upon one's work record. "There are such examples," Sokolov responded, "but I've said, who are these people? There at the Kirov factory, an old man worked for 45 years, lives on the fifth floor. Transfer him to the second floor and that's all, but do not place him on the line. Under the unification of the lists, there must not be a difference of approach between factories and [district soviet] executive committees."[86] Although exceptions could be made to reward valuable workers, the criteria and the method of doing this would remain off the books and hidden under the cover of the unified waiting lists.

Sokolov justified his logic by appropriating arguments favoring native Leningraders. "We give living space to citizens who have been on the list since 1956," he pointed out, "but at the factory there are those who've been in line since 1953—we are obligated to provide them with housing first." He reiterated that most egregious exceptions at workplaces should be sent to the back of the line. Yet there was no escaping the fact that exceptions for more valuable workers were being worked into the reform in an unwritten manner. The city soviet was using the reform to preserve, not eliminate, the prerogatives of workplaces in housing distribution. Much of this had to do with where housing actually came from. Sokolov explained that because many enterprises would still build housing with their resources, district soviets could not indiscriminately expropriate this space. "If we deprive them entirely of the right to settle these buildings with workers," he noted, "then factories will not build. We give factories the right to settle these buildings, but settle with whom? With those persons whom we placed on the waiting list."[87]

A New Line in Distribution

The Leningrad city soviet implemented the waiting list reform in its December 12, 1960, decree, "On the Method of Admission to the List and Allocating Living Space in Leningrad." The decree stated plainly the primary mechanism of the reform: "To establish starting January

1, 1961, at the departments of registry and distribution of housing of district soviet executive committees, a single list of citizens for allocating living space, combining the lines of those standing on the list at district soviet executive committees and at enterprises, institutions and organizations of the city." Workplaces could no longer place people onto their waiting lists after December 15 and had until the end of the month to give the city soviet their lists and "the personnel files of citizens standing in line." The city soviet would then organize and redistribute the workplace lists to the district soviets by January 20, 1961. And the district soviets would have until March 1, 1961, to integrate their waiting lists and bring them in line with new rules to go into effect on July 1, 1961. All residents who were on lists had to reregister between February 1 and March 15 by producing required documentation on the size of their families and their present living space allotments. Failure to reregister would result in being expunged from the waiting list. Temporary instructions for admitting new people onto lists and allocating housing would be in operation for the first six months of the year. After this transition stage, a new set of rules would take effect.[88] In short, the city soviet set up this transitional period to consolidate lists and weed out people it believed did not belong, even if they had been waiting on a list for years.

The December 1960 decree instituted the draft that Sokolov had presented in November with few amendments. Residents would receive housing "strictly in order of the line." In combining the lists, no provisions were included to favor exceptions for people on local soviet lists. Instead, as Sokolov had explained, exceptions that had been made to place people who already had more than 3 square meters per family member, but less than 4.5 square meters, on workplace and local soviet lists would be equally penalized. In its final form, the decree stated that such exceptions "are enrolled at the end of the single line corresponding to the dates of admission to the list." In contrast, district officials could keep on their lists exceptions that fell into the following entitlement categories: families with members who had tuberculosis or mental illness; first- and second-group invalids; families of people who had died in the war; and those who had been brought up in orphanages. The district soviets were also permitted to leave on unified lists people they had taken on as exceptions who "do not have living space" (i.e., who were homeless or renting housing privately) but had held a city registration since at least January 1, 1956.[89]

In consolidating the lists, the decree preserved advantages for workplaces that Sokolov had explained earlier. Workplaces retained authority over distributing housing they had fully or partially built, and only their workers who were on the unified lists could obtain such housing. The decree did not entirely restrict workplaces to draw from the combined lists alone. It included an escape clause for projects enterprises had used to circumvent local soviets (most likely, people's construction). This housing was now vaguely defined as "living space, not foreseen in the state plan of housing construction and built . . . at the expense of other sources." Workplaces could distribute such space based upon their own merit-based criteria. Such space was intended "for improving the housing conditions of members of communist work brigades and the best workers of production." Although the city soviet was still supposed to issue the housing permits for such housing, this was more paper work than real control.[90]

In carrying out the transition to unified lists, the district soviets were supposed to use temporary instructions for admitting new people onto their unified lists until new rules could be worked out. The general qualification for admitting anyone onto the new waiting lists was permanent residence in the city since at least January 1, 1956. Having fulfilled this requirement, a person could get onto a waiting list for one of five reasons. First, persons who "do not have housing" (the homeless or those renting privately) could be admitted. Second, living in local soviet or workplace housing unfit for habitation qualified as a reason for getting onto a list. Third, a person with less than 3 square meters of living space per family member in either soviet or workplace housing could be taken onto a list. Fourth, families with space in dormitories intended for single people could be admitted onto a list. Fifth and finally, people demobilized from the army who "had lost living space in Leningrad in connection with entering the Army" were also allowed onto a waiting list, but without the time requirement of the first four categories.[91]

Purging the Waiting List

The combination of waiting lists put district soviets in charge of enormous lines for housing. In 1957, Sokolov had worried that waiting lists had expanded too much, with 49,000 families. On the eve of the combining of the lists in early 1961, local soviet lists held 69,413 families and workplace lists totaled 178,192 families.[92] By June, the city's lists, now unified, had grown to 180,000 families.[93] The waiting lists grew to 221,209 families by January 1, 1962,[94] the day the space limit for admission onto waiting lists was to be raised to 4.5 square meters.[95] On account of this change, the city soviet projected a total of 300,000 to 310,000 families on waiting lists. With average family size at three persons, roughly 1 million people would be on waiting lists.[96] In a city of 3.3 million individuals, as recorded by the 1959 census, this meant that 30 percent of the population would be on soviet waiting lists.[97] This incredible expansion was well illustrated in the Moscow district. As will be recalled, a mere 1,830 families stood on its waiting list at the end of 1955.[98] The list had grown to 3,892 families at the start of 1958.[99] And by February 1962, it had grown to 18,252 families, which represented a tenfold increase since 1955. Of these families, 11,414 had gotten on since January 1961.[100]

Despite this enormous expansion, the reform's earliest impact on Leningraders was the expulsion of thousands of list waiters during the reregistration process. The main basis for orchestrating this mass purge was people's geographic location. Simply put, if a family lived outside the city limits, it would be kicked off the unified waiting list. Before the lists were combined, many people worked in the city and were registered on a workplace's list but lived in the oblast. When the lists were combined, district officials could only take onto their unified lists residents of their districts. At a December 1960 meeting, Sokolov firmly instructed district officials to leave off the unified lists people who lived outside the city's boundaries, even if they worked in Leningrad.[101]

As a result, these unlucky residents were dropped from the unified lists whether or not they qualified according to the space and time criteria to stay in line. In March 1961, Sokolov explained that approximately 16,000 families found themselves in this situation.[102] At least one outside authority, the All-Union Central Council of Professional Unions (Vsesoiuznyi Tsentral'nyi Sovet Professional'nykh Soiuzov, VTsSPS), was aware of these families' unfortunate situation and noted the injustice of removing people from lists who had already been waiting "for a long time." These families were unable to get onto oblast waiting lists because these were drawn up at one's workplace in the oblast.[103]

The mass purge of the unified lists indicates again how the city soviet used the waiting list reform to excise unwanted residents and henceforth more tightly police residency in the city. But as always, exceptions would be made with native Leningraders in mind. At the March 1961 meeting, Sokolov explained that "it is necessary to place on the list those toilers who lost housing and lived in Leningrad before the war, but now upon returning to Leningrad were not able to set themselves up [in the city], but set themselves up in the oblast." This would apply to about 2,500 people and their families, but even for these the city soviet was reluctant to make concessions. Sokolov explained that nobody was to be informed of this decision and that district soviets were only to reregister such people if they happened to petition again or for the first time for admission onto the lists.[104] By not advertising this concession, city soviet leaders evidently hoped fewer people would come forward. One district official, Makhin, wanted to impose further restrictions and suggested that only those who had returned to the oblast by 1956 be reregistered onto the waiting lists. Another district official, Kolpakov, supported the decision to put the "native Leningrader" back onto the list, but agreed with Makhin's time limit restriction, as did Sokolov.[105] Reluctance to accept the concession without this limit illustrated again that district officials' principled support for native Leningraders waned as waiting lists had gotten longer.

When the city soviet passed its new rules on waiting lists and distribution in a June 1961 decree, it included a special concession for oblast dwellers kicked off the city's lists, but defined them in such a way that failed to privilege native Leningraders who had lived in the city before the war. Those who had lived at some point in the city before January 1, 1956, who presently lived in the oblast, and who had been working in the city since at least January 1, 1956, could be admitted to the waiting lists.[106] The city soviet manipulated even this minor provision to serve the interests of enterprises. At a June 1961 meeting, the city soviet deputy chair, Iu. M. Solomonov, explained how this provision was to be implemented: "Approach the question this way: take on [the waiting lists] all citizens who stood in line at an enterprise, who worked and presently work, who are needed for Leningrad enterprises, who are valuable workers."[107] Similar to countries that regulate immigration with an eye toward a new arrival's economic value, the city of Leningrad wanted to cherry-pick its new residents for the skills they could bring to the city.

Once more, the city soviet was promoting in practice the interests of the workplace in the context of a reform originally intended to make distribution more equitable and transparent. Amazingly, outside authorities such as the VTsSPS misread the Leningrad reform rather superficially as a case of excessive leveling: "Since citizens' housing conditions and the time when one was placed on the waiting list are taken as the basis of establishing one's place in line, the differentiation that makes it possible to realize the socialist principle of distributing material goods according to one's labor is absent." The VTsSPS believed that the city soviet's concessions to workplaces for distributing their own housing to senior workers and shock workers were insufficient.[108] It erroneously concluded that the Leningrad reform had instituted a leveling of differences in housing distribution through objective criteria and had given district soviets unfettered control over the city's housing, including the little permitted workplaces for their own workers. But in December 1960, Sokolov had advised his colleagues to implement precisely the "differentiation" that the VTsSPS believed was missing. He reminded district officials that "we must look after production." And he explained that some people should be put onto the waiting lists even if they had come to the city after the cut off date of January 1, 1956, because their labor was needed: "If they [workplaces] brought him into production in 1956, from this position it'll be necessary in this case to make things right. Those occupying a place in line will not suffer from this, but if they will suffer, then insignificantly."[109]

At a January 1962 meeting, Sokolov emphasized again the unwritten merit-based criteria for distributing housing. He pointed out, as was written in the distribution plan for 1962, that the district soviets were supposed to give housing to all persons who had been taken onto waiting lists before July 1, 1957.[110] The final distribution lists had been drawn up, but Sokolov explained that district officials were not supposed to distribute housing "in the order of the line," as he had previously advised. He said, "You have the [final distribution] lists. Now then it's necessary to see which category of persons is included there who will receive space in 1962. Moreover, I ask you comrades, look more attentively at these lists." In startlingly blunt terms that reflected the enduring priorities of the Soviet command economy, he explained that people indispensable to production should get housing ahead of people in service industries. The reasons he provided for treating the final lists "more attentively" revealed a social hierarchy of access to housing that privileged a resident's perceived economic worth over her needs:

Why is this necessary? In order that we see who gets living space first. Of course he who produces material values must get it first. Count up how many there will be and which workers. [Do it] in order that things don't turn out in such a way that hairdressers will receive [housing] first, but workers will remain at the back of the plan. It's necessary to take this list that goes up to July 1, 1957, work out a small summary and examine it attentively. The purpose [of this] must be clear.[111]

Further defining this unwritten hierarchy, Sokolov added, "First of all workers of leading specialties must receive [housing], then scientific workers, [and] engineering-technical workers."[112] The "hierarchy of civic belonging" (to borrow again Alexopoulos's term) that Sokolov advocated suggested how little had changed since Stalin's rule. Those most likely to contribute to the country's continued industrialization would reap the greatest material rewards, while those in consumer services would continue to wait.

Meetings at the city soviet revealed that complete standardization of distribution was impossible because exceptions would always have to be made and somebody would have to make them. Strict adherence to rules was likewise not desirable because state and party officials with any authority over distribution could not bear subjecting themselves completely to legal norms. Sokolov warned his district subordinates in March 1961 to respect the exceptions to putting people on waiting lists that the city soviet's executive committee handed down, but he chided district officials for making too many of their own: "You have to show self-control and figure things out, what's allowed and what's not allowed and only then to take this or that decision. But when things are going to be sent to you from a member of the Executive Committee, you have to fulfill it."[113] His first point here sounded more like the advice a seasoned veteran of the second economy might give an apprentice on how to game the Soviet system. The district officials of that very system had to learn how to navigate the murky waters of unsanctioned decisions. And who better to teach them than the city's chief authority on housing distribution? Sokolov's second point suggested, however, that gaming the system was not an egalitarian venture. When higher-ups wanted housing distributed outside the rules, district officials had to respect their demands first. The unwritten social hierarchy of access to housing was thus enforced through a political hierarchy that trumped formal rules and laws.

Echoing Sokolov's advice, Communist Party officials in Leningrad were even less amused with having their hands tied by strict standards. A week before the new rules were to come into effect on July 1, 1961, a party member, Verizhnikov, dropped in on a city soviet meeting to spell out how district officials had to carry out the party's exceptions.

> We can't assign ourselves the task of working out such instructions that could replace the head of a district housing department and answer all questions. The city and oblast committees of the party believe that, since we have party people working in this critical area, besides instructions, you still have to decide questions in the field by yourselves. There are cases that can't be placed in any instructions, but decisions have to be made.[114]

District officials were thus obligated to defend the integrity of the Communist Party not by sticking closely to socialist legality, but rather by ensuring that whatever exceptions to the law the party demanded were carried out discreetly. This was a startling twist of logic in the story of reforming housing distribution. Verizhnikov's comments underlined once more how much everyday bureaucratic practice remained untouched by the ideals originally foreseen in reforming housing distribution. He also suggested how little the party had changed when considering its role in this reform. Instead of eliminating practices that undermined transparency and standardization, the party was more interested in reestablishing the proper chain of command in the exercise of discretionary authority that circumvented the letter of the law.

Conclusion

As this chapter has shown, the housing distribution reform in Leningrad allowed city leaders to purge thousands of people from waiting lists for living space and simultaneously institute unofficial criteria in distribution that favored a person's economic worth to the city. These outcomes departed significantly from the original intent of the reform by the leadership in Moscow, including Khrushchev, who called for the creation of objective rules in distribution that emphasized need as defined by how much living space people had and how long they had lived in a city. Centralizing a dysfunctional system of fragmented distribution under local soviets' authority and imposing strict and transparent rules were supposed to fulfill the Russian Revolution's original egalitarian goals in resolving the housing question. Although never repudiating these goals, the Leningrad city soviet used them as a cover for pursuing an agenda that favored one's performance at the workplace and the interests of the city's enterprises and factories, and left plenty of room for city officials to exercise their discretionary authority. The course of the reform demonstrated that Leningrad's leaders used the waiting list as a way of weeding out those who did not deserve housing because they lived in the oblast, were socially undesirable, or were not valuable workers.

Khrushchev's regime had wanted to depoliticize distribution by basing people's claims to housing on objective criteria and emptying the process of its socially and politically charged meanings. Such depoliticization was part of the regime's grander vision of resolving the housing question once and for all. Once people had enough housing, they would no longer view the waiting list as a reflection of their status in relation to others. It would simply be a way to allocate housing rationally. What Khrushchev's regime failed to understand is that as long as the state distributed housing and as long as Communist Party officials like Verizhnikov made exceptions to the rules, ordinary people could rightly assume that another person's will determined what they got. As long as the state allocated housing and as long as the wait proved to drag on for years, the waiting list would always be about more than just getting housing. Ordinary urban dwellers could not help but see in the waiting list a reflection of what the state thought of them, the value it placed on their past sacrifices and contributions, and their station in life in comparison with others. In shaping the meaning of the waiting list as a social register of the regime's failures, urban dwellers exercised one of the few tools at their disposal to shape a process over which they had no direct control. In the end, the Leningrad city soviet grudgingly made some concessions to the needs of the native Leningrader without ever creating a separate category of entitlement. As for those city residents who wanted to circumvent waiting lists for state housing altogether, there remained other options. We now turn to these alternatives in the next chapter, which explores how class and mass housing intersected under Khrushchev.

Chapter 4

Class and Mass Housing

If longer waiting lists and citizens' petitions were any indication, demand for better housing increased rather than decreased in the early years of the mass housing campaign. The government responded to excess demand by supporting alternatives to state housing that required people to contribute labor, money, or both to their housing. It boosted support for citizens who built their own single-family houses in the individual housing sector.[1] It also created two fast-track paths for citizens who desired separate apartments in cities: people's construction and the housing construction cooperative. In people's construction, industrial workers worked on their factories' housing projects in exchange for a single-family apartment in the apartment buildings they constructed collectively. In cooperatives, urban elites purchased shares in a cooperative organization and took out government loans to build housing in which they were guaranteed a separate apartment. In this chapter, I examine why Khrushchev's regime developed these two alternatives to state housing, how they reproduced class differences, and how they allowed ordinary urban residents to shape the reordering of society through the mass housing campaign.

People's construction (*narodnaia stroika*) began early in Khrushchev's tenure in 1955 and was followed by the housing cooperative's establishment in 1958. Both shared the principle that citizens should contribute to the construction of their housing. Propaganda and citizens' petitions alike framed the allocation of state housing from local soviets or the workplace as an indirect exchange, stretched out over many years, of housing for a citizen's labor and sacrifices. In people's construction and the cooperative, the circuit of this exchange was made much more immediate and its currency was now based on labor or labor that had been turned into capital (i.e., income), not sacrifices and sufferings endured under Stalin. Each method also had a distinct class composition. People's construction favored industrial workers especially in midsized cities, while the housing cooperative was meant for the Soviet intelligentsia: white-collar employees in the party-state apparatus and industry, and cultural elites. In 1959, people's construction was terminated, and the cooperative subsequently became the only fast-track option to a separate apartment outside soviet and workplace waiting lists. This chapter examines how the cooperative replaced people's construction as an alternative path to the separate apartment and what this revealed about the intersection of class, housing, and communist ideology under Khrushchev.

From 1955 to 1959, people's construction rode a wave of popular support and a mass media campaign, which reflected and shaped the broader processes of economic de-Stalinization and Khrushchev's thaw. Its unorthodox methods of constructing housing signaled greater liberalization in economic practices, while its class composition and rhetoric of creating new socialist relations reflected Khrushchev's populism and the Communist Party's renewed determination to forge a classless society out of the stratified Stalinist social order.[2] People's construction reflected genuine popular excitement among ordinary workers for trying something new and speaking about it more openly. As discussed in this book's introduction, such opportunities are normally associated with the high cultural politics of Khrushchev's thaw and the cultural intelligentsia. Workers on people's construction projects showed that they, too, could push the boundaries of reform and reflect on what it meant for their everyday lives and sense of self.

In contrast, the housing cooperative lacked the ideological legitimacy and aura of novelty that people's construction enjoyed. Efforts among the top party leadership to create the cooperative initially stalled on account of resistance from Khrushchev over its elite status and cost. Proponents of the cooperative could no longer employ the rhetoric of the Stalin years that justified social hierarchy and differences in wages and access to goods and services. To overcome Khrushchev's resistance, the cooperative's champions cleverly appropriated the rhetoric and principles of people's construction and modified their proposals to address his substantive concerns about the cooperative's financ-

ing. Their success in establishing the cooperative in 1958 was soon
followed by the demise of people's construction in 1959.

Scholars have largely ignored people's construction, depicting it in
passing as a peculiar episode of Khrushchev's mass housing program
in which people built their own housing in the form of apartments. Its
class character, the rhetoric of its media campaign, its impact on Khrushchev's populist beliefs, and ordinary workers' role in it have not been
examined.[3] In contrast, the cooperative has received more attention
from scholars as an alternative method of housing distribution that
favored elites and expanded in the Khrushchev years and beyond.[4] Yet
its relationship to people's construction and the political divide it gen-
erated within the top leadership remain little understood. The high-
level internal debates that accompanied the cooperative's displacement
of people's construction provide us with valuable new insights into the
social content of high politics after Stalin's death. I argue that these
debates over people's construction and the cooperative constituted a
significant rift between Khrushchev and Communist Party leaders over
elite access to housing that shaped broader ideological debates over
class. The outcome of these debates were an early indication, long before his ouster in October 1964, of the obstacles Khrushchev faced in
dismantling the Stalin-era privileges of Soviet elites and meeting the
material needs of the masses. People's construction also legitimized
and advanced Khrushchev's populist beliefs in ways we have not yet
recognized, whereas its displacement by the cooperative simultaneously revealed the limits he encountered trying to implement his vision
for a more egalitarian and materially prosperous society.

Significantly, those who contested Khrushchev over his resistance to
the cooperative were not his political rivals within the ruling Presidium
of the party—such as Georgii Malenkov, Viacheslav Molotov, and
Lazar' Kaganovich, who tried to oust him in 1957.[5] Instead, Khrushchev
was challenged by career party members who had risen to high-level
leadership positions in heavy industry, construction, and the party but
were not contenders in the Presidium. Their chief concern was not
Khrushchev's power and legitimacy, as it was for his Presidium enemies, but the material privileges and social position of those who had
risen into the Soviet intelligentsia under Stalin. These party members
were determined that Khrushchev's populist agenda not come at the
expense of meeting their obligations to the recently upwardly mobile
on whose behalf they sought to establish the cooperative.

Building Mass Housing "On Our Own"

Unlike most innovations of the mass housing campaign, people's construction did not originate in Moscow or Leningrad. It started at the Molotov auto factory in Gor'kii in 1955, and spread to midsized cities such as Perm, Cheliabinsk, and Orenburg. Factory managers and workers organized the projects, used in-house supplies, and bartered for materials in ways that flaunted economic planning. The motto of the people's construction media campaign was that workers built their housing "on our own" (*svoimi silami*). Mass media coverage aimed to draw more workers into people's construction and provide an ideological lesson about its volunteerism and spontaneous forms of exchange. Newspaper accounts and instructional pamphlets chronicled the movement's progress as a harbinger of communist relations, gave practical information on how to start projects, and presented stirring testimonials from workers who lived in separate apartments they had built with their own hands.

Apartment buildings built under people's construction were typically one to two stories and ranged from several to approximately fifty apartments. This distinguished them from the one to two apartment houses that citizens built and owned in the individual housing sector, as well as state construction in Khrushchev's mass housing campaign, which typically produced four- to five-story apartment buildings made of reinforced concrete and prefabricated components manufactured in factories. People's construction was labor intensive and devoid of industrialized and mechanized construction techniques. Its organizers took whatever building supplies they could from their factories and rejected the professional authority of architects and construction firms, relying instead on workers with little or no experience to take charge of their lives and become the makers of their own housing. The results represented a substantial number of newly built apartments in the early years of the mass housing campaign. During its brief existence, people's construction produced approximately 9 million square meters of overall space, or 214,000 apartments, per year, which represented 10 to 13 percent of total state and individual housing construction combined.[6]

Workers joined people's construction projects to move out of overcrowded communal apartments and dormitories and obtain a separate apartment. The first project at the auto factory in Gor'kii showed that making this transition from communal housing to the separate apartment a reality began with changes to existing blueprints for a one-story stone barrack.[7] "By segregating the apartments," one pamphlet explained, "we created more favorable living conditions for each family."[8] Another concluded, "The auto workers now steadfastly observe this principle: a separate apartment for every family."[9] As we saw in chapter 2, large separate apartments were typically distributed as communal apartments. Advocates of people's construction were keenly aware of this problem and devised ways of keeping their apartments separate that echoed the same strategies architects developed since the 1930s.

The plan in figure 4.1 indicated that the participants in this people's construction project had altered an original design from the Gor'kii city soviet to meet their own needs. In reference to the top apartment, the pamphlet describing the project explained, "It consists of a bedroom and a room for daily use (this last room is made to be passed through, which makes it possible to reduce the corridors and excludes the possibility of settling two families in the apartment)."[10] As explained in chapter 2, pass-through rooms legally precluded communal settlement. If a resident had to walk through one room to access a second room, the two rooms could not be settled with a family in each room. Other people's construction apartments in Gor'kii were similarly designed with a pass-through room to ensure single-family occupancy.[11]

As such designs suggested, the main requirement for being included on a people's construction project was having a family; unmarried workers were generally not considered. Reallocations of vacated housing made possible by people's construction followed a similar hierarchy. In late 1959, the Party Control Commission (Kommissia Partiinogo Kontrolia, KPK) praised a people's construction project involving workers and their families in a dormitory of the Moscow factory "Serp i Molot" (Sickle and Hammer). Although less than half the registered residents in the overcrowded dormitory had families, only workers with families would be allowed to work on the project, and eighty-seven families would relocate into newly constructed housing the following year. Single men in the dormitory would remain there along with other workers and their families not included in the project. The space made available by the relocation of the eighty-seven families would go first to these remaining families, not the single men.[12]

In addition to promoting the family, the campaign projected a commitment to gender equality. Like male participants, women workers were frequently described as taking an active role in construction or

Figure 4.1. Design for a one-room apartment and a two-room apartment in a house with eight apartments. The top apartment included an entranceway (2.96 square meters), a pass-through "room for daytime use" (16.60 square meters), and a bedroom (12.5 square meters). The bedroom was altered from the original plan by being split in two and by having a second door added for independent access from the pass-through room. Technically, this would have made the apartment a three-room apartment (the caption below, which credits the Gor'kii city soviet for the original plan, indicates it was a two-room apartment). The word "entresols" describes the space next to the toilet and between the entranceway and the kitchen. It is unclear how far off the ground these entresols were and why they were indicated in the plural. The bottom, one-room apartment included a "kitchen-dining area" (5.95 square meters), suggesting that residents were supposed to eat their meals in it. The design also featured an "alcove" (5.8 square meters) off the main room and two built-in closets on either side of the wall separating the alcove from the entranceway. In both apartments, a semi-enclosed space appears to have been carved out of the kitchen area for a tub or, as is indicated in the bottom apartment, a "place for a half-bath."

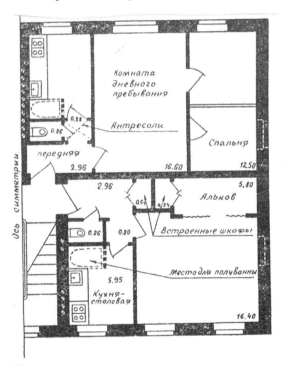

План одно- и двухкомнатных малометражных квартир в восьмиквартирном доме (проект Горьковского горпроекта).

Source: S. Lebedev, ed., *Sila narodnogo pochina: Iz opyta stroitel'stva zhil'ia silami rabochikh kollektivov predpriiatii gor'kovskoi promyshlennosti i narodnoi stroiki avtoguzhevykh dorog i tramvaino-trolleibusnykh putei* (Gor'kii: Gor'kovskaia pravda, 1957), 39–41.

continuing to work in the factory to support existing projects. Unlike men, however, they were also depicted as homemakers, reproducing the "double burden" of Soviet women who held jobs but were chiefly responsible for domestic chores and childrearing.[13]

Although favoring the family was in keeping with profamily policies dating back to the Stalin era, the extension of preferential access to the separate apartment to industrial workers was a dramatic reversal from past practice. Under Stalin, workers had languished in barracks, dormitories, and communal apartments, while party-state and cultural elites had been awarded spacious separate apartments. Like other privileges of Stalin's "new elite," a separate apartment had been a benefit of social mobility. People's construction, in contrast, was not upward social mobility in this earlier sense whereby workers and peasants had risen through higher education to leadership positions in party-state administration and industry.[14] Through people's construction, industrial workers moved to a separate apartment but remained workers. They gained the improved living conditions and *kul'turnost'* (culturedness) that a separate apartment represented without changing jobs or social identity. Under Khrushchev, people's construction was at the forefront of eroding the separate apartment's status as a marker of social difference and making the more civilized and cultured life it embodied ordinary. Unlike past experiments in social mobility, giving factory workers access to something only elites had previously enjoyed was not meant to revolutionize the social order but rather to preserve it.

This was best seen in what factory managers found beneficial about people's construction: reducing high labor turnover, which would also limit workers' physical mobility from one factory or city to another. Since the 1920s, workers had moved from workplace to workplace in search of better housing. Draconian labor laws in the late 1930s and during the war were intended to lower absenteeism and turnover. Nevertheless, turnover continued to be an enormous problem into the early postwar years, and housing remained a chief source of hostility between labor and management.[15] The lack of decent housing was the main reason workers at the Molotov auto factory in Gor'kii petitioned management in the early postwar years to allow them to leave the factory.[16] Until the mid-1950s, the autoworkers lived in the factory's barracks or privately rented rooms.[17] In appealing to the interests of both workers and management, people's construction promised a thaw in labor relations and a less coercive way of restricting workers' physical

mobility. It would keep workers and their families in one place as owners of apartments under the right of "personal property" (*lichnaia sobstvennost'*) and reduce labor turnover.

Another reason factory managers supported people's construction
concerned their institutional dispute with local soviets. Beginning in
September 1945, local soviets were supposed to receive 10 percent of
housing constructed by most enterprises for redistribution to war-
related entitlement groups.[18] People's construction offered enterprises
an easy way out of this obligation. From 1955 to the middle of 1957,
the official property status of people's construction remained unclear,
yet pamphlets loudly proclaimed that all its housing stayed in the
hands of those who built it. One even taunted the Gor'kii city soviet:
"No deductions of the newly built housing in any portion go to the city
soviet, construction organizations, and other organizations. All the
apartments are settled by the builders."[19] Khrushchev's regime clarified
the situation in its July 1957 housing decree by basing people's construction on "the rights of personal property of one builder for one
apartment."[20] This made housing built under people's construction
part of the individual housing sector and made it impossible for local
soviets to claim their 10 percent cut.

People's construction also promised a thaw in social relations by
avoiding the violence and trauma that had characterized reallocations
of housing and privileged access to it in the past. Shortly after the
Russian Revolution, as we saw in chapter 1, workers had forcibly moved
into the single-family apartments of the bourgeoisie and aristocracy
under the banner of class war and abolishing private property. This
was the founding moment of the communal apartment: an act of violence and theft, the fundamental injustice of which was not forgotten
by those who lost out. Under rapid industrialization in the late 1920s
and early 1930s, communal apartments, barracks, and dormitories became increasingly dense as space was divided and redivided to house
the expanding urban workforce. World War II produced the greatest
violence, resulting in the loss of one-third of total housing, leaving 25
million people homeless,[21] and causing bitter disputes when those returning from evacuation tried to reclaim their housing.[22] People's construction, like the broader mass housing campaign of which it was a
critical part, differed from these past experiences for several reasons. It
was conducted in peacetime and under a regime that repudiated terror
as a tool for creating a classless society. Most important, people's con-

struction was not a redistribution of already-existing housing or punishment of undesirable social groups. Ordinary workers now had the
opportunity to obtain new housing that did not come at the direct expense of others.

Selling People's Construction

Pamphlets were an important part of the media campaign that promoted people's construction as the avant-garde of housing construction. Their authors included factory management personnel who organized people's construction projects and explained to others how to do
it. For instance, at the Molotov auto factory in Gor'kii, Petr Cherneev,
the head of the pressing section, and Aleksandr Torbin, the chairman
of the labor union's housing and daily affairs commission, told the
story of the early projects.[23] Pamphlets featured testimonials by workers about their work and their lives after moving to a separate apartment, and claimed that their unorthodox methods were signs that communist economic and social relations were developing before people's
very eyes.[24] Pamphlet writers also developed a discourse on people's
construction centering on its principles of self-interest, initiative, self-
reliance, and mutual obligation.

Celebrations of "self-interest" were particularly striking because
they suggested the displacement of the selfless sacrifice that had been at
the heart of Stalinist industrialization and Soviet socialism. Pamphleteers
unabashedly proclaimed that people's construction worked because of
its "principle of personal self-interest" (*printsip lichnoi zainteresovan-
nosti*).[25] They implied that socialism's methods of resolving the housing
question had thus far been a failure. Previous attempts to enlist workers in housing construction without the payoff of better housing
had failed because they "did not see direct self-interest [*priamaia zainteresovannost'*] in this assistance."[26] People's construction was entirely
different because "participants in the construction are not just building
the houses, but precisely those houses in which they will live with their
families." In keeping with the Soviet discourse on labor, people's construction was supposed to transform a worker's entire approach to
work. People "do not just build houses, but precisely those houses in
which they'll live with their families. Awareness of this produces the
particular self-interest [*osobaia zainteresovannost'*] in participants of

construction in the quicker raising of the residential buildings, and it is the foundation of the creative work of a people's construction collective."[27] Pursuing self-interest, not selfless sacrifice, was the key to greater output and socialist labor organization.

One wonders how America's Cold War warriors would have reacted to such rhetoric coming from the Soviet Union. Were not Soviet propagandists conceding in so many words that socialism could not possibly work because it denied individual self-interest? Widening such cracks in the Soviet veneer of the selfless workers' state was great sport for American journalists, as illustrated in their obsessive coverage of ten Soviet housing delegates who toured the United States in 1955. The ten housing experts' keen interest in the American suburban home, one of which they even bought, and their shopping trips for their families suggested to reporters that further exposure to the American way of life would surely drive a wedge between Soviet citizens and the socialist system that denied their secret material desires.[28] Despite its talk of self-interest, people's construction and its emphasis on working-class collectives building their housing while on the clock may have still sounded too socialist or simply too confusing for such Cold War reporting. American newspapers, as far as I am aware, failed to report on the movement, but this was not because Khrushchev's regime hid the phenomenon for fear that its celebration of "self-interest" might prove embarrassing. On the contrary, the Soviet Union was eager to show people's construction projects to any Westerners who would look at them. Major news organs available to foreigners like *Izvestiia* reported on them.[29] When this media campaign caught the attention of the American Embassy in Moscow in 1957, it sent two individuals on a fact-finding mission to Gor'kii, where local officials graciously received the Americans and took them on a tour of people's construction projects. The Americans even left town with floor plans and photographs as further evidence for the State Department to ponder.[30]

To be sure, self-interest had to be guided toward the greater social good. In some projects, workers knew the size of the apartment they would receive, but not the specific one. This ensured that they worked well on the entire building, not just their own apartments.[31] Self-interest had to be protected to ensure that workers would build good housing. One pamphlet criticized a factory near Gor'kii for making it unclear whether or not workers would receive the housing they built by postponing the allocation of the space until after construction. As a consequence, "this negatively affected labor productivity and the level of the organization of work."[32] The KPK reported on a similar case involving a Muscovite family in 1958, in which a worker was denied a room in a building he had helped construct. The factory director was rebuked "so that in the future they do not make inappropriate commitments and that if they have already engaged a worker, then let them fulfill their obligation to him."[33] Enforcing such obligations was difficult in a labor-for-housing program predicated on informal arrangements. Some proponents advocated written agreements to guarantee the exchange of labor for housing. In Orenburg, written agreements were issued in the form of a "guarantee coupon" that recorded participants' labor in hours and the amount of space to be received. When the building was finished, each family traded in its coupon for a housing permit.[34] At the Leningrad shoe factory "Skorokhod," people's construction projects were incorporated into collective bargaining agreements.[35]

Self-interest also motivated workers to act on their own "initiative" in obtaining supplies and equipment. Celebrations of this aspect of people's construction suggested a new openness in recognizing what was already going on in the second economy. For the second people's construction project in Gor'kii, a building with forty-six apartments, workers recycled waste materials from the factory floor such as packing iron for roofing, bricks, nails, and plywood, and took cinderblocks straight from production. The workers borrowed a circular saw and salvaged a discarded mortar mixer.[36] Such initiatives were sometimes organized through a "council for construction assistance," which included workers, labor union personnel, factory management, and local party organs, and was responsible for allocating supplies, financing, and labor. In delivering supplies, such councils acted like a "pusher" (*tolkach*), the unofficial figure in industry who helped allocate or "push" supplies between enterprises outside official plans.[37] Pamphlets enthusiastically celebrated such deals. A bus conductor in Krasnoiarsk praised her collective's pusher for saving their project:

> Comrade Babii was charged with dealing with the questions of supplying necessary materials. He watched so that there was always lumber and stone at the construction site. In this matter, Comrade Babii showed his talents. One time, for example, lumber at the construction site was suddenly all used up. What to do? Can't give up on the work that's been started. Babii found a way out. He struck an

agreement with the village artisanal cooperative "Kyzyr" in the Karatuzskii district. They quickly delivered the needed amount of lumber to us along the river and for them we completely repaired their automobile during our free time.[38]

Along similar lines, an informal network of exchanging supplies among more than two enterprises in Cheliabinsk illustrated the importance of doing things "by mutual assistance."[39]

Proponents of people's construction celebrated such deals as a sign of new social relations that combined the self-interest inherent in getting a separate apartment with the selfless motivation of helping one's comrades. Construction work was the product of the "*kollektiv*" done through "mutual assistance" among fellow workers and family members.[40] In the first project in Gor'kii, twenty-four workers were chosen for the project. Although sixteen went to work on the construction site, the remaining eight worked overtime in the factory to produce above their regular norms so the section would earn enough money to pay the sixteen workers their salaries.[41] Once construction groups were formed, their family members joined in the construction.[42] As workers relocated to new apartments, their old housing was redistributed to others who worked on the construction sites. Even those with sufficient housing selflessly joined their comrades on a people's construction site. As one pamphlet pointed out, "This is a demonstration of authentic socialist comradely mutual understanding. It's always very crowded at the workers' meetings where they confirm who the future builders will be. Some have personal interest in receiving new housing; others are satisfied because they will receive housing which is being freed up."[43]

Stripped of its ideological veneer, the organization of labor on people's construction projects still surprised the American outsiders who traveled to Gor'kii. The two U.S. Embassy officials were struck to learn that "no attempt was made to hide the fact that the workers are doing house building on the company's time, although there has been no mention of this fact in the press." (The pamphlets examined here actually did report on this aspect.) The American fact-finders speculated that the workers were able to exchange labor among themselves with some doing double duty on the factory floor for others on the construction site because factories had a "surplus of labor on the production lines." This was a theory that nobody in Gor'kii wanted to confirm for the two Americans and one that never showed up in newspaper reports or pamphlets.[44] It nonetheless suggested quite a contrast to the problem of high labor turnover that had plagued Soviet industries in the 1930s. Workers in Gor'kii were staying put in the hopes of gaining a spot on a people's construction brigade and a shot at moving to a separate apartment.

Instead of dwelling on the structural inefficiencies of the Soviet labor market, the media campaign emphasized how workers exercised their agency by negotiating their own terms. In Krasnoiarsk, Tatiana Smirnova explained that she was initially not allowed onto a people's construction project because nobody could do her specific job at the factory in her absence. Smirnova and a friend struck the following deal with a coworker, Tamara Shchukel. Smirnova and her friend continued to work in the factory and fulfilled Shchukel's norm, while Shchukel helped construct the building with Smirnova's future apartment. "Tamara herself did not need an apartment," Smirnova explained, "but I really needed one—I have a baby, a five-year old girl. And so Tamara worked for me. . . . But I nevertheless went to the construction site when I had a free hour. I was there almost every day" (ellipses in the original).[45] In affirming one's mutual obligations to the collective, Smirnova made the rare admission that moving to a private apartment could potentially separate one from the community. "Can these new walls really fence me off from that collective, which took such an active part in my fate?" she asked. "No, I will never forget what my comrades did for me. And I'm not the only one who thinks this. All of us new residents similarly value the care of our comrades and at the necessary moment will answer them: we're coming to help."[46]

Workers like Smirnova, the pamphlet writers insisted, were beginning to see themselves in a different way that harked back to the original promises of the Russian Revolution. They gained "the sense of being the master of an enterprise" as people more in control and more responsible for the spaces and things around them.[47] In a pamphlet from Krasnoiarsk, a former worker at a steam locomotive depot, who had started work there in 1904, invited its current workers to think of their people's construction project and their separate apartments in historical terms. "October transformed the individual from being cowed and bent by necessity into a free and creative worker of society," he explained. "Everything is possible, everything is open for this kind of person. He courageously discovers new lands, he's the first to fly over the North Pole, and he creates a space satellite. . . . This is the chief victory of October. And it's with this that I congratulate you, dear comrades, who celebrate moving into a new home" (ellipses in the original).[48]

Becoming masters of production carried over into workers' new apartments. Nikolai Novikov, a carpenter at the shoe factory "Spartak" in Krasnoiarsk, invited the author of a pamphlet into his new apartment where three of his relatives had come to visit. The pamphlet writer observed, "We understand the legitimate pride of the master of the apartment: Not only was he able to have guests over, but he was able to provide for them comfortably without feeling embarrassed."[49] Acquiring the proper consumer goods facilitated workers' transition to such a well-appointed separate apartment. Having previously rented space privately, Smirnova lacked a table and chairs for her new home, but this only fed her imagination for the future. She recalled what she said on the first day in her new home: "Well now, my daughter, we're going to start to live together now you and me! We're going to have a table, we'll purchase a couple beds for ourselves, and without question we'll bring the sewing machine, we'll sew ourselves some pretty dresses." Mariia Kashina, a worker in the factory's cutting shop, claimed that a lack of space, not money, had prevented her family from purchasing household items while living in privately rented housing: "But now we've been able over the past few months to acquire what's most needed and we even purchased a radio receiver."[50]

According to such vignettes, moving to a separate apartment promised workers a cultural form of social mobility in the confines of their own homes. A pamphlet writer's visit to a residential community of railway workers in Orenburg found them enjoying the new separate apartments they had built by themselves. In one apartment, a young married couple had acquired a clothes closet, a record player, and a mirror piece just in time for their housewarming party. As a sign of the domesticity and coziness they had attained, the young wife emphasized her husband's new slippers: "It's true, he still has some that aren't bad, but one wants everything to be better, indeed even though he's a simple worker, he earns his living well. I also work."[51] Workers thus became masters of their domestic space and attained the finer cultural habits and consumer goods previously reserved for elites under Stalin, while at work they remained "simple workers."[52]

Consumer goods and a well-appointed home were also symbolically important in selling people's construction to the highest levels of the

Soviet leadership. At the December 1956 Party Plenum, H. Kuz'min, a lathe operator from Moscow and Supreme Soviet deputy, gave his perspective on workers' desperate need for better housing. He first placed housing in the official context of greater social and economic concerns. Poor housing was a detriment to culture, the raising of children, productivity, and mental and physical health. He acknowledged that the war's devastation had forced resources to be spent on reconstructing the country and that "the working class knows how much has been done to improve its life." But now it was time to address housing, and he offered his audience this startling image of how out of step with the times the Soviet Union's housing had become for its workers:

> We can observe the following: a family takes a walk on a day off work. The couple is well dressed—a good coat, hats, the children are also well dressed. If the baby is breastfeeding, then he's frequently in a luxurious baby carriage. But they go out for a walk from a broken down barrack. It turns out that somehow one thing has gone forward a long way, but another has lagged behind. And there's more— in such a barrack there's quite often a television on a small table.[53]

The workers imagined here had indeed come a long way. They enjoyed leisure time and had started a new family. They had even acquired one of the newest consumer items for the home: a television set. Now all they needed was to leave their dilapidated barrack for housing that would provide the proper domestic setting for the cultured persons they had become and the objects they had acquired. It was factory workers, not just elites, who were now entitled to acquire these consumer items and move to a separate apartment. Kuz'min criticized enterprises that shifted resources away from housing as something that was "dishonest before the working class" and suggested that any new factory be built with enough new housing for its workers. Naturally, he voiced his support for people's construction.[54]

In addition to its mass media campaign, people's construction gained additional prominence with a conference in Gor'kii in June 1957.[55] The conference was organized by the Gor'kii obkom and praised in a front-page editorial in *Pravda*.[56] In a report on the conference for the Construction Department of the Central Committee of the Communist Party, suggestions were made to bring younger workers into the projects, allow enterprises to redirect more financial resources into people's construction, and extend state loans to individual participants. Architects were to strive for "maximum variation" in their designs, whereas furniture, especially for the kitchen, was to be specifically designed for people's construction apartments.[57] In addition to categorizing people's construction housing as personal property, the July 1957 mass housing decree adopted some of the recommendations of the Gor'kii conference and gave the movement a clearer legal basis as "housing construction collectives."[58]

The final step in the legal codification of people's construction was a government decree issued in July 1959. The decree confirmed that constructors would own their apartments as personal property, but in theory it reduced much of the enterprise's authority in managing people's construction. Constructors would continue to form collectives within their own enterprises, but each collective was supposed to choose a leader and determine the terms of its agreement independently. Loans were to be made available to each constructor, but collectives were to obtain supplies or purchase them independently. In making people's construction less dependent on enterprises, the state was trying to curtail informal and illegal practices in obtaining supplies, labor, and financing, and to simply bring order to a chaotic system of construction.[59] The state's codification of people's construction led, intentionally or not, to its demise. Without access to the levers of the second economy, industrial workers and enterprise managers found it difficult to orchestrate their quasi-legal projects.

Ending a Popular Initiative

Pamphlets promoting people's construction abruptly ceased publication after 1959. Although newspapers noted construction projects resembling people's construction, they lacked the fanfare of the media campaign.[60] Without specifically condemning people's construction, one newspaper article on efforts to tighten housing distribution in Leningrad noted that it "still" occurred.[61] By the early 1960s, failed projects were a further indication of serious problems. In August 1962, a group of "young specialists" in geology from Novosibirsk complained to Khrushchev that poor prospects for better housing affected both families and single people, and caused some to leave the city. Their project to build a house along the lines of people's construction had fallen through because of management foot-dragging.[62] In December 1962, the head of the KGB reported to the Central Committee of the Communist Party on a project in Lipetsk oblast that degenerated into broken promises between labor and management, a mass squatting of the housing in question, and a near riot with the local police.[63] Along with similar declines in individual housing construction, the volume of people's construction fell precipitously in the early 1960s.[64] By 1960, stirring proclamations of building housing "on our own," working out of "self-interest," and developing one's "initiative" in obtaining supplies were gone. An alternative housing system that gave preferential access to industrial workers vanished as quickly as it had appeared.

Three main factors, I argue, explain the collapse of people's construction. First, it was out of step with the overall mass housing campaign that focused on prefabricated housing of five-story buildings based on standardized plans and modern building methods.[65] Second, authorities in Moscow may have targeted people's construction in their broader attacks against informal and illegal economic practices in the early 1960s.[66] As described above, policymakers brought order to people's construction through the July 1959 decree, which distanced workers from their factories' financing and supplies. The decree legitimized people's construction, but it also constrained the informal practices that were at the heart of the movement. Third, whereas enterprises benefited from people's construction, city soviets, such as the one in Leningrad (see chapter 3), found it to be a hindrance in their efforts to allocate housing and worked against it. Whether the rhetoric of people's construction presented a problem that had to be eliminated is a matter of greater speculation. Advocates of people's construction skillfully mixed rhetoric about spontaneous, collective action with celebrations of individual self-interest. Their rhetoric opened a vibrant space for talking openly about individualistic motivations and unorthodox ways of working and procuring materials outside the plan. The abrupt cessation of this discourse after 1959 suggests that it had crossed ideological lines in a state that still prized selfless sacrifices for the good of the whole and was loath to admit the failures of economic planning.

Where did people's construction fit in the overall mass housing campaign? Though it lasted only a few years, it represented the first large wave of workers moving into separate apartments. Looking back in 1972, the ethnographer Sofia Rozhdestvenskaia observed in her study

of housing in Gor'kii that the mass housing campaign produced upward social mobility for workers, insofar as they now lived in the exact
same mass housing of "the intelligentsia, employees, and workers of
the service sphere." Although there were some minor variations in the
size of one's library and interior decoration, workers had moved up in
the world. In moving from peasant dwellings to barracks and now the
separate apartment, they had finally acquired housing that was "identical to the housing of the intelligentsia." This was proof "not only of
the growth of material prosperity but also of the spiritual culture
of workers." People's construction had been the earliest driving force
of this cultural transformation forged through mass housing.[67]

People's construction also transformed the meaning of the separate
apartment. It helped legitimize the notion that moving to a separate
apartment was part of the natural order of things as the country marched
toward communism. It changed the separate apartment from an item
of exclusive privilege for the elite to an object of legitimate desire available to the masses. In short, people's construction helped make the
separate apartment an ordinary feature of Soviet everyday life. But it
also opened up a space in which another form of fast-track access to
the separate apartment, this time catering to urban professionals and
elites, could be created. This was the housing construction cooperative,
to which we now turn.

Co-opting People's Construction

Since at least 1956, a group of top party-state officials sought to establish the cooperative on behalf of urban elites. Most had risen to leadership positions in the economy, such as Vladimir Kucherenko, chairman of the State Committee on Construction for the Soviet of Ministers
of the USSR (Gosstroi), and Ivan Grishmanov, head of the Central
Committee's Department on Construction. Most were born in the first
decade of the twentieth century in peasant or working-class families
and had worked as laborers or served in the Red Army in the 1920s. In
the late 1920s and early 1930s, most of these officials—such as Aleksei
Miurisep, the chairman of Estonia's Soviet of Ministers—went back to
school and got a technical education that propelled them off the factory floor and into their party-state careers.[68] Although none were serious contenders for Khrushchev's job, they banded together to over-

come his opposition to the cooperative and give urban elites the same fast-track access to separate apartments that industrial workers enjoyed through people's construction. The party-state officials in favor of the cooperative initially associated it with the discourse and principles of people's construction in the hopes that the latter's popularity and ideological soundness would legitimize it. Like ordinary Soviet citizens, even party-state elites had to learn the new ways of "speaking Bolshevik" under Khrushchev to get what they wanted out the system they had created under Stalin.[69]

These high-level proponents of the cooperative had been among the beneficiaries of social mobility in the early years of Stalin's rule, whereby workers and peasants were pushed through higher education as part of the regime's efforts to create its own, loyal intelligentsia and provide the technical knowledge for leading the country through industrialization and onward to socialism.[70] Their common background sheds light on the social and political origins of the cooperative's creation under Khrushchev. They were largely motivated, I argue, out of solidarity with the Soviet intelligentsia that had taken shape under Stalin as both its members and its patrons to preserve the privileges of their social class in the face of Khrushchev's populist agenda and resistance to the cooperative. In confronting and ultimately prevailing over Khrushchev, these officials exposed early on behind the Communist Party's closed doors the political opposition among party-state elites that scholars have linked to his ouster in 1964. That opposition was based on elites' perception that Khrushchev's policies threatened their social and political status.[71] The behind-the-scenes debates that went into the cooperative's establishment thus provides us with an early episode, heretofore unexamined by scholars, into the internal political fissures that plagued Khrushchev's tenure and ultimately led to his ouster.

The housing cooperative of the Khrushchev era was not the first in Soviet history. Leasing and housing construction cooperatives had existed in the 1920s and 1930s, but were eliminated by the Stalinist regime's housing decree of October 1937.[72] In light of earlier cooperatives' demise, proponents of a new cooperative under Khrushchev initially avoided discussing them. Instead, they were eager to associate their idea with people's construction because of the legitimacy it conferred on their project. Eliding the differences between people's construction and the cooperative, and borrowing the language and principles of the former, were meant to downplay the latter's professional and elite social composition. Their plan reached its first high point at the Party Plenum held December 20–24, 1956. Before this meeting, lobbying efforts for the cooperative picked up both behind the scenes and in *Pravda*.

In late November, the Ministry of Urban and Village Construction of the RSFSR shared its views on the matter with the Presidium in a report forwarded to three central proponents of the cooperative: Nikolai Baibakov, Vladimir Kucherenko and Ivan Grishmanov. The ministry praised the Moscow city party organization's efforts to promote people's construction and then laid out a plan for reviving cooperatives.[73] It called for cooperatives to be set up with state loans and asked for "the necessary material and technical resources so that members of these cooperatives can feel a real possibility in the next year and a half of receiving living space using their own savings." This was fast-track access in comparison with the ten years Leningrad's city soviet officials believed it took people on their lists to get housing (see chapter 3). The ministry also revealed a critical economic rationale for reviving the cooperative. Having people put their money into housing construction "will be reflected favorably in the general circulation of money in the country since the demand for goods of wide consumption will decrease."[74] In other words, too many rubles were chasing too few consumer goods in the Soviet economy, and cooperatives could help by soaking up excess rubles in the money supply and diverting people's purchasing power from consumer items to housing construction. As a selling point for the cooperative, this argument had its merits. Cooperatives would alleviate shortages in consumer goods and hidden inflation, while contributing to housing construction.

In the weeks before the December 1956 plenum, *Pravda* and *Izvestiia* ran stories praising people's construction as the new wave in housing construction.[75] Interspersed among these stories were articles in *Pravda* touting the cooperative's similarities to people's construction. Whether the cooperative's proponents who spoke at the plenum had a hand in publishing these articles remains a matter of speculation. At the very least, the articles were a fortuitous development that the cooperative's proponents exploited at the plenum.

The *Pravda* article, "Our Worker Housing Cooperative," which was signed by three members of the endeavor in the city of Molotov (Perm), illustrated how the cooperative was legitimized by downplaying its elite class composition and fusing it together with a hybrid version of people's construction and individual housing construction.[76] This so-called cooperative comprised sixty individuals, "ordinary workers, skilled workers, industrial administrators," from different factories. Although it included white-collar employees, its creators wisely chose to call it a "worker housing cooperative," lest anyone think it catered to elites. Its members built individual houses according to the "brigade principle," which resembled people's construction, and secured government loans to supplement their own savings on the grounds that they were individual constructors. As in people's construction, this cooperative proudly described the material and logistical support it received from "the thrifty chiefs of factory shops and enterprises." The authors were convinced they had created a cooperative, although legal recognition would have been welcome because "here and there they will not recognize such a self-sufficient form of organizing working people as a worker housing cooperative."[77]

Two days later, *Pravda* ran a front-page editorial declaring that cooperatives could be enlisted in housing construction alongside people's construction and individual housing construction.[78] Further blurring the lines between cooperatives and people's construction, *Pravda* published a letter from two Gor'kii residents who referred to people's construction projects as "housing construction associations" and cooperatives, and called for the return of the housing construction cooperative.[79]

By publishing these articles, the Communist Party's chief newspaper gave the cooperative's proponents a boost for the case they began to make at the December 1956 plenum. One advocate was Nikolai Baibakov, chief of the State Committee on Future Planning of the National Economy, who explained that people's contribution to housing construction should not be limited to construction work and that more had to be done to draw in "the means of the population"—in other words, money. Baibakov, who was born in Baku to a Russian family of an oil industry worker in 1911, had had an upwardly mobile career that began after graduation from Azerbaidjan's Oil Institute in 1932, spanned twenty years working his way up through the country's oil industry, and now found him working as a chief planner for the Soviet of Ministers of the USSR since 1955. His comments on people's construction suggest that he was thinking of those like himself who had done well under Stalin and wanted the state to continue fulfilling its obligations to them: "Many working people," he said, "express a desire to help in the construction of residential buildings with their own means and in this way to improve their housing conditions, while not every one of them is able to participate directly by means of their own labor in the construction of housing." This was Baibakov's diplomatic way of alluding to elites' aversion or inability to do manual labor given their social status, skills, age, or access to money to purchase their own apartments. The elites in his cohort who had been upwardly mobile in the late 1920s and early 1930s were now in their forties and fifties, and may have found that their age made construction work not only undesirable, but physically impossible. For their sake, he seemed to suggest, there needed to be "a special form of drawing in the means of this part of the population besides the individual construction presently practiced."[80]

Aleksandr Sheremet'ev, chief of the USSR Ministry of Ferrous Metallurgy, cited institutional conflicts over housing as another reason to create an alternative option for those willing to help construct housing. Sheremet'ev was born in Harbin, China, to a family of Russian peasants in 1901, and he successfully worked his way up the ranks of the metallurgy industry after graduating from Moscow's Institute of Steel in 1932.[81] Unlike Baibakov, he seemed less concerned about preserving the privileges of aging elites in his socially mobile cohort than protecting the interests of his enterprise managers, who were eager to control labor turnover by providing workers with housing. He complained at the plenum that "toilers" were not living any better despite a doubling of new construction and attributed this to a 30 percent cut in enterprise housing that went to local soviets and the military. He argued that individual housing construction and the cooperative would help fill this gap, although his version of the latter would draw in both labor and money from its residents.[82] For an industry leader like Sheremet'ev, the form the cooperative would take did not matter as long as his workers got housing.

For other proponents of the cooperative, certain ideological issues had to be addressed to justify it and overcome Khrushchev's resistance. Aleksandr Shelepin, at the time first secretary of the Komsomol's Central Committee, prodded Khrushchev on developing private forms of housing. Unlike other officials who favored the cooperative, Shelepin had been born to a family of white-collar railroad employees in 1918 and graduated from Moscow's Institute of History, Philosophy, and Literature in 1941, after which he followed a career path in the Komsomol and later became head of the KGB in 1958. He was sensitive to the ideological problems inherent in people's construction and the co-operative, but weighed them against the necessity of expanding construction. At the plenum, he argued that married couples should at least be able to live in a room of their own. Khrushchev joked, "Then perhaps there'll be a large increase in the population." Shelepin answered, "Nikita Sergeevich, it'll then be necessary to provide more encouragement to private initiative [*chastnaia initsiativa*], to develop it." He continued, "Maybe the topic isn't timely, we are against private property, but in regards to housing, private initiative must be developed, there's nothing bad about this."[83] In blunting such ideological objections, Shelepin borrowed the language of people's construction that stressed volunteerism and workers' "initiative." His comments in favor of "private initiative" were broad enough to include individual housing construction, people's construction, and the cooperative.

Aleksei Miurisep, chairman of the Soviet of Ministers of Estonia, argued that individual housing constructors should be able to buy more building supplies as part of an effort to provide them with better support and avoid theft of state resources. Like other champions of the cooperative, Miurisep's career path suggested a socially mobile apparatchik with an eye toward pragmatic solutions to economic problems. Miurisep was born in 1902 in Estonia (at the time, part of the Russian Empire) and hailed from the family of a merchant marine. After spending several years in the Red Army in the 1920s, he studied at the Tiumen' Electro-Mechanical Institute of Railway Transport Engineers from 1931 to 1937. He then rose through the ranks of energy industries and held energy and transportation posts in the Estonian party hierarchy.[84] At the December 1956 plenum, he argued that "it would be expedient to allow individual constructors to unite in housing cooperation for the construction of buildings with six to eight apartments." He called for more state credits to individual builders and even suggested that the state sell houses and apartments it built to people.[85] Another selling point for grouping individual builders into cooperatives was its positive impact on urban planning. Before the plenum, the Simferopol city soviet asked Khrushchev and Bulganin "to allow individual constructors to form cooperatives for the construction of residential buildings . . . [and] not just those with one apartment but buildings with four, eight, and sixteen apartments." This would allow the city to save on land, municipal infrastructure, and building supplies.[86]

Others similarly touted savings to the state budget as a selling point for the cooperative. The party boss of the Molotov (Perm) oblast, Aleksandr Struev, lamented that "we want to resolve our problems with housing only at the state's expense as it's been done up to now." Unlike other champions of the cooperative, Struev had only received a primary school education and had spent his career in various local party organs and local soviets. He shared their pragmatic approach to the cooperative that papered over its potential ideological problems. Struev had served under Khrushchev in the Ukrainian party apparatus as the party boss of the Donetsk oblast immediately following the war.[87] This may explain why he felt comfortable enough at the plenum to needle Khrushchev on cooperatives with some good-natured ridicule for the Soviet leader's style. Alluding to an earlier pitch he had made to Khrushchev on the cooperative, Struev explained, "Nikita Sergeevich didn't react as actively to my new proposal as he usually does to everything that's new." Khrushchev responded, "Comrade Struev, you yourself said that it's not new." Indeed, it wasn't new, Struev explained, because his oblast had gone ahead with building the cooperative that *Pravda* had promoted in its article discussed above, "Our Worker Housing Cooperative."[88]

Despite such lobbying efforts by the cooperative's champions, Khrushchev remained circumspect because of its elite status and saw through this group's transparent attempts to pass it off as a version of people's construction. At the plenum, Khrushchev explained, "It's necessary, comrades, to draw the means of the population into construction. Now there the people of Gor'kii have been building. This isn't bad, it's only necessary to be more organized." In contrast, the substance of the cooperative, not the name itself, was a problem. Khrushchev explained,

> The question of housing construction cooperation, about which comrades have come out and spoken. I'm not convinced right now that it's necessary to return to it, and I'm giving my personal opinion on this question. It needs thinking. The question isn't how it's called. Why did they liquidate it? Because [housing construction] cooperation is such, that people became members, but the state gave out credits, and those, who became members, received apartments and materials out of line.[89]

Reflecting his own populist sensibilities, Khrushchev emphasized the unequal advantages earlier cooperatives had given their members.

As explained in the 1937 decree that eliminated them, members of these cooperatives had benefited from state loans covering 80 to 90 percent of construction. The decree concluded that "shareholders of [housing construction] cooperation received apartments at the state's expense for unlimited and irrevocable use and they became in fact privileged owners of living space, having invested little of their own resources."[90] For the time being, Khrushchev successfully shelved the issue. In its decree at the end of the December plenum, the Central Committee only stated the need to "investigate the possibilities for bringing forth additional means into housing construction."[91]

A New Cooperative

Undeterred by Khrushchev's resistance, proponents of the cooperative renewed their efforts in 1957. They tried again to downplay its anticipated social composition and continued to associate it with people's construction. In addition to appropriating the legitimacy of people's construction, the cooperative's proponents tied their project to the regime's seminal July 1957 decree on housing. Within days of the decree's publication, P. Surin, head of the Ministry of the Communal Economy of the RSFSR, cited it as one reason for reinstating the cooperative in detailed briefs he wrote in early August 1957. He legitimized the cooperative by pointing out that it shared the principles of individual housing construction and people's construction whereby people contributed to construction and that the cooperative could contribute to the mass housing campaign outlined in the July 1957 decree. Surin made clear that cooperative housing would be built "at the expense of the means and labor participation of a cooperative's members." He also associated cooperatives with individual housing and people's construction to press for state loans. Members would receive loans similar to those for individual constructors building apartment buildings as mandated by the July 1957 decree. His recommendations were included in a detailed union-level draft decree that suggested the cooperative's champions had been diligently working on legislation to push through when the time was right.[92]

Although the 1937 housing decree had abolished cooperatives, Stalin's regime chose to leave a small set of them intact for elite party, state, and cultural organizations, mostly in Moscow. Such elite cooperatives were made possible by an escape clause in the 1937 decree that allowed them to continue functioning if members repaid all government loans within six months. New cooperatives could not receive state loans or any other assistance and would need to cover all costs independently.[93] According to Surin, some 60 cooperatives functioned in the Russian Republic in 1957, among which 41 were located in Moscow.[94] One inventory showed that 28 of the city's 41 cooperatives had completed construction of their housing, included 2,047 members, and managed 77,597 square meters of living space in 98 buildings. The remaining 13 Moscow cooperatives were still constructing their apartment buildings and included 2,240 members. Of the 28 cooperatives that had built their housing, 13 had been founded in the 1920s, one in 1932, and three in 1940. Although the 1937 decree had spared just over a dozen preexisting cooperatives in the capital and allowed for only 3 new ones before the war, the postwar years of Stalin's rule afforded a modest expansion of these elite cooperatives. Eleven of the 28 Moscow cooperatives that had completed their construction were established between 1945 and 1952. Out of all 41 cooperatives in the city, the 13 that were still constructing their apartment buildings in Moscow had been set up in either 1952 or 1953.[95]

The names of existing cooperatives in Moscow indicated their elite clientele. Some denoted specific professions, such as "Soviet composer," "Moscow writer," "Soviet artist," "medic," "pedagogues of the Moscow Conservatory," "artists of film and drama," and "editorial workers of the Great Soviet Encyclopedia." Some professional groups had more than one cooperative, as illustrated by those named "masters of estrada" and "artists of estrada"; "artists of the GABT [State Academic Bolshoi Theater] Ballet," "the GABT Orchestra," and "workers of GABT"; and "medic" and "professors of medicine." Other names referred to elite institutions, such as "Ministry of Foreign Affairs," "Lenin Pedagogical Institute," and "workers of the Academy of Sciences of the USSR." The Academy of Sciences, which was still constructing its three buildings, had the greatest number of members, at 960; most of these cooperatives had between 50 to 150 members.[96]

With such cooperatives springing up around Moscow's elite institutions and subgroups of the Soviet intelligentsia, it is little wonder that Khrushchev cast a skeptical eye on their proposed institutionalization and the suggestion that they were just like people's construction. Even the cooperative's proponents recognized its elite social composition.

At the very end of one of his briefs, Surin concluded dryly, "A negative moment in the development of housing construction cooperatives is the fact that the most well-to-do part of the population will be seized by cooperatives."[97] Cooperatives' contribution to housing construction would offset this drawback. According to Surin, until most were eliminated in 1937, the original construction cooperatives had succeeded in building 7.27 million square meters of living space and more than a million people had obtained their housing through them. State loans appeared to be the only means to reinstate the construction cooperative. Of the 41 cooperatives in Moscow, 28 were functioning and built as described above, but 13 remained in construction. Surin reported that these 13 cooperatives had benefited from fifteen-year state loans covering as much as 70 percent of construction costs.[98] Such loans were distributed from the center on a strictly ad hoc basis through specific orders from the Soviet of Ministers of the USSR.[99] Surin recommended that cooperative members should receive fifteen-year state loans individually and that the maximum amount of such loans would cover 50 percent of the cost of constructing the member's new apartment. The draft of the union-level decree on cooperatives similarly included provisions for loans. Further illustrating attempts to associate the cooperative with people's construction, the decree would have made loans contingent upon a minimum labor input by the member's family in a cooperative's construction. The draft decree suggested that state loans cover 40 percent of an individual member's cooperative share and that members had to repay them within fifteen years.[100]

Picking up where Surin left off, Vladimir Kucherenko and Ivan Grishmanov made their own case to the Presidium in late August 1957. Their rise to top leadership positions in the construction industry followed a now familiar pattern among proponents of the cooperative. Kucherenko, born into the family of a railway worker in 1909, attended the Kharkov Construction Institute from 1929 to 1933, after which he built a career in the construction industry that eventually brought him to Moscow, where he served as head of housing and civil construction for the city in 1954, and then as chairman of Gosstroi, the government's top construction body, beginning in 1955. Grishmanov, born into a peasant family in 1906, studied at the Leningrad Engineering and Construction Institute from 1931 to 1936, after which he pursued a career in construction that led to positions in Leningrad's city government after the war and eventually the Central Committee's Department on

Construction, where he assumed the top position in 1956.[101] Both men spoke about the cooperative with the authority of years of experience in construction and housing. Their report to the Presidium had the backing of other party-state leaders with similar upwardly mobile careers, such as Ekaterina Furtseva and Frol Kozlov, who had just taken their seats on the Presidium as full members, and Aleksei Kosygin, who had just become a candidate member.[102] Together, their lobbying efforts focused on the cooperative's pragmatic benefits. They were also looking out for the interests of those white-collar employees who had yet to enjoy the housing their social mobility warranted.

In making their pitch to the Presidium, Kucherenko and Grishmanov dutifully repeated Khrushchev's reservations about the disproportionate support cooperatives would receive from the state, but unlike Surin's frank admission, they went to great lengths to downplay the elite social composition of those who wanted cooperatives. They based their claims on two recent surveys. The first was a Gosstroi survey of employees who worked at cultural and educational institutions and had recently written to the Soviet of Ministers of the USSR asking for the establishment of cooperatives.[103] Stretching perceptions about the social status of potential cooperative members as far as they could, Kucherenko and Grishmanov emphasized that it was actually those in the middle ranks of elite institutions, not the elites themselves, who were trying to get into a cooperative. Drawing from the survey, they claimed that "only about 30 percent of the employees [who had wanted to join a cooperative] hold a higher degree, whereas laboratory personnel, mechanics, engineers, technicians, artists, scientific employees without a higher degree, bookkeeping workers, typists and others comprise the remaining contingent of people." They asserted that among scientific employees, "young scientific employees, employees, and workers" far outnumbered senior employees among those expressing an interest in cooperatives. Overstating their point, they explained that twelve soloists at the Bolshoi Theater made up a mere 3.6 percent of those wanting to join cooperatives, compared with the overwhelming number of "ordinary artists and employees of the theater" who made up the remaining 96.4 percent who wanted cooperatives.[104]

The Moscow city soviet conducted a similar survey among seventy families that expressed an interest in cooperatives. Kucherenko and Grishmanov drew an important observation from this study: People who wanted to join cooperatives already enjoyed around 7 square meters of living space per person and as much as 19 square meters.[105] This was far more than most Muscovites, many of whom made do with about 2 square meters.[106] The families that asked for cooperatives likely lived in communal apartments, because they would probably not have expressed an interest if they already lived in a separate apartment. Their space allotments suggest that they had received more space on account of the special benefits reserved for specialists and cultural elites.[107] Although such privileges helped members of the Soviet intelligentsia under Stalin, having 7 square meters per person was a disadvantage for those who wanted to leave their communal apartments for separate apartments under Khrushchev. As we saw in chapter 3, the rules for getting onto a local waiting list were not kind to those who had extra space. A maximum of 3 square meters was set in the late 1950s in Leningrad as the limit beyond which one could not get a spot on a waiting list. Because this maximum limit was only raised slowly over time, those with more space would have to wait for years just to get onto a waiting list, let alone receive a separate apartment. The mass housing campaign produced its share of contradictions, but this one must have seemed particularly ridiculous to those who had benefited from privileges under Stalin. It was now possible to have too much space in the Soviet Union. For these people, the cooperative was attractive because the space one already had would not prevent a family from joining one. Like the seventy families in the Moscow survey, Kucherenko and Grishmanov's report suggests that they, too, were concerned that the professionals and specialists upon whom the state depended would somehow be temporarily bypassed in the allocation of separate apartments.

In their pitch to the Presidium, Kucherenko and Grishmanov remarked that the elite cooperatives set up after 1937 enjoyed far more generous loans than individual housing constructors. They chose not to include loans for a new cooperative, hoping this would convince Khrushchev that they would not be a drain on the state budget.[108] In the absence of a decree on the cooperative in 1957, however, it appears that Khrushchev continued to obstruct its establishment. Kucherenko, Grishmanov, and others redoubled their efforts with a peculiar proposal they brought to the Central Committee in December 1957, for reinstating not one, but two kinds of construction cooperatives. In an allusion to people's construction and the class status of its participants, the report proposed that one kind of cooperative be established for "individual constructors" at their workplace. Their enterprises would assume responsibility for a maximum of 65 percent of the construction work involved and could either assign this task to their own construction sections or contract the work out to construction enterprises. The second proposed cooperative was designed "for the contingent of well-paid workers." These cooperatives would receive no state loans or assistance from the workplaces in which they would be organized. Members would have to pay for a minimum of 75 percent of construction costs up front before construction could begin. The proposal concluded, "The housing construction cooperatives of the forms indicated eliminate those shortcomings which are peculiar to the cooperatives existing now, created on very privileged grounds in comparison to the conditions for individual housing constructors."[109]

Class had apparently remained the main sticking point for Khrushchev. If he could be convinced that workers would get a cooperative on preferential terms, then perhaps he would finally accept a cooperative for elites as well. The fact that such a two-tier system for cooperatives would give in astonishingly stark terms an institutional form to class differences in the Soviet Union evidently did not bother Kucherenko and Grishmanov, nor Furtseva, Kozlov, and Kosygin, who once more backed their latest proposal.[110]

The proposal to the Central Committee showed that Kucherenko, Grishmanov, and others had studied cooperatives in European countries. With the exception of East Germany, they concentrated almost entirely on cooperatives in countries outside the communist bloc, such as Sweden, Norway, Denmark, Italy, Austria, West Germany, Belgium, France, and Finland. They made positive observations about cooperatives in these countries, suggesting that their experience be considered in devising a Soviet cooperative. Foreign cooperatives benefited from state and bank loans, and some received tax breaks. These cooperatives played a factor "in the resolution of a few social questions, which suit the interests of the state. Receiving a loan for the construction of an apartment or house, workers and white-collar employees of enterprises are forced to pay it off with significant interest within strictly established deadlines." Finding ways of ensuring repayment of loans was obviously important to Soviet policymakers eager to demonstrate the cooperative's financial solvency and mitigate any negative impact on the state budget. Their most revealing observation about foreign cooperatives, however, specifically addressed the Soviet Union's chronic problems with high labor turnover. They noted that "in becoming owners of an apartment or house, workers and white-collar employees are territorially fixed in designated areas, which corresponds to the interests of enterprises situated here."[111] The ideal cooperative appeared to be one that encouraged its members to finance housing construction, pay off their debts responsibly, and stay in one place.

When the government finally reinstated the cooperative with a union-level decree in March 1958, it took the conservative approach that Kucherenko, Grishmanov, and others had advanced. Loans were not worked into the cooperative, and the government did not see it as a substantial aspect of the mass housing campaign. Moreover, only one kind of cooperative was created, rather than the two-tier system. It was with these changes that the proponents of the cooperative likely succeeded in overcoming Khrushchev's objections to a new cooperative. Each Soviet republic was charged with coming up with its own model charter for cooperatives that laid out their rights and obligations.[112] The RSFSR's model charter was issued in September 1958.[113]

Perhaps the most significant privilege cooperative members enjoyed, albeit at the price of buying a share in a cooperative, was the guarantee of living in a separate apartment instead of a communal one. As will be recalled from chapter 2, local soviets and workplaces in the 1960s still distributed 5 to 10 percent of new apartments designed for single-family occupancy as communal apartments. When we factor in the communal apartments that local authorities continued to redistribute, the chances of a family actually receiving a separate apartment off a soviet or workplace waiting list was further diminished. As late as 1968 in Leningrad, for example, a family on a local soviet or workplace list had a 61 percent chance of receiving a separate apartment.[114]

Depending upon state housing, therefore, could still easily land a family in a recycled communal apartment or a communalized separate apartment. In contrast, the RSFSR's model cooperative charter in 1958, as well as subsequent ones in 1962 and 1965, formally guaranteed as the first item under "rights and obligations of cooperative members" that a member and his family would obtain "permanent use of a separate apartment."[115] To further preclude the subdivision of apartments, cooperatives enjoyed their own category of property—cooperative property—which separated their housing from the local soviet and workplace distribution networks. Only individual citizens could own shares that gave them the right to an apartment; state organizations could not buy into a cooperative and subdivide its apartments.[116]

Despite the attractiveness of purchasing the right to a separate apartment, the lack of state loans for the cooperative stunted its development. By June 1962, a generous estimate counted 890 cooperatives in the USSR and 530 in the RSFSR.[117] Such lackluster growth convinced the leadership in Moscow to finally introduce state loans. Subsequent decrees in 1962 and 1964 extended generous loans that led to the immediate expansion of the cooperative.[118] In the RSFSR, the cooperative peaked at the end of 1966, with 3,199 cooperatives and approximately 289,000 members.[119]

Class on Tomorrow Street

This chapter has shown how members of the top leadership in the Soviet Union orchestrated a transition from people's construction to the cooperative, through which preferential access to the separate apartment was reallocated along class lines from industrial workers to urban elites. During its brief existence, people's construction epitomized what the thaw was all about and how the liberalization it unleashed could be directed toward (and not away from) the regime's renewed commitment to constructing communism. The unorthodox methods of people's construction reflected the thaw's spirit of experimentation at the local level in midsized cities far from the high cultural centers of Moscow and Leningrad, where we normally situate the thaw. The bread-and-butter goals of people's construction were to raise the living standards of ordinary industrial workers and make society more equitable. It promised to erase the markers of class by raising workers to the material and cultural level of elites, but without disturbing the occupational basis of class. It encouraged mass participation, but without the violence and heavy toll in human life of previous mass campaigns, such as collectivization, industrialization, terror, and the war. It represented a relaxation in state-society relations, whereby housing was no longer a bone of contention between management and labor, but a source of cooperation. And finally, it was interpreted as a harbinger of communist social and labor relations, whereby individual families attained their own apartments and worked harder out of self-interest, but remained selfless members of their communities.

In contrast, the demise of people's construction and its replacement by the cooperative reflected the limits of the thaw, along with the persistence of class differences in housing. The abrupt end of people's construction showed that the Soviet state still exercised phenomenal power over its citizenry. Workers were initially empowered by the discourse of people's construction, but were then just as quickly disempowered when the state decided that it had had enough. The return of the cooperative showed that class-based differences in housing distribution were still possible and even desirable. Members of the top leadership, like Kucherenko and Grishmanov, realized that the cooperative was needed to ensure that white-collar employees and cultural elites received a separate apartment on a fast-track basis. After all, did the state not have a bargain to respect, whereby these elites conferred support on the regime in exchange for a bourgeois lifestyle?[120] Allowing industrial workers the privilege of "jumping the line" through people's construction straight into a separate apartment and leaving urban elites stranded in communal apartments was a violation of that bargain. Even if everyone was to receive a separate apartment eventually, class-based priorities were supposed to be reestablished insofar as fast-track access was concerned. In contrast to their blue-collar counterparts in people's construction, the members of cooperatives enjoyed a well-defined legal framework, which they effectively used to protect their collective rights. As we shall see in chapter 5, they used their rights to build their apartment buildings wherever they desired and even displaced individual housing owners to obtain their land.

The manner in which the shift from people's construction to the cooperative took place tells us much about how political and social life had changed since the first decade of Bolshevik rule and the Stalin era. Khrushchev tolerated challenges and even sarcasm on these issues from subordinates that Stalin would never have allowed without severe retribution. Socially, the cooperative's displacement of people's construction constituted a peaceful transfer of housing privileges (in this case, fast-track access to the separate apartment) along class lines. Before the Khrushchev period, redistributing rights and privileges to housing had often been steeped in violence or coercion. The expropriations of private apartments during and after the Russian Revolution were violent and traumatic episodes of class warfare exacted on the "former peoples" of Tsarist Russia's property-owning classes. Under Stalin, neighbors denounced neighbors in order to obtain their rooms in communal apartments; the state summarily terminated cooperatives in 1937 and expropriated its owners' housing. The vastly different political context of Khrushchev's rule and the regime's repudiation of terror help explain why the cooperative's displacement of people's construction did not end in violence or coercion that deprived someone of the housing they already had. But the fact that new housing was being built under Khrushchev also played a role. In a significant departure from the past, what was being contested were not the privileges to already-existing housing in which people lived and from which they could be forcibly displaced, but privileges to housing yet to be built.

Part III

Living and Consuming the Communist Way of Life

Chapter 5

The Mass Housing Community

In a revealing report to the Communist Party's Central Committee in December 1956, the head of the Central Committee's Department of Construction, Ivan Grishmanov, took the Gosstroi (State Committee on Construction) official A. Ladinskii to task for making exaggerated claims about housing construction in *Izvestiia*.[1] Ladinskii "assures readers that in the next ten years every family will be provided with a separate, fully-outfitted apartment." Grishmanov insisted that mass media pronouncements not overstate present construction targets or get ahead of policymakers in the mass housing campaign.[2] His warnings about raising popular expectations fell on deaf ears in a regime that had already declared behind closed doors in 1955 that "by the end of 1965 every family living in state housing be given a separate apartment, and for the single adult urban dweller—a separate room." The rationale for this declaration was as prosaic as its deadline was daring: Families took better care of their housing when they lived in separate apartments as opposed to communal apartments and dormitories.[3]

By 1957, increasingly hopeful forecasts for resolving the housing question in the near future were widely advertised. The Communist Party framed the mass housing campaign as a race against time with its housing decree of July 1957 that set a ten- to twelve-year deadline for ending housing shortages.[4] People's expectations would now surely be raised, but Khrushchev and the Communist Party were confident that they would succeed. At the Twenty-First Party Congress in 1959, Khrushchev asserted that "the task, set in 1957 by the party and the government to liquidate the shortage in housing and in this very way solve the housing problem in the next ten to twelve years, is being fulfilled successfully."[5]

Deadlines to eliminate the housing question once and for all foreshadowed the most famous deadline of reaching communism by 1980, which Khrushchev's regime announced in the new Party Program of 1961.[6] To be sure, setting a deadline for the arrival of communism was an unusual step for the Communist Party and a politically risky one in the event progress stalled.[7] Similarly risky were declarations by Khrushchev and his Eastern Bloc allies about overtaking the West in production and consumption. Such arbitrarily set deadlines, Greg Castillo observes, touched off "a revolution in rising expectations" among citizens of state socialist regimes.[8] In the long run, the legitimacy of these regimes would depend on whether they could prevent this revolution from turning into a crisis. In the meantime, by putting housing and consumer goods at the forefront of these deadlines, the Soviet Union and other state socialist regimes opened a discursive space for redefining the communist future. Both ordinary urban residents and party-state leaders imagined a well-appointed separate apartment as a critical part of that future. The country's path to communism and the individual Soviet family's journey to a separate apartment and a well-designed neighborhood intersected under Khrushchev, with each shaping the meanings and symbolism of the other. This chapter examines how prescriptions for Communism on Tomorrow Street became intertwined with the ways ordinary residents set about creating community in mass housing neighborhoods.

The Communist Way of Life

On April 12, 1961, Yuri Gagarin took his historic trip into the cosmos, becoming the first person to venture beyond the Earth's atmosphere. The mass press detailed this Soviet first with articles describing the flight and photographs of a clean-cut, smiling Gagarin.[9] Alongside images of futuristic space travel for the masses were stories of the ongoing mass housing campaign,[10] which buttressed the promises of the technologically modern way of life that Soviet man's space travel represented.[11] Apartments were outfitted with the latest amenities, and new buildings were constructed with modern industrial methods. The journal *Architecture of the USSR* (*Arkhitektura SSSR*) idealized well-designed urban microdistricts with their commercial and cultural infrastructure as modern satellites orbiting around older urban centers. They were clean and full of movement, with rapid public transportation and automobiles providing residents with easy access to the entire city or beyond.[12] Khrushchev's regime worked assiduously to represent space exploration and mass housing as parallel Soviet successes paving the way to communism. In 1959, Khrushchev framed the "communist way of life" (*kommunisticheskii byt*) as the eventual outcome of not only giving Soviet citizens their own apartments but also showing them how to "properly use public goods, live properly, and observe the rules of the socialist community."[13]

Propagandists further defined the communist way of life that lay beyond the next street corner.[14] One chronicler of the future, Mikhail Lifanov, began his essay *On Everyday Life under Communism* by melding together images of space-age technology and urban life: "Imagine, reader, that we're walking with you along the streets of the city of the future. Wide thoroughfares filled with light nowhere intersect themselves on one level, and rushing cars, whose form reminds one of rockets, pass by us at great speed."[15] The city of the future, Lifanov explained, would replace the "old city" of the nineteenth century, with its dirty courtyards and tiny streets. Instead, fresh air and sunlight would permeate the city, which "freely and deeply breathes with every particle of its great lungs." In announcing the arrival of this "new way of life," Lifanov explained, "there's no need to make a trip to the far off future, because already today, we now see developed communist construction, which profoundly changes our entire way of life."[16]

Such pronouncements echoed earlier calls in Soviet history to discard the rot of prerevolutionary urban existence in the built environment and everyday social relations.[17] The concept of the microdistrict (figure 5.1) as a residential area outfitted to meet all commercial and social needs grew out of similar ideas in the 1920s and early 1930s for the socialization of everyday life in the designs for the *dom-kommuna* (house commune).[18] As the newspaper *Trud* demonstrated in a 1963 article "The House of Tomorrow," mass housing designs represented the latest "sprouts of the communist way of life." The newspaper invoked the *dom-kommuna* as a precedent for contemporary projects that inculcated proper collectivist values over selfish ones. But there were limits to what should be borrowed from the past. The champions of the *dom-kommuna* had taken the "socialization of a person's personal life" too far and "in-

Figure 5.1. Model of a microdistrict in Novo-Polotsk (architect, Ia. Linev-ich). The description below indicated that this design was meant to house nine thousand residents in four- to five-story buildings in an area covering 32 hectares. Small gardens were interspersed throughout the site and walk-ing paths connected the two main parts of the microdistrict. The design also featured two schools that included a sports facility, five daycare centers, and numerous stores and social services.

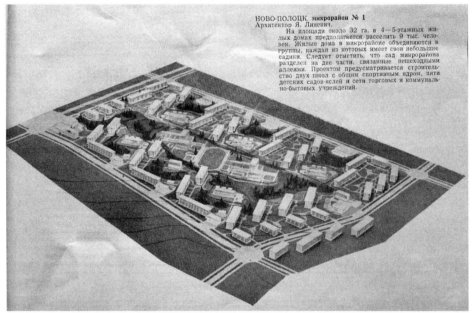

НОВО-ПОЛОЦК. микрорайон № 1
Архитектор Я. Линевич.
На площади около 32 га, в 4—5-этажных жи-лых домах предполагается расселить 9 тыс. чело-век. Жилые дома в микрорайоне объединяются в группы, каждая из которых имеет свои небольшие садики. Следует отметить, что сад микрорайона разделен на две части, связанные пешеходными аллеями. Проектом предусматривается строитель-ство двух школ с общим спортивным ядром, пяти детских садов-яслей и сети торговых и коммуналь-но-бытовых учреждений.

Source: "Zhilye raiony i progressivnye priemy zastroiki mikroraionov," *Arkhitektura SSSR*, no. 7 (1960): 9.

stead of apartments they designed so-called 'sleeping cabins.'"[19] The new mass housing of the Khrushchev period, predicated on the private, sepa-rate apartment, would not risk such excesses. Families would live in their own apartments with the most modern amenities and share communal spaces and facilities with their neighbors.

In claiming to reproduce the collectivist spirit of the past, *Trud* clari-fied the meaning of the communist way of life in ways that suggested additional, subtle revisions to the *dom-kommuna*'s original values. The new housing of the Khrushchev period would ensure that people "lived in one friendly collective according to the principle that a person is a friend, comrade, and brother to another, and not according to the principle—my house is my castle." Bringing this about, it was implied, no longer required the asceticism and collective regulation of everyday life of house communes from the past. All that was needed were well-designed apartment complexes with commercial services, gyms, cafeterias, and cafés so that people could enjoy "the maximum in conveniences and comfort."[20] In this formulation, the communist way of life meant a community whose members got along because the good fences of *separate* apartments made good neighbors and everyone enjoyed all the comforts and consumer items of modern urban life. The separate apartment would engender healthy family relations that expanded outward into harmonious social relations and a collectively shared desire to properly care for housing.

In *House of the Future* (1962), the Soviet architect Aleksandr Peremyslov similarly explored the emerging communist way of life by taking Soviet readers on a futuristic journey to a couple's separate apartment in a newly built microdistrict sometime in the very near but still indeterminate future or, as he put it, in "Moscow, the year 196 . . . ." The microdistrict Peremyslov visited along with a philosophy professor was a harbinger of the communist way of life, where public spaces took pride of place in socializing the new Soviet person. Upon entering the neighborhood, Peremyslov and the philosopher encountered a multitude of vibrant public facilities, including a stadium, club, swimming pool, open-air theater, and greenhouses. The privileging of public over private spaces followed the two men as they entered the building of the couple whose apartment they had come to visit. A café, the building's maintenance office, a drop-off for laundry, and various vending machines greeted them on the first floor. A quick elevator ride brought them to the eighth floor, where each wing featured a common area bedecked with wild grapes. Peremyslov and the philosopher found the couple, Gennadii and Galina, with one of their two children, Lidochka, in the single-family apartment they had "received" (i.e., as a public good, not privately owned property). Their modest two-room apartment featured space-saving and multiuse furniture that contributed to their home's "good taste and great culture." Even though it was a separate apartment, the family's home remained an organic part of the greater, public whole. "Our apartment," Gennadii explained, "isn't just two rooms, an entrance, and a bathroom, but also Lidochka's place at child care, a regular table in the dining hall of the cafeteria, etcetera."

In short, Galina explained, their home comprised their building and the entire microdistrict where their son Andriushka lived in a boarding school. In this expansive definition of home, the private was not divided from the public, but intertwined along a harmonious continuum of well-designed and complementary spaces. In a similar fashion, the microdistrict was situated in a harmonious balance next to a virgin forest, thereby suggesting that the war between town and country, nature and built environment, was finally over.[21]

In framing this view of the future, Peremyslov drew from the Soviet past in a way that revealed the unintended meanings that could surface in defining the communist way of life. Before traveling to the city's outskirts, Peremyslov asked the reader to imagine the bustling downtown of the socialist metropolis at the end of the workday and behold the recently completed Palace of Soviets. This architectural masterpiece of "monumental art" and grand halls served ordinary people with "the most favorable conditions for work and leisure." It fulfilled at last the vision that Sergei Kirov had assigned the project in 1922: as a building that would expand the minds of workers and peasants, and stand as a "triumph of communism." The philosophy professor helpfully explained for readers what this building represented: "A person in the Palace of Soviets already feels as though he lives under communism. You architects need to strive to spread such a feeling to all new buildings, to everything which you have yet to create." The Palace of Soviets, Peremyslov surmised, was the perfect semaphore for introducing readers to the communist way of life in whatever microdistrict and separate apartment they would soon inhabit. By referring to the Palace of Soviets, Peremyslov located the origins of this lifestyle in the unfulfilled dreams of Bolshevik visionaries, which Stalin's regime had impeded along with this particular building. By mentioning Kirov, he let his readers know that the Palace of Soviets was the true embodiment of communism as foreseen by those Bolsheviks who had offered the correct alternative to Stalin. Echoing Ladinskii, Peremyslov was incredibly confident that all three projects—the Palace of Soviets, mass housing, and communism—would soon be achieved.[22]

But it was Grishmanov's fears about mismanaging public perceptions of grand social programs that came true instead. The Palace of Soviets was never completed, and it thus became the symbol of a system that was unable to realize its monumental visions for the future. Serious discussions about the project had actually ceased two years before Peremyslov's book was published in 1962, and the original site had already been converted into a swimming pool.[23] In retrospect, it is easy to see Peremyslov's decision to invoke this unfinished building as a terrible way to begin a popular book about "the house of the future as one of the most important aspects of the communist reconstruction of everyday life."[24] But at the time, when the Soviet Union was surging ahead of the world in space travel, it still made sense to invoke this well-known, if unfinished, project to introduce mass housing as an equally grandiose endeavor to transform people's everyday lives. Peremyslov's unfortunate choice showed that incorporating symbols from the Soviet past in visions of the communist future was a delicate game. The *dom-kommuna*, as the newspaper article "The House of Tomorrow" illustrated, provided with only minor modifications a usable past upon which to build the proper communist credentials of Khrushchev's mass housing. The Palace of Soviets, as Peremyslov must have later realized, was much more problematic.

Communal apartments proved to be another ambiguous legacy for ideologues seeking to define the communist way of life by referring to the Soviet past. According to most mass media representations, the more quickly people moved out of communal apartments and the state prevented communalization of new separate apartments the better. But according to other media reports, the communal apartment could equally be read as symbolizing nostalgia for a way of life that was soon disappearing and as a warning against effusive praise for the separate apartment's privacy and tendency to isolate residents from the socialist whole. As scholars have shown, the privacy and autonomy promised by the separate apartment were checked by the regime's insistence that they not detract from, but rather complement, the creation of a socialist community of good citizens and responsible consumers.[25] The communal apartment was the perfect setting familiar to all urban residents where such a lesson could be taught.[26]

In 1961, for example, *Leningradskaia pravda* chronicled the transformation of communal apartments into paragons of the communist way of life. In some ways, this meant that neighbors had learned to get along: "Noble feelings of comradeship, mutual assistance, and friendship have strengthened; work with children has sharply improved; apartment squabbles have disappeared." The newspaper sang the praises of collectivism and foresaw the erasure of the petty individualism that evoked dysfunctional communal apartments: "Extra mailboxes and doorbells, and 'individual' electric lamps in common spaces are disappearing." Reformed communal apartment neighbors "forgo their personal telephones, add their own personal books to the house libraries, and exhibit for common viewing the collections of rare coins and stamps which they have collected over years and decades."[27] While praising such collectivist spirit, the newspaper did not represent it as a harbinger of the family's withering away as utopian visionaries had done in the 1920s. As we saw in chapter 1, Stalin's regime had quashed such visions, and Khrushchev never revived them. Nevertheless, healthy communal apartments provided the setting for indirect critiques of excessively private lifestyles in separate apartments.

A local "competition" in which communal apartment residents engaged in the "struggle for the communist way of life" further illustrates this point. The competition was featured in a housing and urban affairs journal in 1961, and thus it was placed in the larger context of building communism: "Brigades, construction sites, and entire cities keep the path to communism. *Only everyday life hides as before from public opinion behind a solidly closed door.* And then the idea was born—to draft residents into competing for a new, communist way of life" (emphasis added). Such a claim echoed the heady days of the *dom-kommuna*, with its ominous threats to tear down the public/private divide allegedly impeding the path to the new way of life. The successful competitors were those who shed the outward signs of a dysfunctional communal apartment and transformed themselves into collectives that thrived on the values of communal identity, equality, and sharing: "Under the doorbell, instead of a long list, hangs a small list: '*For all residents ring once.*' A small table has appeared in the hallway on which there is a new telephone. Previously it had belonged to one person" (emphasis in the original). Even their kitchen had undergone a significant makeover: "All the tables are covered with the same oil-cloths. Matches, salt, soda, household soap and a small broom have been turned over for common use."[28]

Although some accounts critiqued yearnings for privacy that lacked socialist consciousness, others unabashedly claimed privacy to be precisely what ordinary residents thought was the *khrushchevka*'s greatest advantage. Playing the privacy card was especially useful when newspapers had to explain to people why their apartments were so small and oddly designed, but still superior to the communal apartment. In a 1956 *Izvestiia* article, Peremyslov, who later wrote *House of the Future*, explained as architects had done since the 1930s that apartments had to be small to avoid communal settlement. Despite their small size, such apartments provided people with "advantages in everyday life" that were "incontrovertible." Describing her family's separate apartment, one housewife told Peremyslov, "I, for example, can arrange my day, my many tasks by my own discretion. It's not necessary to tune yourself to somebody's order and frequently to somebody's mood, like in the communal apartment where we lived previously." Such was the autonomy that the separate apartment promised every family lucky enough to get one, but only as long as it remained separate upon distribution.[29]

Even large families preferred small apartments as long as they were separate. Peremyslov described a factory worker about to retire and his three-generation family of eight—he and his wife, their two daughters, one with a husband and three children—that had moved into a separate apartment. These individuals had gained greater control over their daily lives and could do at home what they wanted, when they wanted. "Each [family member] can rest after the workday as he likes: If you want—sit and watch television in the living room, if you want— lie down, read something in your bedroom." Peremyslov's article told readers that single-family occupancy was worthwhile, but would come at a cost in size, especially in the near future. As the son-in-law in the family of eight that lived in the separate apartment explained, "We're eight, it's kind of tight, but we live amicably, peacefully, like human beings. They should only build houses like ours."[30]

As for new apartments that nonetheless became communal, other press accounts tried to put them in the best possible light by claiming that their neighbors got along well, practically like a family. In 1959, *Leningradskaia pravda* featured a cheerful testimonial from a resident who cast her healthy communal apartment in the likeness of a family living in a separate apartment. Rather than simply aping the separate apartment in a desperate attempt to make a bad situation look good, this testimonial could also be read as a celebration of values that every family was supposed to have, but risked losing by living in a separate apartment. Whereas Peremyslov championed autonomy in separate apartments to the point of making it sound like individualism and atomization—"I, for example, can arrange my day, my many tasks by my own discretion" and "if you want, lie down, read something in your bedroom"—this communal apartment testimonial celebrated the sharing, reciprocity, and openness to newcomers that allowed a community of strangers to create tight family-like bonds out of their everyday lives.[31]

In her testimonial, the resident G. Leonova explained that she lived on Novostroek Street in a communal apartment with the names of three families posted on the door. The street name, meaning "street of newly constructed buildings," and the location of this house among the new housing estates of the Kirov district near the Kirov factory complex strongly suggest that her home was a newly built apartment, which had been communalized. "But, when you come here," she insisted, "it seems that not three families live here, but one." This communal apartment's social life was a hybrid of neighborly and family relations. One family's guest was everyone's guest: "He [a guest] praises the tasty dishes, but it will never occur to him that today Nina Vasil'evna [Pokrusheva] baked the small pies, and that Aleksandra Nikitichna [Gavrilova] prepared the jellied meat." What normally separated communal apartment neighbors brought them together here: "We often sit around at the table here. Any family celebration is marked as a common one for all the residents." In preparation for the Pokrushev daughter's wedding, her apartment neighbors purchased the fabric for a wedding dress, and this was considered "a collective gift to the bride." The groom, Sasha Ivanov, who eventually moved into the apartment, received a silk shirt and tie (presumably also as a gift). The neighbors even helped get him a coat, which revealed this apartment's system of reciprocity: "The Pokrushevs were short of money, but Sasha has not succeeded 'to catch on' properly. This [obtaining a coat] is already not a gift, but, as it's said, credit from neighbors."[32] Leonova's tale was not a sad attempt by the newspaper to put a happy face on the unfortunate communalization of a separate apartment. Her testimonial reminded readers in almost nostalgic terms of their social obligations and communal values lest they revel too much in the privacy of their separate apartments.

Creating Community

In contrast to Peremyslov's visions of pristine microdistricts in *House of the Future*, most residents of the separate apartment moved into new neighborhoods that were a work in progress, as illustrated in Yuri Pimenov's painting *Wedding on Tomorrow Street* (1962), shown in figure I.2 above and on this book's cover. Factories and government institutions built individual apartment buildings for their workers and employees wherever possible, with little attention to neighborhood planning and coordination with local soviets.

In the worst-case scenarios, buildings sprouted up in areas with hardly any infrastructure, public transportation, or access to stores and social services. Unpaved and unlit streets aggravated residents who struggled to find their homes in a sea of similarly designed buildings. Instead of waiting patiently for their apartments and neighborhoods to be fully built and inspected, residents pressured local authorities to let them move in as soon as possible, while others simply squatted illegally in unfinished buildings. The open spaces between apartment houses became empty voids lacking the planned recreational or leisure facilities of a microdistrict's design. Parking and garages were nowhere to be found, forcing car owners to build makeshift garages or leave their cars wherever possible to the great chagrin of their carless neighbors.

The gap between the ideal design of new residential districts and their realities made residents' lives difficult and exposed serious shortcomings in the mass housing campaign. The same gap, I argue, also provided ordinary residents with the necessary space to shape their new communities in ways that had been unforeseen by urban planners, but were not necessarily at odds with the broad ideological vision of building Communism on Tomorrow Street. In the new neighborhoods of the Khrushchev era, "state" and "society" overlapped to constitute the mass housing community in ways that saw residents try to make the architecture, rhetoric, and institutions of the state function as intended. Ordinary residents also acted where the state seemed absent to transform uninhabited and poorly designed spaces into viable communities.

Next to the glowing reports on what life would be like, the Soviet mass media chronicled the shortcomings residents faced in creating a new way of life in mass housing estates.[33] To resolve problems ranging from neighborhood upkeep to hooliganism, Khrushchev's regime bolstered neighborhood "social organizations," such as parents' committees and the more ominous comradely courts and foot patrols (*druzhiny*), which acted as the ground-level organs of municipal government. It did so for practical reasons, such as the lack of resources, but also for the ideological imperatives of constructing communism, whereby the people would progressively take over the functions of the state.[34] As both officeholders in social organizations and residents of new housing, these individuals operated at the very intersection of "state" and "society" in their local communities. For example, two individuals in Leningrad's Kirov district spoke as both residents and members of their local "assistance commission" when they complained about the lack of public spaces for children at a neighborhood meeting in December 1953. Recent construction had changed the face of the neighborhood in ways that disoriented the community. "Before the war," one explained, "it was possible to set up playgrounds, but now they've partitioned everything off, poured asphalt all over. Now you can only walk in courtyards, whereas kids can't run anywhere."[35] A resident of Leningrad's Moscow district, who happened to be head of a local kindergarten, made a similar complaint at a neighborhood meeting of 235 residents in 1957: "In order to exclude the possibility of infection among children, we need an isolated playground for children of the kindergarten to walk around in."[36]

Anecdotal evidence suggests that residents of buildings with communal apartments enacted, perhaps more strongly than residents of separate apartments, the seamless continuum between home and community valued in the discourse on the communist way of life. A meeting in 1957 of 63 residents from a building at 182 Moskovskii Prospekt in Leningrad revealed that creating community was rooted in people's experience of learning to live together in communal apartments. A resident, reporting on what their social assistance commission had done since late 1955, noted neighbors' complaints about "violations of rules on living together in communal apartments" and how the commission worked with communal apartment heads to carry out repair work. One apartment head complained that the commission had not done enough to help resolve problems that communal apartments could not fix on their own. Citing his own communal apartment, he first proudly noted, "We resolve all of our inner-apartment questions at the apartment's general assembly of residents." One of their neighbors, however, decided he would pay less for gas in violation of what was agreed upon at the apartment's general assembly. "If all residents are going to do their own thing," the apartment leader warned, "things will go badly." Their neighbor reportedly laughed at the assembly's next meeting, and for good reason. The commission had failed to answer their request from several months ago for help in this matter and, as a consequence, had only "assisted the misbehaving individual."[37]

At 182 Moskovskii Prospekt, social organizations existed on a continuum of community organization that began in a communal apartment and extended outward to the building, street, and residential area.[38] When problems could not be resolved at one level, residents expected the next-highest authority in the community to step in and reestablish order. Under Khrushchev, engaged residents not only looked to social organizations to put pressure on neighbors unwilling to pay for gas; as the historian Miriam Dobson has shown, they also joined *druzhiny* and comradely courts, created by the state, to police the neighborhood for public drunkenness, violence, and even behavior simply deemed to be "antisocial."[39] For example, at a meeting of fifty-two residents from a microdistrict in Leningrad's Moscow district sometime in the late 1950s, a resident and head of the area's local soviet housing office explained how community members combated hooligans and drunkards, and even simple loafers, by participating in parents' committees, house committees, and comradely courts.[40] In reference to the state's support for such involvement, a certain Metskevich stressed the "new edicts about responsibility for minor hooliganism and beefing up the struggle against those who shy away from socially useful work and carry on an antisocial and parasitical way of life, drunkards, and so on." In response, he called on his community to create a *druzhina*. Metskevich stressed that only "honest and exemplary comrades" would serve on its patrols.[41] Social organizations thus not only enabled residents to constitute a community but also helped identify its internal divisions spanning the self-proclaimed best citizens to those they sought to marginalize.

In addition to social organizations, the discourse on the communist way life proved to be a valuable tool that residents could wield in blaming local housing officials for deficiencies in construction. In 1961, a family living on Tipanova Street in Leningrad's Moscow district seemed only capable of angering neighbors and local housing officials because of water leaking out of their apartment. The Versov family, as they were called, consisted of an elderly couple, their daughter, and two grandsons. They had moved into their new apartment the year before and had constantly run afoul of the local housing office's chief engineer, Volodarets, and the technician-constructor, Sergeeva. According to an acquaintance, a certain G. Aron, who wrote to the head of the Moscow district soviet on the family's behalf, these two officials generally blamed residents for everything:

> These workers got it into their heads that things don't break down
> in new houses; if something happens, it means the residents them-

selves are guilty, who only go on stubbornly in order to break [things] and maliciously take equipment away from a construction site. For them [Volodarets and Sergeeva] residents are an undifferentiated mass of malefactors and people who break the rules.[42]

If he had been speaking on behalf of these local officials, Aron might have argued that new housing did not break down so quickly on its own and that residents bore some responsibility. But like most letters of complaint, Aron was not interested in lower-level state officials' point of view and relished the opportunity to represent them as hapless rubes making the lives of upstanding citizens difficult. After all, the Versov household was full of good people, "neither hooligans, nor drunks-debauched types." Aron himself had been a Communist Party member since 1927 and a senior editor in the sciences at the city's branch office of the Academy of Sciences' publishing house. He sanctimoniously informed his readers, "My heart of an old Communist is filled with anger, and I raise my voice in defense of an honest Soviet family."[43]

Whoever was to blame, the Versov's apartment suffered especially from plumbing problems, such as moisture that leaked from their kitchen to the apartment below. The leak only required minor repairs, but Volodarets had evidently been unhelpful. Aron conceded that the bathroom floor became soaked whenever the Versov grandfather tried to take a bath in the inconveniently small bathtub, but Volodarets accused the Versovs of doing this deliberately and their downstairs neighbor launched his own abuse on the family. "The Versov family is literally terrorized," Aron lamented. "Recently the household head from Apt. 24, V. P. Koliado, a young, healthy man, stormed into their apartment and threatened the Versovs to come with a crowbar and destroy the entire bathroom. Now the Versovs are afraid to use their bathroom." To further emphasize this injustice, Aron insisted that the Versovs adhered to the tenets of the "communist way of life," whereas the housing officials did not.[44]

In his defense of the Versovs, Aron emphasized that they were part of their house's "competition for the title of house of the communist way of life" and that, "having signed this contract, they indeed live and work in a communist way." This distinguished the Versov family from the mean-spirited local housing authorities: "Instead of assisting in every way with the introduction of the communist way of life, these gravediggers deprive people of the elementary comforts of life: plumbing, light, water, a bathroom." Aron was using the "communist way of life" not in a cynical manner, but rather in much the same way that Khrushchev and the mass media employed the term. The Versovs were just good people who wanted to enjoy their new separate apartment, keep it in good repair, and have good neighborly relations, and they were willing to participate in community affairs. The "communist way of life" should mean in practice a fully functioning, modern, single-family apartment, and local officials who failed to maintain housing stood in the way of communism itself. If anyone had to change their behavior, it was the local housing officials, not the Versovs. Aron concluded: "An especial keenness and even particular, sincere qualities are required of workers of housing offices, because if they are going to treat people like Volodarets and Sergeeva do, people's lives will be spoiled."[45]

As the Versovs's story suggests, neighbors sometimes turned on each other when problems with mass housing arose. Neighborhood meetings afforded residents a public forum to criticize one another's parenting skills and simultaneously bond as a community over fears that outside elements had entered their collective space and corrupted their children. In April 1959, a meeting of sixty residents living in Leningrad's Moscow district illustrated how residents could blame their fellow neighbors for children's misbehavior. A certain Potanova lamented, "In the courtyards and the children's playgrounds of houses No. 148-150, the children behave themselves very badly, fight, break equipment, but parents pay no attention whatsoever. The parents' committee needs to work among parents with respect to the conduct of children outside the house." Vasil'ev, a resident and chair of the meeting, similarly noted, "Nobody watches after children, the children act like hooligans, ruin trees and plants and the grass, ring apartment door bells and so on." Suggesting that stairwells were sometimes used for sexual encounters, he continued, "In the stairs of houses, strangers drink wine, sometimes spend the night, and bring young ladies." He reminded his neighbors "to close the entranceway door at night" and then noted the absence of any "cultural-mass work," which he seemed to suggest might prevent such illicit behavior. But some of his neighbors apparently had other priorities for common spaces. A dog-breeding club occupied the only space they had for a "red corner" (i.e., the common space in a residential house or workplace reserved for "cultural-mass work").[46]

As the existence of a dog-breeding club suggests, fixing problems and weeding out the bad elements of the neighborhood were not the only basis for creating community. In reading the minutes of residential meetings, we must keep in mind that the nature of such meetings and the self-selection bias of those present tended to highlight problems instead of successes. The community at 182 Moskovskii Prospekt, however, shed light on the everyday improvements its social assistance commission had made instead of only dwelling on the problems it faced. Television, normally a force that isolates people from one another, united these residents primarily because there appeared to be only one TV set for the entire community. The resident reporting on the commission's work explained that "the viewing of television programs has been set up for residents and children, and someone is put on duty for this everyday." For the past two years, the commission had set up an ice skating rink in the neighborhood and provided for a children's playground. It had teamed up with the parents' committee to organize an unspecified "contest on the ice," as well as a "performance of figure skaters." And it had put together three tours around the city for residents and one out-of-town trip for children. A sewing circle had been set up for interested residents, and the parents' committee had established the group "Capable Hands" made up of children referred to as "Timurovites" (*deti-timurovtsy*), suggesting that its purpose was to lend assistance to elderly residents and war invalids.[47]

Although some residents hoped to use social organizations to rid their communities of individuals engaging in antisocial behavior, others focused on the lack or misuse of recreational spaces in new neighborhoods as the cause of such behavior. At a 1962 meeting of local housing officials and residents in the Vyborg district of Leningrad, a housing committee chairman, Maslennikov, highlighted the issue in his lengthy speech on the many problems of the newly built Lanskii microdistrict. He faulted the neighborhood's designers for not including a club in the microdistrict or reserving 40 square meters of building space for red corners in apartment buildings. "Is it necessary to show," he asked, "how critically the question with child neglect and criminality stands? Do we really not see on a daily basis the loafing herds of 7 to 8, and sometimes 15 to 17 persons, teenagers, idlers, sometimes hooligans?" Maslennikov was sure that a connection existed between the lack of well-regulated public spaces and antisocial behavior. He claimed that their district had seen a higher than average number of such persons arrested by the police.[48]

Another problem was that some neighbors appropriated spaces for their own purposes. Pointing to two lots suitable for volleyball and basketball, he noted, "Mothers and children of all ages naturally gravitate toward these courtyards and the lots became children's playgrounds all by themselves instead of sports lots." Another courtyard had been originally designed as a square, although some people had wanted to transform it into a sports lot, which Maslennikov claimed had "led to a serious quarrel."[49]

As this example indicated, even if urban planners included a clearly demarcated area for recreation, residents' everyday use of such spaces played an equal, if not more important role, in determining its actual function. Likewise, municipal authorities could repurpose existing neighborhood spaces to residents' great chagrin. In a letter to *Trud* published in 1966, a crane operator named Zhigarev from a metallurgical factory in Cherepovets complained about the loss of a sports lot in a neighborhood that had been built up since 1950. "It occupied an honorable place among the residents," he remembered fondly. "It was always full of people here." But the city's chief architect had decided in 1961 to build a kindergarten on the lot. "Good, of course," Zhigarev continued, "but why did they forget about those who like to exercise?" He also complained that other residents monopolized the district's one tennis court for gambling: "Here from morning to late in the evening they shuffle cards, dominos clatter, old and young residents from these places play for money all day long." A small park, which metallurgists had set up "by their own hands, in free time away from work," and was suitable for sports, suffered a similar fate. "But here dominos also reign," Zhigarev continued. "The large pavilion is full. Fifty well-built guys stand at ten small tables." The metallurgists' offer to use the space for basketball or tennis fell on deaf ears among the domino players. Encouraging sports, Zhigarev concluded, came to nothing if there was no place in residential areas reserved for it and little equipment available through one's house committee or children's clubs.[50]

The lack of properly organized social spaces concerned residents when undesirable elements monopolized the empty spaces of a neighborhood. In a letter published in *Trud* in 1966, a Leningrader named Usanov complained that his five-year-old microdistrict on the outskirts of town had "neither a movie theater, nor a theater, nor a cafe, nor a stadium." He contrasted his microdistrict with what one normally thought of as Leningrad, with its "theaters and museums, gardens and parks." Compounding this spatial and cultural rupture between the older and newer parts of town was the fact that going downtown for recreation or entertainment was made difficult by the hour-long commute. This left residents with two options at the end of the work day: "Either sit at home or go to the 'casino'—this is what they call a table and two benches in our courtyard, dug into the ground right near a children's playground." The "lovers of 'kozel,' card players," became a public nuisance. "It's good, if an evening at the 'casino' ends without drunken singing, without police whistles. More often it's the opposite."[51] "Nature, as is well known, does not tolerate emptiness," a reporter added. "And therefore it is not surprising that in new housing estates the notorious 'casinos', about which comrade Usanov writes, grow like poisonous mushrooms after rain."[52] As *Trud*'s reporting suggested, the Soviet mass housing estate was not the paragon of the communist way of life; but neither was it a concrete wasteland lacking in any meaningful human interaction. By playing dominos or setting up a casino, people were creating a community, albeit an illicit one, around a shared activity in urban spaces they had appropriated.

Squatters' Rights

In theory, the distribution of housing was supposed to be a well-organized affair. But in practice, the allocation of space and its effects on organizing the mass housing community were messy. Instead of patiently waiting their turn, some residents rushed to get into their separate apartments before construction was even complete or the local inspection commission had approved their building for habitation. Other residents squatted in new apartment buildings that had not been allocated to them. Still others squatted on unused land and built their own housing, hoping that local authorities would eventually accept their houses as much-needed additions to a scarce housing stock.

Residents who squatted in apartments or on land preempted the rational planning and distribution of new housing estates and exposed the weakness of state authorities to control the allocation of housing and land plots. Residents defied the law, but then just as quickly called upon the government to secure their rights to their newly acquired space or land. Although squatters exploited breakdowns in administrative order, their actions typically did not lead to a breakdown in social order or the violence of a mob taking unclaimed or unprotected property, as had occurred with the mass expropriations of private property in the wake of the October Revolution. At times, squatting was even an organized affair that constituted microcommunities of residents banning together to secure a building and fend off the authorities. In its own, rather extreme way, squatting provides us with another window onto the ways Soviet residents created community in and around the new mass housing estates of the Khrushchev era.

The Soviet leadership was keenly aware of squatting and the related problem of settling housing too early. In 1954, a government inquiry linked squatting in apartments (*samovol'noe zaselenie*) to poor and unfinished construction. Squatters took buildings before they were completed and inspected by local building commissions. New neighborhoods suffered from incompletely built water and sewer lines, unfinished roads, and unfinished hot water lines for heat. Although Pimenov managed to turn such scenes into the setting for his iconic painting of the mass housing campaign, *Wedding on Tomorrow Street*, they remained a colossal headache for local authorities and a ripe target for squatters. Rather than evict them, local soviets often registered squatters as rightful residents. In 1953, the Molotov (Perm) city soviet retroactively approved the settlement of eighty-eight unfinished buildings that squatters had taken. It approved for settlement another forty-three unfinished buildings, which presumably went to their designated residents. In Vladimir, Voronezh, and Syktyvkar, the city soviets settled unfinished housing that had not passed inspection and already needed to be fixed.[53]

Vladimir Kucherenko and Ivan Grishmanov, the Communist Party's point men on new housing construction, similarly linked squatting to poorly built housing and insufficient infrastructure in a 1956 report to their superiors. They concluded, "What is absolutely intolerable is the widespread practice of settling residential buildings with defects, as well as squatters settling in them." In Belorussia in 1955, city soviets allowed squatters to take sixty unfinished buildings that had failed inspection. In Lvov, while the city soviet's chairman was unsuccessfully pressuring inspectors to approve a new building destined for metal workers, squatters had stealthily moved in.[54] Such reports projected an image of new neighborhoods as landscapes of incomplete and already dilapidated housing, which local officials had rushed to settle in order to house people as quickly as possible, even if that meant condoning squatters.

Squatting represented the thin edge of people's desperate desire for better housing and the broader crisis of rising expectations that new housing construction was already stoking even before Khrushchev's regime greatly expanded it in 1957. Instead of brutally cracking down on squatters and sending them to the Gulag, as the Stalinist regime had done to citizens who stole property,[55] Khrushchev's regime handled squatting more calmly by exhorting local soviets to stop the practice and by improving the quality of housing construction that had made unfinished apartment buildings ripe targets for squatters.[56] Ultimately, the Soviet leadership under Khrushchev focused on what Stalin's regime never did: building enough housing. With reports on widespread squatting and early settlements arriving on the desks of top party leaders in the mid-1950s, squatting and its underlying causes likely contributed to the leadership's decision to launch its comprehensive mass housing program in July 1957.[57] To be sure, a boost in housing construction might temporarily lead to even rasher actions by residents desperate to obtain better housing immediately. But in the long run, Khrushchev's regime evidently concluded, sufficient new housing (instead of a violent crackdown) would surely eliminate the main cause of desperate action among residents once more of them enjoyed the modern amenities of mass housing. Such was the formula, in the post-Stalin era, for eliminating apartment squatters and ensuring civil order in the housing distribution process. Dealing with the related problem of squatters taking land to build their own housing proved to be a more complex matter.

According to the Ministry of the Communal Economy (Ministerstvo Kommunal'nogo Khoziaistva), "unauthorized builders" (*samovol'nye zastroishchiki*) were hard at work in the mid-1950s, colonizing empty plots in such cities as Kuibyshev, Saratov, Krasnodar, Sochi, and Stalingrad, and also in the Moscow and Kalinin oblasts. Local authorities failed to pursue criminal cases against these scofflaws and did not follow up on threats to raze their illegally built homes. Not only did the builders "use the absence of control" to construct their homes on empty plots of land, but they even had the gumption to ask local people's courts to register their homes as personal property. Meanwhile, local authorities did not bother to show up in court to contest these petitions and failed to file appeals. Particularly irksome were unauthorized builders' clever use of "documents," which they and the people to whom they sold their houses effectively wielded, thereby "creat[ing] the appearance of legality" and providing them with leverage when they complained about threats to have their homes razed. In short, these squatters played the state every step of the way to get what they wanted and benefited from local authorities that had little intention or incentive to stop them. In response, in early 1954 the Ministry of the Communal Economy proposed a series of measures to crack down on these intrepid squatters, raze their homes, and punish those local authorities that failed to stop them.[58]

The Ministry of Internal Affairs (Ministerstvo Vnutrennikh Del, MVD) for the USSR, however, weighed in with a more conciliatory approach in May 1954. Even though local soviets had done nothing to evict these squatters, the police still had to do its job of keeping track of the population through residency permits. Under a 1940 law, the police were prohibited from issuing residency permits to those who lived in illegally built housing. The MVD now argued that this particular provision of the law was not working as a deterrent and remained "unfulfilled," a not so subtle admission that the police were already issuing residency permits to illegal house builders. The MVD insisted for good measure that such permits technically did not bestow property rights on those who lived in such housing.[59] But extending them would surely give such residents yet another "document" to wield at authorities that threatened to raze their housing.

In fact, the MVD admitted as much by suggesting an amnesty for all people who had been living in illegally built housing before May 1, 1954.[60] This was a May Day present, as it were, from the Soviet Union's internal police to all illegal builders. When the government revised the 1940 law, it went further by eliminating any cutoff date after which an illegal builder could not be registered. It exhorted all relevant government bodies to beef up the "struggle with unauthorized construction."[61] In doing so, Khrushchev's regime chose preventive measures over physical eviction and arrest. In a 1955 decree, the state went even further in its tolerance of unauthorized builders. Instead of threatening them with demolition, it sought to tax them heavily. Local soviets were asked once again to prevent unauthorized construction, but now they were also supposed to gather accurate data on the houses that unauthorized builders constructed.[62] Evidently, the state hoped to use this information to tax them more effectively and find out how much new housing was being built. Khrushchev's regime had taken a pragmatic and civil approach to illegal builders that might bring extra money into state coffers and more living space to the population.

Anecdotal evidence of squatting in new housing sheds additional light on what squatters hoped to gain and what brought them together as a community, as well as the government's civil approach to dealing with them. The incident involving 131 housing sector workers and their families in Moscow, with which this book began, was a striking example of a community that took matters into their own hands in a desperate attempt to obtain housing. Whereas the MVD in that case was eager to brush it off as a local matter, another incident suggests that squatting could attain potentially subversive political meanings that had to be immediately contained.

In late 1962, the KGB got involved in a case of eight workers and their families who had squatted in a new building with eight apartments in the town of Dankov in Lipetsk oblast. The KGB discovered that the squatters in this case were not only motivated by a desire for better housing but had also taken what they considered to be the legitimate fruits of their labor. In exchange for "helping in [their] free time on the construction of the building," the eight families had been promised space in it by the construction organization conducting the work. But before the housing permits were issued, new management arrived at the construction organization. The permits were awarded to another set of workers and their families, thereby breaking the initial agreement. The original eight workers and their families thereupon occupied the building, but were soon visited by the families who had received the housing permits from the new management. These families tried and failed to evict the squatters, and the police were similarly unable to make them leave.[63]

The KGB was fairly uninterested in resolving what had essentially been a breach of an oral agreement between workers and management. This amounted to a failed people's construction project three years after the government had already eliminated the movement, as we saw in chapter 4. What had drawn the KGB's attention was the prospect that this local affair might spin out of control. The attempted eviction drew about two or three hundred residents from the local community. Their harassment of the police and "hooligan and politically unhealthy cries" provoked the KGB to dispatch its officers to the area "for the prevention of possible mass disorders."[64]

The KGB had good reason to fear such an escalation. As Vladimir Kozlov has shown, mass disorders occurred under Khrushchev for reasons ranging from ethnic tensions and discontent with life in the Red Army to poor living conditions and negative popular reactions to Khrushchev's denunciation of Stalin at the Twentieth Communist Party Congress. In many cases, the police themselves became the target of violent mobs, which apparently was on the KGB's mind as it observed the events in Dankov. Having recently dealt with the mass disorders in Novocherkassk in June, the KGB was evidently taking no chances that similar events would escalate elsewhere.[65] KGB chief Vladimir Semichastnyi briefed the Central Committee on events in Dankov and reassured his superiors that the situation was under control.[66]

Although events did not spin out of control and the KGB subsequently lost interest, party officials were left trying to fix what had happened. The party's Central Committee and the Lipetsk obkom (oblast party committee) followed up on the KGB's report with a few corrections. Their detailed investigations found that the apartment building in question was originally to have been constructed for the chemical factory by a construction organization, Otdelstroi No. 1. The managements of Otdelstroi No. 1 and the chemical factory struck a deal "by oral agreement," whereby four apartments would be set aside for the workers of the construction organization if the project was completed by a certain deadline.[67] Deprived of the rhetorical and legal legitimacy that had buoyed people's construction in the past, the players in the Dankov case were operating in the precarious gray area of housing's second economy. The remaining four apartments in their deal would presumably stay in the possession of the chemical factory. Once the deadline passed without completion of the building, the chemical factory balked. Upon learning that the factory would not turn over the four apartments, four Otdelstroi No. 1 workers (not eight) squatted in the building with their families late at night in early November. Four families from the chemical factory likewise squatted in the building at the same time.[68] According to the Central Committee's investigation, "The construction workers say they took their illegal actions because the promises to give them living space in this house were not carried out, and the factory workers—because of difficult housing conditions."[69]

As the squatters settled in, Dankov construction officials secured the district procurator's approval to evict them, but attempts to do so failed.[70] The chemical factory then took a more confrontational approach. In the first week of December, its management issued housing permits to eight of its workers and took them to the apartment building to remove the squatters, presumably by force. But the squatters were saved by their neighbors. Approximately 50 to 70 residents (not 200 to 300) descended upon the scene; some of these neighbors stepped in to block the eviction. The following day the chemical factory turned off the squatters' water, heat, and electricity in a final effort to push them out. But the squatters also won this round by appealing to the Lipetsk obkom, which restored the utilities two days later.[71] Ultimately, the Lipetsk obkom reprimanded the factory's and construction organization's managements and ordered them to "carefully deal with each family, living in the eight-apartment building, to decide the question of each family's accommodation, and to report on January 10 to the obkom bureau on measures taken."[72] Although it was unclear who ultimately received the eight apartments in question, the obkom had demanded that the factory and construction organization make good on their original promises to the workers and provide them with some type of housing.

As a window onto the creation of a Soviet neighborhood, the Dankov affair showed how squatters could suddenly expose for a local community the machinations and personal sacrifices that lay behind new housing. Squatters revealed uncomfortable truths about the winners and losers in the creation of new mass housing communities. The case of the 131 Muscovite workers employed in the mass housing sector exposed the exploitation of those whose labor made such housing possible but were excluded from enjoying it themselves. These and other squatters magnified the desperate desire among all Soviet citizens to obtain a separate apartment and not be left behind in overcrowded communal housing. The deeper Khrushchev's regime committed itself to resolving the housing question for all, the more it raised citizens' expectations that everyone really should get a separate apartment now and not in the far off future. Squatters also revealed the ability of those excluded from new mass housing to form their own communities, through the workplace and where they currently lived, and put their dependence and trust in one another on the line in collective action.

Squatters of all stripes and overly eager residents rushing to get into their separate apartments exposed weak points in the state's local administrative control over housing and land, along with its willingness to take a conciliatory and pragmatic approach when dealing with them. These ordinary residents' actions showed that the path from the construction of new housing to its settlement to the creation of a community was not always smooth, but overlapped in ways that complicated everyday life, bound local residents together or divided them, and compelled local authorities to work with residents to find local solutions to local problems. In the ideal world of urban planning and propaganda on new housing estates, these stages—construction, distribution of apartments, creating community—occurred separately. But in real life, their overlapping was a critical part of what residents found when they arrived in new microdistricts to begin living the communist way of life.

By making these messy circumstances the backdrop to his painting *Wedding on Tomorrow Street*, Pimenov offered in many ways a more realistic impression of new neighborhoods than such works as Peremyslov's *House of the Future*. In his painting, the community came together to witness the union of a newly married couple eager to begin a new life together. Rather than impede their progress, the incompletely built neighborhood reinforced the notion that their life together in the community was a work in progress that the state had made possible, but which they and their neighbors would have to complete.

Getting around Town

In addition to unfinished apartment buildings like those depicted in Pimenov's painting, new mass housing neighborhoods often lacked public transportation and buildings for commercial and cultural uses. Inadequate public transportation made getting to work or enjoying a night at the theater downtown particularly difficult for people now living on the outskirts. Citizens' letters of complaint exposed these structural deficiencies but also revealed how such problems drew residents together as a community.

In November 1963, for example, ten residents living in new housing on Prospekt Geroev in Leningrad's southwest Kirov district sent a letter to the city soviet chairman and the newspapers *Izvestiia* and *Leningradskaia pravda* about transportation problems. In their letter, signed "Workers of the Admiralty factory," the residents explained that only one bus served the area in the southern part of the district known as "Dachnoe," a name whose reference to country cottages reflected how far this neighborhood was from the city center. They estimated that six to seven hundred people tried to use this one bus route in the morning rush hour between 6 a.m. and 8:30 a.m., creating an unpleasant start to their daily routines. "There results a throng [of people], tears, mothers with children and so on." Bus drivers were uncooperative. Before too many people got on, they quickly shut the door and drove off and continued without stopping for more passengers straight to the Avtovo metro station. The individual writing the letter on behalf of his fellow workers estimated that four hours of his day were spent traveling between home and work.[73]

Four residents living on Grazhdanskii Prospekt in Leningrad's Vyborg district described similar problems and a collective consciousness centered on neighborhood life in a letter to *Izvestiia* in December 1964. They wrote, "Grazhdanskii Prospekt, seven o'clock in the morning. Lights turn on in the windows of apartment buildings. Residents of the new quarter get ready for work and each one, exactly each one, has one thought: will he succeed today to sit on the bus, leave on time, take the baby to day care or to school, and not be late for work?" A single bus route provided this area with access to the Lenin Square metro station. Residents were forced to wait for several full buses to pass before they could manage to get onto one. "The working day begins with the storming of bus doors, throngs [of people], arguments, a spoilt mood."[74]

The residents also complained that only light coming from people's apartments illuminated the broad expanses separating the apartment buildings of their microdistrict, which became dark once people turned in for the evening. "It would seem that especially now," the residents continued, "when all around everything isn't set up, construction goes on, foundation plots and trenches have been dug up, asphalted paths begin and break off at the most unexpected places, [that now] good lighting is needed. But no. We get by with the moon."[75] These residents justified their grievances to readers who, they feared, might otherwise take them to be superfluous or simply pass them off as difficulties to be resolved later with extended transportation routes. They continued,

It'll be like that, but in the future. But on Grazhdanskii Prospekt, in the area of new construction, people live now. Today they go to work, today they wait in the evenings for their children, running in the dark courtyards of the neighborhood, today they walk through dirt along the side.[76]

These residents lived on Tomorrow Street, but it was dark and fell far short of the fully developed microdistricts designed by architects and city planners.

Although such deficiencies brought some residents together, other problems risked dividing the mass housing community along new social lines. Residents who owned automobiles had an easier time getting around town than those who relied on public transportation, but they created new tensions within the community when it came time to park. Those who wanted a place to park their cars near their apartment buildings faced off against neighbors who found that automobiles unfairly occupied and ruined a neighborhood's public spaces. Similar to the separate apartment and furniture, the automobile became an item of mass consumption in the Khrushchev period and especially under Brezhnev.[77] Yet most residents of new housing districts did not own cars and found them to be an unwelcome presence in their everyday lives.[78]

Car owners thought differently and took their case to public forums on new mass housing. In a letter to the All-Union Conference of Constructors in December 1954—the same meeting where Khrushchev blasted architects for not designing cheaper, mass housing—a Muscovite by the name of Zhdanov outlined the troubles that "toiling-automobile drivers" (*trudiashchiesia-avtomobilisty*) had with residential parking. He accused city planners of failing to set aside space in new housing districts for single-automobile garages. Pointing to the downtown Kiev district, where he presumably lived, Zhdanov complained that existing garages were being displaced by new housing projects to areas several kilometers away "to uninhabited and unkempt grounds, where there is neither water, nor electricity, where it's impossible to drive through in all weather, and where it's not entirely safe to return from at night."[79] Zhdanov warned that automobile drivers would only increase in number and called for "large, well-organized public garages" to solve the parking problem. The second-best option, according to him, would be sufficient space for single-automobile garages within 500 to 1,000 meters of housing.[80]

Zhdanov's letter suggests a rather strong sense of identity among car owners, reinforced by their sense of being a minority discriminated against by uncaring city planners. Zhdanov complained that the Moscow city soviet's Department of Architectural Affairs neglected "the interests of toilers, owners of light motorcars." Like proponents of the cooperative we saw in chapter 4, Zhdanov grafted working-class labels such as "toiling" onto "automobile drivers" to cast their problems as a legitimate plight worthy of immediate action. Yet his examples of fellow car owners primarily included members of the Soviet intelligentsia: "workers of industry and transport, writers, doctors, artists, composers, performing artists, architects, engineers and technicians, academics."[81]

Publications and institutional support further encouraged car drivers' sense of themselves as a separate group. In the late 1950s, three journals were published for the automotive sector: *Automobile Transport* (*Avtomobil'nyi transport*), *At the Wheel* (*Za rulem*), and *Automobile Roads* (*Avtomobil'nye dorogi*).[82] *Za rulem*, published by the All-Union Volunteer Society of Assistance to the Army, Aviation, and the Navy, was pitched to owners of automobiles and motorcycles, and to aficionados of car and motorcycle racing. Automobile owners' conviction that cars were at the cutting edge of progress further bolstered their sense of self-importance. In his letter, Zhdanov claimed that the Department of Architectural Affairs "forgets that we live in the second half of the twentieth century, in the century of the broad development of automobility [*avtomobilizm*], and carries out city planning without caring about the interests of toiling-automobile drivers."[83] Cars were modern, and disregarding them and their owners was backward.

To their neighbors, car owners, their automobiles, and single-car garages dirtied new housing estates and generally got in the way of people's everyday lives. At a May 1957 residents' meeting of a newly built apartment building on Iakovlevskii Alley in Leningrad's Moscow district, one resident, from 103 in attendance, asked for the removal of garages that had sprung up around their new building. His attempts to secure the district soviet's help in preventing these garages in the first place had been unsuccessful. The situation bothered the resident because the garages "are at the present time not completed and are in an unsanitary state." Although the letter writer Zhdanov had identified himself and fellow drivers positively as "toiling-automobile drivers," this particular resident used a less flattering moniker when referring to "the garages of independent proprietors [*edinolichniki*]." This term, *edinolichniki*, had been used during collectivization in the 1930s to describe peasants who did not join collective farms. They were the only peasants who could possess horses, thereby signifying an appropriate parallel with the automobile situation on Iakovlevskii Alley. By invoking this term, the resident was making an unambiguous point: Through their automobiles and garages that dirtied the common areas of the neighborhood, car drivers went about their business at the community's expense. The resident's use of *edinolichniki* also suggested that car drivers used their automobiles and garages to distinguish themselves materially from their less fortunate neighbors.[84]

Other citizens articulated a similar hostility toward car drivers' ownership of private automobiles in letters to newspapers about the drafting of the Third Party Program in 1961. Their indictment of automobiles fell under more general calls for leveling material differences such as the condemnation of "personal property" (*lichnaia sobstvennost'*) that targeted dachas and individually owned homes; calls for the redistribution of separate apartments; and even the rejection of the separate apartment. A summary of one such letter from a party member living in Moscow oblast described this individual's call "to prohibit the sale of automobiles to private persons," which was condemned together with dachas and "the construction of privately owned houses." This person wanted "legal means limiting the further growth of personal property (houses, dachas, automobiles, and so on)."[85]

Other residents were simply annoyed by the potential dangers and disruption to neighborhood life caused by automobile owners who took public spaces for their garages. At a residents' meeting in Leningrad's Moscow district in 1959, attended by 171 individuals from two apartment buildings on Narymskii Prospekt and Frunze Street, two residents complained about garages being too close to schools, day care centers, and playgrounds.[86] The local press joined in with criticism of car owners' behavior that underlined how they separated themselves from the community. *Leningradskaia pravda* reported in 1961 that car owners in the Vyborg district built small garages seemingly wherever they wanted. Aware of their unpopularity among local communities, some car owners resorted to deceptive tactics to build their garages before anyone could complain. Two men placed a sign in the courtyard of a local housing office indicating where residents could exchange rags and paper waste for cash. While the locals were left believing that such an exchange was being constructed, the two men were busy building their garage after having worked things out with the head of the housing office and gotten an unsuspecting district engineer to approve their plan. According to the newspaper, "Some time passed, and the same people [residents] were extremely surprised: The sign disappeared, the fence was no more, and in their place a garage for two automobiles suddenly appeared."[87]

In the 1950s and 1960s, the social meaning of the mass-produced automobile was shaped in new housing estates, and the automobile likewise played an early role in shaping neighborhood life. Along with makeshift garages, it was a disruptive addition to already badly designed and incompletely built neighborhoods, and created new social divisions within the mass housing community between those who had automobiles and those who did not. The minority who owned automobiles developed a rather strong sense of themselves as a separate, beleaguered group of urban dwellers. As Lewis Siegelbaum points out, car owners were also predominantly men and the attention they spent on their automobiles structured the spaces of neighborhoods along gender lines, so that "garages, makeshift auto parts bazaars, and the interiors of cars themselves served as refuges from the crowded conditions of apartment dwelling."[88] Today, one-car garages and automobiles are standard items in the courtyards (and sidewalks) of Russia's mass housing districts, and the association of men with automobiles has remained strong. According to one long-term resident of Moscow, the courtyard has evolved into a distinctly gendered space, and men long ago established their place in it primarily through their automobiles.[89]

Soviet Gentrification

As we saw in chapter 4, the reintroduction of the cooperative that favored urban professionals and elites displaced the predominantly blue-collar people's construction movement as the best method for fast-track access to a separate apartment. Such class divisions in distribution carried over in shaping the social spaces of the mass housing community. To attract more residents to cooperatives, the state badgered local soviets to ensure that cooperatives received good, empty land plots. When such ideal conditions did not materialize, cooperatives reshaped the social landscape of individual neighborhoods by constructing their housing in areas that required the removal of other buildings and individual housing owners. But they did so only after local authorities extracted hidden fees from cooperative members that effectively taxed their privileged position so that local soviets could cover the economic and social costs that cooperative housing imposed on local communities. Integrating class differences into the built environment of urban communities was thus a product of negotiation between local players over the "just price" of a cooperative's place in the moral economy of Soviet housing.

As the leadership in Moscow soon learned, local soviets resisted the extra workload and strains on their budgets that accommodating cooperatives demanded. Instead of making matters easier for cooperatives, local soviets allocated land plots that required the demolition of existing structures in neighborhoods without such infrastructure as water mains. Cooperatives were sometimes forced to undertake these demolitions at their own expense and find alternative housing for people whose housing was destroyed. Local soviets pressured cooperatives into giving up first-floor units in their buildings for commercial and municipal organizations, sometimes by issuing standardized plans containing such spaces.[90] Although government reports made them appear like helpless victims of local soviet incompetence, cooperatives exercised their agency in negotiating with local soviets. They willingly worked out deals that enabled them to build their privileged housing as soon as possible in the center of town, instead of on the outskirts. Such deals introduced a Soviet version of gentrification in the mass housing community when cooperatives successfully laid claim to choice land plots in exchange for finding new housing for displaced residents.

Government reports rarely mentioned cooperatives' active role in these deals and blamed local soviets instead. In June 1963, for example, Stroibank USSR reported that some cooperatives were forced to cover "the expenses of clearing buildings off their land plots and securing living space for those who live on them" in Sverdlovsk and Moscow.[91] In July, Gosplan of the Russian Soviet Federated Socialist Republic (RSFSR) explained that in addition to these costs, cooperatives in Kuibyshev and Rostov-on-the-Don were forced to cover part or all of the work associated with roads, communication lines, electricity transformer substations, and landscaping new neighborhoods. The city soviet in Kovrov compelled a cooperative to "clear off the existing privately owned home from this land plot and give the residents an apartment as personal property in the cooperative." Gosplan noted that the Moscow city soviet had even managed to shake payments out of a KGB cooperative for "the cost of living space" the city had to find for dislocated individuals, as well as "the balance on the cost of the houses torn down."[92] Despite the government's exhortations to halt these relocation schemes, local soviets and cooperatives continued to negotiate them.[93]

Individual housing owners, however, protested these schemes and the policy of razing their homes for cooperatives or other forms of urban redevelopment. Circumstances in the early 1960s gave them plenty to complain about. When Khrushchev's regime introduced loans for cooperatives in June 1962, it also mandated that cooperatives begin replacing individual housing construction in urban areas.[94] Over the next three years, much housing was demolished to make way for new housing. In the overall stock in the Russian Republic, 775,000 square meters were destroyed in 1962, 846,000 in 1963, and 1,358,000 in 1964. A significant portion of these demolitions occurred in the individual housing stock, which saw 255,000 square meters razed in 1962, 333,000 in 1963, and 508,000 in 1964.[95] Such destruction of existing housing reflected the Khrushchev regime's determination to modernize the Soviet cityscape by replacing makeshift individual houses with the properly planned mass housing estates of the future communist society. As Mark Smith has shown, the mass housing campaign helped secure millions of urban residents' property rights to housing, even in state housing distributed by local soviets and the workplace.[96] But at times, the same campaign threw the property rights of many individual housing owners into jeopardy. Moreover, it was fellow citizens in cooperatives working with local soviets, not the state alone, that deprived individual owners of their property rights.

By the mid-1960s, individual housing owners appealed to the government for a halt to the destruction of their homes and eradication of their communities. Over the course of 1964 and early 1965, owners from more than a dozen cities, including Penza, Tomsk, and Kazan, complained individually and in group letters.[97] Their main grievance was that local soviets had arbitrarily decided to raze their homes to make room for other structures, including cooperatives. In Saratov, nineteen out of sixty-five cooperatives received land plots requiring the clearing of individual housing. This case "naturally roused a large stream of complaints and petitions of working people about this question." Individual owners argued that their homes should not have been razed because they were in good condition; some had only recently been built. Like the residents of mass housing described earlier in this chapter, these individual owners rallied their community around local social organizations. The head of a street committee in Kazan complained that 170 houses dating from the early 1950s had been ear-marked for demolition in his district. Many of these houses had central heating and were constructed out of stone and concrete on land plots that had been allocated for fifty years. The plots were being razed to make room for five-story housing.[98]

Given such developments, individual housing owners viewed co-operatives in increasingly hostile terms. Throughout 1965, individual housing owners complained about cooperatives to the Supreme Soviet of the RSFSR, and to Anastas Mikoian, in his capacity as chairman of the Supreme Soviet of the USSR, and Aleksei Kosygin, as chairman of the Soviet of Ministers of the USSR.[99] They angrily described the ease with which cooperative members had obtained their apartments in con-trast to the hard work they had invested in building their homes. They resented the idea that people with simply more money could waltz into a separate apartment whereas they had labored for years to build a house and, in some cases, the roads and infrastructure surrounding it.[100]

Despite the Soviet leadership's best efforts, cooperatives and local soviets continued to work together to relocate individual owners. In November 1966, the government faulted the city soviets in Kaluga and Saratov for making some cooperatives responsible for clearing land plots and finding housing for dislocated persons. The Saratov city so-viet was accused of delaying the construction of housing for another sixteen cooperatives mainly because of its foot-dragging in finding housing for dislocated people. The government called upon the oblast soviets to bring the city soviets into line and to "punish those guilty of these violations."[101] The Saratov city soviet promptly ignored this de-mand and continued to collude with local cooperatives on an intricate scheme involving the housing exchange system to relocate individual owners. This particular scheme was a revealing, if extreme, example of the extent to which local players determined how the mass housing community was constituted.

When the government checked in on Saratov's housing scene in 1967, the city had succeeded at expanding its cooperative housing. Two hun-dred and forty-five cooperatives had already been organized. Among those that had completed construction, 87 houses (170,000 square meters of living space) were built housing more than 6,500 families. Thirty-four more houses (72,000 square meters of living space) were earmarked for construction in 1967. Cooperatives played a critical role in relocating people who had lost their housing and land plots to such growth. According to a joint report of Gosstroi of the RSFSR and the Ministry of the Communal Economy of the RSFSR in September 1967, a "considerable portion of housing-construction cooperatives" elected to take on this responsibility. The government found that cooperatives sought land plots in the downtown area because their members did not want to be located in areas of new housing. This held true even though new housing areas did not require the razing of existing structures, whereas downtown areas did. Such preferences revealed in rather stark terms how far cooperative members were willing to go in separating themselves spatially and socially from the margins of the mass housing community and its problems in transportation and urban development described earlier in this chapter. Cooperatives wished to remain near their place of work "in the old part of the city." The report found that the Saratov city soviet "as a rule, grants such requests of housing-construction cooperatives," and that district soviets as well as a cooperative's workplace helped to coordinate in one way or another the relocation of the residents of these land plots. Between the start of 1965 and August 1967, cooperatives had relocated more than 600 families, whereas workplaces had found alternative housing for 89 families, and the city and district soviets had relocated 31 families.[102]

The Saratov cooperatives and local authorities brokered the following set of exchanges and relocation plan: A cooperative that had agreed to relocate residents from their land plots searched for people living in town, typically in communal apartments, who were willing to vacate their housing in return for a share in the cooperative at a discount. The cooperative then allocated this vacated space to the residents who were about to lose their housing and land plots to the cooperative. According to the government's inquiry, "This practice . . . in the city of Saratov is widely propagated."[103] Moreover, it was well organized and done in the open:

> In all districts of the city, advertisements are posted on fences, poles, and other places with, for example, this kind of content: "Apartments are needed for the housing-construction cooperative 'Roza' for relocation to permanent place of domicile as well as for temporary residence. Citizens, putting forth their apartments for relocation, will be taken into the cooperative on favorable terms."[104]

Cooperatives earmarked "significant sums" of money to cover such discounts. In one case, a cooperative allocated 75,000 rubles to bring new members into the cooperative and to reallocate these new members' former housing to fifty dislocated families. As a result of this exchange, the cooperative was paying 13 rubles more per square meter of living space. Why cooperatives did not simply bring dislocated individual owners into their cooperatives instead of shuffling them off to other housing was never made clear. Perhaps living with those they had dislocated and deprived of their land plots would have been too awkward. In any event, illustrating once more the city and local soviets' support for such deals, land plots were assigned "in the majority of cases" without the proper paperwork for determining the state of existing structures and whether they should be torn down. With no paperwork to be forwarded to the oblast soviet for review, the city and district soviets kept it all a local matter and watched as housing in good or repaired condition was razed. The investigation found that during the past two years, 188 houses (i.e., 14,000 square meters) in decent condition had been torn down. One hundred and seven of these houses were "privately owned."[105]

As pointed out above, the government demanded in November 1966 that the Saratov oblast and city soviets clean up matters. In his response to the government's inquiry, the Saratov oblast soviet chairman, A. Bochkarev, dutifully reported that everything was being done to end these "serious shortcomings." Yet his account sounded more like a justification of what had happened. Cooperatives preferred land plots in the center of town, not on the outskirts, Bochkarev explained. Without even reflecting on the merits or fairness of razing existing housing, Bochkarev assumed that such housing simply had to go: "In connection with this [i.e., the cooperatives' preference for central city locations] there arose great difficulty with providing living space for citizens relocated from inferior houses earmarked for demolition in the central part of the city." The workplaces of some cooperatives stepped in to find alternative housing for dislocated individuals and cooperatives practiced their exchange schemes described above. Bochkarev stressed that such schemes were of the cooperatives' own making. "In these cases," he wrote, "cooperatives accepted additional expenses connected with relocation voluntarily, by decision of the general assemblies of cooperative members." Cooperatives were now receiving fewer central city land plots that required demolition. Consequently, Bochkarev noted, "This has led to somewhat of a reduction in newly established cooperatives."[106]

Individual housing owners were at a clear disadvantage in these relocation schemes. They had little choice about where they would ultimately live and ended up at times in the communal apartments of state housing, which was a far cry from the single-family homes they had enjoyed as personal property. The Saratov cooperative plan demonstrated that creating the very foundations of a community, and determining who would live next to whom and where, were by far not arbitrary processes dictated by planners in Moscow. Local residents negotiated over the location of buildings and the costs associated with relocating displaced persons. The city center in places like Saratov became a site of Soviet gentrification as cooperative members gladly paid extra to stay near their place of work and the cultural life of the city, rather than trek to the outskirts. In doing so, some cooperatives managed to maintain a spatial and social distance from the mass housing estates being built on the city's periphery.

Conclusion

This chapter has explored the different ways residents shaped mass housing communities out of the incompletely built environments they entered when moving to the separate apartment. Some joined the lowliest organs of state power, "social organizations," and drew upon official rhetoric about the communist way of life in making their grievances heard. In such cases, the lines between state and society blurred together, and residents more often found themselves demanding greater government involvement than shunning it or trying to escape from it. Others took the extraordinary step of squatting in apartments or on plots of land, and then defending their microcommunities through legal appeals and civil disobedience. Defying the law in very different ways, cooperative members brokered deals with local soviets that reshaped the social landscape of the mass housing community along class lines that reinforced the division between the privileged city center and its surrounding marginalized outskirts. Once they were living in their new homes, some residents bonded over the deficiencies of neighborhood infrastructure, whereas others turned on their car-driving neighbors for cluttering neighborhoods with garages. Mass housing estates formed a new social space in the post-Stalinist Soviet Union. A new and diverse social group, the residents of mass housing, created their own communities in ways that sometimes bolstered the volunteerism inherent in the Khrushchevian ideal of creating the communist way of life but at other times ran against its egalitarian values and visions of a classless society.

In contrast to the uniformity suggested by the aesthetics and organization of microdistricts, the mass housing community evolved into a heterogeneous body with new social divisions rooted in both the distribution of new housing and the ways residents made use of its public spaces. Mass housing estates were the site of new social identities centered in the neighborhood and the home that differed from how people had represented themselves when trying to get housing. As we saw in chapter 3, residents identified themselves as war invalids, the rehabilitated, or Leningrad blockadeers in asking for new housing from local and central authorities. In seeking a separate apartment, Soviet citizens identified themselves in reference to social identities and personal experiences that had little or nothing to do with being a resident. But when they settled in a new mass housing estate and turned once again to the state to lodge complaints, citizens now talked about themselves as residents, homemakers, cooperative members, consumers, and even "toiling-automobile drivers." Rooted in the everyday life of mass housing estates, these social identities were part of the broader evolution of mass consumerism also taking place in postwar Europe and the United States. In the final two chapters, I examine these social identities in greater detail as we enter the new domestic world of the separate apartment and explore its new consumer items and furniture.

Chapter 6

New Furniture

In December 1954, a Muscovite, E. Lashun, wrote to the All-Union Conference of Constructors in Moscow to tell the architects and builders what she expected from new housing. Lashun, who was living with her husband and two daughters in an 8.85-square-meter room of a wooden house, explained that they had been on their local soviet's waiting list for four years and that "not a few years will probably still pass when we will live normally, as it befits a Soviet toiling person, to whom the Stalin Constitution has given the right: to labor, study and cultured rest!"[1]

The December conference meant different things to different members of the Soviet polity. For Khrushchev, it presented the opportunity to declare a clear break from Stalin's expensive architectural aesthetics and insist that architects take up economical mass housing designs. For architects beholden to Stalinist aesthetics, the meeting was a bruising experience, whereas for others it opened a space for reexamining their constructivist past.[2] For an ordinary Muscovite like Lashun, the conference unleashed a cathartic torrent of complaints about her family's everyday existence and her expectations for the future: "One can hardly believe that one day we will not in fact freeze in a damp and cramped kennel, that we will stop to wallow on the floor, underfoot, but that we will rest on a couch in a cultured way, for which there will be space in the room." Looking to the future, she imagined that "arriving from work and school, we will sit as an entire family at the table and not eat in line one after another."[3]

Alongside more space in a private apartment, furniture was a critical part of what ordinary citizens like Lashun expected from Khrushchev's mass housing campaign. Her letter depicted what she believed would be her family's transition from its present, cramped housing to a "normal" domestic sphere. Objects and spaces would no longer serve multiple functions. It would be possible, she mused, "to do homework quietly without harassment like our seventh grade schoolgirl does her homework now—she studies, but she's pushed and everything gets poured onto her books and notebooks, which is on the only table, where the kitchen and the dining room and the bedroom and so on and so forth are situated." This multifunctional table and their lack of space only served to frustrate her family. She continued:

Imagine our family at the table: the father eats his meal, the schoolgirl does her homework, and as the housewife I'm cooking at one and the same table, yes and the younger daughter also climbs up to the table, and under the table there's all the kitchenware, that is, a tea kettle, a pot, and a frying pan and the rest, since we don't have a kitchen, but just a narrow passageway where there are gas stoves . . . and all the gas emissions and the steam from boiling linens gets into our room.[4]

If meals and homework were not difficult enough, the cramped conditions of their remaining dilapidated furniture made sleeping impossible. "At night we settle down 'comfortably,'" Lashun added sarcastically, "the children sleep on the bed, and my husband and I sleep on the floor under the children's feet, because there is no more free space."[5] The Soviet state's answer to Lashun's demands was a small, single-family apartment with all the technological amenities and consumer goods of modern urban life. A new line of furniture was likewise part of its long-awaited answer to the housing question.

This chapter examines the role that furniture played in the construction of the *khrushchevka* as a new space in which the values and social norms of the communist way of life were defined. The millions of new small apartments required entirely new consumer items that would correspond to the dimensions and aesthetics of mass housing, shape people's everyday behaviors according to the values of the communist way of life, and remain distinct from consumerism in the capitalist West. What this new furniture would look like and what these values and behaviors would be were neither predetermined nor decided by the Communist Party's top leadership. As scholars have argued, the separate apartment did not signify the end of the revolutionary process, but rather its reinvigoration under Khrushchev's regime, which mobilized mass housing and the consumer items that went with it to fulfill the Revolution's project of creating the New Soviet Man and Woman.[6] Although Khrushchev's regime boosted production of consumer items and defined the broad ideological contours of the communist way of life, it delegated furniture design and defining the new Soviet home's communist content to architects, furniture designers, and taste arbiters. With the regime's blessing, these members of the cultural intelligentsia tied such tasks to the broader processes of de-Stalinization and the Cold War struggle with the West over standards of living, to reexaminations of early Soviet design aesthetics and their relationship to modernist design, to women's role within the home, and to what a classless society looked like at home.

This chapter also explores the new furniture designs that residents of the *khrushchevka* were promised and the meanings that members of the cultural intelligentsia ascribed to these new household goods. And it delineates what ordinary urban dwellers actually brought to their new homes. Internal government reports on Soviet citizens' consumption patterns for furniture and other household goods in the early 1960s, examined here for the first time, revealed to Khrushchev's regime that the state of people's household possessions diverged significantly from ideal images of the modern Soviet home as the site of a rationally organized and aesthetically modern domesticity fit for the transition to communism. Despite expansions in production, chronic shortages prevented many people from finding new furniture and household consumer items in stores, forcing them to make do with older makes. People's continued reliance on mechanical consumer goods instead of electrical ones undermined propaganda that celebrated the scientific and modern direction of the Soviet household. Social differentiation in consumption patterns undercut the egalitarian ethos in the rhetoric on new furniture and the *khrushchevka*. Comparisons with consumption patterns in the capitalist West revealed to the leadership how far behind the Soviet Union really was, and how foolish Khrushchev had been to declare otherwise during his famous "Kitchen Debate" with Richard Nixon in 1959. In short, as this chapter demonstrates, two starkly different images of ordinary people's furniture and household consumption patterns emerged in the 1950s and 1960s: The first comprised ideal representations of the new Soviet home and its household objects; the second included the realities residents faced in trying to find new furniture and consumer goods for their new homes. Each played a significant role in shaping what Communism on Tomorrow Street promised to be and how it turned out in practice.

In Search of New Furniture

Like all consumer goods, furniture was an item of extreme scarcity under Stalin. Before World War II, the furniture industry was based largely on handmade methods of production and was insufficiently mechanized.[7] Khrushchev's regime faced an uphill battle when it committed itself to meet ordinary citizens' furniture needs. In March 1955, an audit found that supply was still slipping further behind "the growing needs of the population" because the industry was based on "handicraft methods, predominantly with the use of manual labor." Factories with technology "for the mechanization of production processes" continued to depend upon labor-intensive techniques.[8] The Soviet leadership redoubled its efforts in 1957 to "organize the manufacture of small-sized furniture and built-in kitchen equipment for apartments of the new type in the necessary quantity."[9] But government agencies inexplicably lowered production targets during the next couple of years, despite evidence of increasing demand. The Central Committee of the Communist Party soon learned that "the production of furniture by far will not satisfy the needs of the population of the republic [Russian Soviet Federated Socialist Republic, RSFSR], and the shortage of furniture will be felt all the more sharply."[10]

As the domestic embodiment of Communism on Tomorrow Street, the well-appointed separate apartment was supposed to come with its own line of furniture that met every family member's needs. Internal government reports and empty store shelves, however, indicated that there would be many sparsely furnished *khrushchevki*. In February 1957, for example, the director of a furniture retailer, Mosmebel'torg, reported on the uncoordinated state of his industry to the Soviet of Ministers of the RSFSR. The director, a certain Fokin, explained how problems with dinner tables had worsened considerably during the past two years. Mosmebel'torg had obtained and sold 94,000 dinner tables in 1955, and 77,000 in 1956. For 1957, it would handle only about 55,000 to 60,000 dinner tables, falling far short of the 150,000 it had ordered.[11] Fokin explained that increases in the city's housing stock had given rise to a high demand for dinner tables and somehow caught planners off guard: "They have forgotten that a person who has just moved into an apartment obtains in the first place a dinner table and they have completely forgotten about this dinner table." The industry's lack of coordination was impossible for even him to understand. One of his local suppliers, Moscow Furniture Factory No. 2, had even ceased being a furniture factory altogether:

> At the present time, for reasons we can't fathom [Moscow Furniture Factory No. 2] has begun to call itself the "Lira" factory and by now doesn't produce tables, but pianos. We are not against pianos, but we will not stop repeating this until they hear us and understand the simple truth, that having received a new apartment, the majority of Soviet people need in the first place a dinner table and in the last place a piano.[12]

Fokin also accused national furniture producers of dropping tables in favor of other consumer goods, such as television cases and sewing machine benches.[13] Although Soviet consumers were unable to influence furniture production, as their capitalist counterparts did in a buyer's market, their frustration could nonetheless be repurposed to legitimize a retailer's main points. Thus, to illustrate people's frustration, Fokin quoted from letters to newspapers, identifying each person as a "customer." In a letter to *Soviet Trade* (*Sovetskaia torgovlia*), one Muscovite wrote, "Five o'clock in the morning. Moscow sleeps, there is only cold wind penetrating into one's bones, but 'seekers' of furniture are sadly awake on the streets of the sleeping city." In a letter to *Evening Moscow* (*Vecherniaia Moskva*), another lamented, "Well, for already four months I try to obtain a round table. . . . But unfortunately my search has not been crowned with success."[14]

The Soviet leadership—undeterred, or perhaps spurred, by such reports—launched a comprehensive reorganization and expansion of furniture manufacturing in March 1958.[15] The government highlighted the connection between "the population's broad demand for furniture" and more mass housing. It directed the furniture industry to focus on "the massive output of inexpensive sets and individual objects of household furniture for one-room and two-room apartments." Set to expand was furniture built into apartments, a key space-saving device for already-small apartments. The industry was also supposed to widen the variety of furniture and adopt new synthetic materials such as plastic, rubber, and artificial resins for varnish. Machine-building enterprises were charged with providing the industry with a sufficient supply of woodworking machines in order to transform it from handicraft production to mechanized mass production. To educate the public, Gosstroi of the USSR (State Committee on Construction) was charged with setting up a permanent furniture exhibit in Moscow and managing "an all-union competition in 1958 for the creation of better furniture models for new apartments, intended for one family."[16]

The new way of life was about to go on display, but reports on the ground told a familiar story. Although production showed steady increases after 1958 for tables, hutches, and cupboards, other makes such as couches and sofas experienced periodic decreases (see table 6.1[17]). The rapid pace of furniture manufacturing led to severe deficiencies in quality that mirrored those in housing construction. By 1961, 90 percent of the products coming out of seven Moscow oblast factories were defective. Factories in the Gor'kii and Novosibirsk regions had similarly high rates of deficient products.[18]

By 1963, the usual problems persisted. Most of the 3,000 furniture manufacturers in the Russian Republic were "small, of a partial handicraft type." The government ordered an end to the manufacturing of 296 outdated makes and urged that obsolete designs with low demand be pulled from production. The industry's heavy reliance on handmade production resulted in too many different designs. There were 156 kinds of chairs, 116 makes of dining tables, 222 sorts of clothes closets, and 217 kinds of beds in production.[19] In short, the furniture destined for people's homes under Khrushchev was an eclectic assortment of older, handmade makes lacking any recognizable style. This is something we must keep in mind before turning to the furniture exhibitions and mass media propaganda that presented the new furniture as factory-produced makes based on standardized designs and modernist aesthetics. Such ideal representations projected a harmonious alignment between modern apartments and new furniture. The reality was more of a mismatch between apartments that already afforded little space and furniture items that were not designed for them in either size or aesthetics. Like the communal apartment, as we saw in chapter 5, outdated furniture lingered in the Soviet everyday as a sign that leaving behind an older, dysfunctional lifestyle for a new way of life would not be as

Table 6.1. Annual Furniture Production in the Soviet Union, 1940–70 (thousands of pieces or sets of furniture)

Year	Tables	Chairs and Armchairs	Hutches and Cupboards	Wardrobes and Closets	Couches and Sofas	Metal Beds	Furniture Sets
1940	2,226	10,267	148	638	628	6,157	...
1950	2,198	12,395	54	834	446	4,357	...
1952	2,753	15,000	116	1,434	743	6,298	...
1953	2,781	14,543	158	1,698	915	9,128	...
1955	3,265	16,143	287	2,259	1,381	11,268	...
1956	3,400	16,805	334	2,430	1,392	10,499	...
1957	3,771	18,362	363	2,583	1,525	11,238	30.6
1958	4,492	22,000	470	2,932	1,947	12,309	31.6
1959	5,416	26,000	703	3,620	2,478	13,251	38
1960	6,467	29,000	964	4,229	2,683	13,365	30.9
1961	7,376	32,000	1,256	4,814	2,689	11,542	28.1
1962	8,222	33,000	1,569	5,121	2,674	10,670	31.6
1963	8,823	34,000	1,850	5,159	2,657	12,000	29
1964	9,600	35,000	2,188	4,969	2,349	12,400	34.7
1965	10,400	35,000	2,381	4,807	2,078	11,700	44.7
1966	11,000	35,000	2,429	4,970	1,757	11,800	80.3
1967	11,500	36,000	2,536	4,984	1,469	12,900	135
1968	11,700	37,000	2,772	5,161	1,297	13,700	170
1969	11,800	38,000	2,901	5,278	1,116	...	215
1970	12,100	40,000	3,091	5,704	994	...	275

Sources: Narodnoe khoziaistvo SSSR v 1958 godu (Moscow: Gosudarstvennoe statisticheskoe izdatel'stvo, 1959), 299. This source is hereafter cited as Nkh SSSR, followed by the year reported: Nkh SSSR v 1959 godu, 266; Nkh SSSR v 1960 godu, 341; Nkh SSSR v 1961 godu, 262; Nkh SSSR v 1962 godu, 202; Nkh SSSR v 1963 g., 203; Nkh SSSR v 1964 g., 225; Nkh SSSR v 1965 g., 239; Nkh SSSR v 1967 g., 306; Nkh SSSR v 1968 g., 300; Nkh SSSR v 1969 g., 264; Nkh SSSR v 1970 g., 252.

immediate as the regime's deadline for achieving communism by 1980 suggested.

Despite these problems, increases in consumer goods production opened new opportunities for architects, designers, and taste arbiters to shape the design and meaning of the Soviet home. They sought to define the contours of the communist way of life with as much pent-up excitement as ordinary urban dwellers had trying to get a separate apartment and shop for new furniture. For these makers of the Soviet home, scholars have argued, Khrushchev's mass housing campaign provided unprecedented opportunities to act out the Russian intelligentsia's traditional role of telling ordinary people how to live their lives; liberate themselves from the banality of the everyday, now associated with the "petit bourgeois" tastes that bureaucratic elites had enjoyed under Stalin; and raise themselves to a higher state of being or "new way of life."[20] Designers under Khrushchev adopted the *khrushchevka* as the organizing principle of furniture design, and set about telling people how to use it in a tasteful and culturally edifying manner worthy of a society well on its way to communism.

Furniture designers found inspiration in both the Soviet past and the contemporary world beyond their borders as they searched for furniture that fit the small dimensions of the *khrushchevka*. This placed their work at the intersection of two critical currents in Khrushchev's thaw: the rehabilitation of cultural trends repressed under Stalin and greater openness toward the West. Similar to the fate of constructivist architecture, the Soviet avant-garde's furniture projects had fallen victim to the Communist Party's attacks against constructivism in the early 1930s. Those designers who were still interested in producing inexpensive and functional furniture under Stalin quietly developed ideas about streamlining production and integrating design with small separate apartments, thereby following a path similar to their colleagues in architecture, as explained in chapter 2. In 1941, for example, the Architects' Union promoted "furniture types and models that are coordinated with contemporary, small dwellings."[21] A catalogue of furniture designs, written during the war, similarly recommended designing furniture for small separate apartments.[22]

As with architects' small apartment designs in the 1930s, ideas on designing "mass furniture" were not implemented until the Khrushchev era.[23] The models of avant-garde architects and artists from the 1920s and early 1930s—such as Aleksandr Rodchenko, El Lissitzky, and Moisei

Ginzburg—served as one source of inspiration.[24] Like the architects who looked back to the constructivist tradition and international style in designing mass housing,[25] furniture designers under Khrushchev drew from these earlier experiments at home and abroad.[26] The modernist aesthetics and production principles they incorporated included the development of form from function, simplicity and lightness of form, a rejection of ornamentation and figurative representation, adoption of industrial materials such as steel, the fusion of art with everyday life, and mass production of inexpensive objects available to the wider public.

In addition to past experiments, a contemporary source of inspiration (and competition) for Khrushchev's furniture designers and architects came from the capitalist West and the state socialist regimes of Eastern Europe. Designers on both sides of the Iron Curtain produced mass housing, furniture, and consumer items that fused the modernist aesthetics of the prewar avant-garde with postwar mass production. By sharing ideas and models through publications, exhibitions, and tours, furniture designers and architects across the Cold War's political divide advanced an international style for the interior of the postwar home. The American Exhibition in Moscow in 1959—where Khrushchev had his ill-fated debate with Richard Nixon over an American kitchen—was perhaps the most famous encounter that permitted Soviet architects, furniture designers, and ordinary people to see, touch, and borrow ideas about American domestic design. Soviet architects and furniture designers, scholars have recently shown, enjoyed many other opportunities to exchange and borrow ideas (and technology) from their state socialist satellites and the capitalist West.[27]

As Greg Castillo has convincingly demonstrated, each side in the Cold War laid claim to the modernist aesthetic of midcentury domestic design as a symbol of its socioeconomic system's superiority over the other. Americans mobilized modernist design in countless exhibitions to promote the internationalism of the Atlantic Alliance and the material benefits that European integration and economic ties with the United States would produce. They used the modernist aesthetic to convince skeptical Western European critics that the American way of life coming over the borders represented a sophisticated consumerism instead of a descent into tasteless kitsch. The Soviet Union and its Eastern European satellites similarly promoted modernist design as a sign of transnational unity and economic integration within their camp.

In the socialist home, modernist aesthetics promoted a proper scientific and rational (one might say planned) approach to consumerism in the face of capitalism's chaotic and excessive version. In short, there was a socialist path to mass consumerism, and modernist design was its ideal aesthetic. Getting there, however, would require Soviet architects and furniture designers to purge themselves of the consumer tastes and aesthetics that had evolved under Stalin.[28]

Designs for the New Way of Life

For some members of the cultural intelligentsia, letting go of Stalinist excesses in domestic design was hard to do. A 1954 collection of essays on apartment and furniture design, *Interior of a Residential House*, still celebrated elite, Stalin-era apartments. The larger the apartment, the more likely it was that each of its rooms would have its own, separate function. A spacious apartment could include a kitchen, a common room, a bedroom, a children's room, a dining room, an office, a living room, a vestibule, an entranceway, a hallway, and various connecting spaces. Furniture was assigned the single function of the room it occupied, and every room contained one piece or set of furniture that served as its "compositional center."[29] One contributor, Lazar' Cherikover, recognized that times were changing and furniture design was to be conditioned by the dimensions and layout of smaller apartments. Apart from serving set functions—the storage of objects, eating, and sitting—furniture was to be "at the same time capable of decorating the interior of the modern mass apartment." He warned residents that large furniture and household objects "visually reduce the already small size of rooms of the mass apartment and create in it an impression of things being too narrowly packed." Aesthetics and function had to be brought into balance with one another because the home was supposed to be characterized by "the absence of unneeded splendor and at the same time of unjustified simplification of forms." Here Cherikover was negotiating a middle position by reminding readers that rooting out Stalinist "excesses" should not swing the pendulum back to the asceticism of constructivism. Ideally, spaces and objects were equal partners that together constituted the new Soviet home.[30]

As one of the last publications of its kind to celebrate the domestic interiors of elite, Stalin-era apartments, *Interior of a Residential House* simultaneously looked ahead, if somewhat grudgingly, to the aesthetics and prototypes of the new furniture. At the heart of the transition was an evolving relationship between objects and space, whereby the latter came to dominate the former. In much the same way that architects simplified larger, elite apartments to arrive at the *khrushchevka*'s basic design (see chapter 2), proponents of the new furniture reshaped objects and their relationship to space. The result in ideal representations of the *khrushchevka* was a home that resembled a well-calibrated machine whose parts all fit together perfectly to produce the New Soviet Man and Woman. The scales soon tipped decidedly in favor of smaller separate apartments as the organizing principle of furniture. In drawing conclusions from a furniture exhibition in Moscow in 1956, Cherikover approvingly described the emerging changes as a consequence of smaller domestic spaces, arguing that

> the dimensions and composition of new furniture, and its technical and artistic forms, must to a maximum degree correspond to the parameters of apartments of the new type and to the architecture of interiors of modern housing; and . . . the increase in the amount of manufactured furniture, improvement in its quality, and lowering of its cost can be reached only through maximum industrialization of production and furniture finishings.[31]

Proponents of the new furniture categorized it according to its functions and relationship to the mass apartment's dimensions. One of the most widespread was sectional furniture (*sektsionnaia mebel'*), which applied especially to bookcases and cupboards in living rooms (figure 6.1).

Such furniture was composed of two or more distinct sections that could be dismantled and rearranged in whole or separately.[32] Sectional furniture was devoid of excess decoration and all its surfaces were flat, making it possible to save space.[33] Collapsible and folding furniture (*universal'naia razbornaia mebel'* and *skladnaia mebel'*) was similarly designed to conserve space and alter a room's function. Examples included tables with collapsible sections to make them larger or smaller and a bookcase with a section that folded out to serve as a small desk.[34] Shelf furniture (*stellazhnaia mebel'*), such as shelves attached to walls, was another flexible space saver.[35] With rooms doubling or tripling in function, combined or transformative furniture (*kombinirovannaia mebel'* and *tranformiruiushchaiasia mebel'*) was the order of the day. The couch-

Figure 6.1. Sectional furniture in a living/dining room with dining table and chairs. The furniture and this room were part of the 1959 furniture exhibition in Moscow discussed below.

Source: N. Luppov, "O vsesoiuznom konkurse na luchshuiu mebel'," *Dekorativnoe iskusstvo SSSR*, no. 5 (1959): 9.

bed (*divan-krovat'*), which was used during the day as a couch, became a bed in the evening.[36] Pillows and sheets were conveniently hidden from view during the day in a space under or behind the couch-bed. An alternative design was the trundle bed, which was well suited for a bedroom shared by more than one person.[37] Another variant was a bed that folded out of a large case that served as a desk and bookshelf. Likewise, armchairs could be opened and extended in the evening to serve as a bed for one.[38] Built-in furniture (*vstroennaia mebel'* and *pristennaia mebel'*) was a critical space saver already included in an apartment's design.[39]

To introduce the Soviet public to the new furniture and spur architects and designers to produce it, Khrushchev's regime organized several home and furniture exhibitions. These exhibitions announced that
the state was serious about meeting people's consumer needs and incorporating their input drawn from comment books. They also had a
didactic function: to teach urban dwellers about proper consumption
and homemaking for the communist way of life. Such exhibitions
revealed the broader tensions between the consultative and didactic
aspects of promoting the new furniture and the *khrushchevka*. The regime was declaring its willingness to cater to consumers' tastes, but
only within certain boundaries that members of the cultural intelligentsia were only too happy to articulate.[40] The architects' reactions to the
1958 Gosstroi furniture competition and its exhibition in 1959 (figures
6.1 and 6.2) reveal that the new furniture was as much a novelty for
them as it was for consumers, whose comments will be examined in
chapter 7.

Gosstroi organized the 1959 exhibition in Moscow in time for the
Twenty-First Communist Party Congress in early 1959, where Khrushchev described the broad outlines of the communist way of life.[41]
Gosstroi chief Vladimir Kucherenko explained its purpose to the
Central Committee: "The participants in the competition were given
the task to create new models of inexpensive mass furniture, meeting
the growing needs for well-furnished and well-equipped housing and
corresponding to the dimensions and layout of apartments of the new
type."[42] The competition featured sixty-six different sets of furniture,
twenty-four sets for kitchens, and fourteen designs for built-in closets.
It stressed the importance of integrating furniture and apartment design, rather than treating these separately. All entries were put on display in one-, two-, and three-room apartments in Moscow's poster-
child district for new mass housing, Novye Cheremushki.[43] The Moscow
exhibit featured the main types of new furniture discussed above,
including beds that could be raised into closets during the day, dinner
tables that could be extended or shortened with folding parts, and a
desk attached to a bookcase. The models were made from modern,
factory-produced materials such as plastics, light steel frames, and
aluminum.[44]

Publications such as *Architecture of the USSR* (*Arkhitektura SSSR*)
and *Decorative Arts of the USSR* (*Dekorativnoe iskusstvo SSSR*) praised
the exhibit as a major turning point.[45] The architects, designers, and

Figure 6.2. Part of the interior of a living room. This room and its furniture were displayed at the 1959 furniture exhibition in Moscow.

Source: N. Luppov, "O vsesoiuznom konkurse na luchshuiu mebel': Novye resheniia," *Dekorativnoe iskusstvo SSSR* no. 5 (1959): 9.

manufacturers at the Leningrad affiliate of the Union of Architects in April 1959 echoed the sentiment at a meeting to discuss the competition, to which some in attendance had contributed designs. Their discussion revealed much excitement at witnessing and participating in the furniture industry's recent transformation. As one architect, a certain Belov, explained, "It is now clear to everyone that for the apartment of the new type a new furniture is required, that is organically tied to the layout and sizes of spaces." Another architect, A. Liubosh, exclaimed that "we have seen a revolution in this matter; there had not yet been an exhibit that broke to such an extent the old traditions and habits and ended up on the right path." A new type of furniture had at last been made that fit the dimensions of the separate apartment. Liubosh enthusiastically predicted that they could supply at least 40 percent of new apartments in Leningrad with the new furniture by 1960 and, thereafter, shoot for 70 percent. This implied, of course, that a substantial portion of new apartments would not have the new furniture but rather, as suggested above, an eclectic mix of furniture not designed for the *khrushchevka*'s dimensions or aesthetics. Such realities did not dampen the architects' sense of accomplishment. Belov explained that designers from the local furniture manufacturer he represented, Lenobldrevmebel'prom, had tried to balance comfort, attractiveness, cost, and availability of raw materials in their competition entries. Simplicity and efficiency, which were core ideas of modernist design, had fully informed their work. Belov's designers had reduced the different types of furniture they made, developed multifunctional models, and simplified designs to increase output.[46]

The recent competition put to shame the last major exhibit held in Moscow in 1956. One architect, I. Gol'verk, explained that "our furniture seemed primitive at that time in comparison with those foreign makes that were presented."[47] Cultural progress on the world stage intersected at home with the arduous task of lifting the ordinary person's domestic tastes. The architect A. Macheret explained that the latest competition had given him "an impression first of all of a correctly chosen direction"—all the better because he believed that some urban dwellers desperately needed to improve their interior decorating skills. Drawing attention to recently settled apartment buildings in Leningrad, Macheret explained that "the picture looks plain awful. You can't imagine what goes on there, not because people don't want to get other furniture or don't have the means to do so, but because they can't get it anywhere." Shortages notwithstanding, Macheret believed in the power of the cultural intelligentsia to save ordinary people from their poor interior decorating decisions: "I'm not going to say that the broader masses' taste is less than polished, but they need to be shown what to get. Just go [to their apartments] and see what they acquire!"[48]

As the Leningrad architects pointed out, the new furniture's relationship to space had to be highly efficient and simplified. In 1954, Cherikover had written in *Interior of a Residential House* that furniture typically covered 35 to 40 percent of an apartment's floor space.[49] By 1959, Gol'verk claimed that furniture actually took up more space, usually 50 to 60 percent, but that the designs on display in the Novye Cheremushki apartments offered a positive step forward. He explained that the furniture models covered 33 percent, and in some cases only 27 or 28 percent, of an apartment's space. He assured his colleagues that "these small-sized objects entirely satisfy all the needs of the population" and would even improve people's psychological well-being. In his view, the 1959 exhibit illustrated the benefits of uncluttered interior spaces characterized by flat, uninterrupted surfaces. He explained that "for a person who stands over the course of the workday in front of a constantly moving lathe or rides on fast transportation, it's necessary to create in the domestic setting some kind of release, conditions in which a quiet scene has an impact on domestic life."[50] The benefits of a well-furnished and properly arranged single-family apartment had been noted in the past as a way of mitigating the psychological harm of war.[51] In Gol'verk's vision, a soothing, uncluttered domestic sphere similarly shielded residents from the turbulence of modern life in peacetime.

Proponents of the new furniture asserted that the domestic interior of the separate apartment should reflect the production aesthetic of contemporary factories in order to emphasize its modernity. Gol'verk explained that "the simplicity and economical efficiency of the method of production without a doubt draws with it the economical efficiency and simplicity of the interior's resolution." With production having such an influence on the composition of interior space, there seemed to be no other option than to recognize it as part of the aesthetic of domestic space. Gol'verk continued: "Precisely in this organic link, so to speak, of the interior's aesthetic with the method of production are laid those progressive foundations, which we see now in the architecture of the interior." The aesthetics of interior design had been fundamentally shaken. Domestic objects could no longer be created apart from their interior and the production process, and the basic structure of the apartment was now the central organizing force of household furniture design. The architecture of the separate apartment, its objects, and mass production now formed an organic whole.[52]

Teaching Good Taste

Architects and designers like Gol'verk were eager to explain to the general population what to do with the new furniture and what to think about it. Through advice pamphlets, newspapers, and magazines, they showed consumers how to construct a tasteful domestic interior. This expert advice intertwined prescriptions on proper socialist taste with the most practical matter at hand: how to comfortably arrange one's new furniture in the tiny spaces of the separate apartment. But this literature also revealed a fundamental tension between the self-appointed and state-supported taste arbiters of the cultural intelligentsia who wrote it and the ordinary urban dwellers who were supposed to read it. On the one hand, homemaking experts insisted that tastes were diverse and that individual consumers played a key role in developing them. On the other hand, domestic design experts never failed to set ground rules for what was acceptable. Like their counterparts in other Eastern Bloc countries such as East Germany, many of their ideas were rooted in the revival of prewar modernist aesthetics that emphasized the minimalist and functional décor of the international style.[53] But Soviet advice literature also had domestic influences, such as the Russian intelligentsia's traditional view of itself as arbiter of cultural norms.[54] The communal apartment, whose lingering influence on the symbolic construction of the new Soviet home we already saw in chapter 5, similarly served as an alternative source of inspiration for arranging furniture in the *khrushchevka*.

In the communal apartment, families living in one room used furniture to demarcate areas for different family members and for sleeping, eating, studying, and leisure. Although the separate apartment gave a family more privacy than had ever been imaginable in a communal apartment, its small number of rooms and dimensions continued to force families to use rooms for two or more functions. Rather than lament this continuity, the authors of domestic advice literature presented it as a new and refreshing lesson in modest taste and overcoming spatial limitations through the practical arrangement of furniture.

In fact, such advice was hardly novel. It had already been part of architects' recommendations for coping with life in cramped communal apartments, as illustrated in a Leningrad furniture exhibition in 1951. Upon its review of this exhibit, a city commission stressed that "in choosing designated forms of furniture, it follows to consider the character of contemporary housing space that the basic mass of the population has." It noted that "in general a room serves at one and the same time as a bedroom and as a place where one spends the day, therefore the production of a combined complex of furniture should be developed at the present time."[55] The same year, Leningrad designers looked to collapsible furniture (*skladnaia mebel'*) as a way to help residents make do with the spatial restrictions of the communal apartment. They explained that "the population has to reconcile itself for now with the restrictions of living space, searching for various ways to use it more rationally." Furniture could play a key role in making "comforts and coziness in our rooms" possible. "With the skillful arrangement [of furniture] it is possible to save floor space in any room either for children to play, or for dancing, or as free space for passing through."[56] Making efficient and rational use of space through well-designed furniture was thus not only an invention of modernist design. Residents of communal apartments had already grown accustomed to using furniture for different functions, such as the round dining table in the middle of a room at which people ate, studied, and wrote.[57] Such practices had been a necessity for communal apartment dwellers, who reproduced them in the tight confines of the *khrushchevka*.

The domestic advice literature eased the transition by framing such compensatory practices as harbingers of a new, modern way of life. In the small separate apartment, tables served more than one function, and to save space they became rectangular and gravitated to a wall. Such arrangements divided up rooms into functional zones, which the advice literature touted as a critical principle in a rationally and efficiently organized home.[58] The division of urban space into functional zones, such as those for work and residence, was a central idea of modernist urban planning, which extended here from the city straight into the home.[59] Alternately hiding and revealing certain household objects was a critical feature of functional zones. If the common room doubled as a bedroom, sheets, pillows, and covers needed to be stored away during the day. A resident could change a space's function by opening or folding up a couch-bed, and the sleeping zone of a common room could be hidden from view behind a curtain. A combined dresser included a vanity that could be pulled out or stored away, thereby hiding toilet articles. Residents could discreetly keep alcoholic beverages, shot glasses, and wine glasses in a specially made box designed into one of the sides of a couch-bed. The box's top and side sections opened up, with the latter serving as a small table.[60]

Under the banner of modest taste, homemaking specialists also urged residents to use furniture and other household objects to make their small apartments appear larger. Mirrors could visually expand the dimensions of the combined bathroom and toilet unit. To offset the cramped feeling that several doors in one entranceway created, a mir-

ror could be attached to the bathroom and toilet door, thereby covering up one door and giving this space greater visual depth.[61] Children's
furniture offered additional opportunities for the rational division of
scarce space.[62] Because a child was unlikely to have his or her own
room, children's furniture demarcated a child's corner in a common
room or bedroom.[63] A combined foldout bed, desk, and bookcase
saved space when a child shared the common room with parents.[64]
Whereas homemaking specialists recommended that pre-school-aged
children have a minimal amount of furniture and a corner in a room, a
school-age child could have a transformable zone in a common room
or share a room with a sibling. In a two-bedroom apartment, children
and a grandparent could occupy the smaller room, while parents lived
in the common room. In a three-room apartment, parents and children
lived in separate rooms and a grandparent resided in the common
room. The grandparent's space was to be cordoned off by a curtain
during the day so as not to be seen by "an outsider's eyes."[65]

Acceptable Social Divisions

As these examples illustrate, an apartment's properly arranged spaces
and objects divided the social world of the separate apartment along
generational lines. The conjugal pair had priority in occupying its own
space, followed by children, and then the grandparent. The inclusion
of three-generation families was an allusion to the actual presence of
grandmothers in many Soviet families.[66]

  In homemaking advice literature, such generational differences were
acceptable because they were deemed to be universal and would naturally continue to exist when Soviet society reached communism. Differences in nationality and ethnicity were another matter. Homemaking
literature, at least what was published in Russian, showed individuals
in either photographs or drawings wearing exclusively modern
European clothing. Such images were not intended to mean that only
ethnically European Soviet citizens belonged in separate apartments.
On the contrary, the separate apartment was supposed to be a universal form of housing available to all. Instead, such images suggested
that the ideal separate apartment would eventually be the home of an
ethnically homogenous and egalitarian society. The persons depicted
in Soviet homemaking advice literature were thus white, middle-class

Europeans posing as a universal standard. This mirrored the international style of mass housing and new furniture, which was likewise more European and North American in origin than its universalist claims pretended to be.

Homemaking specialists' ideal visions of the *khrushchevka* signaled a sharp reduction in the number of social divisions and identities that Soviet citizens had come to expect, especially in communal housing. In a communal apartment, gender and generation had intersected with other social cleavages, such as class, education, ethnicity, and religious belief. Chroniclers of the communal apartment's early existence—such as Mikhail Bulgakov in his play *Zoya's Apartment*, and in his novella *Heart of a Dog*—represented such social mixing as a central part of this unique urban milieu. In the homemaking literature of the Khrushchev era, the move to the separate apartment effectively purged these social divisions from the domestic sphere and mass housing estates. As we saw in chapter 3, Khrushchev's regime had attempted but failed to strip the waiting list for housing of the social and historical meanings that urban residents projected onto it. Homemaking advice specialists were attempting something similar by presenting the *khrushchevka* as a domestic space that had filtered out the messy social complexities of communal apartment life in the old city center. Their efforts left gender and generation as the only recognizable and legitimate social divisions in the separate apartment and the future communist society. Their textual and visual representations advanced the Soviet project of cleansing the social body of its impurities in order to produce a hygienically fit and homogenous society that just happened to look middle class and European. This was strikingly different from the Stalinist regime's violent methods of remaking society, especially in the wake of World War II, and the coercive measures that Khrushchev's regime periodically undertook against criminals and social undesirables.[67] The homemaking literature under Khrushchev was a decidedly benign and peaceful method of reshaping society, which residents could simply ignore.

In contrast to generational differences, homemaking advice literature treated gender in a more complex manner, alternately constructing the separate apartment as a genderless space and then emphasizing the role of the housewife within it. With the major exception of the kitchen, most of an apartment and its furniture tended to be gender neutral. Unlike the bourgeois apartment of the nineteenth century, the *khrushchevka* provided no specifically male space like an office.[68] A

1968 sociological survey of a cooperative building in Moscow even found that both men and women took an active role in setting up domestic interiors.[69]

Although homemaking advisers likewise addressed both men and women, their prohibitions on questionable behavior, especially the kind that perpetuated class differences, focused more on women. What women allegedly did to beds was particularly troublesome. One advice specialist lamented their unfortunate desire to construct mountains of decorative pillows on beds. Peasants of long ago had allegedly laid the foundations for such misuse of beds by sleeping on wooden benches, while placing sheets and covers on a real bed during the day. This piece of furniture became "the designator of the masters' status." Given the spatial limitations of a separate apartment, no space or object could have a purely decorative function. Doing so would transform its ideological content. This adviser concluded that "when a household object acquires the sense of being put on display, which does not correspond to its real function, that bad taste appears, which is now called petit bourgeois."[70]

Two taste arbiters further derided such use of beds as the ostentatious display of a family's material wealth: "At times you come across apartments in which the bed stands in the foreground, decorated with an atlas-sized cover and an entire mountain of pillows, as if proudly announcing the family's prosperity reigning in the house."[71] Other accounts specifically identified women with conspicuous forms of domestic consumption. The 1968 sociological study in Moscow claimed that women had become the prime "victim of the cult of the object" in new housing. They were "guilty of 'the disposition to put things on display' [*vystavochnost'*] in their home" and were more likely to allow an object to "stand outside of time and function like an exhibition object on display."[72] Such criticisms alluded to the modernist ethos of collapsing the division between art and everyday life that had informed Soviet and Western avant-garde experimentations of the 1920s. Whereas the bourgeoisie and capitalism had been to blame at that time for dividing art from everyday life, it was now Soviet women who stood in the way of this modernist vision for the new Soviet home.

Of course, a woman could redeem herself by properly working in the kitchen. In no other unit of the separate apartment was as much attention paid to integrating space and the female body in a rational system replete with the latest amenities and appliances. Sinks, a stove and an oven, a refrigerator, counters for food preparation, a table and chairs, storage spaces, cooking and eating equipment, a radiator, and even sometimes a washing machine for clothes all had to fit in a space of about 5.5 square meters.[73] The rationally organized kitchen resembled an assembly line, allowing the scientific organization of the outside world to permeate and shape the new Soviet home.[74] The rational arrangement of kitchen objects facilitated the housewife's daily work and rationalized her bodily movements. A poorly arranged kitchen forced a woman to walk "several kilometers" while preparing food. In such a kitchen (figure 6.3), the housewife wastefully contorted her body, bending, kneeling, and reaching for things.

In a well-arranged kitchen, however (figure 6.4), the lower half of a woman's body remained stationary, while her movements were confined to the upper body.[75] The rationally organized kitchen promised

Figure 6.3. A housewife working in a poorly and inefficiently organized kitchen.

Source: Boris Merzhanov and Konstantin Sorokin, *Eto nuzhno novoselam* (Moscow: Ekonomika, 1966).

Figure 6.4. A housewife in a rationally organized kitchen.

Source: Boris Merzhanov and Konstantin Sorokin, *Eto nuzhno novoselam* (Moscow: Ekonomika, 1966).

to make the housewife's movements more efficient. It disciplined her body, making it resemble that of a worker standing before a lathe on the factory floor. Like the excesses of ornamental architecture under Stalin, the housewife's body would be purged of unnecessary movements in the name of domestic efficiency and a new way of life.

As the image shown in figure 6.4 suggests, the perfect housewife's body was the desired social product of the *khrushchevka*'s kitchen factory. So too was the efficient assembly-line production of family meals. Food preparation counters with compact storage spaces were conveniently situated next to the stove and sink. A cutting board that slid out from under a counter allowed the housewife to prepare food while sitting down. Hanging cupboards above the main working areas decreased excessive walking.[76] The chair in one kitchen (figure 6.5) suggested its transformation into a laboratory of everyday life, where meals were prepared with clinical precision.

Some visionaries of the communist way of life foresaw an ever-smaller kitchen that would eventually disappear into the walls of people's apartments as residents, especially women, spent more of their every-day lives in the workplace and in the neighborhood's public spaces. In the futuristic apartment Aleksandr Peremyslov featured in his book *House of the Future* (see chapter 5), the kitchen was reduced in space-age efficiency to "a built-in compact aggregate for storing and warming up food" featuring a refrigerator, sink, electric stove, and pull-out table. This compact unit "replaced" the kitchen as a separate social space within the apartment, allowing at most for preparing and con-suming small meals like breakfast. A family took its real meals in the communal dining hall and called ahead to place its orders. The nine dining facilities in Peremyslov's imagined microdistrict "at the very least replace three thousand individual kitchens and make it possible to feed the entire population."[77] In dreaming of the day when communal dining halls would forever replace the kitchen, Peremyslov echoed Soviet designers of the kitchen-less *dom-kommuna* and prewar modernist vi-sionaries such as Karel Teige. In his treatise *The Minimum Dwelling* (1932), Teige had lamented the continued presence of the "live-in kitchen" as a holdover from the past that exceeded minimal functions and served as a social space separating the family from the community. A kitchen reduced to a compact nook, similar to the one Peremyslov found, was at worst "a throwback to the old live-in kitchen" and at best "a transi-tion to a higher form of apartment (i.e., without a kitchen)."[78]

Other homemaking experts under Khrushchev did not believe that the kitchen needed to be eliminated and were much less willing than Peremyslov to entertain the radical stances of such prewar modernists as Teige. These experts contended that, in addition to cooking and cleaning, the Soviet housewife used the kitchen for ironing and sewing clothes, and the family took its meals in it. One homemaking specialist noted that "under the settling of an apartment by one family, the kitchen becomes not only a place where they prepare food but also eat. In the absence of a separate working room, the majority of all work con-nected to household labor also takes place in the kitchen." Given its added functions, the kitchen of the separate apartment was increas-ingly referred to as a kitchen–dining room (*kukhnia-stolovaia*) and took on the "appearance of living space."[79] A well-arranged kitchen was the anchor of a separate apartment that ensured a family's bliss and al-lowed its members to regenerate psychologically. A homemaking ad-

Figure 6.5. Kitchen equipment with standardized sectional components. This model kitchen was designed at the Building Academy in East Germany, demonstrating that Soviet architects drew upon the models of other socialist countries for their own designs.

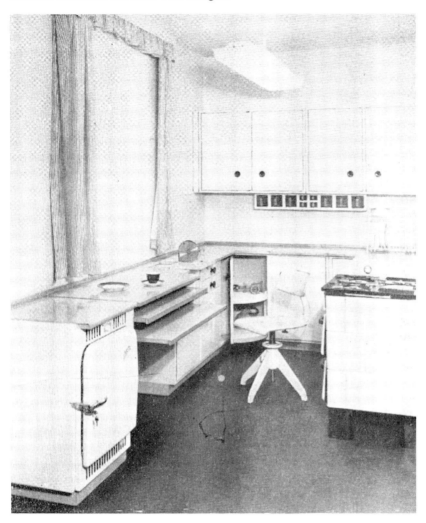

Source: Bruno Artmanis and Aleksei Nikolaev, *Sovremennaia mebel' i kvartira* (Riga: izdatel'stvo Akademii nauk Latviiskoi SSR, 1959), photograph at end of the book.

viser explained that "here the family gets together in a scene of coziness and warmth that furthers rest and the relaxing of one's nerves after the working day."[80]

Such advice implied that communal dining rooms and laundries had not developed sufficiently to liberate the housewife from such chores. Even if they had, homemaking experts likely would have still advocated the "live-in kitchen," pace Teige, as a progressive social space suitable for the communist way of life. As we saw in chapter 1, the kitchen had long since returned as a legitimate space in apartment designs. Although architects and housing propaganda under Khrushchev drew some inspiration from such radical models as the *dom-kommuna*, eradicating the kitchen was simply off the table. In more prosaic terms, homemaking specialists simply reflected what ordinary urban dwellers were doing once they got into a *khrushchevka*. In the communal apartment, residents had typically used the kitchen for cooking and other domestic chores but returned to their private rooms for eating and socializing. In the separate apartment, this critical auxiliary space was suddenly in the hands of just one family, and no matter how small it was, urban residents would make the most of it.

New Things in Life

As noted above, the furniture that residents of the *khrushchevka* brought home was often unlikely to be the kind advertised in homemaking advice literature and in exhibitions. Although shortfalls in production suggest how widespread this problem was, the data on household consumption illustrate it even more vividly. Several years into the mass housing campaign, the leadership in Moscow got its most comprehensive look at what people were consuming from a 1962 study done by the Central Statistical Administration of the Russian Republic (Tsentral'noe statisticheskoe upravlenie RSFSR) on the household items of people in different employment categories. The Soviet government discovered that not everyone's household consumer needs were the same and that some social groups had obtained more goods than others. Evidence that class mattered in obtaining new furniture and household goods stood in sharp contrast to homemaking advice literature, which saw gender and generation as the only legitimate social divisions. It undermined the egalitarian values of Khrushchev's regime and reproduced in consumption the class-based differences that we have already seen in housing distribution.

The 1962 study was based on a sample of 28,700 families, broken down into the following categories: 11,100 families of workers, 700 families of permanent *sovkhoz* (state farm) workers, 300 families of construction workers, 300 families of railway system workers, 13,100 *kolkhozniki* (collective farm families), and 3,200 families of engineering-technical personnel (*inzhenerno-tekhnicheskie rabotniki,* ITRs) and white-collar workers. The surveyors wanted to know about practically everything that people had accumulated, and they broke down respondents' possessions into five main categories: furniture, items bearing a "cultural" value (e.g., musical instruments, but also audiovisual electronics), household appliances, forms of transportation, and reading materials. They also asked respondents whether anyone in their families went to the library. In addition to reporting what people presently had in their homes (see tables 6.2, 6.3, and 6.4), the surveyors asked respondents what percentage of their household items they had acquired from January 1958 to June 1962 (see table 6.5). The data from this question allowed the surveyors to infer the impact of mass housing on consumers' purchases: Most people had obtained most of their furniture "in the past four years, in other words, in the period that saw the most rapid housing construction and the greatest mass-scale allocation of apartments to workers and white-collar employees."[81]

The survey also revealed which social groups were likely to have more consumer goods. As illustrated in table 6.2, ITRs and white-collar employees were the most privileged possessors of furniture. Although they had the smallest families (along with construction workers), they had more items per family than any other social group for all furniture except beds and dining tables, which was most likely a function of their small family size. In contrast, *sovkhoz* workers and *kolkhoz* members, the two groups with the largest families, possessed the most beds and dining tables. For almost all other furniture, these two rural groups had less than anyone else.[82] ITRs and white-collar employees similarly came out ahead of all other groups in the possession of most consumer items and reading materials (table 6.3).

The urban/rural divide, which had long been considered a holdover of social inequality from the capitalist past that would wither away under communism, reproduced itself in people's household possessions. In due deference to egalitarian ideals, the surveyors claimed that every-

Table 6.2. *Possession of Furniture among Six Soviet Employment Groups in 1962 in the Russian Soviet Federated Socialist Republic (average number of items per 100 families in each group as reported on June 1, 1962; highest amounts for each furniture item are shaded)*

Family Characteristics or Type of Furniture	Industrial Workers	Construction Workers	Railway Workers	Sovkhoz Workers	ITRs[a] and White-Collar Employees	Collective Farm Workers
Average family size	3.2	2.96	3.11	4.01	2.97	3.77
Clothes closets	87.1	69.7	89.9	61.1	93.4	30.2
Bookcases	3.4	2.8	6.8	1.4	15.6	1.3
Beds	165.6	144.4	161.5	219.1	166.7	180.8
Couches and sofas	74.6	69.7	79	43.5	84	16.4
Hutches and cupboards	32.9	25.9	37.2	13.1	42.6	12.7
Chests of drawers	43.2	25.3	40.2	20.8	44.5	15.2
Tables for eating	114.7	105.6	112.8	150.1	121.2	158.2
Tables for writing	10.4	6.6	11.8	12.7	21.8	12.3
Tables for televisions and radio sets	26.8	32.5	25.3	13.4	33.7	4.3
Chairs and armchairs	356.2	315.9	410.1	235.7	450.3	176.6
Vanities and mirror pieces	14.9	12.8	21.6	9.1	21.9	8.5

[a]ITRs = inzhenerno-tekhnicheskie rabotniki (engineering-technical workers).

Source: Gosudarstvennyi arkhiv Rossiiskoi Federatsii (State Archive of the Russian Federation), f. A-259, op. 42, d. 9114, l. 63.

Table 6.3. *Possession of Household Consumer Goods among Six Soviet Employment Groups in 1962 in the Russian Soviet Federated Socialist Republic (average number of items per 100 families in each group as reported on June 1, 1962; highest amounts for each consumer good are shaded)*

Family Characteristics or Type of Good	Industrial Workers	Construction Workers	Railway Workers	Sovkhoz Workers	ITRs[a] and White-Collar Employees	Collective Farm Workers
Average family size	3.2	2.96	3.11	4.01	2.97	3.77
Cable radio receivers	45.1	32.2	34.5	41.4	54.4	70.5
Radio sets and radiolas	54.4	50	54.7	58.6	53	18.7
Televisions	28.9	35.9	41.9	9.6	36.3	1.3
Tape recorders	0.7	0.3	1.4	—	1.6	0.03
Electronic record players	7.5	3.8	6.8	1.8	8.9	0.5
Portable gramophones	4.6	2.2	3.4	6.8	4.9	7.8
Accordions	8.9	6.6	9.8	11.2	8.4	9.6
Pianos and grand pianos	0.6	0.6	1.4	—	4.1	—
Other musical instruments	6.4	3.8	3.7	4.9	9.2	2.6
Refrigerators	2.9	4.4	8.4	—	8.1	0.03
Washing machines	10.1	10	21.3	2.9	18.6	0.5
Electrical vacuum cleaners	2.3	1.9	5.1	—	6.8	0.04
Electrical floor polishers	0.1	0.6	0.3	—	0.7	0.01
Cameras	12.1	8.1	15.2	5.6	21.4	2.3
Sewing machines	69.7	55.3	72.3	68.3	70.8	56.5
Light automobiles	0.8	0.6	1	0.5	1.7	0.2
Motorcycles and motorscooters	3.5	2.2	4.1	9.7	3	4.8
Bicycles and motorized bicycles	23.2	10	19.2	46.9	24.7	50.2
Books	3,807	2,315	5,117	1,527	9,217	1,125
Families that subscribe to or regularly buy:						
Newspapers	96	62	126	107	139	88
Periodicals	36	13	34	20	93	13
Number of family members who go to the library	90	38	77	98	127	71

[a]ITRs = inzhenerno-tekhnicheskie rabotniki (engineering-technical workers).

Source: Gosudarstvennyi arkhiv Rossiiskoi Federatsii (State Archive of the Russian Federation), f. A-259, op. 42, d. 9114, ll. 63–64.

one was getting more household items across the board and that "differences in providing separate social groups with the goods indicated here are smoothing out." Despite this good news, the surveyors admitted, "the urban population is provided with more than the rural population. There are also differences in what separate urban groups surveyed here have."[83]

Indeed, the data revealed significant differences within the social groups (table 6.4). Among ITRs and white-collar employees, for example, the families of doctors had the most furniture, were most likely to have a television and a piano, had obtained the most refrigerators and vacuum cleaners, owned the most books, read the most newspapers and periodicals, and got around town on the most bicycles. The families of ITRs working in industry and schoolteachers tended to have the most household goods after doctors. Schoolteachers were the most likely to have family members who used the local library, while ITRs had the greatest number of automobiles. The bottom of this scale was shared by white-collar workers in industry and midlevel medical personnel. Although both lagged behind in various furniture items, the white-collar employees fell behind the most in home electronics like televisions and possessed the fewest musical instruments. Meanwhile, the midlevel medical personnel had the fewest home appliances like refrigerators, the smallest book collections, and the fewest subscriptions to print media.[84]

The surveyors' data showed patterns that already existed under Stalin: City dwellers tended to have more household consumer goods than peasants, while engineering specialists and other well-educated groups in the Soviet intelligentsia tended to have more than anyone else. Additional data revealed the amount of consumer items people had obtained in the previous four years (table 6.5). As one would expect, most people had obtained most of their new furniture in the past several years. Furthermore, every social group was spending more per family member, as measured in two bundled categories of all household items surveyed, than they had in the recent past (see table 6.6).[85]

The surveyors' data suggested revealing trends about who first obtained the everyday artifacts of the communist way of life. The data given in table 6.5 suggest that some social groups had obtained more of their overall furniture possessions in the recent past than others, for reasons that the data presented in table 6.6 help elucidate. According to table 6.5, the families of construction workers and the families of

Table 6.4. *Possession of Furniture and Household Consumer Goods among Engineering-Technical Workers (Inzhenerno-Tekhnicheskie Rabotniki, ITRs) and White-Collar Employees in 1962 in the Russian Soviet Federated Socialist Republic (average number of items per 100 families in each group as reported on June 1, 1962; highest amounts for each furniture item are shaded)*

Family Characteristics or Type of Furniture or Good	All ITRs and White-Collar Employees	ITRs in Industry	From All ITRs and White-Collar Employees:			
			White-Collar Employees in Industry	Teachers in Primary and Secondary Schools	Doctors	Middle Medical Personnel
Average family size	2.97	3.48	2.91	2.75	2.91	2.68
Clothes closets	93.4	99.1	92.1	97.1	101.4	87.1
Bookcases	15.6	21.5	8.8	37.6	54.3	11.1
Beds	166.7	185.1	164.5	165.9	172.9	150.3
Couches and sofas	84	92.8	80.9	92.2	112.9	74.3
Hutches and cupboards	42.6	51.2	38.4	47.8	55.7	39.8
Chests of drawers	44.5	43.4	48.1	36.6	37.1	40.4
Tables for eating	121.2	130.7	118.5	125.9	138.6	112.9
Tables for writing	21.8	28.7	17.3	38	54.3	13.5
Tables for TVs and radio sets	33.7	43.5	29.6	36.6	41.4	31
Chairs and armchairs	450.3	512.5	423.6	486.3	592.9	415.2
Vanities and mirror pieces	21.9	25.6	20.3	23.9	30	19.9
Cable radio receivers	54.4	47.3	57.1	57.1	64.3	52.6
Radio sets and radiolas	53	63.5	49.6	51.2	48.6	51.5

Televisions	36.3	46.9	30.7	35.6	60	37.4
Tape recorders	1.6	2.1	0.6	3.9	7.1	2.3
Electronic record players	8.9	12.4	6.1	10.2	17.2	11.1
Portable gramophones	4.9	5	3.9	8.8	7.1	5.3
Accordions	8.4	9.7	8	10.7	7.1	7
Pianos and grand pianos	4.1	5.9	1.7	12.7	17.1	2.3
Other musical instruments	9.2	11.2	7	11.2	17.1	11.1
Refrigerators	8.1	16.5	4.9	9.3	31.4	4.1
Washing machines	18.6	28.3	16.5	23.4	27.1	8.8
Electrical vacuum cleaners	6.8	12.2	4.1	12.2	20	3.5
Cameras	21.4	30.3	15.8	33.7	45.7	16.9
Sewing machines	70.8	82.4	71.3	65.9	64.3	58.5
Light automobiles	1.7	3.1	1.1	2.9	1.4	1.2
Motorcycles and motorscooters	3	4.9	2.7	0.5	2.9	2.9
Bicycles and motorized bicycles	24.7	32.3	22.4	24.4	38.6	20.5
Books	9,217	10,849	5,935	23,226	35,193	5,736
Families that subscribe to or regularly buy:						
Newspapers	139	174	125	191	216	98
Periodicals	93	110	87	136	156	61
Number of family members who go to the library	127	141	119	166	160	105

Source: Gosudarstvennyi arkhiv Rossiiskoi Federatsii (State Archive of the Russian Federation), f. A-259, op. 42, d. 9114, l. 71.

Table 6.5. *Percentage of Furniture Obtained between January 1958 and June 1, 1962, in the Russian Soviet Federated Socialist Republic (highest percentages for each furniture item are shaded)*

Type of Furniture	Industrial Workers	Construction Workers	Railway Workers	Sovkhoz Workers	ITRs[a] and White-Collar Employees	Collective Farm Workers
Clothes closets	38	58.2	37.9	72.3	33.3	57.5
Bookcases	58.8	67.9	39.7	57.1	48.1	25
Beds	25.6	49.1	20.7	32.4	24.7	29.5
Couches and sofas	38.2	61.8	37.6	73.6	33.3	67.1
Hutches and cupboards	53.5	73.7	50.8	67.2	48.6	31.8
Chests of drawers	24.5	49.4	14.2	59.6	18	36.9
Tables for eating	28.3	52.9	26.9	28.7	26.2	15.4
Tables for writing	45.2	75.8	37.3	37.8	33	21.4
Tables for televisions and radio sets	56	72	52.2	63.4	47.2	41.2
Chairs and armchairs	36.5	56	31.6	52.7	31.3	43.6
Vanities and mirror pieces	50.3	51.6	36.1	54.9	44.7	36

[a]ITRs = inzhenerno-tekhnicheskie rabotniki (engineering-technical workers).

Source: Gosudarstvennyi arkhiv Rossiiskoi Federatsii (State Archive of the Russian Federation), f. A-259, op. 42, d. 9114, l. 66.

sovkhoz workers were most likely to have obtained higher proportions of their overall furniture possessions in the past four years, whereas *kolkhoz* members and ITRs/white-collar workers had obtained the smallest proportions of their furniture in the recent past. The Soviet intelligentsia had not obtained less furniture in recent years for lack of money, whereas it appears that was the fate of *kolkhozniki*. As the surveyors noted in table 6.6, ITRs and white-collar employees spent the most amount of money per family member on furniture and other household goods in 1961 and had increased their expenditures the most among all groups in comparison with 1958.[86] Yet according to table 6.5, between 1958 and 1962 they had obtained less than half of their current furniture possessions. In conjunction with table 6.5, therefore, table 6.6 suggests that the Soviet intelligentsia (ITRs and white-collar employees) had obtained most of their furniture before the high years of Khrushchev's housing boom but still spent more per family members on all consumer goods than all other social groups. But do the data really tell us that construction workers and *sovkhoz* workers purchased a higher proportion of their furniture in recent years than other social groups and that most of their new purchases were of the new style? This is a more difficult question to answer because older models continued to be manufactured and families may have bought older,

Table 6.6. Money Spent by Soviet Families on Household Consumer Items in 1961 in the Russian Soviet Federated Socialist Republic

	Average Amount Spent in 1961 per Family Member on These Goods (rubles):		Expenditures in 1961 on These Goods as a Percentage of Expenditures in 1958 on the Same Goods:	
Employment Group	Furniture and Household Appliances	Items of a Cultural Value and Means of Transportation	Furniture and Household Appliances	Items of a Cultural Value and Means of Transportation
Industrial workers	24.7	21.3	129	119
Sovkhoz workers	16.1	14.5	141	120
Collective farm workers	9.5	7.4	128	116
ITRs[a] and white-collar employees	33.1	30.9	145	122

[a]ITRs = inzhenerno-tekhnicheskie rabotniki (engineering-technical workers).

Source: Gosudarstvennyi arkhiv Rossiiskoi Federatsii (State Archive of the Russian Federation), f. A-259, op. 42, d. 9114, l. 52.

secondhand items. Nonetheless, the data indicate that most Soviet citizens, even peasants, were benefiting from a wave of increased consumer goods production that was triggered by Khrushchev's mass housing campaign.

The surveyors found that people in some groups had not only obtained most of what they possessed in the past four years but had also acquired some goods for the very first time. Purchasing new consumer items they had never before enjoyed or even seen—such as refrigerators and vacuum cleaners—was another aspect of the emerging communist way of life that Khrushchev's regime celebrated and ordinary people had come to expect. As explained in table 6.7, construction workers obtained several items for the first time, including tape recorders, pianos, refrigerators, vacuum cleaners, and motorcycles. Most families surveyed had likely obtained most of their electronic devices only recently, if not for the first time. This was especially true for television sets, tape recorders, electronic record players, refrigerators, washing machines, vacuum cleaners, motorcycles, and automobiles. In addition, the data reveal the objects most families were likely to have already possessed before 1958, including cable radio receivers, portable gramophones, a musical instrument, sewing machines, and bicycles. These broad patterns suggested that electrical devices were just beginning to make their way into Soviet homes in the late 1950s and early 1960s. In contrast to homemaking advice literature, which celebrated the modernity of electronic goods in the scientifically organized home, most families still relied on mechanical goods in their everyday lives.

The fact that more ordinary Soviet citizens from different social groups were obtaining more household consumer goods, despite lingering social stratification, was surely a good sign. But the real victory of the communist way of life, as Khrushchev famously saw it, could only come once the Soviet Union surpassed its capitalist rivals in the West. The surveyors for the 1962 study were attuned to this measure of success, but they only had bad news to share. Without offering much commentary, they provided two tables (adapted here as tables 6.8 and 6.9) showing that a far greater percentage of families in the United States, England, France, and West Germany possessed major household appliances than did families in the Soviet social groups surveyed.

The surveyors curtly interpreted the grim statistics in table 6.8 by noting that "only 3 percent of families of industrial workers and 8 per-

Table 6.7. Percentage of Furniture and Household Consumer Goods Obtained between January 1958 and June 1, 1962, in the Russian Soviet Federated Socialist Republic (highest percentages for each consumer good are shaded)

Type of Furniture or Good	Industrial Workers	Construction Workers	Railway Workers	Sovkhoz Workers	ITRs[a] and White-Collar Employees	Collective Farm Workers
Cable radio receivers	18.8	49.4	18.6	26.8	15.8	37.6
Radio sets and radiolas	43.7	58.8	43.1	63.7	39.8	56.7
Televisions	70.9	84.4	66.8	83.3	65	82.6
Tape recorders	71.4	100	100	—	75	66.7
Electronic record players	38.7	89.5	60.3	61.1	38.2	66
Portable gramophones	10.9	40.9	8.8	25	10.2	20.2
Accordions	46.1	66.7	52	43.7	56	47.6
Pianos and grand pianos	66.7	100	—	—	43.9	—
Other musical instruments	32.8	34.2	37.8	59.2	33.7	40.5
Refrigerators	89.7	100	92.9	—	74.1	66.7
Washing machines	86.1	88	93.4	100	77.3	94.3
Electrical vacuum cleaners	78.3	100	80.4	—	70.6	75
Cameras	50.4	69.1	40.1	80.4	47.2	65.3
Sewing machines	34	54.2	36	42.6	27.5	37.6
Light automobiles	50	50	70	60	64.7	70.6
Motorcycles and motorscooters	71.4	100	48.8	60.8	83.3	68.5
Bicycles and motorized bicycles	42.7	56	26.6	55.5	40.5	46.8

[a]ITRs = inzhenerno-tekhnicheskie rabotniki (engineering-technical workers).

Source: Gosudarstvennyi arkhiv Rossiiskoi Federatsii (State Archive of the Russian Federation), f. A-259, op. 42, d. 9114, l. 66.

cent of ITRs and white-collar employees have refrigerators." Their inclusion of sewing machines in this table went without commentary, but the implication in comparison with what capitalist families had (table 6.9) was fairly clear. Most Soviet families got by with mechanical devices from the nineteenth century, while their capitalist counterparts had surged ahead into the twentieth-century world of electrical goods.[87]

The surveyors moved on without further comment, but the numbers alone spoke volumes to the leadership in Moscow. The data confirmed any sense of inferiority that Khrushchev and his inner circle might have experienced, but which they hid when Nixon met him during their famous "Kitchen Debate" at the American Exhibition in Moscow in 1959. The United States was so thoroughly routing the Soviet Union in getting electronic goods into the hands of its citizens that the same paltry number of Soviet families that somehow had them tended to equal the tiny number of American families that somehow avoided them. Even the presentation of the capitalist countries' data on the page of the surveyors' report suggested the greater inferiority the further one moved east. The United States stood in the middle of the page at the head of the West brandishing its latest crushing data, followed to its right by its faithful British allies with their lower, but still respectable, figures. The French came next, already woefully behind in televisions, and the West Germans were not far behind, even with three-year-old figures. Someone reading this report could have

Table 6.8. Possession of Electrical Appliances and Sewing Machines among Six Soviet Employment Groups in the Russian Soviet Federated Socialist Republic (average number of items per 100 families in each group as reported on June 1, 1962)

Appliance or Machine	Industrial Workers	Construction Workers	Railway Workers	Sovkhoz Workers	ITRs[a] and White-Collar Employees	Collective Farm Workers
Refrigerators	2.9	4.4	8.4	—	8.1	0.03
Washing machines	10.1	10	21.3	2.9	18.5	0.5
Floor polishers	0.1	0.6	0.3	—	0.7	0.01
Vacuum cleaners	2.3	1.9	5.1	—	6.8	0.04
Sewing machines	69.7	55.3	72.3	68.3	70.8	56.5

[a]ITRs = inzhenerno-tekhnicheskie rabotniki (engineering-technical workers).

Source: Gosudarstvennyi arkhiv Rossiiskoi Federatsii (State Archive of the Russian Federation), f. A-259, op. 42, d. 9114, l. 57.

Table 6.9. Percentage of Families in Capitalist Countries in Possession of Durable Goods

Type of Good	United States, End of 1961	England, January–March 1961	France, June 1961	West Germany, End of 1958
Radio sets	94	76	85	86
Televisions	89	78	19	13
Refrigerators	98	20	32	23
Washing machines	96	39	28	22
Vacuum cleaners	76	71	32	54

Source: Gosudarstvennyi arkhiv Rossiiskoi Federatsii (State Archive of the Russian Federation), f. A-259, op. 42, d. 9114, l. 58.

only guessed how depressing the data were for countries just beyond the Iron Curtain.

Conclusion

No matter how much the Soviet state increased the manufacture of consumer goods, the data presented above show that unsatisfied consumer demand continued to plague the Soviet economy. Increases in the variety and amount of consumer goods, coupled with persistent shortages, created a troubling contradiction. Although Khrushchev's regime had significantly increased the production of consumer goods, it still retained the features of the command economy forged under Stalin to which economists have pointed in explaining state socialist regimes' persistent shortages. These included manufacturers' tendency to hoard supplies and goods, unforeseen changes in economic plans, official prices that failed to accurately reflect demand, and the fact that consumers faced a seller's market. For many ordinary urban dwellers, waiting for the state to manufacture furniture and consumer goods was becoming with each passing year as much a part of the communist way of life as the dream world envisioned in homemaking advice literature.

Retaining control over the symbolic construction of the *khrushchevka* and its furniture as the new spaces and objects of the communist way of life was critically important to a regime that increasingly staked its legitimacy on improving ordinary citizens' standard of living. Despite their embrace of a rational and scientifically organized domestic life, the advice specialists on the new Soviet home hid a deeper anxiety, which was shared especially among mass housing architects, about the limitations they faced. As we saw in chapter 2, underneath the scientific veneer of the well-planned *khrushchevka* were a series of decisions about apartment design dating back to the 1930s that ultimately delimited what architects could do with this space and how furniture makers could design new furniture. Ordinary residents, to whom we turn in chapter 7, politicized architects' inability to resolve the design shortcomings that plagued separate apartments, and many were less than enamored by the modernist turn in furniture design. Rather than embrace the minimalist dimensions of the *khrushchevka* as a harbinger of a more rational and scientific way of life, many residents wondered why their apartments simply could not be a bit larger and better designed to meet their needs, and why furniture was still so difficult to obtain.

Chapter 7

The Politics of Complaint

The Soviet home remained a politically charged field under Khrushchev as the regime mobilized it for the broader goals of creating a classless society, shaping the New Soviet Man and Woman, and showing the world that socialism was superior to capitalism. The communist way of life (*kommunisticheskii byt*) would be the final victory of this politics of transformation. It would be achieved not through repression and war as Stalin's regime had tried, but through the peaceful, consensus-building project of moving people into their own apartments, proper socialization through neighborhood organizations, and a deluge of advice literature on how to live the good life of a Soviet citizen.

At the same time, by resolving the housing question through the mass housing campaign, Khrushchev's regime sought to depoliticize its most socially divisive features, such as the waiting list and the cooperative, as we saw in previous chapters. The regime looked forward to a future communist way of life without a housing question once urban residents all lived in separate apartments. What Khrushchev's regime found, however, was that ordinary people were not as prepared to abandon the politics of complaint and blame once they passed through the process of housing distribution and moved into their separate apartments. Urban residents at times even echoed the language of a Stalinist purge in trying to force the state to resolve a housing question they believed remained unanswered.

Residents of the *khrushchevka* found a host of problems when they moved to their new homes, ranging from incompletely built neighborhoods to shortages of furniture in stores. Rather than sheepishly accept their fate or simply make do on their own, however, ordinary people vigorously confronted architects, furniture designers, and housing officials to force them to fix problems. This chapter explores the new opportunities urban dwellers enjoyed under Khrushchev to voice their complaints, focusing in particular on residential meetings with architects and housing officials, comment books from housing and furniture exhibitions, and citizens' letters to architectural congresses. Their appropriation of these encounters tells us much about how ordinary people experienced and shaped Khrushchev's thaw beyond high cultural politics and the regime's relationship with the cultural intelligentsia. Upon moving to the separate apartment, many urban dwellers were far from satisfied with what they got and were intent on keeping the housing question on the front burner by projecting new desires and needs onto it. They directed their ire not so much at the top leadership or the Soviet system but rather toward representatives of the state responsible for the design and upkeep of mass housing. By blaming architects in particular, ordinary residents anticipated and may have even encouraged Khrushchev's own impatience with these members of the cultural intelligentsia. In short, there was a popular dimension to Khrushchev's attacks against architects and the cultural authority upon which they drew to dictate the design of the Soviet home and tell urban dwellers how to live.

Meet the Architects

Among the ways residents complained to state authorities about their housing, residential meetings stand out as a particularly contentious setting. Two such meetings, held in Leningrad in December 1953 and May 1954, provide us with a unique window onto the ways residents confronted architects and displayed their knowledge about apartment design, bringing us back to design issues examined in chapters 1 and 2. The apartments of these residents were at the threshold of transformations in design toward smaller apartments. Some were too large and hence communal, while others had too much living space, but tiny auxiliary units. Regardless of how they had been distributed, these residents believed their apartments should be separate. Apart from the fact that the Leningrad branch of the Union of Soviet Architects organized the meetings, their stenographic reports shed little light on their background. Both meetings, however, occurred *before* Khrushchev's regime issued its first post-Stalin housing initiatives, such as the December 1954 All-Union Conference of Constructors and a November 1955 decree that faulted architects for their "excesses" in costly designs and pressed them to build cheaper and less ornate apartments for the masses.[1] As illustrated in the Leningrad meetings, ordinary residents hardly needed direction from above to tell architects what was wrong with housing.

To be sure, the meetings cannot account for all residents' experiences or opinions. Like other sources examined in this chapter, the meetings encouraged the self-selection of residents eager to complain and their frequency still needs to be determined. With such qualifications in mind, these encounters can tell us much about the range of issues that plagued new housing at the dawn of the post-Stalin era and how these issues subsequently shaped contact between architects and residents under Khrushchev. The two meetings were local examples of the thaw that occurred before its seminal moments, such as the publication of Ilya Ehrenburg's novella *The Thaw* (1954) and Khrushchev's "Secret Speech" in 1956. As open-ended forums for critical input on housing, they stood in contrast to ritualized meetings between party-state bureaucrats and citizens under Stalin. They also foreshadowed the Khrushchev regime's populist commitment to answer ordinary citizens' demands for improvements in everyday material life.[2]

But the meetings also reflected the punitive tendencies and scapegoating of Khrushchev's populism that threatened, like housing deficiencies themselves, to become a permanent fixture in the communist way of life instead of being discarded as part of the Stalinist past. Architects had little control over the underlying problems of mass housing, especially the distribution norms that constrained their design work. But as the only authority figures at these meetings, they became the target of residents' discontent. From the state's perspective, architects' cultural capital and professional status were expendable. Bringing them down a notch deflected popular criticism and presaged Khrushchev's own decision to favor engineers and constructors over architects in the mass housing campaign.[3]

At the first meeting in December 1953, architects met with residents of the city's Kirov district. As home of the prerevolutionary Putilov (now Kirov) factory, this industrial district in southwestern Leningrad became a site of mass housing construction under Khrushchev.[4] Residents posed questions on issues that architects were at pains to answer. "How many movie theaters and libraries are there going to be in the district?" one resident asked. "Have you heard the complaints about the great noise in houses and is anything being done about it?" another wanted to know. "Are they going to build baths in our district?" Responding to a question about heat, one architect lamented that the authorities refused to expand existing capacity. Addressing a question about telephones, another explained that a new telephone station would meet demand in only two years.[5]

Chairmen of residential "assistance commissions" offered longer descriptions of problems. One chairman, Iakovlev, emphasized the obvious discrepancies between representation and reality. "In newspapers and everywhere else," he explained, "we talk about the need to create coziness for the toilers of the Soviet Union, so that they can rest well coming home from work." In reality, new apartments suffered from excessive reductions in size. Iakovlev lamented one apartment building's "small two- to three-room apartments," which he described as "small dormitories." He asked architects to imagine a birthday with five guests in a particular apartment: "I would like to know how Comrade Designer would receive them right there in the entrance. I'm sure that he would have to receive guests in the corridor one at a time in line! Is this the way to go? Is this really coziness!"[6]

Although the separate apartment gave families exclusive use of domestic space and encouraged them to acquire consumer goods, its dimensions left little room for these objects. At the meeting in May 1954, a planning official noted that the dimensions of entranceways in communal apartments were not that important because "residents keep their outer clothes and galoshes in their rooms." In contrast, the width of a separate apartment's entranceway mattered because a family made full use of it. An architect conceded that small entranceways prevented residents from organizing them as they wanted and lacked space for objects like bicycles. She explained, "[People] hang a coat in the entranceway of individual apartments. Then residents will want to place furniture—a mirror piece or a small table. Given current dimensions, it's impossible to find space for any of this."[7]

The auxiliary space that especially concerned residents was the kitchen. At the 1953 meeting, Iakovlev complained that in one apartment "the kitchen was made so small, you can't turn around in it." He recognized that apartment design, as explained by architects in chapter 2, was subject to peculiar cost pressures that had to do with the proportion of living to auxiliary spaces: "Apparently the question consists of the need to increase the amount of living space and to decrease the amount of unpaid for space [i.e., auxiliary space], but nobody thinks that living this way is difficult."[8] Iakovlev also found that the small windows (*fortochki*) that were placed within the frame of larger windows were located too high. He asked a designer at the opening of a new house to open such a window and found that she had to climb from a stool to the window ledge in order to reach the small window. "This is how she had to climb up, moreover she was rather tall, but what will a short person do?" Another assistance commission chairman, Dmitriev, found that the typical kitchen in one house "looks like a matchbox." This was especially onerous in six-room apartments, which he explained had been designed for the communal settlement of single persons. Such apartments were an extreme example of how pressures to reduce costs produced more living space in proportion to auxiliary space.[9] At the 1954 meeting, a resident identified as an engineer reasoned that three-room apartments would hold larger families and thus require larger kitchens than two-room apartments. Instead, he found that two-room apartments had kitchens with 8 to 10 square meters, whereas three-room apartments had kitchens with 8.1 square meters.[10]

A planning official at the 1953 meeting, Drebezgov, acknowledged residents' concerns about small spaces but explained that norms came from the center and kitchens would not exceed 7 to 8 square meters: "The State Committee on Construction Affairs and the Soviet of Ministers establish a fundamental task: the maximum output of living space, the maximum reduction of auxiliary space, because not only in Leningrad, but throughout the Soviet Union an acute shortage in living space is felt."[11] As explained in chapter 1, shortages were measured and apartments were distributed in units of living space per person (i.e., the floor space of rooms not including auxiliary units). Although more living space was needed overall, its amount per apartment had to be reduced to ensure single-family occupancy. Meanwhile, cost estimates favored high yields of living space in proportion to auxiliary space, requiring the latter to be heavily reduced. Drebezgov's brief explanation suggested that the trade-offs between living space and auxiliary space inherent in the design of separate apartments were well known, but not accepted by those in attendance at the meeting.

The architect chairing the 1954 meeting, A. S. Gintsberg, an early designer and proponent of mass housing in Leningrad, tried to dampen residents' expectations and steer them away from such questions:[12] "Each person, of course, thinks that the more living space a person has, the better. But we all know that for now living space is limited in a definite way, therefore we must orient ourselves to existing norms and therefore it's necessary to discuss other questions." Gintsberg also deflected responsibility for communally distributed apartments with small kitchens: "There are frequent reprimands that the kitchen is small, that it's difficult to accommodate three or four housewives. That's right, it's difficult to accommodate them, but we design on the basis of one family. And what's done now, that it's necessary to accommodate not one family—this does not arise from the architect's work, but the established circumstances."[13] The "established circumstances" were the distribution norms and practices that turned separate apartments into communal ones. In a 1950 article for a local architectural journal, Gintsberg had alluded to similar circumstances to explain why larger apartments were settled communally.[14] Although he was right that architects had no power over distribution, this mattered little to residents living with the consequences.

Rejecting Gintsberg's request for limiting discussion, residents focused on communal settlement and construction defects. One resident, Lebedev, explained why apartments had to become small: "A minimal design is desirable for apartments by virtue of the fact that it is not a secret that if an apartment has five rooms, then five families live in it." To avoid communal distribution, he called for "a minimum quantity of rooms, to design apartments of two to three rooms." And he also wanted apartments of higher quality. Soundproofing was a chronic problem, and walking on poorly installed floors was like "playing a piano."[15] Although residents understood why an apartment's living space had to become smaller to ensure it remain separate and why auxiliary spaces had to be reduced to keep costs down, they nonetheless lamented an apartment's shrunken dimensions that lowered basic human dignity. At the 1953 meeting, Dmitriev explained that residents of small apartments could not respectfully remove a dead body: "Someone here said that if a person dies, then it's impossible to remove him, it's necessary to carry him out standing up, but they don't carry corpses standing up, and yet people also need to die! It's natural."[16]

After hearing Lebedev's complaints, Gintsberg asked, "Is the entranceway sufficient? How many rooms do you have?" Lebedev answered, "We have three rooms. The entranceway is not sufficient, yet we have three families. The kitchen is also very small." Uninterested in its communalized state, Gintsberg wanted Lebedev to ignore reality and critique his apartment from the vantage point of its intended settlement. The kitchen was small "only because three families live there, but if there were one—would the one [kitchen] be sufficient?" To Lebedev, Gintsberg utterly missed the point: "But you see in reality the housing question is not resolved, so then one family lives in each room. If one family of five gets a 22-meter room, three persons live in a 12-meter room, and four persons in an 18-meter room. Here's what is done in the apartment, here are the kind of inconveniences!"[17] The members of Lebedev's family lived a familiar contradiction: Their apartment's large living spaces led to communal distribution, yet its auxiliary spaces were designed for one family.

Even when architects managed to keep apartments separate, residents remained discontent with the design solutions employed to bring this about. As we saw in chapter 2, architects included "pass-through" rooms to cut down on auxiliary spaces and, alongside reductions in living space, to prevent communalization. Residents disliked this feature, desiring instead separate rooms with their own doors onto the corridor. Bezzubov, a housing constructor and resident at the 1954 meeting, explained that one factory's apartments were large, but presumably because they had "pass-through" rooms, they were settled with single families. He estimated that approximately 20 percent of the living space was "lost" because single families had obtained more living space than the factory could afford. To remedy the situation, someone had added doors to connect the isolated rooms with corridors. The factory management may have initiated this in order to transform the apartments into communal ones to house as many workers as possible. But residents may have done so themselves as a way of refashioning their apartments to fit their own tastes. In either case, Bezzubov was confident that such reconfigurations would cease in the future when distribution norms would increase so that "a single family will live in a two- to three-room apartment" and each room would have its own access to the corridor.[18]

Bezzubov's comments articulated urban residents' rising expectations for apartments that would be spacious *and* separate, not require major reconstruction, and conform to people's needs, not distribution norms. He explained, "People want to live large [*liudi khotiat zhit' bogato*]. They want to have things, but there's no place to put them." He recommended that apartment designs be vetted to ensure they matched the number of family members. Constructors should be permitted to communicate directly with future residents to change designs according to their needs. In response to Gintsberg's question about where to put built-in closets, Bezzubov said, "This depends upon what kind of residents there are, what kind of settlement. We need to get closer to those for whom we are designing."[19] Such a scenario was unlikely in a housing system that would soon be predicated on standardization and mass construction where the left hand of design had no control over the right hand of distribution.

Like Lebedev, Bezzubov displayed a keen interest in the kitchen. He explained to Gintsberg, "In relationship to kitchens the majority of housewives think, and I share this opinion, that the calculation is done incorrectly, architects don't look to the future." The future was consumerist, and the separate apartment was already behind the times: "If material life will improve, a person will obtain objects, household equipment, but there won't be any place to put it. Therefore, one mustn't fear that the kitchen be made larger." Bezzubov pointed to a friend's separate apartment where the kitchen was 10 to 12 square meters, thereby allowing the family to use it as a dining room with space for a refrigerator, sink, and a stove. Yet the kitchens of most apartments were so small that "in the future there won't be any space to put anything in them." To underline his criticism of such Spartan dimensions, Bezzubov urged architects to develop decorative elements, such as cornices, and to "reject that simplicity that was necessary in the past." This was a reference to constructivist aesthetics, which he evidently disliked in favor of an architectural style more in line with elite apartment houses built under Stalin. "This is housing, not a theater," Gintsberg lectured Bezzubov, and noted that flat walls without cornices avoided dust buildup.[20]

Their brief exchange over aesthetics suggests that Bezzubov and Gintsberg were already having the architectural debate, heretofore kept within professional circles, that Khrushchev would dramatically turn into a public issue at the December 1954 All-Union Conference of Constructors.[21] Gintsberg's negative response to Bezzubov's suggestions foreshadowed in rough outline Khrushchev's comments at this conference, in which he pushed for standardized models of minimalist design, acknowledged the positive attributes of the constructivist heritage, and rejected decorative elements as the architectural "excesses" of the Stalinist legacy. In doing so, Khrushchev sincerely believed he was acting in the ordinary Soviet citizen's best interest to bring him the separate apartment he had always wanted. What he did not anticipate were individuals like Bezzubov, who were not excited by the straight lines and flat surfaces of new apartments and household wares but actually would have liked some of those Stalinist excesses for themselves. Visitors to furniture exhibitions, to which we will turn later in the chapter, were similarly skeptical of the modernist turn in mass housing design and consumer goods.

First Days in the Separate Apartment

Many residents experienced the move to the separate apartment as a two-step process of joy followed by disappointment. After waiting years to get a separate apartment, many opened the doors to their new homes only to find design peculiarities, construction defects, and, in some cases, communal settlement. In a letter to the December 1954 All-Union Conference of Constructors, a Muscovite Communist Party member, V. Ganicheva, wrote, "In 1951, I encountered great happiness— they issued a housing permit for a small separate apartment. My gratitude is great." But soon thereafter, troubles began with the heat and plumbing in her bathroom. Crevices appeared between doors and their frames because the latter were warped. Finding a comfortable place to be seated at her piano gave her particular problems. She complained of "my sufferings with which I sit at this instrument!" Sound traveled between apartments, a phenomenon she found "insulting." At the end of her letter, she pleaded with her readers to "show more care for a person" (a boilerplate slogan from the Stalin era) and asked that they prevent defects in construction. She concluded, "Don't spoil the happiness of 'new residents' by repeating old mistakes!"[22]

Ganicheva was a well-to-do member of the Soviet intelligentsia. As a party member living in Moscow, she had secured a separate apartment all to herself, which was highly unusual not only in 1951 but also for the entire Khrushchev era. Her piano suggested a cultural refinement that set her off from the masses. Yet in writing to the December 1954 meeting, she joined ordinary Muscovites like the Lashuns we saw in the last chapter. Dealing with the shortcomings of mass housing was an experience that cut across social lines. To borrow Ganicheva's words, they were all "new residents" now.

As the Party Control Commission (Kommissia Partiinogo Kontrolia, KPK) found in 1960, Ganicheva's experience became the norm for many urban dwellers. Lengthy repairs on the construction defects of a newly built building on Bol'shaia Kashenkinskaia Street in Moscow were keeping its new residents from relocating to their new apartments. The investigator quoted from their group letter:

> Our initial happiness to live in a new building turned out to be in vain. It turns out that in order to move in, it is necessary to endure yet more sufferings and torments, but most importantly, nowhere will you find either a person in authority or an institution that would answer [for this], that would take responsibility for this mess.[23]

Residents' inability to pin down precisely who was to blame suggests that there was plenty to go around. When residents tried to fix problems themselves, the outcomes lent credence to local officials' frustration with ordinary people's inability to take care of their homes. For example, in another group letter included in the KPK's investigations, fifty-five residents living on Novo-Mikhalkovskii Passage complained, "It's now already a few months since we've settled in a new, well-outfitted house. It appeared possible to live and be happy and thank the Timiriazevskii district Soviet Executive Committee, but instead of this we are only nervous and tormented." Because bureaucratic red tape had held up access to gas, the residents depended on electricity for cooking and washing clothes. Having evidently adjusted their electrical wiring for these purposes, their electricity was now "in a chaotic condition, tangled up" and the residents lamented, "we sit without light."[24]

The mass media similarly featured the two-step process of moving into new housing. In 1961, *Pravda* painted this image of new housing in Khabarovsk:

> When a building is settled, everything in it shines, everything appears to have been made [to last] for many years. In reality, it is not rare that this outer gloss is made only so that the building can be turned over to the organization that ordered it, as it's said, to get rid of it. But after a few months, many defects are discovered.[25]

In reviewing construction problems in Ufa, *Pravda* quoted from the following group letter: "'In receiving the housing permits for new apartments with all the amenities, we were happy. But disappointment soon overtook us: In the building there was much that was not yet finished, badly done work.'"[26] Before describing heating and water problems, a resident of Iaroslavl wrote that "hundreds of thousands of Soviet citizens celebrate settling in, others await it. My dream was fulfilled. I received an apartment. Great comforts, however. . . ."[27] As such letters suggested, it was the problems, not the benefits, of the separate apartment that could bring residents together. Complaining about design abnormalities and construction defects gave people a collective sense of identity as residents in opposition to state officials who, they firmly believed, had acted either through neglect or malicious intent to make their everyday lives difficult. In a planned economy that did not fall prey to the impersonal market forces of capitalism, someone somewhere must have done something to cause design flaws and construction defects.

The most common problems were covered in the press and chronicled in residents' meetings and letters of complaint. They included floors and walls with uneven surfaces, and warped window frames that made it difficult to close them. Kitchens had warped linoleum floors, bathrooms had peeling paint, and both spaces were sometimes overly damp on account of poorly installed plumbing.[28] Some apartment buildings were settled without running water or electricity, and drainage pipes were improperly installed, making apartments damp.[29] Rain water seeped into top-floor apartments because of poorly constructed roofs.[30] Residents moved into new apartments in which doors and floors had not been painted, sinks and pipes had yet to be installed, and basements lacked concrete floors.[31] Telephone lines were not set up, and the installation of televisions damaged stairwell walls.[32] Residents on top floors complained of periodic interruptions of running water and poor water pressure. Elevators, which were included in apartment buildings with more than five floors, were known to break down soon after people moved in.[33] In a 1960 report on Muscovites' complaints, a KPK investigator wrote, "In the examination of these buildings, one gets the impression that they have already been used many years. . . . New residents are not happy for long. A new apartment 'grows old' before one's eyes."[34]

Khrushchev's regime published much propaganda about the prefabrication technology and factory production of standardized mass housing assembled at breakneck speed on construction sites.[35] In the tradition of Soviet industrialization campaigns in the 1930s, the mass media placed enormous emphasis on high yields of square meters of living space, completing projects early, and quickly overcoming unforeseen difficulties.[36] More critical assessments of the campaign in the mass media pointed out that the rush to complete construction within quarterly and yearly time tables led to last-minute "storming" and, consequently, badly built housing.[37] Other media accounts conceded the shortcomings in the technological modernization of mass housing.[38] Constructors often made parts out of available materials to compensate for shortfalls in factory-produced elements.[39] Defective prefabricated parts were delivered to construction sites.[40] Labor-intensive and nonindustrialized methods of construction were roundly condemned.[41] Construction defects plagued state housing, distributed through local soviets or the workplace, along with cooperative housing. Although people bought into cooperatives to expedite the process of obtaining a separate apartment, their investment did not make them immune to the defects and delays that residents of state housing experienced.[42] In short, construction defects had the unintended effect of creating a common experience across all urban social groups as they moved to the separate apartment and became "new residents" with much to complain about.

Critics at an Exhibition

In addition to writing letters to newspapers, Soviet citizens had other opportunities to communicate their rising expectations about new housing. Exhibitions that were meant to promote new furniture and instruct residents on proper consumer habits drew many visitors eager to examine the new way of life and share their opinions when comment books were available. The exhibits "Urban Planning" ("Gradostroitel'stvo"), held in 1960 in Moscow, and "Art into Life" ("Iskusstvo v byt"), held the following year in Moscow, showed visitors new furniture in domestic settings.[43] Their comment books provide us with a unique window onto popular reactions to new furniture and new housing. Similar to residential meetings and letters, comment books do not account for all experiences and opinions or indicate how widely they were shared. They provide valuable clues, however, about the range of opinions urban dwellers had about housing and consumer goods, many of which were not anticipated by advice literature but resonated with the findings of the statistical survey on people's household possessions examined in chapter 6.

When set against the backdrop of these two sources, the exhibits and people's comments reveal a central tension of Khrushchev's mass housing campaign and its place in the emerging communist way of life: More consumer goods were becoming available, close enough for someone to see and touch, but frustratingly hard to actually purchase and bring home. The statistical survey, which quantified such troublesome results as socially differentiated shortages, was kept from the public eye. In contrast, furniture exhibitions had the unintended consequence of reminding individual visitors of the chronic shortages they experienced in their everyday lives.

Visitors at the two exhibitions typically praised the new furniture and then complained about its shortages. At the "Gradostroitel'tvo" exhibit (figure 7.1), one wrote,

One only hears all around: "Marvelous!" "Delightful!" And this is right. Good objects and deeds should elicit good impressions. All that remains is to thank the engineers and constructors. However, there's a "but" here. Where can one find such furniture? Why do they only produce it in Estonia, Moscow, Leningrad? It should also be produced in the south. It would be good to give out apartments with furniture and pay for the furniture in installments.[44]

At the "Iskusstvo v byt" exhibit, a person noted the necessity of producing the new furniture for those receiving smaller apartments. She wrote,

Everything at the exhibit is ideal, but one would like to see all of this on sale in our stores. For example, I would personally like to obtain furniture similar to the kind on display, but it's impossible to purchase it. The furniture on display here is very comfortable, especially for a one-room apartment. I received such an apartment, but furniture [i.e., what was presently available] is bulky and does not correspond to the sizes of the apartment.[45]

Another visitor echoed the didactic message of the advice literature, which lectured homemakers on good taste. The new furniture sent this

Figure 7.1. Visitors at the "Gradostroitel'stvo" exhibit in Moscow, 1960.

Source: "Vystavka po gradostroitel'stvu," *Arkhitektura SSSR*, no. 6 (1960): 63.

person into a daydream about practicing her consumer autonomy, albeit within the bounds of good taste, in a land without shortages. She wrote,

> The exhibit is wonderful, more such exhibits are needed, they cultivate our taste. We hope that the shift to improving our everyday life has been done and that the time is not far off when we will be able to buy (without lines and according to one's taste and means) the furniture, fabrics, and dishware that are on display here.[46]

Other visitors alluded to the socioeconomic differences in consumption of furniture. At "Gradostroitel'stvo," one visitor noted, "It's such,

such a pity that all of this is a dream for now, a beautiful dream. And very expensive for the simple worker, since furniture and everything that goes into apartments in general are still very expensive and difficult to access."[47] Others revealed popular frustration over unsatisfied consumer demand, which they assumed would continue into the foreseeable future: "Good, but inaccessible. I received a new apartment recently, ran about furniture stores to buy some contemporary furniture. It's difficult; you have to sign up on some kind of lines for one or two years. And then, purchasing anything from the exhibition—don't even think about it. Only frustration."[48] An engineer visiting "Iskusstvo v byt" lamented, "It's incomprehensible why *such exhibitions* are put on, when buying anything easily from what was on display will remain impossible for years to come. People leave the exhibit even more irritated" (emphasis in the original).[49]

Some visitors faulted the new furniture and small apartments for being inadequate and thus unable to accommodate the different needs of the Soviet intelligentsia. At "Iskusstvo v byt," an engineer named Zhemchuzhin complained that

> the furniture won't satisfy anyone whose life is his work. There's almost no space for books, a television, a radio set—likewise, writing tables aren't well suited for more or less serious work. There's no furniture for clothes. The rooms are suitable only for receiving guests (to drink coffee). It's a shame, comrades, to recommend such nonsense! I'm an engineer; this doesn't satisfy me. I work at home. I think that it also doesn't satisfy a working person who rests and works with books.[50]

As a single person with his own apartment, Zhemchuzhin should have considered himself lucky because separate apartments were meant for families, not individuals. Families had it worse, squeezing into *khrushchevki* with new furniture that, despite its compact design, still took up too much space. One visitor to "Iskusstvo v byt" wrote, "Most of the furniture, particularly for small-sized apartments, is uncomfortable. Indeed, in reality we have families with 4 to 5 people living in such apartments, not newlyweds, old folks, and pensioners all over the place."[51] Unable to imagine how one could live in new apartments, two visitors commented, "Apartments? The kitchens are good. But the rooms? Where can one put a television, a radio receiver? Well, and what if there's a piano? How would it fit in? Beds—one or two. And what if there are children?"[52]

Another visitor to "Iskusstvo v byt" similarly complained, "The modern apartment is small in size, but the furniture presented here uses spaces far too uneconomically." The person offered some friendly, if somewhat contradictory advice. "Comrade designers! Don't lose touch with reality," the visitor implored. "Furniture should not only be beautiful, but capacious." But how would this work if apartments were only getting smaller? The visitor continued, "Indeed, in any one apartment there's only one wall closet, but of the things that need to be placed in it, there are many. For example, shoes, a bicycle, and seasonal things and many others. Put some thought into this. Then it'll be spacious even in a small apartment." In a final dig at designers, the visitor noted, "But instead you copy foreign objects, not taking into consideration that they have more floor space in apartments than we have."[53] This remark threw cold water on the exhibit by alluding to the paltry amount of living space the Soviet state provided to its citizens. Such resignation to the Soviet Union's inferiority in comparison with the outside world was not what Khrushchev's regime or furniture designers wanted to hear. For this visitor, it was self-evident.

Other visitors were incredibly critical of the aesthetic quality of the new furniture and kitchenware makes, suggesting that the new style was not for everyone. They took designers to task for what they perceived was a sharp turn toward a modernist aesthetic, elitism, and a desire to imitate the West blindly. Like their American counterparts, Khrushchev's architects and furniture designers appropriated the international style in furniture and housing exhibitions to advertise the superiority and modernity of their socioeconomic system, but the message appeared to fall on deaf, even hostile ears.[54] One visitor to "Iskusstvo v byt" wrote, "Ultramodernistic furniture gives an impression of impermanence, it's not cozy. One wouldn't want to live in a room arranged with such furniture."[55] An engineer wrote, "We don't need that which is presented at this exhibition! Take note of this comrades. Don't imitate the West, create that which is yours, that which is realistic. Shame! Utter imitation of feudal Greece of the times of Pompeii, and of abstract Americanism [*amerikanshchina*]!"[56] This last comment suggests the engineer may have been aware that American propagandists drew on modernist aesthetics in presenting the American way of life at exhibitions to European audiences.[57] The notion that such furniture could represent the Soviet way of life was not well received.

Other visitors did not seem to have a clear idea of what Americanization meant in aesthetic terms and simply used the association with the Soviet Union's Cold War adversary to smear the furniture on display. "What's this?" a visitor to "Iskusstvo v byt" asked. "Art into life? No, it's the long known *amerikanshchina*, the penetration of which into Soviet everyday life is somehow tolerated." This individual's animosity toward all things American was particularly intense and served as the lens through which he or she criticized other exhibition objects including jewelry. The visitor called upon the satirical magazine *Krokodil* to investigate "the monstrous things they're recommending that women wear under the name 'necklace' [*kol'e*] and 'brooches' [*broshi*]." The exhibition's samples represented not just "a simple monstrosity, but the dragging in of perverted tastes from America." Pointing to one necklace with metal plating, the visitor even likened it to the collar "on which was engraved the last name of a black slave's owner in the American South." Bringing matters closer to home, the same visitor equated the modernist aesthetic of the furniture on display with efforts at making do under conditions of poverty: "There was a time when poor people got this advice from magazines: If you don't have the means to buy furniture, then make it out of boxes. They showed the furniture models that were recommended from boxes: The drawings had the very same objects that we now see at the exhibit."[58] Such visitors could be forgiven their inability to celebrate the new furniture's modernity. Many saw in its minimalist and standardized designs little else than the Soviet state's tendency to do everything on the cheap.

Articulating similar hostility to the exhibit, another visitor claimed its modernist aesthetic had no place in the communist future. He lamented "the defeat of individual artists by abstraction [*abstraktizm*]. Most probably, these comrades still don't understand that a Soviet person who is building communism needs beauty, reality." As a remedy, this visitor suggested that designers and the exhibit's organizers, not ordinary people, be transformed: "Most likely it's necessary to present them all on a 'decorative dish' to the minister of culture for an operation on the brain. This is putting it crudely, but justly. The people hope that abstraction will not continue beyond this exhibit."[59] Another visitor complained,

A plain taste is being inculcated consciously in the people. It's understandable that this was brought forth out of necessity. Not everyone can have expensive furniture. But if one talks about a true name of the exhibit "Iskusstvo v byt" then the exhibit, unfortunately, is far from art.[60]

The assumptions behind this person's comments were quite different from those of the advice literature, examined in the last chapter, which predicted that inexpensive, well-designed furniture could refine ordinary people's taste. In this visitor's opinion, good taste was necessarily expensive; debasing taste was the inevitable cost that came with making consumer items such as furniture available to the masses.

In contrast, other visitors who liked the exhibit echoed advice pamphlets by noting how the new furniture was distinct from older makes. An architect visiting "Iskusstvo v byt" wrote, "When will these pretty things replace this vulgarity and petit bourgeois filth which is sold in our stores?"[61] Along similar lines, a person noted, "I liked the exhibit. But it's only an exhibit. It's funny after this to see orange lampshades in stores. It's necessary to hurry things up."[62] Most visitors, however, came away from the exhibits feeling alienated for one reason or another. For some, the exhibits were full of objects that they could not afford or find in stores. Others saw the furniture makes as markers of social status that excluded them. One visitor to "Iskusstvo v byt," signing as Colonel Smirnov, reflected upon furniture as a marker of class. "For whom are [the furniture] and its pieces meant?" he asked. "Most probably, only for people of intellectual labor, because the working people—workers, peasants, yes and midlevel employees, there are only a few who can find here that which can be introduced into life and our present everyday."[63] Yet as we saw with the engineer Zhemchuzhin, some in the Soviet intelligentsia did not like what they saw either.

Those visitors who still lived in communal housing felt similarly marginalized. The new furniture, they lamented, was only designed for small, single-family apartments and did not answer the needs of residents living in communal housing. In fact, there was no practical reason why someone could not use the new furniture in a communal apartment. Its small scale and multifunctional design were ideally suited for the cramped living arrangements of a *kommunalka*, where a family's room served as living room, bedroom, and dining room all in one, not unlike the overlapping spaces of a *khrushchevka*. But as a communal apartment resident who visited "Iskusstvo v byt" noted, the exhibition evoked a strong sense of alienation: "Unfortunately, after seeing the exhibit, I had a feeling and others as well that artists and architects have oriented themselves in their work on creating the contemporary housing interior exclusively for families living in separate apartments." Perhaps the modernist aesthetic of the new furniture was simply too incongruous for a communal apartment located in a prerevolutionary apartment building with decorative architectural motifs and ceilings that dwarfed those of the *khrushchevka*. This visitor saw in the objects on display a sign that the lives of separate apartment residents were moving forward, while those in communal apartments were falling behind. Designing for the separate apartment "needs to be done, it's our outlook," he conceded, "but for now those who are forced to live in one room in the conditions of a common communal apartment should not be removed from consideration; this exhibit will help them very little on a practical level."[64] The visitor did not explain what such consideration would mean in practice. Did he expect designers to come up with furniture just for communal apartments and, if so, what would it look like? A separate line of furniture had never been manufactured for the *kommunalka*, and Khrushchev's regime was not about to start one now.

Older residents likewise felt marginalized by new furniture that was poorly suited to meet their needs. This compounded their broader sense of alienation from Khrushchev's mass housing campaign, which they believed bestowed separate apartments only on young couples with children.[65] As the comment books revealed, pensioners feared that given their age and the slow rate of production, they would never live to see the new furniture. One pensioner named Grishin sarcastically remarked, "Looking at the exhibit, there arises a vain thought—I'll have these pretty objects in my daily life (in 50 years)."[66] Another person, signing as a professor, saw age discrimination inherent in the new furniture. He or she explained that an elderly person's difficulties in moving about were not accounted for in new furniture design. "If everything is meant only for young married couples up to twenty-five to thirty years of age," the professor lamented, "then this furniture is justified. For people of an older age, especially above forty to forty-five years of age, it's unlikely that this furniture is comfortable. Beautiful—

yes, but not very comfortable, since it's necessary to bend over low all the time. For people of an older age constructors and artists need to work out furniture models whose lines are entirely modern, but taller."[67]

"Not by Square Meters of Living Space Alone"

The residential meetings and furniture exhibitions discussed above opened a space that residents exploited to challenge the authority of architects and furniture makers over designing the new Soviet home. The central authorities followed suit in well-publicized events such as the December 1954 All-Union Conference of Constructors and two All-Union Congresses of Soviet Architects in 1955 and 1961. A dialogue between urban dwellers, the Soviet leadership, and the architectural profession over mass housing was conducted through these high-profile events.

Following the December 1954 conference, for example, the government issued a scathing indictment of architectural "excesses" in a November 1955 decree, "On Eliminating Excesses in Design and Construction," which announced the firing or demotion of specifically named architects and blasted other officials such as Moscow's city soviet head, Mikhail Iasnov.[68] With this decree, Khrushchev's regime joined the ordinary residents of the Leningrad meetings in 1953 and 1954 in heaping abuse upon architects for past failures to resolve the housing question. Although the decree echoed the Stalinist practice of blaming those in between the leadership and the people for the shortcomings of Soviet socialism, nobody was shot or sent to the Gulag. Journalists who read the decree on the other side of the Iron Curtain were betting otherwise, based on their assumption that little had changed since Stalin's death two and a half years earlier.

The November decree concerned internal Soviet matters, but unexpectedly touched off an embarrassing international incident that sent Khrushchev into a public rage over the Western media's suggestion that one of his cultural elites wanted to defect. One of the architects denounced for his Stalin-era excesses was Alexander Vlasov, who was touring the United States as part of a Soviet housing delegation when the decree was issued. American journalists immediately assumed that he would defect in the wake of such a harsh denunciation, only to find that this elite architect just wanted to go home. The affair drew sensational Western media coverage when journalists' last ditch effort to have Vlasov defect ended in an ugly scene at a Paris train station. Nothing bad happened to Vlasov upon returning home, where he had already been eased out of his elite posts as an unapologetic practitioner of Stalin-era architecture before the November decree. The incident showed how the cultural politics of moving away from Stalinist aesthetics toward mass housing could take unpredictable turns and assume international dimensions over which the Soviet leadership did not have full control.[69] Whereas Western journalists interpreted the November 1955 decree through a lens of Cold War intrigue, ordinary residents in the Soviet Union referenced it to blast architects for their work.

The November decree truly hit a raw nerve among some urban dwellers writing to the 1955 Congress of Soviet Architects. A Muscovite by the name Shcherbakov praised the decree in his letter and angrily charged that with the money wasted on one particular building, "AN ADDITIONAL 30,000 MUSCOVITES COULD HAVE BEEN MOVED OUT OF BARRACKS AND BASEMENTS." Shcherbakov was furious and produced his own detailed calculations citing architecture and construction periodicals to make his point. This highly engaged Muscovite explained that such an outcome had occurred "only because the architects who designed this building and the higher-ups in the Moscow soviet who approved it are hardly bothered by the hundreds of thousands of Muscovites who LIVE IN BARRACKS AND BASEMENTS, where often THE MOST BASIC AMENITIES ARE LACKING, LIKE WATER AND SEWERAGE, and where as a rule, RESIDENTS ARE STUFFED LIKE CANNED HERRINGS." He asked architects at the congress to get out and see how poorly people lived, extending the invitation as well to Iasnov, "whose lordly and scornful approach to those who desperately need improved living conditions is well known."[70]

Another equally incensed Muscovite, who identified herself as a stay-at-home housewife, angrily set pen to paper upon hearing one of the congress participants explain on the radio that it was fine to build housing "10 to 15 kilometers out of town since people who have a television go to the movies and theater less often." Were architects so out of touch with reality, she wondered, that they missed the greater concern about the commute people like her husband endured getting to and from work? Whereas Shcherbakov accused architects of depriving

Muscovites of necessary living space, this housewife bitterly charged them with stealing something just as valuable, their time. "Comrade architects," she wrote, "everybody at work, at the factory, counts the minutes and the seconds; why do you take away from people's personal lives something of such worth—two to three hours of a person's life?" Instead of wasting it on the commute, a person could use his time "to go to the movies, or read a book, or learn something on his own, or just relax with the family, but you don't even want to think about this."[71] Fears about losing control over the little time people had to themselves were shared by others, such as women in Leningrad who challenged a citywide change to the beginning of the workday that upset their daily routines.[72]

Some urban dwellers wrote to the architects at the congress in favor of small apartments as an antidote to the communal apartment.[73] An engaged resident from Leningrad wrote in with a theory about the congress: "It's clear from the press that there's a debate going on at the congress between those who support the large apartment intended for a few families and architects who defend the principle of a small apartment for one family." There was really no choice in the matter as far as this communal apartment dweller was concerned. Smaller apartments were the way to go. This person invited architects to see what life was like in a communal apartment to understand what large apartments produced. Like Shcherbakov and the Muscovite housewife, the underlying point echoed Khrushchev and the November 1955 decree in depicting architects as elitists hopelessly out of touch with ordinary people's current conditions. "Only people who've never lived in communal apartments and don't know all their discomforts and squabbles could defend large apartments," the Leningrader concluded. Although architects likely did not make house calls, this person did get a written response from a certain P. Abrosimov of the Union of Architects in which he wholeheartedly agreed with the person's complaints: "You're absolutely right about the advantages small apartments have for one family." Moreover, he assured the person that these were precisely the kinds of apartments that architects were now designing.[74]

Architects who supported Khrushchev's turn to mass housing undoubtedly appreciated letters from Shcherbakov and this Leningrader because they confirmed that the "people" were wholeheartedly behind the new direction in housing design. But how would the Union of Architects respond to the angry reactions and astute criticisms that small separate apartments provoked in others? Would they even be open, let alone able to change designs and to meet people's requests within the already-restricted boundaries Khrushchev and the Communist Party had set? If anything, the mass housing campaign was already showing architects in 1955 that the more housing they built, the more people were articulating an increasingly diversified and sometimes conflicting range of needs and tastes. Instead of just complaining, many people wanted to sustain their dialogue with architects that local-level meetings in Leningrad had opened up and written correspondence made possible. Without a market mechanism through which to influence what was built, urban dwellers jumped at the opportunities that events such as the November 1955 decree and the Congress of Architects afforded to continue communicating their desires.

Another person from Leningrad named Raigorodskaia wrote to the 1955 congress after reading an article in *Izvestiia* about how living and auxiliary spaces in apartments were going to get smaller. She insisted that this was the wrong way to go and that tighter corridors, smaller kitchens, front doors without vestibules, lower ceilings, and thinner walls made life difficult, especially when such apartments were settled communally. These apartments were best for single families, she asserted, but their auxiliary spaces should get bigger, not smaller. She suggested that architects keep lines of communication open to find out what people wanted through conferences and newspapers. In this case, a certain D. Khodzhaev from the Union of Architects responded. "You rightly note," he respectfully began his letter to Raigorodskaia, "that architects must everyday take into consideration the population's requests and needs." Khodzhaev nonetheless asserted that smaller, one- to two-room single-family apartments would effectively fulfill what people wanted, as evidenced by the many "letters working people send to the congress" in support of such apartments. Addressing her concerns about small auxiliary spaces—she had called for a 10-square-meter kitchen—Khodzhaev assured Raigorodskaia that "a small kitchen with 5 to 6 [square] meters of floor space can be used very well, if there's only one housewife in it." This subtle allusion to preventing communal settlement brought the conversation back to the fundamental reasons that apartments were getting smaller. The *Izvestiia* article to which she had referred, Khodzhaev explained, had thus correctly promoted the design of "small apartments, intended exclusively for single-family occupancy."[75]

This official response politely, but effectively absorbed Raigorod-skaia's criticism and turned it, along with an appeal to the people's will, into support for the new line in housing architecture. In search of an open dialogue with architects, Raigorodskaia had gotten instead a Soviet lesson in discursive jujitsu. Other residents pressed on, although it is unclear from the archival record how many received personalized responses. Along similar lines as Raigorodskaia, another Muscovite housewife decried the uncomfortable dimensions of small apartments and argued that larger ones would help three-generation families stay and live comfortably together.[76] In his criticism of small apartments, a Moscow-based biologist derisively noted, "One-room apartments can only be intended for old maids and bachelors, or for sterile, old couples, and also perhaps for architects, who design these apartments."[77] Other residents raked architects over the coals for the poor quality of new housing construction.[78] A Leningrader contrasted the shoddy construction of contemporary housing with the city's prerevolutionary architecture he admired, in particular a house dating back to 1875 now under preservation according to its commemorative plaque. The city's prerevolutionary housing was a disorienting reminder that the past had produced higher-quality and longer-lasting housing than the present. But all was not yet lost. This Leningrader held out hope that the Soviet building industry could improve so that by the year 2055, a visitor to the city might stumble across a building's plaque like he had done and read the following inscription: "This house was built in the winter of 1955 and is under state preservation."[79]

Others looked to the Soviet past to criticize what was going on in the present. Looking beyond the boundaries of the apartment, two Muscovite women wrote to remind the congress that new neighborhoods required good eating establishments like cafés and cafeterias, as well as home delivery of prepared meals, so that women would not have to constantly cook at home. In an allusion to the original goals of the Russian Revolution, they charged that architects "don't remember Lenin's orders on the necessity of freeing women from the mind-numbing, nerve-racking, unproductive work of preparing food in their kitchen." Their explanation for architects' failure in this regard touched on one of the great gender divides shaping the mass housing campaign: an architectural profession consisting primarily of men who designed domestic interiors where women were supposed to do most of the housework. The women wrote, "The majority of you are men led by an egotistical desire to have a tastier home-cooked meal." Catering to such men and living in a city with such poor public food services did not constitute the communist way of life these two women were hoping for. "What do you want," they angrily asked architects, "TO DOOM US WOMEN EVEN UNDER COMMUNISM TO FIXING BREAK-FAST, LUNCH, AND DINNER EVERYDAY AT HOME!?"[80] The two women would have found a comrade-in-arms in a certain Sergei Iulanov from Leningrad, who likewise called upon the architects at the congress to improve new housing estates with more public establishments like bath houses and "large cafeterias that emancipate women by improving what one can eat out."[81] In a response to their letter, the same Abrosimov of the Union of Architects told the women that their demands for more eating establishments were "absolutely correct." The union also sent their letter to the Moscow city soviet, whose office of commercial trade wrote to the women with the good news that five new public eating establishments were to be built in a microdistrict they had complained about in their letter.[82]

Six years later, urban dwellers wrote to the Union of Architects once again on the occasion of the Congress of Architects in 1961. Among their complaints were the usual suspects, including shoddy construction, painfully small apartments with tiny auxiliary spaces, pass-through rooms, low ceiling heights, and toilets combined with bathrooms.[83] One individual reported the small dimensions of his apartment's auxiliary spaces down to the square centimeter and lamented that new consumer items—such as "a refrigerator, washing machine, vacuum cleaner, baby carriage, sleds, skis . . . and other household things"—ended up in people's rooms instead of auxiliary units. "Not by bread alone is a person fed," he opined. "Not by square meters of living space alone must a person be content. This is a truth everyone should know." Looking to the future, he cast the problem of inconveniently small apartments in generational terms to suggest that demands for more spacious apartments would only increase with time. Although his generation had put up with worse conditions, he predicted that the younger generation simply would not suffer tiny apartments, which "history will judge as a pointless waste of the people's resources."[84]

Instead of writing individual responses as it did in 1955, the Union of Architects streamlined that process in 1961 with a standard letter, suggesting they had either received too many letters to answer or become too disenchanted with complaints to respond to them individually. In any event, the Union of Architects continued to validate people's criticisms and guide them toward the current line in housing architecture. The union explained more than it had in 1955 that apartment designs were changing to meet popular demands. The formula letter read, "A number of letters, including yours, have been addressed to the Third All-Union Congress of Soviet Architects, in which people have pointed out the shortcomings in the design of new apartments: pass-through rooms, combined bathrooms and toilets, a door connecting a kitchen and a room." The response letter condemned reductions in auxiliary space and promised reforms to meet residents' criticisms.[85] Whether architects could fulfill such promises given the restrictions they faced in designing separate apartments was an entirely different matter.

Who Is to Blame?

Before and after the 1961 Congress of Architects, architects and constructors found themselves to be the targets of increasingly pointed and at times politicized criticism by residents eager to find someone to blame. At a meeting of 235 residents from apartment house No. 21 on Leningrad's Narymskii Prospekt in April 1957, residents complained bitterly about constructors. "Who, and at whose cost, will fix the defects in the constructors' work?" one resident wanted to know. Another suggested, "The constructors must take into account all the defects in the construction of the house and not repeat them. Doors and small windows are overly slanted and don't close. Radiators are installed in such a way that crevices remain that mice slip into. The work of constructors has to be considered careless."

Such residents seemed to forget that all the pressure they had put on architects and constructors to finish projects early may have contributed to poor-quality housing. One resident asked, "Where exactly do they [defects] come from? Why weren't they eliminated over the course of construction; surely the project's author, inspectors, as well as many controllers watch over the construction site? This means that all of these authorized people didn't use their rights." Another resident added, "The 102nd construction trust already built many houses along Narymskii Prospekt before house No. 21, but it repeated here again the defects in previous construction."[86] At least one person, likely associated with a construction trust, objected to such criticism. "The poor quality of materials, interruptions in their supply, and storming, which we were forced to do because of the interruptions, very much hindered things," he pointed out. An architect at the meeting similarly pointed to the difficult circumstances under which the apartment house had been built. Problems would be taken care of, he assured the residents, but then tried to shift some of the blame onto them, or at least those who had participated in the building's construction. He pointed out, "The tenant-constructors speaking here sharply judged the quality of work, but it would have been good if they also had thought like residents while working—the quality of work would have been incomparably better."[87]

Such comments revealed this apartment house to have been a hybrid of people's construction and the more modern method of having a construction trust build a structure. Because constructors in people's construction were also the housing's future residents, as we saw in chapter 4, they alone would be responsible for the quality of its projects. In contrast, when a construction trust built housing with factory-produced materials, the distinction between residents and constructors was redrawn. At the meeting on Narymskii Prospekt in 1957, the architect's point about "thinking like residents while working" was promoted as one of the main advantages of people's construction because it was said to improve quality. In the hybrid case examined here, however, residents clearly preferred the sharp distinction between themselves and construction trust No. 102 now that they were residents. The architect sought in vain to remind them that they, too, bore responsibility for the poor state of their housing. In other cases, neighbors blamed one another in addition to outside authorities for the construction defects that appeared in new housing.

The residents of apartment house No. 182 on Moskovskii Prospekt, whose strong sense of community we saw in chapter 5, combined a collective concern for the physical upkeep of their building with a willingness to criticize their own neighbors that would have made Khrushchev gush with pride had he read the minutes to their December 1957 meeting. Residents asked their district soviet deputy at the meeting why it had not been possible to evict a cleaners that had installed itself in "our laundry." "Who's to blame for this?" one resident asked. Without access to their building's laundry room, he explained, residents were damaging the building by washing their clothes at home. Another complained that nothing had happened even though the local party bureau and four district deputies were looking into the matter. To expedite the eviction of the unwanted cleaners, a third resident invited "the [district] deputies [to] go through apartments and see how the house is being ruined from the dampness brought on by housewives washing linens in apartments." Such knowledge about neighbors' housework was easy to come by in a building with communal apartments. Rather than simply complain about what her neighbors were doing, this last resident used the fix they were in as leverage to get local authorities to give these residents back their laundry room and help keep their building in good physical shape.[88]

In new housing with separate apartments, residents similarly took their neighbors to task for doing things that damaged their building. A meeting of 103 residents from a recently constructed building on Leningrad's Iakovlevskii Alley in May 1957, shows that residents could be very critical of others who only complained. The head of the building's assistance commission opened the meeting with a few comments on repair work, residents' written complaints, and difficulties in getting the laundry operating. Residents then launched into their complaints about construction defects that echoed media reports. The building suffered from the usual problems: Water heaters in bathrooms were not functioning, floors were already damaged, whitewashing and plaster work were shoddy, and frames (presumably of windows and doors) were defective. Residents called for the local office of capital construction (*upravlenie kapital'nogo stroitel'stva,* or UKS), the local municipal housing authority (*zhilishchno-kommunal'nyi otdel,* or ZhKO), and other outside authorities to answer for these problems.[89]

The chairman of the meeting agreed that having UKS personnel present would have been helpful (the most guilty parties in such meetings were, of course, never present). He pointed out that the UKS had left residents with plenty of defects in an apartment building that had been rejected on two occasions before being approved. Other residents, however, came to the defense of the UKS and ZhKO. Although conceding that the constructors' work was poor, one explained that "a number of shortcomings depends also on residents, washing the floor is not allowed but it frequently gets washed and from this comes the ruin." Another approved of the assistance commission's efforts and chastised his neighbors. He pointed out that "there are few people in attendance at the meeting, but a lot of petitions come in from residents that apartments get flooded, they blame the UKS, but individual residents do not handle the plumbing well, they throw cans, rags, peelings, and so on into toilets." He singled out one resident in particular for her constant complaining about the allegedly noisy boiler room and "all kinds of trifles, such as, for example, a handle that had come off in the bathroom." Furthermore, this resident stored heating wood for her sister, who lived somewhere else, in her bathroom, and could not seem to take advantage of modern amenities properly: "Comrade Zakharova, living with all the comforts, taps into the heating system to get hot water for her personal needs."[90]

Whether the guilty parties were architects, constructors, or neighbors, residents demanded that the housing system—from design and construction to distribution—function as intended. In expressing their discontent, they drew upon laws, party decrees, and an accusatory discourse rooted in Stalinism. For ordinary citizens, experiencing the thaw did not mean that they were or even wanted to be free from "speaking Bolshevik."[91] For some, the thaw meant that they were able to invoke the punitive language of Stalinism in new contexts.[92] To examine these dynamics, we turn to a neighborhood meeting in Leningrad in April 1962.

Four hundred residents attended this meeting on new housing along Lanskii Road in the Vyborg district. Also in attendance were district and city soviet officials, building committee chairmen, a party member from a housing office, engineers, and a labor union representative. Residents grew so incensed with these officials that they took over the meeting and amended its resolution to call for the criminal prosecution of those responsible for having built such poor housing, including architects. Noticeably shaken, the officials nervously regurgitated the official line on housing whereby the state provided millions of apartments to the needy masses whose job it was to show gratitude.[93] But there were other, similarly "official" ways people could discuss housing. Residents voiced complaints that echoed newspaper coverage of mass housing's problems in an accusatory manner worthy of a 1930s purge hearing.[94]

A building committee chairman, Maslennikov, began the meeting by reviewing the area's housing. Fifty-nine new buildings, with approximately 4,500 new apartments, had been settled during the previous four years, but they now exhibited many problems, including leaking roofs, faulty electrical wiring, and poorly asphalted balconies. Buildings had not been equipped for telephones, there were not enough laundries, and the neighborhood suffered from insufficient heat and hot water. According to Maslennikov, the purpose of the meeting was to pass a constructive resolution identifying major problems and the means to address them. He warned his audience, "This meeting must have a business-like character and end with passage of the corresponding decision entered into the protocol."[95] Residents responded with familiar criticisms. One complained of the combined bathroom and toilet, calling it an "unsuccessful innovation," and noted its presence in a communalized apartment with three families. Poor sound insulation was also cited: "When you go along the stairs, the impression is such that it's a nuthouse—all around voices, laughter, music, shouts. Everything can be heard on the stairs." Another complained about poor ventilation, while others blasted the small dimensions of auxiliary spaces: "In apartments there are absolutely no auxiliary units; children's strollers have to be kept in the stairwell. Who planned it like this?" Another asked, "Will there be a redesigning of apartments; corridors are so narrow that it's impossible to take out a coffin?!"[96]

The meeting began to unravel over hot water. One resident asked, "Why do they collect so much for hot water? Ten kopecks for one day from one person?" A local housing official explained that the cost would actually be 40 kopecks per person, but that this initial estimate would be reconsidered in May once they knew rates of consumption. Audience members protested loudly. The stenographic record read, "/In the hall a very strong noise, shouts of protest. 'The baths cost less,' 'turn off the water' and so on/" (slash marks are in the original to denote audience interruptions). When the official turned to another question, residents interrupted again. "/All the time in the hall there's an awful noise, shouts: 'Explain about the water, why does water cost so much?'/." The flustered official exclaimed, "There are no more questions. . . . I ask these comrades to come by the office and we'll reach an agreement together."[97]

This only antagonized residents further. Someone exclaimed, "They're asking you and you hear them: Why did they raise prices on heating and hot water?" The district soviet's deputy chair, Racheev, admonished residents with little success. Drawing from the media's positive discourse on mass housing, he stressed how severe residents' needs had been and how grateful they should be. He started, "Thanks to the vast care, of great decisions in the area of housing construction," but was interrupted again: "/The orator talks under ceaseless outcries of those in attendance/." He continued, "providing a wide front of housing construction was successful, on Lanskii Road, in particular. In a little over three years in the Vyborg district there has been built around / the number is inaudible because of the awful noise /." An audience member shot back, "We know all about this from the newspapers, answer the concrete questions." Racheev pointed out that construction had made it possible for 12,500 residents to move into the area. Promising to address problems later, he implored them not to focus entirely on the negative: "It's necessary to say something, above all, about the great care, which has been displayed for those of you who have received living space." The audience response: "/Shouts, noise/."[98]

When Racheev eventually addressed hot water, he chastised residents for wanting to pay whatever they felt was right, but promised that prices would be reassessed. Shortly thereafter, the chair tried to end the meeting by calling a vote on the resolution, but residents still insisted on answers and finding people to punish. As the authorities lost control, residents invoked their own order drawn from law and party policies, and switched to an accusatory discourse peppered with colorful terms about negligence and deception. One noted that "sloppiness" (*khalatnost'*) was punishable under law: "The assembly thinks it necessary to give a copy of the protocol to the Leningrad city procurator in order that the guilty be punished. For sloppiness, for wasting state resources." Others followed with broader suggestions: "Put the question about calling the guilty to account to a vote." "We need to BRING [to account] specific guilty persons, but whom?" (emphasis in the original) Another suggested a public and democratic effort: "I sent a note up to the presidium and proposed to elect here at the meeting an accusatory commission that must find the guilty. Whoever it pleases can get into the commission, this question needs to be covered in the press."[99] Only a couple of residents resisted such calls. One rejected the last suggestion, arguing that almost everybody was guilty of defective work and that constructors were primarily but not solely to blame. The audience ignored him, while another pressed on: "There's a decree of the Central Committee of the Party: for widely misleading people into thinking things are more advantageous for them than they really are [*ochkovtiratel'stvo*], for deceit, two years imprisonment is doled out." Backing the idea of an accusatory commission and involving the procuracy, he added, "Houses are not built according to the schedules indicated and there are many elements of deception."[100]

When the chair suggested that the city soviet investigate instead, people shouted, "No! No!" As one resident demanded that the procu-

racy take charge, another decried the moblike mentality of his neighbors. Having worked construction himself, he declared, "never have I
seen or heard such an attitude toward toilers." He continued, "Of
course, you can pass such a decree because there are people here who
are in a very zealous state of mind, bloodthirsty, if one can put it like
this. But we are more humane than we are right now." His call to appeal to the city soviet fell on deaf ears and others pressed on, aiming
now at architects. "We need to punish at least one designer for this
'lovable' project. For they'll design like this later." Ultimately, the audience voted to send the matter to the procuracy instead of the city
soviet. The meeting finally ended when the chair resubmitted the resolution for a vote: "Nobody against. No abstentions. The resolution is
passed unanimously."[101]

The residents of Lanskii Road highlighted the separate apartment's
small dimensions and bizarre layouts, much like residents did in letters
of complaint and at the other residential meetings examined above.
Yet their sense of entitlement and resentment was more pronounced,
and they infused this meeting with the persecutory language of Stalinism punctuated by such words as "carelessness" and "deception." As
they had done under Stalin, some residents continued "speaking
Bolshevik" during the thaw in complaining about the separate apartment's many flaws.[102] Living in a separate apartment may have also
provided them with the assertiveness that inflected their words and actions. Such instances as the meeting on Lanskii Road provide us with
a window onto the unintended and contradictory ways that mass housing shaped ordinary citizens and the thaw. The separate apartment's
deficiencies were a source of discontent, but the separate apartment
was also a source of an invested self-interest, sense of entitlement, and
autonomy that drove residents to express that discontent against the
makers of the Soviet home and those responsible for its upkeep.

Conclusion

Unlike their counterparts a generation later in the waning days of the
Soviet Union, urban residents under Khrushchev were far from ready
to explore the alternatives and declare the quest for the communist way
of life a failure. As they had done on questions of housing distribution,
ordinary urban dwellers demanded that the Soviet system work as

planned and respond to their growing list of desires for larger apartments and better household goods that met their socially differentiated needs for modern urban life. This chapter has shown how engaged urban residents actively pursued and widened new lines of communication between themselves and representatives of the state responsible for mass housing. They anticipated and even shaped how Khrushchev's regime itself sought to bring pressure upon architects to redirect their efforts and meet the housing needs of ordinary urban dwellers. Their voices and actions in this chapter reveal a popular dimension to the Khrushchev regime's tense relationship with architects. They broaden our understanding of the thaw beyond its traditionally understood place in cultural high politics that pitted the state against the cultural intelligentsia. A new social actor, ordinary residents of the *khrushchevka*, emerged in such milieus as residential meetings and furniture exhibitions as critical players in the politicization of mass housing under Khrushchev.

Residents' complaints to architects bring our examination back to the fundamental design principles of the separate apartment that we explored in the first part of this book. Urban dwellers' discontent also puts the advice literature examined in chapter 6 in a different light. Homemaking brochures told Soviet citizens that their apartments were smaller and their furniture was compact by design because this was the modern, properly socialist way to live. The urban dwellers examined in this chapter were rather skeptical of this line. To architects' dismay, they displayed a clearer understanding of the real reasons behind the odd designs and tiny dimensions of their separate apartments than what they were being fed by the advice literature. They knew, for instance, that living space was reduced to prevent communalization and that auxiliary spaces were likewise simplified and reduced to lower costs. Urban residents took architects and furniture designers to task for their inability to reform or work around these obstacles. They blamed the makers of the Soviet home for being out of touch with people's ordinary lives and for attempting to impose material standards on people with different needs and means. As reflected in urban dwellers' own words, the politics of complaint was thus not simply a matter of "society" resisting or challenging the "state." Instead, design oddities and construction defects engendered a repoliticization of mass housing and furniture that pitted ordinary residents against those members of the cultural intelligentsia who thought they knew better than anyone how they should live.

Conclusion:
Soviet Citizens' Answer
to the Housing Question

Lessons Learned

In January 1967, the editors of *Leningradskaia pravda* informed the Leningrad city soviet of the many letters residents had sent the newspaper about two recent articles regarding new housing and new neighborhoods.[1] They asked the city to submit an article explaining the measures that were being taken to address residents' major complaints. In early March, the deputy chairman of the city soviet, G. Kochkin, wrote a response that reflected upon the worst aspects of housing design and construction. His letter's tone suggested the end of the most difficult part of a long campaign, when the pressure to succeed at all costs had lessened and mistakes could be more soberly discussed in the past tense. Extreme measures could now be checked by a more balanced approach, and major problems could be analyzed to produce better housing in the future. For Kochkin and his fellow Leningraders, a corner had been turned and it was time to take stock of the lessons learned and move forward.[2] His letter invites us to look back on what the Soviet state and its citizens had been through in making the *khrushchevka* their definitive answer to the nineteenth century's housing question.

Speaking on behalf of the Soviet state, Kochkin readily acknowledged that urban dwellers had much to complain about: "Indeed, there were serious shortcomings in the projects of the years 1958–59—pass-through rooms, the small floor space of auxiliary spaces, the absence of storage spaces." As this book has shown, the *khrushchevka*'s design problems originated primarily in the formula architects devised in the 1930s to balance the conflicting imperatives of distribution norms, single-family occupancy, and cost. The history of this "Soviet minimum dwelling," as Karel Teige might have grudgingly called it, stretched back to the pan-European housing reform movement of the nineteenth century, and took a fateful turn in 1919, when the Bolshevik adaptation of minimum living space norms turned them into a maximum, with long-term consequences for housing design. Kochkin summarized this long history by simply observing that quantity had been placed above quality.

As we have seen in this book, some mass housing architects were reluctant to admit that their design formula created inconveniences that outweighed the success of ensuring single-family occupancy. But by the late 1960s, Kochkin suggested, a general consciousness about the roots of these problems had taken hold. It was now easier to see that "the quality of an apartment, and its level of comfort, are determined not only (and not even so much!) by the size of rooms, but by the rational organization of everyday life, which demands large auxiliary spaces." Who could better speak to people's preference for such changes in design than those who actually had to pay for housing? "It's not by accident," he observed, "that members of housing cooperatives, paying for all the floor space, prefer apartments with more spacious entranceways and kitchens."[3]

Looking toward the future, Kochkin explained that residents had been heard and that better apartments were being designed with larger kitchens (7 to 8 square meters in size), larger entranceways, and built-in closet spaces. Larger auxiliary spaces would finally accommodate people's new household consumer goods, such as refrigerators and washing machines. The apartments of the future would be designed so that "for each person, besides 9 square meters of living space, there should be another 5 square meters of auxiliary space." Quality had a legitimate place in answering the housing question, after years of focusing only on construction and single-family occupancy. As Kochkin explained, "A design's quality should be appraised not by the output of living space, but by conveniences and comforts."[4]

Kochkin's hopeful outlook notwithstanding, would it really have been possible to guarantee residents 5 square meters of auxiliary space in addition to the 9 square meters of living space they were originally promised in the 1920s? Had architects not tried and failed before to reform spatial categorizations and distribution to provide greater flexibility in design? And if quality was now the goal, why fall back once again on a quantitative measurement to represent it? Was this not precisely what they were trying to escape? Kochkin's article may have reflected a broader awareness of design problems, but his solutions instead conjured up the specter of long-familiar limits to what could be reformed. And when it came to citizens' complaints about neighborhood infrastructure, transportation, and telephone lines, Kochkin was even less sanguine. He blandly explained that "coordinating the activities of many actors is extremely difficult."[5]

In many histories of the Khrushchev period, it is frequently some version of the state ("conservatives" within the party-state apparatus, the "Soviet system," Marxist-Leninist ideology, or at times Khrushchev) that eventually imposed limits on reforms in the face of a population that we assume only wanted more. This book has certainly shown this to be true in many instances. When the architects of mass housing proposed reforms to calculating cost, they got nowhere with a state content that most new apartments were allocated to single-families and uninterested in uprooting the fundamental principles of distribution. The state abruptly ended people's construction, despite its popularity among workers and factory managers. This book has also shown, however, that limits on reforms had broader origins that complicate our understanding of what this state and its society were all about.

Khrushchev, who normally was the champion of reforms, especially in housing, found himself imposing limits on those within his regime who sought to bring back the housing cooperative. Was the cooperative then truly a reform that the people wanted? The answer depends on whose perspective one examines. For those professionals and cultural elites on whose behalf party-state leaders like Kucherenko and Grishmanov spoke, it certainly was. In the spirit of de-Stalinization, recreating the housing cooperative reversed the Stalinist regime's decision to eradicate it in 1937. The cooperative's backers succeeded in reinstating it by initially associating it with people's construction and depoliticizing its elite connotations. By the time Kochkin wrote his response, the cooperative even served as the measure of what ordinary people truly wanted. But for the blue-collar workers of people's construction, and also the individual housing constructors who lost their land plots to cooperative projects, the cooperative was the antithesis of reform and prevented them from solving their own housing question. In short, reforms for some could come at the expense of others, in the form of limits on what they could say and do. This had little to do with whether they were "conservatives" or "liberals."

In calling for the housing cooperative, urban professionals, cultural elites, and their party-state patrons were undermining yet another reform that Khrushchev personally championed: the egalitarian distribution of housing based on rational and transparent mechanisms. Khrushchev's regime soon found, however, that even ordinary citizens resisted this idea. In Leningrad, urban dwellers and district officials speaking on their behalf believed that access to better housing was not a right of citizenship to be shared equally, but should reflect social differences based upon who they had become in Soviet society in relation to others. Looking toward the future instead of the past and to the kinds of professionals and skilled workers it wished to bring to the city, the Leningrad city soviet further eroded Khrushchev's egalitarian vision by advocating a merit-based approach to allocating housing.

The limits placed on housing reform reveal more about the different visions and purposes that various state and social actors projected onto the *khrushchevka* than a debate on whether to continue building single-family apartments. Nobody suggested that the regime abandon the separate apartment and reverse course back to communal forms of housing. The single-family apartment was here to stay, and every family would eventually have one. But who would get there first, what part of town it would be in, and who would fix housing deficiencies remained heavily contested issues. Instead of finally resolving the housing question and allowing the regime to move on, the *khrushchevka* and its neighborhoods opened a space for ordinary people to speak and act in unpredictable ways as they searched for a new way of life after Stalin. The *khrushchevka* democratized and made ordinary not only access to single-family apartments but also participation in a phenomenon normally seen as the exclusive domain of the cultural intelligentsia under Khrushchev: the thaw.

Experiencing the Thaw

From joining a people's construction project to visiting an exhibit of new furniture, urban dwellers experienced the thaw by trying new things and shaping their meaning. In meetings with the architects of mass housing and letters to architectural congresses, residents proved themselves to be fully engaged with the intricacies of the separate apartment's design. At furniture and apartment exhibitions, they voiced a range of comments on the aesthetics and suitability of new designs. Members of the cultural intelligentsia involved in the making of the separate apartment and its household objects were likewise trying new things. Khrushchev's mass housing campaign gave architects, furniture designers, and taste arbiters an unprecedented opportunity to shape the built environment and the aesthetics of Communism on Tomorrow Street. The designers of the *khrushchevka* ensured that it remained a politicized space where the social and cultural transformations set in motion by the Russian Revolution would at last be fulfilled.

The dialogue that the city's ordinary people had with the makers of their new homes further politicized the *khrushchevka* in ways that embarrassed the members of the cultural intelligentsia and undercut their position as arbiters of everyday life. These urban dwellers' complaints often brought discussions with the architects back to the design origins of the *khrushchevka*, thereby revealing the limitations on the latter's agency as they struggled to design better apartments. Some who attended furniture exhibitions mocked the aesthetic choices of the designers and politicized them in a Cold War context as the signs of a cultural intelligentsia subservient to the West. Others simply lamented that the furniture designers had uselessly raised people's expectations by exhibiting models that few were able to find in stores. Finally, on Lanskii Road in Leningrad, residents dramatically transformed a meeting to discuss housing problems with local officials into an intensely politicized space resembling a Stalin-era purge meeting. The words and actions of these ordinary urban dwellers repoliticized the meaning of the housing question in ways that Khrushchev's regime had hoped to avoid in resolving this nineteenth-century question of social reform.

Among its many unintended consequences, the mass housing campaign created links and lines of communication bridging various levels of state and society. In the absence of a civil society standing apart from the state, this was one of the campaign's most fascinating aspects. By moving to the separate apartment, urban dwellers sought out a dialogue with many different state actors in addition to the campaign's architects and furniture designers. They complained to their district deputies, city leaders, and sometimes even Khrushchev about not having been placed on a waiting list. They wrote to newspapers and municipal authorities about the lack of transportation and infrastructure in their new neighborhoods. And closer to home, they turned to the low-level state organizations in which they or their neighbors had a role, such as comrades' courts, street patrols, and residential assistance commissions.

As represented in this book, the many dialogues that these urban dwellers held with representatives of the state over housing enrich our understanding of who was speaking or listening to whom in creating new communicative links across the state/society divide. Instead of speaking in one voice, the state in Khrushchev's mass housing campaign had many different voices—with sometimes conflicting agendas. While the architects were trying to fulfill Khrushchev's vision to put all families in single-family apartments, the local soviet officials were allocating housing by the square meter. The district deputies cared little if apartments remained separate or became communal, but they seemed quite concerned about those residents who considered themselves "native Leningraders." Many of the state actors we have seen were themselves ordinary residents hoping to resolve their housing question through Khrushchev's mass housing campaign. They spoke from both sides of the state/society divide and could see the *khrushchevka*'s problems as both residents and state actors with a hand in its making.

Communism on Tomorrow Street

In its dialogue with urban residents about mass housing, Khrushchev's regime (including Khrushchev himself) presented the *khrushchevka* as a critical element in the creation of the communist way of life. According to this rhetoric, mass housing would create a happy balance between people's private lives and their obligations to the community and the construction of communism. It would not tempt them to withdraw into the private world of their separate apartments. According to the furniture exhibitions and homemaking pamphlets, the well-designed apartment with its modern amenities and new consumer items would not make urban dwellers, especially housewives, run rampant with consumer lust, but it would teach them to become restrained and rational consumers. The problem, many urban dwellers told the state, was not so much the didactic message they were hearing but the fact that much of what had been promised seemed impossible to find. Instead of steadily becoming a reality, the communist way of life as envisioned by Khrushchev's regime and represented in exhibits and homemaking pamphlets seemed forever stalled in a visible, but still distant, future.

While experimental houses and exhibitions provided visions of the future, the country's urban dwellers filled in the content of the communist way of life with the lived reality they found and constructed in new mass housing estates. At times, this hardly conflicted with the values that Khrushchev's regime promoted under the rubric of the communist way of life. By taking the initiative to create livable communities where the state was seemingly absent, urban dwellers acted out what the discourse on the communist way of life foresaw. But what was becoming increasingly apparent to the residents of the *khrushchevka* was that its chronic design and construction deficiencies, along with problems with neighborhood infrastructure and shortages of consumer goods, were beginning to constitute what the communist way of life really looked like in practice. These problems served as legitimate grounds for politicizing the mass housing campaign and looking for someone to blame. Having set out to resolve the housing question once and for all, Khrushchev's regime had instead produced post-Stalinist subjects who persistently came back to remind it that much remained to be done.

What were the longer-term social and political consequences of these problems that Khrushchev's mass housing campaign engendered as it tried to solve the housing question of the nineteenth century and create a new way of life after Stalin? Although a study of the separate apartment in the Soviet Union's last generation lays beyond the scope of this book, reflections on its long-term effects are in order. Since the collapse of the Soviet Union in 1991 looms in the foreground of research on the Khrushchev and Brezhnev periods, one question easily presents itself: Did mass housing and mass consumption prop up the regime in its remaining years, or did their shortcomings—especially in comparison with life in the West—undermine the legitimacy of the Soviet system and ultimately contribute to its collapse? Insofar as this study is concerned, Khrushchev's mass housing campaign did more to prop up the Soviet system than undermine it, at least in his time. Its successes bolstered the regime's legitimacy, while its shortcomings did little to encourage citizens to think seriously about alternatives. Millions of urban families improved their living standards and gained an apartment of their own. The *khrushchevka* gave them a stake in Soviet socialism, which was reflected in how ordinary residents chose to deal with its problems.

The crisis of rising expectations and the politics of complaint that emerged from the *khrushchevka*'s deficiencies did little to create an alternative form of politics that could challenge the Soviet system's foundations as a one-party state running a command economy. Despite repudiating Stalinist terror, Khrushchev's regime retained the coercive tools of control and punishment that made such a challenge a costly affair. Yet fear of the state's reprisals does not fully explain why Soviet citizens chose to channel their discontent within the accepted practices and discourses of complaint, as illustrated in their petitions, residential meetings, and comments at furniture exhibitions. Many urban dwellers chose these avenues under Khrushchev because they wanted the Soviet state to finish what it had started and to remain more, not less, involved in resolving their housing question. These residents also engaged the state through residential meetings, architects' congresses, and furniture exhibitions, in part because these were new opportunities to express themselves in a time of intense political change. Some were even willing to defend the state's organs of housing construction from frustrated neighbors. Under Khrushchev, ordinary people wanted to see how far the politics of complaint would take them with a regime that still seemed willing to improve their living standards and build Communism on Tomorrow Street.

Notes

Introduction

1. State Archive of the Russian Federation (Gosudarstvennyi arkhiv Rossiiskoi Federatsii), fond 9401, opis' 2, delo 482, listy 216–17.

2. Ibid.

3. Ibid.

4. These figures were tabulated using official statistics in *Narodnoe khoziaistvo SSSR v 1959 godu* (Moscow: Gosstatizdat TsSU SSSR, 1960), 568; *Narodnoe khoziaistvo SSSR v 1967 g.* (Moscow: Statistika, 1968), 677, 681; *Narodnoe khoziaistvo SSSR v 1974 g.* (Moscow: Statistika, 1975), 581, 585.

5. Greg Castillo presents a fascinating transnational history of mid-twentieth-century domestic design, including East Germany, in which he demonstrates how Cold War warriors on both sides of the Iron Curtain claimed the mantle of the international style in staking the superiority of their socioeconomic systems after World War II. See Greg Castillo, *Cold War on the Home Front: The Soft Power of Midcentury Design* (Minneapolis: University of Minnesota Press, 2010). See also Kimberly Zarecor's recent history of mass housing and architecture in the postwar construction of socialism in Czechoslovakia: Kimberly Zarecor, *Manufacturing a Socialist Modernity: Housing in Czechoslovakia, 1945–1960* (Pittsburgh: University of Pittsburgh Press, 2011).

6. Blair Ruble, "From *Khrushcheby* to *Korobki*," in *Russian Housing in the Modern Age: Design and Social History*, edited by William Brumfield and Blair Ruble (Cambridge: Cambridge University Press, 1993), 232–70.

7. In a recent study that locates the origins of Khrushchev's mass housing campaign in the late Stalin era, Mark Smith focuses on the evolution of property rights in mass housing and what they reveal about the Soviet Union's status as a welfare state under Khrushchev. Mark Smith, *Property of Communists: The Urban Housing Program from Stalin to Khrushchev* (DeKalb: Northern Illinois University Press, 2010). Lynne Attwood has recently examined the intersection of mass housing and gender in tracing women's evolving role in Soviet society. Lynne Attwood, *Gender and Housing in Soviet Russia: Private Life in a Public Space* (Manchester: Manchester University Press, 2010).

8. Stephen Bittner, *The Many Lives of Khrushchev's Thaw: Experience and Memory in Moscow's Arbat* (Ithaca, N.Y.: Cornell University Press, 2008); Stephen Bittner, "Remembering the Avant-Garde: Moscow Architects and the 'Rehabilitation' of Constructivism, 1961–1964," *Kritika: Explorations in Russian and Eurasian History* 2, no. 3 (2001): 553–76.

9. Victor Buchli, "Khrushchev, Modernism, and the Fight against Petit-Bourgeois Consciousness in the Soviet Home," *Journal of Design History* 10, no. 2 (1997): 161–76; Christine Varga-Harris, "Constructing the Soviet Hearth: Home, Citizenship and Socialism in Russia, 1956–1964" (Ph.D. diss., University of Illinois at Urbana-Champaign, 2005); Christine Varga-Harris, "Homemaking and the Aesthetic and Moral Perimeters of the Soviet Home during the Khrushchev Era," *Journal of Social History* 41, no. 3 (2008): 561–89.

10. Susan Reid, "Who Will Beat Whom? Soviet Popular Reception of the American National Exhibition in Moscow, 1959," *Kritika: Explorations in Russian and Eurasian History* 9, no. 4 (Fall 2008): 855–904; Susan Reid, "Khrushchev Modern: Agency and Modernization in the Soviet Home," *Cahiers du monde russe*, 47, nos. 1–2 (January–June 2006): 227–68; Susan Reid, "The Khrushchev Kitchen: Domesticating the Scientific-Technological Revolution," *Journal of Contemporary History* 40, no. 2 (2005): 289–316; Susan Reid, "Cold War in the Kitchen: Gender and the De-Stalinization of Consumer Taste in the Soviet Union under Khrushchev," *Slavic Review* 61, no. 2 (2002): 211–52.

11. On the role that World War I played in shaping early Bolshevik state formation, see Peter Holquist, *Making War, Forging Revolution: Russia's Continuum of Crisis, 1914–1921* (Cambridge, Mass.: Harvard University Press, 2002).

12. For a study that emphasizes the origins of Khrushchev's mass housing campaign in the late Stalin years after the war, see Smith, *Property*.

13. "O razvitii zhilishchnogo stroitel'stva v SSSR," July 31, 1957, *Sobranie postanovlenii pravitel'stva SSSR*, no. 9 (1957).

14. *Kommunisticheskaia partiia sovetskogo soiuza v resoliutsiiakh i resheniiakh s"ezdov, konferentsii i plenumov TsK* (Moscow: Izdatel'stvo politicheskoi literatury, 1972), 8:245.

15. On the ways in which the cultural intelligentsia took advantage of the mass housing campaign to pursue their ideas on transforming the Soviet everyday, see Buchli, "Khrushchev, Modernism"; Reid, "Khrushchev Modern"; and "Reid, Khrushchev Kitchen."

16. Oleg Kharkhordin, *The Collective and the Individual in Russia: A Study of Practices* (Berkeley: University of California Press, 1999); Miriam Dobson, *Khrushchev's Cold Summer: Gulag Returnees, Crime, and the Fate of Reform after Stalin* (Ithaca, N.Y.: Cornell University Press, 2009); Buchli, "Khrushchev, Modernism"; Reid, "Khrushchev Modern"; Varga-Harris, "Homemaking"; Mark Smith, "Khrushchev's Promise to Eliminate the Urban Housing Shortage: Rights, Rationality and the Communist Future," in *Soviet State and Society under Nikita Khrushchev*, edited by Melanie Ilič and Jeremy Smith (London: Routledge, 2009), 26–45.

17. E.g., Mark Meerovich, *Biografiia professii: Ocherki istorii zhilishchnoi politiki v SSSR i ee realizatsii v arkhitekturnom proektirovanii (1917–1941 gg.)* (Irkutsk: Izdatel'stvo IrGTU, 2003).

18. On neighborhood social organizations, see Theodore Friedgut, *Political Participation in the USSR* (Princeton, N.J.: Princeton University Press, 1979), 235–88.

19. General histories of the Khrushchev era adopt the label to cover a range of social, political, economic, diplomatic, and cultural topics. See Aleksandr Pyzhikov, *Khrushchevskaia "Ottepel'"* (Moscow: Olma-Press, 2002); and Iurii Aksiutin, *Khrushchevskaia "Ottepel'" i obshchestvennye nastroeniia v SSSR v 1953–1964 gg.* (Moscow: Rosspen, 2004).

20. Ilya Ehrenburg, *Ottepel'* (Moscow: Sovetskii pisatel', 1954).

21. Others have similarly noted the importance of housing in Ehrenburg's story. See Geoffrey Barraclough, "Late Socialist Housing: Prefabricated Housing in Leningrad from Khrushchev to Gorbachev" (Ph.D. diss., University of California, Santa Barbara, 1997), 6–7.

22. For an example of this use of the term, see Elena Zubkova, *Russia after the War: Hopes, Illusions, and Disappointments, 1945–1957*, translated and edited by Hugh Ragsdale (Armonk, N.Y.: M. E. Sharpe 1998), 149–201.

23. E.g., see Eleonory Gilburd and Larissa Zakharova's introduction and the essays in the collection "Repenser le Dégel: Versions du socialisme, influences internationales et société soviétique," in the special edition of *Cahiers du monde russe* 47, nos. 1–2 (2006).

24. Donald Filtzer, *Soviet Workers and De-Stalinization: The Consolidation of the Modern System of Soviet Production Relations, 1953–1964* (New York: Cambridge University Press, 1992).

25. See Polly Jones's introduction and the essays in *The Dilemmas of De-Stalinization: Negotiating Cultural and Social Change in the Khrushchev Era*, edited by Polly Jones (London: Routledge, 2006).

26. Smith, *Property*.

27. Bittner, *Many Lives*; Varga-Harris, "Constructing the Soviet Hearth."

28. For an early analysis that privileged Communist Party officials and the cultural intelligentsia as the main players in the thaw, but also included other social groups such as youth, see the chapter "The Great Thaw" in *Khrushchev's Russia*, by Edward Crankshaw (Baltimore: Penguin Books, 1959), 100–140. For more recent examples that focus on the cultural intelligentsia, see Mariia Zezina, *Sovetskaia khudozhestvennaia intelligentsiia i vlast' v 1950-e–60-e gody* (Moscow: Dialog-MGU, 1999); Nancy Condee, "Cultural Codes of the Thaw," in *Nikita Khrushchev*, edited by William Taubman, Sergei Khrushchev, and Abbott Gleason (New Haven, Conn.: Yale University Press, 2000), 160–76; and Karl Lowenstein, "Ideology and Ritual: How Stalinist Rituals Shaped the Thaw in the USSR, 1953–54," *Totalitarian Movements and Political Religions* 8, no. 1 (2007): 93–114; Bittner, *Many Lives*.

29. Stephen Bittner explains how the thaw's meaning as a metaphor for the Khrushchev period has changed over time and how the cultural intelligentsia's collective memory of the thaw shapes scholars' understanding of it. Bittner, *Many Lives*, 1–18.

30. Nataliia Lebina and Aleksandr Chistikov, *Obyvatel' i reformy: Kartiny povsednevnoi zhizni gorozhan v gody nepa i khrushchevskogo desiatiletiia* (Saint Petersburg: "Dmitrii Bulanin," 2003).

31. Vladimir Kozlov, *Massovye besporiadki v SSSR pri Khrushcheve i Brezhneve (1953–nachalo 1980-kh gg.)* (Novosibirsk: Sibirskii khronograf, 1999), 155–83; Iurii Aksiutin, "Popular Responses to Khrushchev," in *Nikita Khrushchev*, 177–208; Polly Jones, "From the Secret Speech to the Burial of Stalin: Real and Ideal Responses to De-Stalinization," in *Dilemmas*, ed. Jones, 41–63; Miriam Dobson,

"Contesting the Paradigms of De-Stalinization: Readers' Responses to *One Day in the Life of Ivan Denisovich,*" *Slavic Review* 64, no. 3 (2005): 580–600.

32. Varga-Harris, "Constructing the Soviet Hearth"; Varga-Harris, "Forging Citizenship on the Home Front: Reviving the Socialist Contract and Constructing Soviet Identity during the Thaw," in *Dilemmas*, ed. Jones, 101–16.

33. Dobson, "'Show the Bandit-Enemies No Mercy!': Amnesty, Criminality and Public Response in 1953," in *Dilemmas*, ed. Jones, 21–40.

34. Ann Livschiz, "De-Stalinizing Soviet Childhood: The Quest for Moral Rebirth, 1953-1958," in *Dilemmas*, ed. Jones, 117–34.

35. Katerina Clark includes these dynamics in her typology of the thaw, in which she focuses primarily on literature and film. Katerina Clark, "Rethinking the Past and the Current Thaw: Introduction," *Studies in Comparative Communism* 21, no. 3-4 (1988): 241–53.

36. In his study of Khrushchev's mass housing campaign, Mark Smith provides other critiques of the welfare state model insofar as it applies to the Soviet Union. First, he notes that the Stalinist state never provided the degree of welfare the model would suggest in the West or what the regime called for, whereas Khrushchev's regime exceeded the model by including so many of its citizens as beneficiaries. Smith additionally argues that the transformation of welfare entitlements to housing into stable property rights further differentiated the Soviet case from Western models of the welfare state. Smith, *Property.*

37. On the origins of the Soviet intelligentsia, see Sheila Fitzpatrick, "Stalin and the Making of a New Elite" and "Becoming Cultured: Socialist Realism and the Representation of Privilege and Taste," in *The Cultural Front: Power and Culture in Revolutionary Russia*, by Sheila Fitzpatrick (Ithaca, N.Y.: Cornell University Press, 1992), 149–82, 216–37. For a standard list of the types of employment that qualified one to be a member of the Soviet intelligentsia, see the entry for "intelligentsia" in *Sovetskaia istoricheskaia entsiklopediia*, edited by E. Zhukov (Moscow: Izdatel'stvo "Sovetskaia entsiklopediia," 1965), 6:119.

38. On the cultural intelligentsia's role under Stalin, see Sheila Fitzpatrick, "Cultural Orthodoxies under Stalin," in *Cultural Front*, 238–56.

39. Yanni Kotsonis, "Ordinary People in Russian and Soviet History," *Kritika: Explorations in Russian and Eurasian History* 12, no. 3 (2011): 739–54.

40. Sheila Fitzpatrick, *Everyday Stalinism: Ordinary Life in Extraordinary Times— Soviet Russia in the 1930s* (New York: Oxford University Press, 1999).

41. For a discussion of other ways that class reemerged in shaping Soviet society under Khrushchev, see Amir Weiner, "The Empires Pay a Visit: Gulag Returnees, East European Rebellions, and Soviet Frontier Politics, *Journal of Modern History* 78, no. 2 (2006): 333–76.

Chapter 1

1. Russian State Archive of Literature and Art (Rossiiskii gosudarstvennyi arkhiv literatury i iskusstva), fond (f.) 674, opis' (op.) 4, delo (d.) 12, list (l.) 44.

2. Regulations on minimum living space in July 1919 mandated that "when establishing local norms, take into account the professional circumstances and way

of life of separate groups of the population that allow for one or another increase in these norms." A. Sysin et al., *Sanitarnoe zakonodatel'stvo: Sbornik vazhneishikh zakonov i rasporiazhenii po voprosam sanitarno-profilakticheskogo dela* (Moscow, 1926), 77.

3. I thank Alexander Vlasov for this illustrative joke.

4. Blair Ruble, "From *Khrushcheby* to *Korobki*," in *Russian Housing in the Modern Age: Design and Social History*, edited by William Brumfield and Blair Ruble (Cambridge: Cambridge University Press, 1993), 232–70; Stephen Bittner, *The Many Lives of Khrushchev's Thaw: Experience and Memory in Moscow's Arbat* (Ithaca, N.Y.: Cornell University Press, 2008), 113–17.

5. János Kornai, *Economics of Shortage* (Amsterdam: North-Holland, 1980).

6. Victor Buchli, "Khrushchev, Modernism, and the Fight against Petit-Bourgeois Consciousness in the Soviet Home," *Journal of Design History* 10, no. 2 (1997): 161–76; Susan Reid, "The Khrushchev Kitchen: Domesticating the Scientific-Technological Revolution," *Journal of Contemporary History* 40, no. 2 (2005): 289–316. On "austere consumerism," see David Crowley and Susan Reid, "Style and Socialism: Modernity and Material Culture in Post-War Eastern Europe," in *Style and Socialism: Modernity and Material Culture in Post-War Eastern Europe*, edited by Susan Reid and David Crowley (Oxford: Berg, 2000), 12.

7. Bittner, *Many Lives*, 115–19. I borrow here Bittner's translation of *tipovoe proektirovanie*.

8. An exception in the scholarship is Geoffrey Barraclough, who notes how distribution norms shaped design and the dimensions of rooms in his study of mass housing under Khrushchev and through the Gorbachev era. His analysis, however, does not trace the origins of this relationship between distribution and design further back than the Khrushchev era. Geoffrey Barraclough, "Late Socialist Housing: Prefabricated Housing in Leningrad from Khrushchev to Gorbachev" (Ph.D. diss., University of California, Santa Barbara, 1997), 188–205.

9. In relating the *khrushchevka* to the pan-European history of minimum living standards, this chapter and the next draw in particular on the study by Dana Simmons, "Minimal Frenchmen: Science and Standards of Living, 1840–1960" (Ph.D. diss., University of Chicago, 2004).

10. E.g., see Daphne Spain, "Octavia Hill's Philosophy of Housing Reform: From British Roots to American Soil," *Journal of Planning History* 5, no. 2 (2006): 106–25.

11. *Congrès international des habitations à bon marché* (Paris: Imprimerie nationale, 1889); *Actes du Congrès international des habitations à bon marché tenu à Bruxelles (juillet 1897)* (Brussels: Hayez, imprimeur de l'Académie royale de Belgique, 1897); *Compte rendu et documents du Congrès international des habitations à bon marché tenu à Paris les 18, 19, 20 et 21 juin 1900* (Paris: Secrétariat de la société française des habitations à bon marché, 1900); *Papers Submitted to the 8th International Housing Congress, Held in London, August 1907* (London: National Housing Reform Council, 1907); *International Housing and Town Planning Congress, Paris 1928* (Paris: Imprimerie Chaix, 1928).

12. The 1897 congress, attended by a delegation from Russia, featured state intervention as its first question. *Actes du Congrès international*, v, xxv. The question was also featured at the congress in 1900. *Compte rendu et documents du Congrès international*, 6.

13. On nineteenth-century housing reform, see John Burnett, *A Social History of Housing, 1815–1970* (London: David and Charles, 1978); Nicholas Bullock and James Read, *The Movement for Housing Reform in Germany and France, 1840–1914* (Cambridge: Cambridge University Press, 1985); and Ann-Louise Shapiro, *Housing the Poor of Paris, 1850–1902* (Madison: University of Wisconsin Press, 1985).

14. Elizabeth Lebas, Susanna Magri, and Christian Topalov, "Reconstruction and Popular Housing after the First World War: A Comparative Study of France, Great Britain, Italy and the United States," *Planning Perspectives* 6, no. 3 (1991): 249–67.

15. Burnett, *Social History*, 41.

16. Nancy Stieber, *Housing Design and Society in Amsterdam: Reconfiguring Urban Order and Identity, 1900–1920* (Chicago: University of Chicago Press, 1998), 19.

17. Joseph Bradley, *Muzhik and Muscovite: Urbanization in Late Imperial Russia* (Berkeley: University of California Press, 1985), 194–238.

18. Shapiro, *Housing the Poor*, 17–32.

19. Burnett, *Social History*, 64.

20. Max von Pettenkofer, *The Value of Health to a City: Two Lectures Delivered in 1873*, translated by Henry Sigerist (Baltimore: Johns Hopkins University Press, 1941), 1–14, 45.

21. Sigerist, in his introduction to the work by von Pettenkofer, *Value of Health*, 4–10.

22. Heinz Müller-Dietz, "Zur Tätigkeit des Hygienikers F. Erismann in Moskau" (Unveröffentlichte Dokumente und Briefe an M. V. Pettenkofer)," *Clio Medica* 4, no. 3 (1969): 203–10; Laura Engelstein, *The Keys to Happiness: Sex and the Search for Modernity in Fin-de-Siècle Russia* (Ithaca, N.Y.: Cornell University Press, 1992), 174.

23. Blair Ruble, *Second Metropolis: Pragmatic Pluralism in Gilded Age Chicago, Silver Age Moscow, and Meiji Osaka* (New York: Woodrow Wilson Center Press and Cambridge University Press, 2001), 280–82.

24. M. Dikanskii, *Kvartirnyi vopros i sotsial'nye opyty ego resheniia* (Saint Petersburg, 1908); Ia. Littauer and N. Sopikov, *Rabochii zhilishchnyi vopros* (Astrakhan, 1909).

25. William Brumfield, "Russian Perceptions of American Architecture, 1870–1917," in *Architecture and the New Urban Environment: Western Influences on Modernism in Russia and the USSR* (Washington, DC: Woodrow Wilson International Center for Scholars, 1988), 51–70.

26. Ann-Louise Shapiro, "Housing Reform in Paris: Social Space and Social Control," *French Historical Studies* 12, no. 4 (1982): 490–91.

27. Ibid., 490–91. See her extended discussion of Le Play and other like-minded reformers in *Housing the Poor*, 84–110.

28. In the Soviet case under Stalin, see David Hoffmann, *Stalinist Values: The Cultural Norms of Soviet Modernity, 1917–1941* (Ithaca, N.Y.: Cornell University Press, 2003), 15–26.

29. Bullock and Read, *Movement for Housing Reform*, 52, 79.

30. Burnett, *Social History*, 63–64, 173–75.

31. Shapiro, "Housing Reform," 491.

32. Burnett, *Social History*, 176–80.

33. Ibid., 180–82.

34. Shapiro, "Housing Reform," 496.

35. Shapiro, *Housing the Poor*, 147–53.

36. Stieber, *Housing Design and Society*, 20.

37. Bullock and Read, *Movement for Housing Reform*, 273–75; Burnett, *Social History*, 175, 181.

38. Shapiro, "Housing Reform," 497.

39. Bullock and Read, *Movement for Housing Reform*, 272.

40. Ibid.; Burnett, *Social History*.

41. This is as discussed and quoted by Burnett, *Social History*, 175.

42. Shapiro, "Housing Reform," 498.

43. Ibid., 494–96; Stieber, *Housing Design and Society*, 23-25.

44. Friedrich Engels, *The Housing Question* (Moscow: Cooperative Publishing Society of Foreign Workers in the USSR, 1935).

45. *Kommunisticheskaia partiia Sovetskogo Soiuza v rezoliutsiiakh i resheniiakh s"ezdov, konferentsii i plenumov TsK* (Moscow: Izdatel'stvo politicheskoi literatury, 1970), 1:59–66.

46. Engels, *Housing Question*, 54–55.

47. Vladimir Lenin, *Gosudarstvo i revoliutsiia* (Moscow: Politizdat, 1975), 58.

48. Engels, *Housing Question*, 98.

49. Lenin, *Gosudarstvo i revoliutsiia*, 59.

50. Modris Eksteins, *Rites of Spring: The Great War and the Birth of the Modern Age* (New York: Anchor Books, 1990); Maureen Healy, *Vienna and the Fall of the Habsburg Empire: Total War and Everyday Life in World War I* (Cambridge: Cambridge University Press, 2004).

51. Jack Roth, ed., *World War I: A Turning Point in Modern History* (New York: Alfred A. Knopf, 1967); Richard Wall and Jay Winter, eds., *The Upheaval of War: Family, Work and Welfare in Europe, 1914–1918* (Cambridge: Cambridge University Press, 1988).

52. Peter Holquist, *Making War, Forging Revolution: Russia's Continuum of Crisis, 1914–1921* (Cambridge, Mass.: Harvard University Press, 2002).

53. Burnett, *Social History*, 215.

54. Lebas, Magri, and Topalov, "Reconstruction."

55. Stephen Kotkin, *Magnetic Mountain: Stalinism as a Civilization* (Berkeley: University of California Press, 1995), 469.

56. Charles Hardy and Robert Kuczynski, *The Housing Program of the City of Vienna* (Washington, D.C.: Brookings Institution Press, 1934).

57. Gregory Andrusz, *Housing and Urban Development in the USSR* (Albany: State University of New York Press, 1984), 12–13.

58. Burnett, *Social History*, 217; Tyler Stovall, "Sous les Toits de Paris: The Working Class and the Paris Housing Crisis, 1814–1924," *Proceedings of the Annual Meeting of the Western Society for French History* 14 (1987): 267–68.

59. Burnett, *Social History*, 221–43.

60. Bullock and Read, *Movement for Housing Reform*, 263–72.

61. Horst Matzerath, "Berlin, 1890–1940," in *Metropolis, 1890–1940*, edited by Anthony Sutcliffe (Chicago: University of Chicago Press, 1984), 305–8.

62. Stieber, *Housing Design and Society*, 21.

63. Michael Geyer, "The Stigma of Violence, Nationalism, and War in Twentieth-Century Germany," *German Studies Review* 15 (Winter 1992): 84.

64. Lebas, Magri, and Topalov, "Reconstruction," 255, 262.

65. Ibid., 257.

66. Eric Karolak, "'No Idea of Doing Anything Wonderful': The Labor-Crisis Origins of National Housing Policy and the Reconstruction of the Working-Class Community, 1917–1919," in *From Tenements to the Taylor Homes: In Search of an Urban Housing Policy in Twentieth-Century America*, edited by John Bauman, Roger Biles, and Kristin Szylvian (University Park: Pennsylvania State University Press, 2000), 60–80.

67. Lebas, Magri, and Topalov, "Reconstruction," 249–67.

68. Holquist, *Making War*.

69. Denis de Rougemont, "Minds and Morals: The Conquest of Anarchy," in *America and the Mind of Europe* (London: Hamish Hamilton, 1951), 31–32.

70. Holquist, *Making War*; Lars Lih, *Bread and Authority in Russia, 1914–1921* (Berkeley: University of California Press, 1990).

71. Hubertus Jahn, "The Housing Revolution in Petrograd, 1917–1920," *Jahrbücher für Geschichte Osteuropas* 38, no. 2 (1990): 212–27; Svetlana Boym, "Everyday Culture," in *Russian Culture at the Crossroads: Paradoxes of Postcommunist Consciousness*, edited by Dmitri Shalin (Boulder, Colo.: Westview Press, 1996), 157–83; Nataliia Lebina, *Povsednevnaia zhizn' sovetskogo goroda: Normy i anomalii. 1920–1930 gody* (Saint Petersburg: Zhurnal Neva, Izdatel'sko-torgovyi dom Letnii Sad, 1999), 178–204; Mark Meerovich, *Biografiia professii: Ocherki istorii zhilishchnoi politiki v SSSR i ee realizatsii v arkhitekturnom proektirovanii (1917–1941 gg.)* (Irkutsk: Izdatel'stvo IrGTU, 2003).

72. Hardy and Kuczynski, *Housing Program*, 46–47.

73. Jahn, "Housing Revolution," 215–17.

74. Ibid., 217–18; Timothy Colton, *Moscow: Governing the Socialist Metropolis* (Cambridge, Mass.: Belknap Press of Harvard University Press, 1995), 119–23.

75. "Dekret o zemle," October 26, 1917, *Sobranie uzakonenii i rasporiazhenii rabochago i krest'ianskago pravitel'stva* (hereafter, *SU*), no. 1 (1917): 4–5.

76. The decree released from rent families with members fighting in the war and persons with a monthly income of less than 400 rubles; the moratorium would last until three months after the war's end. "O zhilishchnom moratorii," October 28, 1917, *SU*, no. 1 (1917): 14–15.

77. See points 6–8 of the decree's regulations in "O zhilishchnom moratorii."

78. In accordance with whatever "rules and norms" they devised, local authorities could relocate people in need of housing into the confiscated dwellings. In addition, they were given the power to establish "housing inspection," "house committees," and "housing courts." The decree, published October 30, 1917, left it up to local authorities to define what exactly these bodies would do. "O peredache zhilishch v vedenie gorodov," *SU*, no. 1 (1917): 15.

79. "Ob otmene prava chastnoi sobstvennosti na nedvizhimosti v gorodakh," August 20, 1918, *SU*, no. 62 (1918): 743–46.

80. Jahn, "Housing Revolution," 218–21.

81. Meerovich, *Biografiia professii*.

82. Nikolai Bukharin and Evgenii Preobrazhenskii, *Azbuka kommunizma: Populiarnoe ob"iasnenie programmy rossiiskoi kommunisticheskoi partii bol'shevikov* (Gomel': Gosudarstvennoe izdatel'stvo, 1921), 273–76, 295, 315–16.

83. V. Sviatlovskii, *Kvartirnyi vopros* (Saint Petersburg: M. M. Stasiulevich, 1898).

84. Bukharin and Preobrazhenskii, *Azbuka kommunizma*, 273–75.

85. Ibid., 275–76.

86. Ibid., 276, 315–16.

87. Simmons, "Minimal Frenchmen," 225–50.

88. Ibid., 233–39.

89. Shapiro, *Housing the Poor*.

90. Sviatlovskii, *Kvartirnyi vopros*; Dikanskii, *Kvartirnyi vopros*; Ia. Littauer and N. Sopikov, *Rabochii zhilishchnyi vopros* (Astrakhan, 1908).

91. Simmons, "Minimal Frenchmen," 237.

92. Ibid., 248–54.

93. J. Calvert Spensley, "Urban Housing Problems," *Journal of the Royal Statistical Society* 81, no. 2 (1918): 181.

94. Bullock and Read, *Movement for Housing Reform*, 263–66.

95. For a standard definition of an apartment's spatial units, see *Narodnoe khoziaistvo SSSR v 1959 godu* (Moscow: Gosstatizdat TsSU SSSR, 1960), 843. "Podsobnye pomeshcheniia" was used in addition to "podsobnaia ploshchad'" to describe auxiliary spaces. E.g., see L. Bumazhnyi and A. Zal'tsman, "Perspektivnye tipy zhilykh domov i kvartir," *Arkhitektura SSSR*, no. 1 (1959): 2–9.

96. The figures in parentheses were prerevolutionary units of measurement and appear in the original text.

97. "Vremennye pravila ustroistva i soderzhaniia zhilykh pomeshchernii i organizatsii zhilishchno-sanitarnogo nadzora," Sysin, *Sanitarnoe zakonodatel'stvo*, 76–79.

98. "O merakh pravil'nogo raspredeleniia zhilishch sredi trudiashchegosia naseleniia," in Sysin, *Sanitarnoe zakonodatel'stvo*, 83–84.

99. Clause 1 of "Instruktsiia o merakh uluchsheniia zhilishchnykh uslovii rabochikh," issued by the People's Commissariat of Internal Affairs, the Central Commission on Improving Workers' Daily Lives, and the Commissariat of Health on June 4, 1921, in *Sbornik dekretov i vazhneishikh rasporiazhenii po zhilishchnomu voprosu: Vypusk vtoroi. Za period s oktiabria 1920 g. po oktiabria 1921 g.* (Moscow, 1921), 17–20. These regulations listed the minimum norm only in the prerevolutionary unit of measurement as "1.8 square *sazheni* per person." As noted above, its equivalent in the metric system was 8.25 square meters.

100. David Broner, *Kurs zhilishchnogo khoziaistva* (Moscow: Izdatel'stvo Ministerstva kommunal'nogo khoziaistva RSFSR, 1948), 90; T. Alekseev, ed., *Zhilishchnye zakony: Sbornik vazhneishikh zakonov SSSR i RSFSR, postanovlenii, instruktsii i prikazov po zhilishchnomu khoziaistvu* (Moscow: Izdatel'stvo Ministerstva kommunal'nogo khoziaistva RSFSR, 1958), 326.

101. Aleksandr Marzeev, *Kommunal'naia gigiena* (Moscow: Gosudarstvennoe izdatel'stvo meditsinskoi literatury, 1951), 422.

102. Broner, *Kurs zhilishchnogo khoziaistva*, 90.

103. The average amount of living space per person in cities of the USSR declined from 6.45 square meters in 1923 to 5.91 in 1928, 4.17 in 1937, and 4.09 in 1940. Timothy Sosnovy, "The Soviet Housing Situation Today," *Soviet Studies* 11, no. 1 (1959): 4.

104. Regulations issued by the People's Commissariat of the Municipal Economy and the People's Commissariat of Justice (Russian Republic) from 1934 invoked the "housing-sanitary norm" to define what constituted "extra space": amounts above 9 square meters of living space per person and any legally obtained additional space. Regulations issued by the People's Commissariat of the Munici-

pal Economy from 1947 similarly defined extra space explicitly as amounts exceeding the sanitary norm of nine square meters. Alekseev, *Zhilishchnye zakony*, 323, 326, 355. On the norm's increase to 9 square meters, see the explanation below.

105. The 1922 Civil Code defined the maximum limit as "the established norms." See clause 173 of *Grazhdanskii kodeks RSFSR* (Leningrad: Izdatel'stvo "Rabochii Sud," 1925), 41. An important 1937 housing decree defined it as "the established housing norms." See clause 27 of "O sokhranenii zhilishchnogo fonda i uluchshenii zhilishchnogo khoziaistva v gorodakh," *Sobranie zakonov i rasporiazhenii raboche-krest'ianskogo pravitel'stva SSSR* (hereafter, *SZ*), no. 69 (1937).

106. For regulations that expected such distribution, see the 1921 regulations cited above, "Instruktsiia o merakh uluchsheniia zhilishchnykh uslovii rabochikh." For regulations that allowed it, see the 1934 regulations of the People's Commissariat of the Municipal Economy and People's Commissariat of Justice, cited above.

107. This was still stated as a matter of fact in 1965 by Izrail Martkovich et al., *Zhilishchnoe zakonodatel'stvo v SSSR i RSFSR* (Moscow: Izdatel'stvo literatury po stroitel'stvu, 1965), 94–95.

108. Whereas the sanitary norm applied to state housing, cooperatives and individual housing had different limits. In the cooperatives of the 1920s and 1930s, limits on space were pegged to the space norms of their localities established for state housing. "O zhilishchnoi kooperatsii," August 19, 1924, *SZ*, no. 5 (1924): 65–72. Cooperatives of the 1960s were bound by a cap of 60 square meters of living space. See clause 16 of "Ob individual'nom i kooperativnom zhilishchnom stroitel'stve v RSFSR," October 5, 1962, *Sobranie postanovlenii pravitel'stva Rossiiskoi Sovetskoi Federativnoi Sotsialisticheskoi Respubliki* (hereafter, *SP RSFSR*), no. 21 (1962): 386–97. The maximum amount of living space in individually constructed houses was set at 60 square meters in 1958. Martkovich et al., *Zhilishchnoe zakonodatel'stvo*, 25.

109. On the increase to 9 square meters in 1929, see Marzeev, *Kommunal'naia gigiena*, 422. Another source dates this increase to 1926. David Broner, *Zhilishchnoe stroitel'stvo i demograficheskie protsessy* (Moscow: "Statistika," 1980), 23. The Housing Code of 1983 set the norm at 12 square meters. *Zhilishchnyi kodeks RSFSR* (Moscow: "Iuridicheskaia literatura," 1985), 16. No unionwide norm existed. Each Soviet republic set its norm at or below the Russian Republic's with the exception of Ukraine where the norm was 13.65 square meters since before World War II. Valerii Litovkin, *Zhilishchnoe zakonodatel'stvo: Spravochnoe posobie* (Moscow: Profizdat, 1988), 40; Broner, *Kurs zhilishchnogo khoziaistva*, 90.

110. Marzeev, *Kommunal'naia gigiena*, 421–22. Sosnovy cites this source in linking the origins of the 9-square-meter norm to Pettenkofer. Timothy Sosnovy, *The Housing Problem in the Soviet Union* (New York: Research Program on the USSR, 1954), 4–5.

111. I. Vainshtein, "Zhiloi dom dlia inzhenerno-tekhnicheskikh rabotnikov," *Arkhitektura SSSR*, no. 12 (1935): 38–41; L. Karlik, "Sektsionnyi zhiloi dom novogo tipa," *Arkhitektura SSSR*, no. 9 (1959): 56–57; Natalia Lebina and Aleksandr Chistikov, *Obyvatel' i reformy: Kartiny posvednevnoi zhizni gorozhan v gody nepa i khrushchevskogo desiatiletiia* (Saint Petersburg: Izdatel'stvo "Dmitrii Bulanin," 2003), 175.

112. Simmons, "Minimal Frenchmen," 255–96.

113. The term "the right to use living quarters" is from clause 24 of the 1937

housing law, "O sokhranenii zhilishchnogo fonda." The 1964 Civil Code employs "the right to use living space" in clause 302 and specifies the exclusion of auxiliary spaces in the rental agreement in clause 300. *Grazhdanskii kodeks RSFSR* (Moscow: Izdatel'stvo "Iuridicheskaia literatura," 1968), 82. For further explanation, see Martkovich et al., *Zhilishchnoe zakonodatel'stvo*, 100–104.

114. Izrail Martkovich and Vitalii Skripko, *Kvartirnaia plata* (Moscow: Izdatel'stvo literatury po stroitel'stvu, 1965), 5, 11.

115. *Konstitutsiia (osnovnoi zakon) Soiuza Sovetskikh Sotsialisticheskikh Respublik* (Moscow: "Iuridicheskaia literatura," 1978), 16.

116. Sosnovy, "Soviet Housing Situation," 3.

117. Wendy Goldman, *Women, the State and Revolution: Soviet Family Policy and Social Life, 1917–1936* (Cambridge: Cambridge University Press, 1993).

118. Kotkin, *Magnetic Mountain*, 157–97.

119. On the Stalinist state's profamily policies, see Sheila Fitzpatrick, *Everyday Stalinism: Ordinary Life in Extraordinary Times—Soviet Russia in the 1930s* (New York: Oxford University Press, 1999), 139–63; and Hoffmann, *Stalinist Values*, 88–117.

120. Kotkin, *Magnetic Mountain*, 157–97.

121. Bukharin and Preobrazhenskii, *Azbuka kommunizma*, 273–76, 315–16.

122. On the origins and history of the communal apartment, see Jahn, "Housing Revolution"; and Lebina, *Povsednevnaia zhizn' sovetskogo goroda*, 178–204. On communal apartment life, see Ekaterina Gerasimova, "Sovetskaia kommunal'naia kvartira kak sotsial'nyi institut: Istoriko-sotsiologicheskii analiz" (Candidate diss., European University in Saint Petersburg, 2000); Ilia Utekhin, *Ocherki kommunal'nogo byta* (Moscow: OGI, 2001); and Ekaterina Gerasimova, "Public Privacy in the Soviet Communal Apartment," in *Socialist Spaces: Sites of Everyday Life in the Eastern Bloc*, edited by David Crowley and Susan Reid (Oxford: Berg, 2002), 207–30.

123. Gerasimova, "Sovetskaia kommunal'naia kvartira," 35–47.

124. On the laboring classes' prerevolutionary experience with communal forms of housing, see Lebina, *Povsednevnaia zhizn' sovetskogo goroda*, 160; and Ruble, *Second Metropolis*, 267–72.

125. Gerasimova, "Sovetskaia kommunal'naia kvartira," 35–47.

126. Engels, *Housing Question*, 101.

127. Friedrich Engels, "Socialism: Utopian and Scientific," in *The Marx-Engels Reader*, edited by Robert C. Tucker (New York: W. W. Norton, 1978), 715–16.

128. For a study of Soviet everyday life, including the communal apartment, that emphasizes its origins in the prerevolutionary intelligentsia's obsessions with transforming the everyday, see Svetlana Boym, *Common Places: Mythologies of Everyday Life in Russia* (Cambridge, Mass.: Harvard University Press, 1994).

129. Richard Stites, *Revolutionary Dreams: Utopian Vision and Experimental Life in the Russian Revolution* (New York: Oxford University Press, 1989), 197–204.

130. Hugh Hudson Jr., *Blueprints and Blood: The Stalinization of Soviet Architecture, 1917–1937* (Princeton, N.J.: Princeton University Press, 1994), 52–67; Milka Bliznakov, "Soviet Housing during the Experimental Years, 1918 to 1933," in *Russian Housing*, ed. Brumfield and Ruble, 101–18.

131. S. Frederick Starr, "Visionary Town Planning during the Cultural Revolution," in *Cultural Revolution in Russia, 1928–1931*, edited by Sheila Fitzpatrick

(Bloomington: Indiana University Press, 1978), 207–40; Barbara Kreis, "The Idea of the *Dom-Kommuna* and the Dilemma of the Soviet Avant-Garde," *Oppositions*, no. 21 (Summer 1980): 53–77.

132. Carol Hayden, "The Zhenotdel and the Bolshevik Party," *Russian History* 2 (1976): 150–73; Choi Chatterjee, *Celebrating Women: Gender, Festival Culture, and Bolshevik Ideology, 1910–1939* (Pittsburgh: University of Pittsburgh Press, 2002), 106–7, 113–19; Wendy Goldman, *Women at the Gates: Gender and Industry in Stalin's Russia* (Cambridge: Cambridge University Press, 2002), 40–42, 51–56.

133. Kotkin, *Magnetic Mountain*, 157–97.

134. Sheila Fitzpatrick, *The Cultural Front: Power and Culture in Revolutionary Russia* (Ithaca, N.Y.: Cornell University Press, 1992).

135. Starr, "Visionary Town Planning."

136. Goldman, *Women at the Gates*, 51–52, 56–57.

137. "O rabote po perestroike byta," *Partiinoe stroitel'stvo*, nos. 11–12 (June 1930): 86. On the decree's significance as part of the government's turn against utopian projects, see Starr, "Visionary Town Planning," 237–38.

138. Hudson, *Blueprints and Blood*.

139. "O rabote po perestroike byta."

140. Ibid.

141. In April 1931, the Main Administration for the Communal Economy made "a residential building with individual apartments" the central focus for new housing. Not to be outdone, the Leningrad city soviet passed a similar provision in 1934 making the separate apartment for single-family occupancy the central basis of new housing. As quoted by Gerasimova, "Sovetskaia kommunal'naia kvartira," 63. The Moscow city soviet announced in a 1932 housing decree that "each flat with its own bath or shower will, as a rule, accommodate one family." As quoted by Andrusz, *Housing*, 121. Union-level decrees on standardized housing in 1939 called for apartments ranging in size from one to three rooms with smaller floor space and a kitchen, bathroom, and toilet. "O tipovykh proektakh zhilishchnogo stroitel'stva," May 21, 1939, *Sobranie postanovlenii i rasporiazhenii pravitel'stva SSSR* (hereafter, *SP SSSR*), no. 33 (1939): 487–90. See also "O tipovykh proektakh zhilishchnogo stroitel'stva," July 21, 1939, *SP SSSR*, no. 45 (1939): 667–68.

142. Fitzpatrick, *Everyday Stalinism*, 139–63.

143. Colton, *Moscow*, 168–69; Fitzpatrick, *Everyday Stalinism*, 98–99; Gerasimova, "Sovetskaia kommunal'naia kvartira," 63–64.

144. Kotkin, *Magnetic Mountain*, 125–29.

145. Sheila Fitzpatrick, "Becoming Cultured: Socialist Realism and the Representation of Privilege and Taste," in *Cultural Front*, 216–37.

146. Vera Dunham, *In Stalin's Time: Middle-Class Values in Soviet Fiction* (Durham, N.C.: Duke University Press, 1990).

147. Hudson, *Blueprints and Blood*, 80–81.

148. R. Khiger, "Zhilishche kvartirnogo tipa," *Sovetskaia arkhitektura*, no. 4 (1933): 18–33.

149. P. Blokhin, "Trudiashchiesia poluchili novye zhilishcha," *Arkhitektura SSSR*, no. 10 (1937): 32.

150. Monique Eleb and Anne Debarre, *L'Invention de l'habitation moderne: Paris 1880–1914* (Paris: Hazan, 1995); François Loyer, *Paris Nineteenth Century: Architecture and Urbanism*, translated by Charles Clark (New York: Abbeville Press Publishers, 1988).

151. *Voprosy zhilishchnoi arkhitektury: III plenum orgkomiteta soiuza sovetskikh arkhitektorov SSSR, 3–5 iiunia 1936 goda* (Moscow: Izdatel'stvo vsesoiuznoi akademii arkhitektury, 1936), 17–18.

152. V. Blokhin, "Otdelka i detali," *Arkhitektura SSSR*, no. 6 (1934): 25. Whether this was the same Blokhin cited above is unclear. This article is the only one I am aware of that identifies the author's first name with the initial "V."

153. *Voprosy zhilishchnoi arkhitektury*, 61–62.

154. Ibid., 62–63.

155. Jürgen Habermas, *The Structural Transformation of the Public Sphere: An Inquiry into a Category of Bourgeois Society*, translated by Thomas Burger and Frederick Lawrence (Cambridge, Mass.: MIT Press, 1996), 45.

156. *Voprosy zhilishchnoi arkhitektury*, 63.

157. Ibid., 63.

158. Ibid., 25, 27.

159. Blokhin, "Trudiashchiesia poluchili novye zhilishcha," 34.

160. Hudson, *Blueprints and Blood*, 118–216.

161. Iu. Shass, "Malometrazhnaia kvartira," *Arkhitektura SSSR*, no. 5 (1940): 12.

162. S. Alekseev et al., *Inter'er zhilogo doma* (Moscow: Gosudarstvennoe izdatel'stvo literatury po stroitel'stvu i arkhitekture, 1954), 10.

163. Blokhin, "Otdelka i detali," 25.

164. Zholtovskii received his architectural training in Saint Petersburg from 1887 to 1898. In his pre-1917 work, he had preferred the Renaissance style and designed at least one private residence in Moscow. *Bol'shaia sovetskaia entsiklopediia*, 3rd ed. (Moscow: Izdatel'stvo "Sovetskaia entsiklopediia," 1972), 9:231.

165. *Voprosy zhilishchnoi arkhitektury*, 18.

166. R. Khiger, "Dom na Mokhovoi," *Arkhitektura SSSR*, no. 6 (1934): 23; Blokhin, "Otdelka i detali," 25.

167. V. Kusakov, "Zhiloi dom na Zemlianom valu," *Arkhitektura SSSR*, no. 6 (1934): 29–30.

168. *Voprosy zhilishchnoi arkhitektury*, 59–61.

169. Ibid., 59–61.

170. Ibid., 19.

171. Ibid., 59–60.

172. Hudson, *Blueprints in Blood*, 118–216.

173. Russian State Archive of Socio-Political History (Rossiiskii gosudarstvennyi arkhiv sotsial'no-politicheskoi istorii; hereafter, RGASPI), f. 81, op. 3, d. 192, ll. 57–60, 70, 130. See also *Otchet gruppy rabotnikov, komandirovannykh Len. gorkomom VKP(b) dlia oznakomleniia s zhilishchno-kommunal'nym khoziaistvom gorodov zapadnoi Evropy.* This unpublished and undated version of their report, preserved in the National Library in Saint Petersburg, concentrates mostly on technical aspects of housing construction.

174. RGASPI, f. 81, op. 3, d. 192, ll. 132–33.

175. *Otchet gruppy rabotnikov*, 2–3.

176. Designed by Grete Schütte-Lihotsky in the mid-1920s, the Frankfurt Kitchen was a formative model in modernist architecture for a compact, rationally designed kitchen. Nicholas Bullock, "First the Kitchen—then the Façade," *Journal of Design History* 1, nos. 3–4 (1988): 177–92.

177. RGASPI, f. 81, op. 3, d. 192, ll. 57–60, 68, 70, 130–31.

178. Hudson, *Blueprints and Blood*, 69–70, 131; Bittner, *Many Lives*, 139.

179. Greg Castillo, *Cold War on the Home Front: The Soft Power of Midcentury Design* (Minneapolis: University of Minnesota Press, 2010).
180. *Voprosy zhilishchnoi arkhitektury*, 50–51.
181. *Zhilishche: Voprosy proektirovaniia i stroitel'stva zhilykh zdanii—Materialy II plenuma pravleniia Soiuza sovetskikh arkhitektorov SSSR, 23–27 dekabria 1937 goda* (Moscow: Izdatel'stvo vsesoiuznoi akademii arkhitektury, 1938), 47.
182. *Voprosy zhilishchnoi arkhitektury*, 17.
183. Ibid., 63.
184. Ibid., 75.
185. Ibid., 75.
186. Yves Cohen, "Circulatory Localities: The Example of Stalinism in the 1930s," *Kritika: Explorations in Russian and Eurasian History* 11, no. 1 (Winter 2010): 11–45.

Chapter 2

1. Sheila Fitzpatrick, "Becoming Cultured: Socialist Realism and the Representation of Privilege and Taste," in *The Cultural Front: Power and Culture in Revolutionary Russia*, by Sheila Fitzpatrick (Ithaca, N.Y.: Cornell University Press, 1992), 216–37.
2. A. Urban, "'Minimal'naia' zhilaia iacheika," *Arkhitektura SSSR*, no. 5 (1936): 14–17.
3. *Voprosy zhilishchnoi arkhitektury: III plenum orgkomiteta soiuza sovetskikh arkhitektorov SSSR, 3–5 iiunia 1936 goda* (Moscow: Izdatel'stvo vsesoiuznoi akademii arkhitektury, 1936), 23, 26.
4. P. Blokhin and A. Zal'tsman, "O tipovykh proektakh zhilykh sektsii dlia massovogo stroitel'stva 1939 goda," *Arkhitektura SSSR*, no. 2 (1939): 29. For other cases in which architects discussed the problem of large separate apartments turning into communal apartments, see D. Fridman, "Proekt tipovoi kvartiry," *Arkhitektura SSSR*, no. 9 (1936); 13; M. Barshch, "Individual'naia kvartira," *Arkhitektura SSSR*, no. 9 (1937): 37; and Iu. Shass, "Dom na Maloi Nikitskoi ulitse," *Arkhitektura SSSR*, no. 1 (1939): 69.
5. Hugh Hudson Jr., *Blueprints and Blood: The Stalinization of Soviet Architecture, 1917–1937* (Princeton, N.J.: Princeton University Press, 1994), 78–79, 125.
6. The fact that some elites lived in communal apartments suggests their homes had undergone communalization. See Sheila Fitzpatrick, *Everyday Stalinism: Ordinary Life in Extraordinary Times—Soviet Russia in the 1930s* (New York: Oxford University Press, 1999), 98–99. Because the quantitative data cited below on the communalization of new apartments do not indicate their residents' social status, it is not possible to determine how many apartments inhabited by elites became communal.
7. *Voprosy zhilishchnoi arkhitektury*, 19.
8. *Zhilishche: Voprosy proektirovaniia i stroitel'stva zhilykh zdanii—Materialy II plenuma pravleniia Soiuza sovetskikh arkhitektorov SSSR, 23–27 dekabria 1937 goda* (Moscow: Izdatel'stvo vsesoiuznoi akademii arkhitektury, 1938), 51.
9. Iu. Shass, "Malometrazhnaia kvartira," *Arkhitektura SSSR*, no. 5 (1940): 7.
10. L. Gel'berg and B. Plessein, "O tipe odnosemeinoi kvartiry," *Arkhitektura SSSR*, no. 5 (1940): 3.

11. The source was a 1955 report to the Ministry of the Communal Economy of the Russian Soviet Federated Socialist Republic (RSFSR), which explained that 48 percent of families occupied apartments or houses as one family in 1926. By 1955, as shown in Moscow, "separate apartments are used by only 16 percent of families (renters) in the housing stock of local soviets that makes up two thirds of the entire stock." State Archive of the Russian Federation (Gosudarstvennyi arkhiv Rossiiskoi Federatsii; hereafter, GARF), fond (f.) A-314, opis' (op.) 3, delo (d.) 1392, listy (ll.) 22, 27.

12. A. Zal'tsman, *Klassifikatsiia zhilykh domov*, no. 2, *Soobshcheniia Instituta massovykh sooruzhenii* (Moscow: gosudarstvennoe arkhitekturnoe izdatel'stvo Akademii arkhitketury SSSR, 1943), 5.

13. M. Ginzburg, "Puti razvitiia massovogo zhilishchnogo stroitel'stva," *Arkhitektura SSSR*, no. 2 (1943): 8–12.

14. P. Blokhin, *Maloetazhnyi zhiloi dom* (Moscow: Izdatel'stvo Akademii arkhitektury SSSR, 1944), 58.

15. Barshch, "Individual'naia kvartira," 37; P. Blokhin, "Trudiashchiesia poluchili novye zhilishcha," *Arkhitektura SSSR*, no. 10 (1937): 33–34; Blokhin and Zal'tsman, "O tipovykh proektakh," 29.

16. Gel'berg and Plessein, "O tipe odnosemeinoi kvartiry," 3.

17. Barshch, "Individual'naia kvartira," 37. Other architects similarly advocated the broader availability of separate apartments. See Fridman, "Proekt tipovoi kvartiry," 13; Blokhin, "Trudiashchiesia poluchili," 30–35; N. Bylinkin, "Arkhitektura massovogo zhilishchnogo stroitel'stva," *Arkhitektura SSSR*, no. 2 (1938): 10–21; and P. Blokhin and A. Zal'tsman, "Tipy zhilykh domov i problema malometrazhnoi kvartiry," *Arkhitektura SSSR*, no. 3 (1940): 4–6.

18. "Ob uluchshenii zhilishchnogo stroitel'stva," April 23, 1934, *Sobranie zakonov i rasporiazhenii raboche-krest'ianskogo pravitel'stva SSSR* (hereafter, *SZ*), no. 23 (1934): 318–19. In addition to smaller-sized apartments, the decree recommended the construction of apartments with individual rooms for one or two people that could accommodate bachelors and small families.

19. Barshch, "Individual'naia kvartira."

20. Blokhin, "Trudiashchiesia poluchili," 32–34.

21. Blokhin, *Maloetazhnyi zhiloi dom*, 59.

22. Zal'tsman, *Klassifikatsiia zhilykh domov*, 6, 13, 15.

23. Blokhin, *Maloetazhnyi zhiloi dom*, 59.

24. Gel'berg and Plessein, "O tipe odnosemeinoi kvartiry"; D. Lomonosov and A. Shapiro, "Kak otsenivat' ekonomichnost' proekta zhilogo doma?" *Arkhitektura SSSR*, no. 11 (1958): 33–37; A. Shutov, "Krupnopanel'noe stroitel'stvo na Maloi Okhte," *Arkhitektura SSSR*, no. 6 (1959): 24–26; A. Vlasov's explanation of comparing costs between projects at the 1961 Congress of Architects, *Tretii vsesoiuznyi s'ezd sovetskikh arkhitektorov, 18–20 maia 1961 g. Sokrashchennyi stenograficheskii otchet* (Moscow: Gosudarstvennoe izdatel'stvo literatury po stroitel'stvu, arkhitekture i stroitel'nym materialam, 1962), 16; A. Shutov and B. Banykin, "Novye varianty tipovykh proektov zhilykh domov serii 1–335," *Arkhitektura SSSR*, no. 8 (1962): 14–21.

25. These included the coefficient of living space to overall space, the coefficient of living space to auxiliary space, and the coefficient of the cubic space of a building to living space. Blokhin and Zal'tsman, "O tipovykh proektakh," 31; G. Lavrik,

"K voprosu ob otsenke ekonomichnosti proekta zhilogo doma," *Arkhitektura SSSR*, no. 9 (1963): 14–18.

26. Blokhin and Zal'tsman, "O tipovykh proektakh," 29–41.

27. On both coefficients' advantages and disadvantages, see Lavrik, "K voprosu," 14–18.

28. Blokhin and Zal'tsman, "O tipovykh proektakh."

29. *Voprosy zhilishchnoi arkhitektury*, 20.

30. Barshch, "Individual'naia kvartira."

31. R. Khiger, "Zhilishche kvartirnogo tipa," *Sovetskaia arkhitektura*, no. 4 (1933): 23.

32. Bylinkin, "Arkhitektura," 18.

33. *Zhilishche: Voprosy proektirovaniia*, 44-46.

34. Gel'berg and Plessein, "O tipe odnosemeinoi kvartiry."

35. According to regulations from the 1930s, if a family occupied a "pass-through room" (*prokhodnaia komnata*), through which communal apartment neighbors had to walk to access a second room that did not have its own door onto the hallway, then the second room could not be settled with another family, even in the event that the first family's living space exceeded local norms. On these regulations, see T. Alekseev, ed., *Zhilishchnye zakony: Sbornik vazhneishikh zakonov SSSR i RSFSR, postanovlenii, instruktsii i prikazov po zhilishchnomu khoziaistvu* (Moscow: Izdatel'stvo Ministerstva kommunal'nogo khoziaistva RSFSR, 1958), 355; clause 27 of "O sokhranenii zhilishchnogo fonda i uluchshenii zhilishchnogo khoziaistva v gorodakh," *SZ*, no. 69 (1937); Iu. Tolstoi, *Zhilishchnye prava i obiazannosti grazhdan SSSR* (Moscow: Gosudarstvennoe izdatel'stvo iuridicheskoi literatury, 1960), 29–32; Izrail Martkovich et al., *Zhilishchnoe zakonodatel'stvo v SSSR i RSFSR* (Moscow: Izdatel'stvo literatury po stroitel'stvu, 1965), 95. Architects recognized the ability of pass-through rooms to prevent communal settlement. At the 1961 All-Union Congress of Architects, the architect V. Kamenskii noted the practice, although he argued that communal settlement be simply outlawed instead of having to rely on pass-through rooms, which residents disliked in any case. *Tretii vsesoiuznyi s"ezd*, 37–38.

36. Barshch, "Individual'naia kvartira"; Zal'tsman, *Klassifikatsiia zhilykh domov*, 6.

37. Blokhin, *Maloetazhnyi zhiloi dom*, 45.

38. According to architects, these measures defined housing architecture under Khrushchev. L. Gel'berg and G. Fedorov, "Puti snizheniia stoimosti i uluchsheniia kachestva zhilishchnogo stroitel'stva," *Arkhitektura SSSR*, no. 5 (1964): 5–8. By the 1960s, some architects began to criticize these results and the system of cost estimates that helped produce them. Lavrik, "K voprosu," 14; B. Rubanenko, B. Kolotilkin, and D. Meerson, "Ob opredelenii ekonomichnosti zhilogo doma," *Arkhitektura SSSR*, no. 10 (1966): 6–9; G. Fedorov and N. Lazareva, "Ob ekonomicheskoi otsenke planirovochnykh reshenii zhilykh domov," *Arkhitektura SSSR*, no. 1 (1967): 27–30.

39. Rossiiskii gosudarstvennyi arkhiv ekonomiki, f. 339, op. 1, d. 1073, ll. 7–8.

40. Ibid., l. 9.

41. L. Karlik, "Sektsionnyi zhiloi dom novogo tipa," *Arkhitektura SSSR*, no. 9 (1959): 56.

42. A. Ladinskii, "Razvivat' vse vidy zhilishchnogo stroitel'stva," *Izvestiia*, De-

cember 12, 1956. Ladinskii was not identified as an employee of Gosstroi USSR in the article; this was noted in a Central Committee report, discussed in chapter five, which rebuked him for his overly optimistic predictions. Rossiiskii gosudarstvennyi arkhiv noveishei istorii, f. 5, op. 41, d. 52, l. 174.

43. Martkovich et al., *Zhilishchnoe zakonodatel'stvo*, 80–81.

44. Rubanenko, Kolotilkin, and Meerson, "Ob opredelenii," 6.

45. Nikolai Dmitriev, *Zhilishchnyi vopros: Dva mira—dva podkhoda* (Moscow: Moskovskii rabochii, 1973), 152–53.

46. Nikita Khrushchev, *O shirokom vnedrenii industrial'nykh metodov* (Moscow: Gosudarstvennoe izdatel'stvo politicheskoi literatury, 1955).

47. Stephen Bittner, *The Many Lives of Khrushchev's Thaw: Experience and Memory in Moscow's Arbat* (Ithaca, N.Y.: Cornell University Press, 2008), 105–40; Susan Reid, "Khrushchev Modern: Agency and Modernization in the Soviet Home," *Cahiers du monde russe*, 47, nos. 1–2 (January–June 2006): 227–68; Victor Buchli, "Khrushchev, Modernism, and the Fight against Petit-Bourgeois Consciousness in the Soviet Home," *Journal of Design History* 10, no. 2 (1997): 161–76.

48. I draw here on Bittner's emphasis on ideological transformation over liberalization for explaining the thaw and differentiating the Khrushchev from the Stalin eras. Bittner, *Many Lives*, 215–16.

49. Ibid., 137.

50. Dana Simmons, "Minimal Frenchmen: Science and Standards of Living, 1840–1960" (Ph.D. diss., University of Chicago, 2004), 262, 296.

51. Avraam Shneerson, *Chto takoe zhilishchnyi vopros* (Moscow: Izdatel'stvo VPSh i AON pri TsK KPSS, 1959), 63; Dmitriev, *Zhilishchnyi vopros*, 120–22.

52. David Broner, *Zhilishchnoe stroitel'stvo i demograficheskie protsessy* (Moscow: "Statistika," 1980), 25.

53. "O razvitii zhilishchnogo stroitel'stva v SSSR," July 31, 1957, *Sobranie postanovlenii pravitel'stva SSSR*, no. 9 (1957): 332. I arrive at my estimate of 96 million square meters of overall space destroyed in the following way. A November 1966 report of the Central Statistical Administration of the Russian Republic indicated the amounts of overall space and living space in the state and individual housing sectors at the end of the following years: 1926, 1940, 1949, 1960, and 1965. Calculating the proportion of living space to overall space from this data reveals that living space accounted for 73 percent of overall housing space at the end of 1926 and 1940, 74 percent at the end of 1949, and 70 percent at the end of 1960 and 1965. Consequently, one can estimate on the basis of the data for 1926 and 1940 that during the war in the Russian Republic, living space was approximately 73 percent of overall space. Assuming this reflected the Soviet Union as a whole, then 70 million square meters of destroyed living space represent approximately 96 million square meters of overall space. See the archival data upon which these calculations are based in GARF, f. A-374, op. 36, d. 2093, ll. 1, 13.

54. Shneerson, *Chto takoe zhilishchnyi vopros*, 63.

55. Richard Anderson, "USA/USSR: Architecture and War," *Grey Room* 34 (Winter 2009): 80–103.

56. The statistical sourcebook lists housing construction figures for individual years starting with 1961. It was in this year that state housing produced more (56.6 million square meters of overall space) than the combined total of individual housing constructors (23.6 million) and collective farms, collective farmers, and the

rural intelligentsia (22.5 million). *Narodnoe khoziaistvo SSSR v 1967 g.* (Moscow: Statistika, 1968), 675. This sourcebook hereafter is cited as *Nkh SSSR*, followed by the year of the specific volume.

57. K. Chernenko and M. Smirtiukov, eds., *Resheniia partii i pravitel'stva po khoziaistvennym voprosam. 1941–1952 gody* (Moscow: Izdatel'stvo politicheskoi literatury, 1968), 3: 246, 267, 287.

58. Andrew Elam Day, "Building Socialism: The Politics of the Soviet Cityscape in the Stalin Era" (Ph.D. diss., Columbia University, 1998), 209–51; Mark Smith, *Property of Communists: The Urban Housing Program from Stalin to Khrushchev* (DeKalb: Northern Illinois University Press, 2010), 25–69.

59. Smith, *Property of Communists*, 9–12, 25–99.

60. Ann Livschiz, "Growing Up Soviet: Childhood in the Soviet Union, 1918–1958 (Ph.D. diss., Stanford University, 2007).

61. Mefodii Terent'ev, *Milliony novykh kvartir* (Moscow: VTsSPS Profizdat, 1958).

62. N. Karpov, "Stroitel'stvo zhilishch: Postoiannaia zabota partii," *Leningradskaia pravda*, January 23, 1958; "Za 700 tysiach kvadratnykh metrov novoi zhiloi ploshchadi!" *Leningradskaia pravda*, March 26, 1958; V. Vlasovskii, "Komnata: Za 20 minut," *Leningradskaia pravda*, November 15, 1960; V. Butuzov, E. Smirnov, and N. Poriadkov, "Pust' zavody delaiut kvartiry," *Izvestiia*, October 26, 1960; "Primer dlia stroitelei vsei strany," *Pravda*, January 3, 1961; V. Kolpakov, "Kogda dom dostraivaetsia . . .," *Leningradskaia pravda*, June 18, 1961.

63. Stephen Kotkin, *Magnetic Mountain: Stalinism as a Civilization* (Berkeley: University of California Press, 1995), 37–71.

64. I have generally found that archival data confirm what was reported in published sources. E.g., a report by the Central Statistical Administration in 1966 reported the same figures on the total amount of existing housing in the RSFSR as its published sourcebook reported for years that could be compared. GARF, f. 374, op. 36, d. 2093, l. 13. Compare with *Nkh SSSR v 1967 g.*, 682–83.

65. *Nkh SSSR v 1959 godu*, 843.

66. Lomonosov and Shapiro, "Kak otsenivat'," 33–37.

67. Lavrik, "K voprosu," 14–18.

68. For other proposals from architects, see Rubanenko, Kolotilkin, and Meerson, "Ob opredelenii," 6–9; and Fedorov and Lazareva, "Ob ekonomicheskoi otsenke," 27–30.

69. V. Ivkin, *Gosudarstvennaia vlast' SSSR: Vysshie organy vlasti i upravleniia i ikh rukovoditeli, 1923–1991 gg. Istoriko-biograficheskii spravochnik* (Moscow: Rosspen, 1999), 381.

70. Kucherenko's proposal was sent to the Soviet of Ministers of the USSR and circulated to the Ministry of the Communal Economy of the RSFSR. GARF, f. A-314, op. 3, d. 2211, ll. 23–25.

71. Aleksandr Saltykov, *O khudozhestvennom vkuse v bytu* (Moscow: Gosudarstvennoe izdatel'stvo "Iskusstvo," 1959); Iurii Sharov and Galina Poliachek, *Vkus nado vospityvat' (besedy dlia molodezhi)* (Novosibirsk: Novosibirskoe knizhnoe izdatel'stvo, 1960), 66–79.

72. N. Narin'iani and B. Dmitriev, "Pod igom koeffitsienta," *Izvestiia*, March 3, 1960.

73. V. Lagutenko et al., "V plenu abstraktsii," *Izvestiia*, March 15, 1960.

74. Ibid.

75. M. Orlov, "O chem zhe spor?" *Izvestiia*, March 27, 1960.

76. Narin'iani and Dmitriev, "Pod igom koeffitsienta"; Orlov, "O chem zhe spor?"

Chapter 3

1. E.g., Gregory Andrusz, *Housing and Urban Development in the USSR* (Albany: State University of New York Press, 1984), 46–81.

2. Stephen Bittner, "Exploring Reform: De-Stalinization in Moscow's Arbat District, 1953–1968," (Ph.D. diss., University of Chicago, 2000), 101–48.

3. Christine Varga-Harris, "Forging Citizenship on the Home Front: Reviving the Socialist Contract and Constructing Soviet Identity during the Thaw," in *The Dilemmas of De-Stalinization: Negotiating Cultural and Social Change in the Khrushchev Era*, edited by Polly Jones (London: Routledge, 2006), 101–16.

4. Steven Harris, "'We Too Want to Live in Normal Apartments': Soviet Mass Housing and the Marginalization of the Elderly under Khrushchev and Brezhnev," *Soviet and Post-Soviet Review* 32, nos. 2–3 (2005): 143–74.

5. In contrast, Rebecca Manley has examined how settling housing claims after World War II was intertwined with reshaping the postwar social body. Rebecca Manley, "'Where Should We Resettle the Comrades Next?': The Adjudication of Housing Claims and the Construction of the Post-War Order," in *Late Stalinist Russia: Society between Reconstruction and Reinvention*, edited by Juliane Fürst (London: Routledge, 2006), 233–46. On weeding out socially undesirable elements under Khrushchev, see Miriam Dobson, *Khrushchev's Cold Summer: Gulag Returnees, Crime, and the Fate of Reform after Stalin* (Ithaca, N.Y.: Cornell University Press, 2009).

6. Golfo Alexopoulos, "Soviet Citizenship, More or Less: Rights, Emotions, and States of Civic Belonging," *Kritika: Explorations in Russian and Eurasian History* 7, no. 3 (2006): 487–528.

7. On the state's continued backing of the proposed reform into the post-Khrushchev era, see Andrusz, *Housing*, 57–81.

8. Iasnov and Mikhailov outlined their ideas in two reports to Malenkov and Khrushchev in late March and mid-April 1953. Russian State Archive of Contemporary History (Rossiiskii gosudarstvennyi arkhiv noveishei istorii; hereafter, RGANI), fond (f.) 5, opis' (op.) 30, delo (d.) 19, listy (ll.) 28–35, 47–50.

9. Ibid., ll. 33–34, 48–49, 51–52.

10. Ibid., ll. 136–39.

11. For a critique of scholars' assumption that centralization encouraged social inequalities rather than egalitarianism, see Bittner, "Exploring Reform," 147.

12. The instructions to Leningrad's leaders were communicated in a July 19, 1955, decree of the RSFSR Council of Ministers, "On the Method of Distributing Living Space in the City of Leningrad," State Archive of the Russian Federation (Gosudarstvennyi arkhiv Rossiiskoi Federatsii; hereafter, GARF), f. A-259, op. 7, d. 6151, ll. 1–2.

13. A Soviet of Ministers of the RSFSR decree from September 1954 outlined the course of action for the Briansk, Velikie Luki, Kalinin, Lipetsk, Novgorod, Orel, Pskov, and Smolensk oblasts. GARF, f. A-259, op. 1, d. 674, ll. 1–4.

14. The RSFSR Ministry of State Control reported in November 1955 on implementation of the September 1954 decree. GARF, f. A-314, op. 3, d. 1393, ll. 2, 11.

15. GARF, f. A-339, op. 1, d. 8964, ll. 61–62.

16. Ibid., l. 116.

17. GARF, f. A-314, op. 3, d. 1393, ll. 2, 5, 9, 11.

18. RGANI, f. 5, op. 41, d. 102, ll. 177–78.

19. "O sokhranenii zhilishchnogo fonda i ulushchenii zhilishchnogo khoziaistva v gorodakh," October 17, 1937, *Sobranie zakonov i rasporiazhenii rabochekrest'ianskogo pravitel'stva SSSR*, no. 69 (1937): 746–55.

20. GARF, f. A-314, op. 3, d. 321, l. 45.

21. Ibid., ll. 43–45.

22. RGANI, f. 5, op. 41, d. 102, ll. 151, 171–75.

23. Such practices were noted in 1951, when the government considered, but eventually abandoned proposals to tighten the 1939 regulations on exchanges. See the materials related to this proposal in GARF, f. A-259, op. 6, d. 8356.

24. GARF, f. A-339, op. 1, d. 8964, ll. 64–65.

25. Archival materials on the draft decree include commentaries from Moscow and Leningrad city leaders, as well as opinions by the Chairman of the Supreme Court and the chairman of the Juridical Commission. RGANI, f. 5, op. 41, d. 102, ll. 151–56, 161–84.

26. RGANI, f. 5, op. 41, d. 102, ll. 157–60.

27. Ibid., ll. 158–59.

28. Central State Archive of Saint Petersburg (Tsentral'nyi gosudarstvennyi arkhiv Sankt-Peterburga; hereafter, TsGA SPb), f. 103, op. 5, d. 330, ll. 66–67.

29. For Leningrad as a whole, reports on distribution in the 1950s accounted for lists dating back to no earlier than 1944. TsGA SPb, f. 3343, op. 1, d. 55, l. 2; TsGA SPb, f. 3343, op. 1, d. 70, l. 1.

30. TsGA SPb, f. 103, op. 5, d. 330, ll. 66–67.

31. Tikhon Alekseev, *Zhilishchnye l'goty grazhdan SSSR* (Moscow: Gosudarstvennoe izdatel'stvo iuridicheskoi literatury, 1962).

32. TsGA SPb, f. 103, op. 5, d. 330, ll. 66–67.

33. Andrusz, *Housing*, 33, 55.

34. TsGA SPb, f. 103, op. 5, d. 330, ll. 66–67.

35. Ibid.

36. Ibid.

37. Ibid.

38. Leningrad city soviet decree of August 27, 1956, "On the Method of Inventory and Distribution of Living Space in the City of Leningrad." TsGA SPb, f. 7384, op. 37, d. 263, ll. 7–9.

39. Ibid., ll. 9–10, 20–21.

40. Ibid., l. 20.

41. TsGA SPb, f. 7384, op. 37, d. 625, ll. 1, 23–24.

42. Ibid., ll. 15–16.

43. Ibid., ll. 3–4, 17.

44. Ibid., ll. 3–4.

45. TsGA SPb, f. 103, op. 5, d. 707, ll. 1–3, 7.

46. TsGA SPb, f. 7384, op. 37, d. 625, ll. 3–4.

47. Miriam Dobson, "Contesting the Paradigms of De-Stalinization: Readers'

Responses to *One Day in the Life of Ivan Denisovich*," *Slavic Review* 64, no. 3 (2005): 580–600.

48. Amir Weiner, "The Empires Pay a Visit: Gulag Returnees, East European Rebellions, and Soviet Frontier Politics," *Journal of Modern History* 78, no. 2 (2006): 333–76.

49. TsGA SPb, f. 7384, op. 37, d. 625, ll. 17–19.

50. Ibid., ll. 6–7.

51. Ibid., ll. 12–14.

52. Ibid., l. 7.

53. TsGA SPb, f. 7384, op. 37, d. 2046, ll. 320–21.

54. Ibid., ll. 320–21.

55. TsGA SPb, f. 7384, op. 37a, d. 47, l. 115.

56. TsGA SPb, f. 7384, op. 37a, d. 69, ll. 93–94ob.

57. TsGA SPb, f. 7384, op. 42, d. 343, ll. 132–33.

58. Her biographical information was reported in a city soviet housing department memo. TsGA SPb, f. 7384, op. 37, d. 2046, ll. 307, 320.

59. For examples of petitioners who relied on their rehabilitated status in making their case, see two letters in 1965 (in TsGA SPb, f. 7384, op. 42, d. 1004, ll. 51–53; TsGA SPb, f. 7384, op. 42, d. 1004, ll. 89–93) and one in 1967 (in TsGA SPb, f. 7384, op. 42, d. 1759, l. 5).

60. TsGA SPb, f. 7384, op. 41, d. 765, l. 185.

61. TsGA SPb, f. 7384, op. 37, d. 2046, ll. 86, 88–88ob.

62. Ibid., ll. 88–88ob.

63. Enterprises were obligated to contribute 10 percent of housing they constructed to local soviets since September 1945. Andrusz, *Housing*, 70.

64. TsGA SPb, f. 7384, op. 37, d. 829, ll. 1, 5–7.

65. The Central Committee gathered input on the proposed decree in July 1958. The Leningrad obkom head, Spiridonov, had contributed to this discussion, making it likely that the city's leadership knew the government was planning to give local soviets more control over housing. RGANI, f. 5, op. 41, d. 102, ll. 151–84.

66. TsGA SPb, f. 7384, op. 37, d. 1007, ll. 1–9.

67. TsGA SPb, f. 3343, op. 1, d. 95, ll. 1–6.

68. Ibid., ll. 6–7.

69. Ibid., ll. 6–7.

70. TsGA SPb, f. 7384, op. 37, d. 1179, ll. 1–4, 39–40.

71. Ibid., l. 10.

72. Ibid., ll. 18–19.

73. Ibid., ll. 18–20.

74. Ibid., ll. 24, 41.

75. Ibid., l. 22. Belov was identified only by name at this meeting. He was identified as the Kalinin district representative at the 1957 meeting cited above. TsGA SPb, f. 7384, op. 37, d. 625, l. 2.

76. TsGA SPb, f. 7384, op. 37, d. 1179, l. 23.

77. Ibid., ll. 73–74, 93–94.

78. Ibid., ll. 82–83.

79. Ibid., l. 83.

80. Ibid., ll. 87–88.

81. Ibid., ll. 90–92.

82. Ibid., l. 92.

83. Ibid.

84. Ibid., l. 100.

85. Ibid., l. 76.

86. Ibid., l. 94.

87. Ibid., ll. 75–76, 95.

88. TsGA SPb, f. 7384, op. 37, d. 1146, ll. 7–11.

89. Ibid., ll. 8–9.

90. Ibid., l. 8.

91. Ibid., ll. 8, 10.

92. The source was a report on the Leningrad reform by the All-Union Central Council of Professional Unions. GARF, f. 5451, op. 30, d. 449, ll. 85, 91.

93. TsGA SPb, f. 7384, op. 41, d. 255, ll. 26, 28.

94. GARF, f. 5451, op. 30, d. 449, l. 85.

95. The June 24, 1961, city soviet decree delayed until January 1, 1962 the anticipated shift to 4.5 square meters as the maximum space beyond which one could not get onto a waiting list. TsGA SPb, f. 7384, op. 41, d. 64, ll. 2–3.

96. TsGA SPb, f. 7384, op. 41, d. 255, ll. 26, 28–29.

97. *Itogi vsesoiuznoi perepisi naseleniia 1970 goda, tom 1: Chislennost' naseleniia SSSR, soiuznykh i avtonomnykh respublik, kraev i oblastei* (Moscow: "Statistika," 1972), 22.

98. TsGA SPb, f. 103, op. 5, d. 330, l. 66.

99. TsGA SPb, f. 103, op. 5, d. 707, l. 3.

100. TsGA SPb, f. 103, op. 5, d. 893, l. 1.

101. TsGA SPb, f. 7384, op. 37, d. 1146, ll. 24, 30–31.

102. TsGA SPb, f. 7384, op. 41, d. 255, ll. 1, 6.

103. GARF, f. 5451, op. 30, d. 449, l. 87.

104. TsGA SPb, f. 7384, op. 41, d. 255, ll. 1, 6.

105. Ibid., ll. 12–14.

106. TsGA SPb, f. 7384, op. 41, d. 64, ll. 2, 5–5ob.

107. TsGA SPb, f. 7384, op. 41, d. 255, ll. 26, 50.

108. GARF, f. 5451, op. 30, d. 449, l. 87.

109. TsGA SPb, f. 7384, op. 37, d. 1146, l. 36.

110. See this point in the 1962 distribution plan in TsGA SPb, f. 7384, op. 41, d. 280, l. 28.

111. TsGA SPb, f. 7384, op. 41, d. 280, ll. 37, 46.

112. Ibid., l. 47.

113. TsGA SPb, f. 7384, op. 41, d. 255, l. 19.

114. Ibid., l. 60.

Chapter 4

1. "O razvitii zhilishchnogo stroitel'stva v SSSR," July 31, 1957, *Sobranie postanovlenii pravitel'stva SSSR* (hereafter, *SP SSSR*), no. 9 (1957).

2. The reemergence of class in shaping Soviet society after Stalin appeared in other politically charged contexts. See Amir Weiner, "The Empires Pay a Visit: Gulag Returnees, East European Rebellions, and Soviet Frontier Politics, *Journal of Modern History* 78, no. 2 (2006): 333–76.

3. Alfred DiMaio Jr. and Gregory Andrusz, writing before access to archives, guessed correctly that the leadership's efforts to promote "housing-construction collectives" (a term that included people's construction) were a step in the direction of the cooperative. Alfred DiMaio Jr., *Soviet Urban Housing: Problems and Policies* (New York: Praeger, 1974), 23, 109–10; and Gregory Andrusz, *Housing and Urban Development in the USSR* (Albany: State University of New York Press, 1984), 82–83. More recently, Lynne Attwood mentions people's construction; see Lynne Attwood, "Housing in the Khrushchev Era," in *Women in the Khrushchev Era*, edited by Melanie Ilič, Susan Reid, and Lynne Attwood (New York: Palgrave, 2004), 187. See also Mark Smith, *Property of Communists: The Urban Housing Program from Stalin to Khrushchev* (DeKalb: Northern Illinois University Press, 2010), 75, 163.

4. For examinations of the cooperative, see DiMaio, *Soviet Urban Housing*, 175–98; Andrusz, *Housing*, 82–98; and Smith, *Property*, 161–65.

5. Roy Medvedev and Zhores Medvedev, *Khrushchev: The Years in Power*, translated by Andrew Durkin (New York: W. W. Norton, 1978), 75–79.

6. The following is my explanation for how these statistics were derived. Soviet statisticians did not record construction figures for people's construction as a separate category. Because the housing constructed under people's construction was supposed to be registered as personal property (*lichnaia sobstvennost'*), and because the main source of housing that fell under this category was individual housing, an analysis of the statistics on the individual housing sector can provide a reasonable estimate of how much was built through people's construction. The data on individual housing construction (table 2.4 in chapter 2) reflect noticeable increases in construction for 1956 and 1957, at the start of the people's construction campaign, followed by a remarkable surge in 1958. People's construction most likely accounted for this surge, and the high volume of individual housing construction in the following years. Statisticians may have begun adding people's construction to individual construction statistics in 1956 and 1957. This would be plausible only if its levels of construction were quite low in these years and suddenly skyrocketed in 1958. Because the campaign was already in full swing by 1957, the data more strongly suggest that people's construction was added to statistics on individual housing construction beginning in 1958. And because individual housing construction accounted for yearly increases of 2 to 2.9 million square meters from 1956 to 1959 (excluding the bulk of the surge in 1958), one can estimate that people's construction produced approximately 9 million square meters of overall housing space per year. This is a conservative estimate, because it assumes that individual construction alone accounted for the annual increases from 1956 to 1959 of 2 to 2.9 million square meters. It also assumes that all people's construction projects were registered as personal property and none as state property; if some projects had been registered as the state property of factories and enterprises, the volume of people's construction would be higher than estimated here. As further evidence that people's construction most likely accounted for most of the 1958 surge, the data show that construction in the individual housing sector peaked in 1959 and fell precipitously after 1960. This turn of events coincided with the end of the people's construction campaign.

Using the conservative estimate of housing built through people's construction at 9 million square meters of overall space per year, one can estimate its share of overall housing construction. For total state and individual housing construction (as shown in table 2.4, this total did not include collective farm housing), people's construction accounted for approximately 10 to 13 percent of new housing construction during the years for which the data here reflect its growth from 1958 to 1960. This contribution to the mass housing campaign can be illustrated in an additional way. Data from the statistical sourcebook *Narodnoe khoziaistvo SSSR* (hereafter, *Nkh SSSR*) allow one to estimate that the average size of an apartment constructed from 1956 to 1960 was 42 square meters of overall space (see *Nkh SSSR v 1965 g.*, 611); these data represent the annual construction of apartments in the state housing sector and the individual housing sector for 1956 to 1965, and these data are also rendered in square meters of overall space, from which the average amount of square meters of overall space in one apartment can be calculated. If people's construction produced 9 million square meters of overall space annually, then one can estimate that it produced approximately 214,000 apartments a year from 1958 to 1960. Once more, this is a conservative estimate that assumes no growth above 9 million square meters a year after 1958.

   7. N. Paushkin, *Formy organizatsii truda na narodnykh stroikakh v g. Gor'kom (Doklad na sektsii 'Formy organizatsii stroitel'stva i metody proizvodstva stroitel'nykh rabot' konferentsii po massovomu stroitel'stvu zhilykh domov metodom narodnoi stroiki)* (Gor'kii: Gor'kovskaia oblastnaia tipografiia, 1957), 4.

   8. Petr Cherneev and Aleksandr Torbin, *Svoimi silami* (Moscow: Izdatel'stvo VTsSPS Profizdat, 1957), 8.

   9. S. Lebedev, ed., *Sila narodnogo pochina: Iz opyta stroitel'stva zhil'ia silami rabochikh kollektivov predpriiatii gor'kovskoi promyshlennosti i narodnoi stroiki avtoguzhevykh dorog i tramvaino-trolleibusnykh putei* (Gor'kii: Gor'kovskaia pravda, 1957), 15–16.

   10. Ibid., 40.

   11. Cherneev and Torbin, *Svoimi silami*, 25–26.

   12. Russian State Archive of Contemporary History (Rossiiskii gosudarstvennyi arkhiv noveishei istorii; hereafter, RGANI), fond (f.) 6, opis' (op.) 6, delo (d.) 1776, listy (l.) 56–56ob.

   13. *Svoimi silami: Iz opyta stroitel'stva zhil'ia khoziaistvennym sposobom na Orenburgskom uzle* (Orenburg: Dorprofsozh i redaktsiia gazety "Orenburgskii zheleznodorozhnik," 1959), 19, 29, 36; L. Perepelov, *Stroim dlia sebia* (Moscow: Gosudarstvennoe izdatel'stvo politicheskoi literatury, 1958), 23, 39; P. Petrov, "Metodom narodnoi stroiki," in *My sebe khoroshii dom postroim*, edited by I. Grebtsov (Krasnoiarsk: Krasnoiarskoe knizhnoe izdatel'stvo, 1958), 35–39; V. Savinov, "Za schet sverkhplanovykh nakoplenii," in *My sebe khoroshii dom postroim*, 54–58; F. Grishin, "Nasha pochetnaia zadacha," in *My sebe khoroshii dom postroim*, 64–70; Fedor Kopeikin, *Kollektivnoe stroitel'stvo individual'nykh domov* (Leningrad: Gosudarstvennoe izdatel'stvo literatury po stroitel'stvu, arkhitekture i stroitel'nym materialam, 1958), 19, 35, 39–41.

   14. Sheila Fitzpatrick, *Education and Social Mobility in the Soviet Union, 1921–1934* (Cambridge: Cambridge University Press, 1979).

   15. Sheila Fitzpatrick, "Postwar Soviet Society: The 'Return to Normalcy', 1945–1953," in *The Impact of World War II on the Soviet Union*, edited by Susan J. Linz (Totowa, N.J.: Rowman & Allanheld, 1985), 140–41; Donald Filtzer, *Soviet Workers and Stalinist Industrialization: The Formation of Modern Soviet Produc-*

tion Relations, 1928–1941 (Armonk, N.Y.: M. E. Sharpe, 1986), 95; Donald Filtzer, *Soviet Workers and Late Stalinism: Labour and the Restoration of the Stalinist System after World War II* (Cambridge: Cambridge University Press, 2002), 158–76.

16. Filtzer, *Soviet Workers*, 94–95.

17. Lebedev, *Sila narodnogo pochina*, 10–11; Cherneev and Torbin, *Svoimi silami*, 5.

18. Andrusz, *Housing*, 70.

19. Cherneev and Torbin, *Svoimi silami*, 12.

20. "O razvitii zhilishchnogo stroitel'stva v SSSR," clause 24. The main journal of the Ministry of the Communal Economy of the RSFSR already claimed in March 1957 that people's construction projects were exempt from the 10 percent rule. "Ob osvobozhdenii ot 10-protsentnoi peredachi zhiloi ploshchadi," *Zhilishchno-kommunal'noe khoziaistvo*, no. 3 (1957): 30.

21. Avraam Shneerson, *Chto takoe zhilishchnyi vopros* (Moscow: Izdatel'stvo VPSh i AON pri TsK KPSS, 1959), 63.

22. Rebecca Manley, "'Where Should We Resettle the Comrades Next?': The Adjudication of Housing Claims and the Construction of the Post-War Order," in *Late Stalinist Russia: Society between Reconstruction and Reinvention*, edited by Juliane Fürst (London: Routledge, 2006), 233–46.

23. Cherneev and Torbin, *Svoimi silami*.

24. Print runs were as low as 1,000 and as high as 25,000 copies, but were usually around 5,000. In addition to the pamphlets discussed in this chapter, see I. Medvedev, *Za 3 goda vmesto 12 let* (Khar'kov: Khar'kovskoe knizhnoe izdatel'stvo, 1959); V. Kozmenkov, *O praktike massovogo stroitel'stva zhil'ia silami rabochikh zavoda 'Krasnyi iakor'" (Doklad na plenarnom zasedanii konferentsii po massovomu stroitel'stvu zhilykh domov metodom narodnoi stroiki)* (Gor'kii, 1957); and V. Konev, *Istochniki finansirovaniia narodnykh stroek i stoimost' rabot (Doklad na sektsii "Formy organizatsii stroitel'stva i metody proizvodstva stroitel'nykh rabot" konferentsii po massovomu stroitel'stvu zhilykh domov metodom narodnoi stroiki)* (Gor'kii: Gor'kovskaia oblastnaia tipografiia, 1957).

25. Lebedev, *Sila narodnogo pochina*, 13.

26. V. Maksimenko, *O praktike massovogo stroitel'stva zhil'ia silami rabochikh zavoda (Doklad na plenarnom zasedanii konferentsii po massovomu stroitel'stvu zhilykh domov metodom narodnoi stroiki)* (Gor'kii: Gor'kovskaia oblastnaia tipografiia, 1957), 16.

27. Maksimenko, *O praktike massovogo stroitel'stva zhil'ia*, 10.

28. Greg Castillo, *Cold War on the Home Front: The Soft Power of Midcentury Design* (Minneapolis: University of Minnesota Press, 2010), 130–36, 161; Steven Harris, *Two Lessons in Modernism: What the* Architectural Review *and America's Mass Media Taught Soviet Architects about the West*, Trondheim Studies on East European Cultures and Societies 31 (Trondheim: Norges Teknisk-Naturvitenskapelige Universitet, 2010).

29. "Rabochie stroiat doma svoimi silami," *Izvestiia*, December 20, 1956; V. Baiderina, "Svoimi rukami," *Izvestiia*, December 27, 1956.

30. David Mark, "The 'Gorki Initiative' in Housing," Embassy Dispatch 150, September 26, 1957, document 861.02/9-2657 in *Confidential U.S. State Department Central Files: The Soviet Union, 1955–1959, Internal Affairs*.

31. Paushkin, *Formy organizatsii truda*, 13.

32. Lebedev, *Sila narodnogo pochina*, 13.

33. RGANI, f. 6, op. 6, d. 1721, ll. 28–29.

34. K. Lazarev, "Massovo-politicheskaia rabota na stroike," in *Svoimi silami: Iz opyta stroitel'stva zhil'ia*, 25–26.

35. Kopeikin, *Kollektivnoe stroitel'stvo*, 10.

36. Lebedev, *Sila narodnogo pochina*, 17–18.

37. Joseph Berliner, *Factory and Manager in the USSR* (Cambridge, Mass.: Harvard University Press, 1957), 207–30; Sheila Fitzpatrick, "After NEP: The Fate of NEP Entrepreneurs, Small Traders, and Artisans in the 'Socialist Russia' of the 1930s," *Russian History* 13, nos. 2–3 (1986): 187–233.

38. Petrov, "Metodom narodnoi stroiki," in *My sebe khoroshii dom postroim*, 37–38.

39. G. Klimenko, *Metodom narodnoi stroiki (Iz opyta stroitel'stva zhilykh domov v Cheliabinskoi oblasti)*, 16.

40. F. Grishin, "Nasha pochetnaia zadacha," in *My sebe khoroshii dom postroim*, 67; Lebedev, *Sila narodnogo pochina*, 30.

41. Lebedev, *Sila narodnogo pochina*, 15.

42. Cherneev and Torbin, *Svoimi silami*, 15; Lebedev, *Sila narodnogo pochina*, 29, 31; Paushkin, *Formy organizatsii truda*, 4; A. Guseva, "Zhiznennost' initsiativnogo stroitel'stva," in *My sebe khoroshii dom postroim*, 20; M. Gorev, *O praktike massovogo stroitel'stva zhil'ia silami rabochikh na Gor'kovskom avtozavode (Doklad na plenarnom zasedanii konferentsii po massovomu stroitel'stvu zhilykh domov metodom narodnoi stroiki)* (Gor'kii: Gor'kovskaia oblastnaia tipografiia, 1957), 5.

43. Gorev, *O praktike massovogo stroitel'stva zhil'ia*, 5.

44. Mark, "'Gorki Initiative.'"

45. I. Urazov, "U novoselov," in *My sebe khoroshii dom postroim*, 59–62.

46. Urazov, "U novoselov," 63.

47. Lebedev, *Sila narodnogo pochina*, 24.

48. V. Irmolinskii, "Neissiakaemyi rodnik," in *My sebe khoroshii dom postroim*, 40–41.

49. Urazov, "U novoselov," 60.

50. Ibid., 62–63.

51. I. Kalinin, "V novom dome," in *Svoimi silami: Iz opyta stroitel'stva zhil'ia*, 35–36.

52. Sheila Fitzpatrick, "Becoming Cultured: Socialist Realism and the Representation of Privilege and Taste," in *The Cultural Front: Power and Culture in Revolutionary Russia* (Ithaca, N.Y.: Cornell University Press, 1992), 216–37.

53. RGANI, f. 2, op. 1, d. 198, ll. 32, 34–36.

54. Ibid., ll. 36–38.

55. RGANI, f. 5, op. 41, d. 89, l. 61.

56. Ibid., ll. 53, 61. "Zamechatel'naia narodnaia initsiativa," *Pravda*, June 10, 1957. See also the article published the next day: "Rasshiriat' stroitel'stvo zhilishch silami rabochikh i sluzhashchikh: na konferentsii v g. Gor'kom," *Pravda*, June 11, 1957.

57. RGANI, f. 5, op. 41, d. 89, ll. 68–78.

58. "O razvitii zhilishchnogo stroitel'stva v SSSR."

59. "O merakh sodeistviia kollektivnomu stroitel'stvu mnogokvartirnykh i od-

nokvartirnykh individual'nykh zhilykh domov," July 9, 1959, *Sobranie postanovlenii pravitel'stva RSFSR* (hereafter, *SP RSFSR*), no. 9 (1959).

60. G. Meshcheriakov, "Kvartiry raspredeliaet obshchestvennost'," *Pravda*, February 3, 1961; A. Papko, "Pis'ma v redaktsiiu: S vodoi i . . . bez vody," *Leningradskaia pravda*, April 1, 1961.

61. V. Kolpakov, "Kogda dom dostraivaetsia . . .," *Leningradskaia pravda*, June 18, 1961.

62. State Archive of the Russian Federation (Gosudarstvennyi arkhiv Rossiiskoi Federatsii; hereafter, GARF), f. A-259, op. 45, d. 1058, ll. 75–77.

63. RGANI, f. 5, op. 41, d. 204, ll. 108–17.

64. See the explanation above on people's construction statistics.

65. This was the reason cited in an ethnographic study of housing in Gor'kii in the nineteenth and twentieth centuries. Sof'ia Rozhdestvenskaia, *Zhilishche rabochikh Gor'kovskoi oblasti (XIX–XX vv.)* (Moscow: Izdatel'stvo "Nauka," 1972), 96.

66. Rudol'f Pikhoia, *Sovetskii Soiuz: Istoriia vlasti, 1945–1991* (Novosibirsk: Sibirskii khronograf, 2000), 218–23.

67. Rozhdestvenskaia, *Zhilishche rabochikh Gor'kovskoi oblasti*, 95–96, 150–52.

68. For Kucherenko's, Grishmanov's, and Miurisep's professional biographies, see Vladimir Ivkin, *Gosudarstvennaia vlast' SSSR. Vysshie organy vlasti i upravleniia i ikh rukovoditeli 1923–1991 gg. Istoriko-biograficheskii spravochnik* (Moscow: Rosspen, 1999), 276–77, 381, 434–35.

69. I borrow the term "speaking Bolshevik" from Stephen Kotkin, *Magnetic Mountain: Stalinism as a Civilization* (Berkeley: University of California Press, 1995), 198–237.

70. Fitzpatrick, *Social Mobility*.

71. Carl Linden, *Khrushchev and the Soviet Leadership, 1957–1964* (Baltimore: Johns Hopkins University Press, 1966), 202–21; Medvedev and Medvedev, *Khrushchev*, 143–70.

72. "O sokhranenii zhilishchnogo fonda i uluchshenii zhilishchnogo khoziaistva v gorodakh," October 17, 1937, *Sobranie zakonov i rasporiazhenii rabochekrest'ianskogo pravitel'stva SSSR*, no. 69 (1937): 746–55.

73. RGANI, f. 5, op. 41, d. 59, ll. 126–33.

74. Ibid.

75. "Tsennyi opyt zhilishchnogo stroitel'stva," *Pravda*, December 7, 1956, I. B. Shelepenkov, "Sobstvennymi silami," *Izvestiia*, December 9, 1956; K. Pogodin, "Pochin avtozavodtsev v zhilishchnom stroitel'stve vyzval shirokii otklik," *Pravda*, December 13, 1956; A. Mokhova, "Raionnyi Sovet i voprosy zhilishchnogo stroitel'stva," *Pravda*, December 15, 1956; "Opyt svidetel'stvuet: Mozhno stroit' bol'she zhilishch, vozvodit' doma gorazdo bystree i deshevle," *Pravda*, December 16, 1956; "Aktivno podderzhivat' narodnuiu initsiativu v zhilishchnom stroitel'stve," *Pravda*, December 18, 1956; "Tsennaia initsiativa v zhilishchnom stroitel'stve," *Izvestiia*, December 20, 1956; "Rabochie stroiat doma svoimi silami," *Izvestiia*, December 20, 1956; "Delo bol'shoi vazhnosti," *Pravda*, December 20, 1956; S. Bakhtiarov, "Kollektiv zavoda postroil chetyre doma," *Pravda*, December 21, 1956.

76. Perm was named Molotov between 1940 and 1957. A. Prokhorov, ed., *Bol'shaia Sovetskaia Entsiklopediia*, 3rd ed., no. 19 (Moscow: Izdatel'stvo "Sovetskaia Entsiklopediia," 1975), 432.

77. S. Pautov, G. Proskuriakov, and E. Gilev, "Nash rabochii zhilishchnyi kooperativ," *Pravda*, December 14, 1956.

78. "Vsemerno podderzhivat' initsiativu trudiashchikhsia v zhilishchnom stroitel'stve," *Pravda*, December 16, 1956.

79. A. Shul'pin and N. Dem'ianov, "Shiroko razvernut' deiatel'nost' zhilishchno-stroitel'noi kooperatsii," *Pravda*, December 17, 1956.

80. RGANI, f. 2, op. 1, d. 192, ll. 25–26. On Baibakov's biographical information, see Ivkin, *Gosudarstvennaia vlast' SSSR*, 211.

81. See Sheremet'ev's biographical information in Ivkin, *Gosudarstvennaia vlast' SSSR*, 601.

82. RGANI, f. 2, op. 1, d. 195, ll. 106, 108.

83. RGANI, f. 2, op. 1, d. 196, ll. 158–59. On Shelepin's career, see Ivkin, *Gosudarstvennaia vlast' SSSR*, 599.

84. Ivkin, *Gosudarstvennaia vlast' SSSR*, 434–35.

85. RGANI, f. 2, op. 1, d. 197, ll. 66–67.

86. RGANI, f. 5, op. 41, d. 72, ll. 119, 123–25.

87. See Struev's biographical details in Ivkin, *Gosudarstvennaia vlast' SSSR*, 547.

88. RGANI, f. 2, op. 1, d. 197, ll. 120, 134.

89. RGANI, f. 2, op. 1, d. 198, l. 82.

90. See the introduction of the 1937 decree, "O sokhranenii zhilishchnogo fonda."

91. RGANI, f. 2, op. 1, d. 189, ll. 13, 19.

92. GARF, f. A-314, op. 3, d. 3151, ll. 1–4, 21–23, 48–50, 72–75.

93. See points 1–3 on the dismantling of leasing and construction cooperatives, and point 4 for the escape clause for the latter in "O sokhranenii zhilishchnogo fonda."

94. GARF, f. A-314, op. 3, d. 3151, l. 73.

95. Ibid., l. 78.

96. The following is a list of each cooperative's name with the year in which it was established: Sokol, 1940; Zaria, 1927; im. Krasina, 1922; Kislovskoe, 1926; Kooprabotnik, 1926; Ob"edinenie 214, 1928; Mastera estrady, 1940; Medik, 1945; Oblkoopstroi, 1926; Inzhkoopkhimstroi, 1947; Orkestr GABT, 1946; Professorov meditsiny . . . [*sic*], 1940; Rabotniki GABT, 1946; Sovetsk. rabotnik, 1923; Sovetskii truzhennik, 1926; Solomennaia storozhka, 1926; Truzhennik iskusstv, 1925; Zhilishche, 1932; 50 let MkhAT, 1947; Nauch. rabotnik VNIIRO, 1951; Sovet.uchen./geologii/, 1950; Vzaimnost', 1927; RANIT, 1924; Lesnoi rabotnik, 1929; Sovetskii kompozitor, 1950; Pedagogi Moskovskoi konservatorii, 1951; Nauchnyi rabotnik /VIMS/, 1952; and Rab. redaktsii BSE, 1952. Cooperatives that were still constructing their housing included the following: Artisty baleta GABT, 1952; Artisty Estrady, 1953; Sovetskii uchen. medik, 1952; Rab. Akadem. nauk SSSR, 1952; Min-vo inostran. del, 1952; Sovetskii khudozhnik, 1952; Ped. in. im. Lenina, 1952; Komitet Radionformatsii [*sic*], 1952; Muz. teat. Nemir. Danchenko, 1953; Moskovskii pisatel', 1953; Ped. inst. im. Potemkina, 1953; Art. kino i dramy, 1953; and Proek. ugl. promyshlen., 1953. GARF, f. A-314, op. 3, d. 3151, l. 78.

97. Ibid., l. 75.

98. Ibid., ll. 72–73.

99. Surin explained the ad hoc basis of these loans in a second report on cooperatives dated August 12, 1957. Ibid., l. 48.

100. Ibid., ll. 2–3, 22.

101. Ivkin, *Gosudarstvennaia vlast' SSSR*, 276–77, 381.

102. These individuals' names were included among others at the end of the report. RGANI, f. 5, op. 30, d. 215, l. 98. On Furtseva, Kozlov, and Kosygin's careers, see Ivkin, *Gosudarstvennaia vlast' SSSR*, 351–52, 362–63, 570.

103. These included the State Academic Bol'shoi Theater, the Krzhizhanovskii Energy Institute, the All-Union Energy Institute, the Administration of Radio Communication, chemical industry institutes, and economics, law, and philosophy institutes. RGANI, f. 5, op. 30, d. 215, ll. 91–92.

104. Ibid.

105. This average level was further broken down as follows: 26 percent (18 families) averaged 9 to 19.2 square meters per person; 33 percent (23 families) averaged 5 to 9 square meters; and 41 percent (29 families) averaged under 5 square meters. RGANI, f. 5, op. 30, d. 215, l. 91.

106. Among 32,000 families wanting more housing on Moscow's local soviet waiting lists in 1953, the average amount of living space per person was under two square meters. RGANI, f. 5, op. 30, d. 19, l. 52.

107. On these special benefits, see A. Sysin et al., *Sanitarnoe zakonodatel'stvo: Sbornik vazhneishikh zakonov i rasporiazhenii po voprosam sanitarno-profilakticheskogo dela* (Moscow, 1926), 77. Sosnovy's small survey of displaced persons after the war showed that specialists and scientific workers had about 7.6 square meters per family member. Timothy Sosnovy, *The Housing Problem in the Soviet Union* (New York: Research Program on the USSR, 1954), 128–31.

108. RGANI, f. 5, op. 30, d. 215, ll. 86–87, 90–91, 97.

109. Russian State Economic Archive (Rossiiskii gosudarstvennyi arkhiv ekonomiki; hereafter, RGAE), f. 339, op. 3, d. 349, ll. 285–87.

110. Ibid., ll. 286–87.

111. Ibid., ll. 301–2.

112. "O zhilishchno-stroitel'noi i dachno-stroitel'noi kooperatsii," March 20, 1958, *SP SSSR*, no. 5 (1958).

113. "O zhilishchno-stroitel'nykh i dachno-stroitel'nykh kooperativakh," September 24, 1958, *SP RSFSR*, no. 13 (1958).

114. The source was a city soviet report on distribution in 1968. It found that among the 59,995 families to which housing was allocated in that year, 61.4 percent moved into separate apartments. Central State Archive of Saint Petersburg (Tsentral'nyi gosudarstvennyi arkhiv Sankt-Peterburga), f. 7384, op. 43, d. 396, l. 2.

115. See point 17 of the 1958 model charter in "O zhilishchno-stroitel'nykh i dachno-stroitel'nykh kooperativakh." See point 16 in both the 1962 and 1965 charters in "Ob individual'nom i kooperativnom zhilishchnom stroitel'stve v RSFSR," October 5, 1962, *SP RSFSR*, no. 21 (1962); and "O khode vypolneniia plana kooperativnogo zhilishchnogo stroitel'stva v 1965 godu," October 2, 1965, *SP RSFSR*, no. 23 (1965).

116. See the section "Purpose, Rights and Obligations of a Cooperative" in each of the three charters cited above.

117. The figures presented here are an estimate based on information in GARF, f. A-259, op. 45, d. 1086, ll. 53–56.

118. "Ob individual'nom i kooperativnom zhilishchnom stroitel'stve," June 1, 1962, *SP SSSR*, no. 12 (1962); "Ob individual'nom i kooperativnom zhilishchnom stroitel'stve v RSFSR"; "O dal'neishem razvitii kooperativnogo zhilishchnogo

stroitel'stva," November 19, 1964, *SP SSSR*, no. 25 (1964); "O khode vypolneniia plana kooperativnogo zhilishchnogo stroitel'stva v 1965 godu." By May 1963, 988 cooperatives existed in the RSFSR with a total membership of 76,692. GARF, f. A-259, op. 45, d. 1086, l. 53.

119. GARF, f. A-259, op. 45, d. 7424, ll. 97, 100. It subsequently dropped to 2,573 with about 251,000 members at the close of 1969. DiMaio, *Soviet Urban Housing*, 187.

120. Vera Dunham, *In Stalin's Time: Middle-Class Values in Soviet Fiction* (Durham, N.C.: Duke University Press, 1990).

Chapter 5

1. A. Ladinskii, "Razvivat' vse vidy zhilishchnogo stroitel'stva," *Izvestiia*, December 12, 1956.

2. Russian State Archive of Contemporary History (Rossiiskii gosudarstvennyi arkhiv noveishei istorii; hereafter, RGANI), fond (f.) 5, opis' (op.) 41, delo (d.) 52, list (l.) 174.

3. The source was an internal memo of the Ministry of the Communal Economy of the RSFSR, whose job maintaining state housing likely explains its support for this rationale. State Archive of the Russian Federation (Gosudarstvennyi arkhiv Rossiiskoi Federatsii; hereafter, GARF), f. A-314, op. 3, d. 321, ll. 188–95.

4. N. Karpov, "Stroitel'stvo zhilishch: Postoiannaia zabota partii," *Leningradskaia pravda*, January 23, 1958; S. Verizhnikov, "Polnee ispol'zovat' rezervy v zhilishchnom stroitel'stve," *Leningradskaia pravda*, February 14, 1958; "O razvitii zhilishchnogo stroitel'stva v SSSR," July 31, 1957, *Sobranie postanovlenii pravitel'stva SSSR* (hereafter, *SP SSSR*), no. 9 (1957).

5. *Vneocherednoi XXI s'ezd kommunisticheskoi partii sovetskogo soiuza, 27 ianvaria–5 fevralia 1959 goda—Stenograficheskii otchet* (Moscow: Gosudarstvennoe izdatel'stvo politicheskoi literatury, 1959), 1:51.

6. *Kommunisticheskaia partiia Sovetskogo Soiuza v resoliutsiiakh i resheniiakh s'ezdov, konferentsii i plenumov TsK* (Moscow: Izdatel'stvo politicheskoi literatury, 1972), 8:245.

7. I thank Amir Weiner for his comments on the risks Khrushchev ran in setting deadlines.

8. Greg Castillo, *Cold War on the Home Front: The Soft Power of Midcentury Design* (Minneapolis: University of Minnesota Press, 2010), 189.

9. *Izvestiia*, April 13, 1961; "Pervyi polet cheloveka v kosmicheskoe prostranstvo," *Pravda*, April 25, 1961.

10. *Izvestiia*, April 13, 1961; I. Semenov, "Vsled za Gagarinym (pervomaiskaia shutka)," *Pravda*, May 1, 1961.

11. I thank Vadim Volkov for suggesting the connection between mass housing and space flight.

12. D. Burdin and Iu. Umanskaia, "Arkhitektura zhilykh kvartalov Leninskogo prospekta," *Arkhitektura SSSR*, no. 2 (1958): 12–14; I. Fomin, "Pervichnye arkhitekturno-planirovochnye kompleksy zhiloi zastroiki," *Arkhitektura SSSR*, no. 7 (1961): 21–27; I. Kontorovich, "Voprosy planirovki i zastroiki zhilykh raionov i mikroraionov," *Arkhitektura SSSR*, no. 7 (1962): 6–29.

13. *Vneocherednoi XXI s"ezd*, 1:51–52.

14. "Dom za Moskovskoi zastavoi," *Leningradskaia pravda*, December 25, 1960; G. Gradov, "Gorod i byt," *Izvestiia*, January 13, 1960.

15. Mikhail Lifanov, *O byte pri kommunizme* (Moscow: Gosudarstvennoe izdatel'stvo politicheskoi literatury, 1961), 3.

16. Lifanov, *O byte pri kommunizme*, 3–4. An updated version of Lifanov's pamphlet was published as Mikhail Lifanov, ed., *Za kommunisticheskii byt* (Leningrad: Obshchestvo po rasprostraneniiu politicheskikh i nauchnykh znanii RSFSR, Leningradskoe otdelenie, 1963).

17. S. Frederick Starr, "Visionary Town Planning during the Cultural Revolution," in *Cultural Revolution in Russia, 1928–1931*, edited by Sheila Fitzpatrick (Bloomington: Indiana University Press, 1978), 207–40; Richard Stites, *Revolutionary Dreams: Utopian Vision and Experimental Life in the Russian Revolution* (Oxford: Oxford University Press, 1989).

18. Gregory Andrusz, *Housing and Urban Development in the USSR* (Albany: State University of New York Press, 1984), 127–28.

19. A. Kuz'michev, "Dom zavtrashnego dnia," *Trud*, May 31, 1963.

20. Kuz'michev, "Dom zavtrashnego dnia."

21. Aleksandr Peremyslov, *Dom budushchego (Zametki arkhitektora)* (Moscow: Gosudarstvennoe izdatel'stvo politicheskoi literatury, 1962), 8–11.

22. Peremyslov, *Dom budushchego*, 7–8.

23. Timothy Colton, *Moscow: Governing the Socialist Metropolis* (Cambridge, Mass.: Belknap Press of Harvard University Press, 1995), 365–67.

24. Peremyslov, *Dom budushchego*, 4.

25. Susan Reid, "Women in the Home," in *Women in the Khrushchev Era*, edited by Melanie Ilič, Susan Reid, and Lynne Attwood (New York: Palgrave, 2004), 149–76; Christine Varga-Harris, "Constructing the Soviet Hearth: Home, Citizenship and Socialism in Russia, 1956–1964" (Ph.D. diss., University of Illinois at Urbana-Champaign, 2005), 132–86.

26. On the communal apartment's continued importance in defining communal values under Khrushchev, see Deborah Field, *Private Life and Communist Morality in Khrushchev's Russia* (New York: Peter Lang, 2007), 27–37.

27. M. Maksimov, "Zhit' khorosho, druzhno, po-kommunisticheski," *Leningradskaia pravda*, February 17, 1961.

28. Alla Efremova, "Byla obyknovennaia kvartira," *Zhilishchno-kommunal'noe khoziaistvo*, no. 6 (1961): 4, 33.

29. A. Peremyslov, "Kvartira v novom dome," *Izvestiia*, December 27, 1956.

30. Ibid.

31. G. Leonova, "Tak i nado zhit'," *Leningradskaia pravda*, November 12, 1959.

32. Ibid.

33. E. Iashmanov, "Pis'ma v redaktsiiu: Nash schet stroiteliam," *Leningradskaia pravda*, June 12, 1957; N. Makarova et al., "Pis'ma v redaktsiiu: Torgashi i ikh pokroviteli," *Leningradskaia pravda*, July 3, 1957; N. Milash and A. Zaitsev, "Plan formal'no vypolnen . . . Pokonchit's nedodelkami v zhilishchnom stroitel'stve," *Leningradskaia pravda*, February 14, 1961; M. Sharipov et al., "Zabota o byte liudei: Delo bol'shoe, vazhnoe," *Pravda*, April 4, 1961.

34. On social organizations under Khrushchev, see Theodore Friedgut, *Political Participation in the USSR* (Princeton, N.J.: Princeton University Press, 1979), 235–88.

35. Central State Archive of Literature and Art, Saint Petersburg (Tsentral'nyi gosudarstvennyi arkhiv literatury i iskusstva Sankt-Peterburga), f. 341, op. 1, d. 357, ll. 42–43.

36. Central State Archive of Saint Petersburg (Tsentral'nyi gosudarstvennyi arkhiv Sankt-Peterburga; hereafter, TsGA SPb), f. 103, op. 5, d. 464, ll. 23, 25, 28.

37. TsGA SPb, f. 103, op. 5, d. 495, ll. 62–64.

38. For an analysis of this continuum of community relations that extended out from their origins in the communal apartment into the broader public spaces and institutions of everyday life, see Ilia Utekhin's study of the post-Soviet communal apartment in Leningrad. Ilia Utekhin, *Ocherki kommunal'nogo byta* (Moscow: OGI, 2001), chap. 11, "Outside the Apartment."

39. Miriam Dobson, *Khrushchev's Cold Summer: Gulag Returnees, Crime, and the Fate of Reform after Stalin* (Ithaca, N.Y.: Cornell University Press, 2009), 133–55.

40. The minutes for this meeting were undated. The contents of its discussion suggest it occurred sometime in the late 1950s. Another set of minutes in the same archival file was recorded in 1959. TsGA SPb, f. 103, op. 5, d. 663, ll. 79, 203.

41. Ibid., ll. 79, 203.

42. TsGA SPb, f. 103, op. 5, d. 829, l. 90.

43. Ibid., ll. 90, 93.

44. Ibid., ll. 90–93.

45. Ibid., ll. 92–93.

46. TsGA SPb, f. 103, op. 5, d. 663, ll. 79–81.

47. TsGA SPb, f. 103, op. 5, d. 495, l. 62. Inspired by Arkadii Gaidar's 1940 story, "Timur and His Team," Timurovites were patriotic children who helped those affected by the war. On the Timurovites, see their definition in *Bol'shoi tolkovyi slovar' russkogo iazyka* (Saint Petersburg: Norint, 2000), 1323.

48. TsGA SPb, f. 6276, op. 273, d. 1270, ll. 1, 3, 5, 22–23.

49. Ibid., l. 23.

50. L. Zhigarev, "Riadom s domom," *Trud*, September 7, 1966.

51. Evgenii Nikolin, "Chelovek prishel s raboty . . .," *Trud*, September 11, 1966.

52. Nikolin, "Chelovek prishel s raboty."

53. The source was a June 21, 1954, Soviet of Ministers of the RSFSR decree, "On Serious Shortcomings in Housing and Civil Construction in Cities of the RSFSR," in GARF, f. A-259, op. 1, d. 663, ll. 89–90.

54. They sent their report, "On Improving the Quality of Construction," to the Central Committee and the Soviet of Ministers USSR. RGANI, f. 5, op. 41, d. 57, ll. 2–4.

55. Steven Barnes, *Death and Redemption: The Gulag and the Shaping of Soviet Society* (Princeton, N.J.: Princeton University Press, 2011), 159–60.

56. E.g., see Kucherenko and Grishmanov's proposed decree, "On Improving the Quality of Construction" and an additional proposed set of regulations on the settlement of new housing in RGANI, f. 5, op. 41, d. 57, ll. 16–22, 80–81.

57. "O razvitii zhilishchnogo stroitel'stva v SSSR."

58. GARF, f. A-314, op. 3, d. 321, ll. 108–10.

59. MVD memo originally sent to the Soviet of Ministers of the RSFSR and forwarded to the Ministry of the Communal Economy. GARF, f. A-314, op. 3, d. 321, l. 105.

60. Soviet of Ministers of the RSFSR, draft decree, included with the MVD memo, GARF, f. A-314, op. 3, d. 321, l. 107.

61. Soviet of Ministers of the RSFSR, decree of July 3, 1954, "On Measures for Struggling with Unauthorized Construction," GARF, f. A-259, op. 1, d. 664, l. 39.

62. Soviet of Ministers of the RSFSR, decree of November 4, 1955, "On the Taxation of Citizens, Who Constructed Buildings in an Unauthorized Manner on Land Plots That Were Not Given to Them," GARF, f. A-259, op. 1, d. 766, ll. 59–60.

63. RGANI, f. 5, op. 41, d. 204, ll. 108–9.

64. Ibid.

65. Vladimir Kozlov, *Massovye besporiadki v SSSR pri Khrushcheve i Brezhneve (1953–nachalo 1980-kh gg.)* (Novosibirsk: Sibirskii khronograf, 1999).

66. RGANI, f. 5, op. 41, d. 204, ll. 108–9.

67. Ibid., ll. 114, 116.

68. Ibid.

69. Ibid., l. 116.

70. Ibid.

71. Ibid., ll. 110, 114–16.

72. Ibid., ll. 112–13.

73. TsGA SPb, f. 7384, op. 42, l. 339, ll. 114–15.

74. TsGA SPb, f. 7384, op. 42, d. 1002, ll. 7–8, 10.

75. Ibid., l. 9.

76. Ibid., ll. 9–10.

77. Lewis Siegelbaum, *Cars for Comrades: The Life of the Soviet Automobile* (Ithaca, N.Y.: Cornell University Press, 2008).

78. A study published in 1971 found a mere 1.93 automobiles for every 1,000 residents in Moscow, 1.11 in Leningrad, and 1.10 in Kiev. The average for "large cities of the USSR" was 0.76 automobiles for every 1,000 residents. D. Velikanov, "Vazhneishie voprosy razvitiia avtomobil'nogo transporta v SSSR," in *Voprosy razvitiia avtomobil'nogo transporta*, edited by D. Velikanov (Moscow: Izdatel'stvo "Transport," 1971), 20–21.

79. Russian State Economic Archive (Rossiiskii gosudarstvennyi arkhiv ekonomiki; hereafter, RGAE), f. 339, op. 1, d. 1098, ll. 24–26.

80. Ibid.

81. Ibid.

82. Vitalii Filippov, *Avtomobil'nyi transport SSSR (Khronologicheskii obzor)* (Moscow: Avtotransizdat, 1957), 101.

83. RGAE, f. 339, op. 1, d. 1098, l. 24.

84. TsGA SPb, f. 103, op. 5, d. 495, ll. 48–49. On independent peasants in the 1930s, see Sheila Fitzpatrick, *Stalin's Peasants: Resistance and Survival in the Russian Village after Collectivization* (Oxford: Oxford University Press, 1994), 128, 152–58.

85. See the summary of this letter in RGANI, f. 1, op. 4, d. 74, ll. 54–55, 96. For two other examples of letter writers condemning automobiles, see the report on letters sent to *Pravda* in RGANI, f. 1, op. 4, d. 73, ll. 8–9. For examples of letters condemning people's ownership of individual houses, see the summary reports of citizens' letters about the Party Program in the Russian State Archive of Socio-Political History (Rossiiskii gosudarstvennyi arkhiv sotsial'no-politicheskoi istorii; hereafter, RGASPI), f. 586, op. 1, d. 297, ll. 2–3, 30. On a call for the redistribution of separate apartments to more needy groups, see RGANI, f. 1, op. 4, d. 73, l. 34. On someone condemning the separate apartment itself, see RGASPI, f. 586, op. 1, d. 296, l. 43.

86. TsGA SPb, f. 103, op. 5, d. 663, ll. 188–89.

87. V. Mikhailovskii, "Pora i vlast' upotrebit'," *Leningradskaia pravda*, July 19, 1961.

88. Siegelbaum, *Cars for Comrades*, 7.

89. Evgeniia Pishchikova, "Moskovskii dvorik," *Moskovskie novosti*, November 29–December 6, 1998, 27. I thank Sheila Fitzpatrick for drawing my attention to this article.

90. For reports that the Soviet of Ministers of the RSFSR received on these problems, see GARF, f. A-259, op. 45, d. 1086, ll. 57–61, 65–67, 74–81, 91–94, 105–9.

91. Ibid., ll. 45–49.

92. Ibid., ll. 30–33.

93. See point 3 of the decree "O khode vypolneniia plana kooperativnogo zhilishchnogo stroitel'stva v RSFSR v 1963 godu," September 3, 1963, *Sobranie postanovlenii pravitel'stva RSFSR* (hereafter, *SP RSFSR*), no. 16 (1963). See also point 2 of the decree "O dal'neishem razvitii kooperativnogo zhilishchnogo stroitel'stva," November 19, 1964, *SP SSSR*, no. 25 (1964).

94. "Ob individual'nom i kooperativnom zhilishchnom stroitel'stve," June 1, 1962, *SP SSSR*, no. 12 (1962); "Ob individual'nom i kooperativnom zhilishchnom stroitel'stve v RSFSR," October 5, 1962, *SP RSFSR*, no. 21 (1962).

95. The source was an undated report of the Soviet of Ministers of the RSFSR Department of Planning and Construction of Cities and Populated Areas. GARF, f. A-259, op. 45, d. 4110, ll. 95, 99.

96. Mark Smith, *Property of Communists: The Urban Housing Program from Stalin to Khrushchev* (DeKalb: Northern Illinois University Press, 2010).

97. Other cities cited in this report included Stavropol', Volgograd, Gor'kii, Saratov, Ivanovo, Kolomna (Moscow oblast), Mtsensk (Orlov oblast), Nevinnomyssk (Stavropol' krai), and the village Kargapol'e (Kurgansk oblast). GARF, f. A-259, op. 45, d. 4109, ll. 70–71, 74.

98. Ibid., ll. 118–20, 127.

99. For a letter to Kosygin, see GARF, f. A-259, op. 45, d. 4108, l. 69. For letters to Mikoian and reports about letters, see GARF, f. A-259, op. 45, d. 4109, ll. 70–71, 74, 134–35, 138–39; and GARF, f. A-259, op. 45, d. 4113, ll. 2–3, 9–13.

100. See the group letter of eighty individual housing owners in Volgograd to Mikoian in which they described the infrastructure they set up for their houses in an area that was now set aside for cooperatives. They wrote their letter in late 1964. GARF, f. A-259, op. 45, d. 4113, ll. 2, 9–10.

101. See the Soviet of Ministers of the RSFSR decree of November 11, 1966, "On the Further Development and Improvement of the Quality of Cooperative Housing Construction," in GARF, f. A-259, op. 1, d. 2293, ll. 175, 177, 180.

102. GARF, f. A-259, op. 45, d. 1091, ll. 42–44. This particular investigation was done in response to an individual letter of complaint addressing the city soviet's activities. The Russian Republic office of Stroibank USSR had earlier submitted a report with many of the same details to the Soviet of Ministers of the RSFSR in early June 1967. Ibid., ll. 47–50.

103. Ibid., l. 43.

104. Ibid.

105. Ibid., ll. 43, 44ob.

106. Ibid., ll. 45–46.

Chapter 6

1. Russian State Economic Archive (Rossiiskii gosudarstvennyi arkhiv ekonomiki; hereafter, RGAE), fond (f.) 339, opis' (op.) 1, delo (d.) 1101, listy (ll.) 86–87.

2. Stephen Bittner, *The Many Lives of Khrushchev's Thaw: Experience and Memory in Moscow's Arbat* (Ithaca, N.Y.: Cornell University Press, 2008), 115–16.

3. RGAE, f. 339, op. 1, d. 1101, ll. 86–87.

4. Ibid., ll. 87–88.

5. Ibid., l. 88.

6. Victor Buchli, "Khrushchev, Modernism, and the Fight against *Petit-bourgeois* Consciousness in the Soviet Home," *Journal of Design History* 10, no. 2 (1997): 161–76; Susan Reid, "Women in the Home," in *Women in the Khrushchev Era*, edited by Melanie Ilič, Susan Reid, and Lynne Attwood (New York: Palgrave Macmillan, 2004), 149–76; Christine Varga-Harris, "Constructing the Soviet Hearth: Home, Citizenship and Socialism in Russia, 1956–1964" (Ph.D. diss., University of Illinois at Urbana-Champaign, 2005), 6–8.

7. John Bowlt, "The Ideology of Furniture: The Soviet Chair in the 1920s," *Soviet Union/Union Soviétique* 7, pts. 1–2 (1980): 138–56; Architects' Union, resolution of April 1941, "O merakh po podniatniiu arkhitekturno-khudozhestvennogo kachestva massovoi mebeli," in *Soveshchanie po voprosam arkhitekturno-khudozhestvennogo kachestva mebeli i otdelochnykh materialov* (Moscow, 1941), 2–6.

8. March 1955 report by the Ministry of State Control of the USSR on the October 1953 decree, "On Increasing the Production and Improving the Quality of Furniture for Sale to the Population," Russian State Archive of Contemporary History (Rossiiskii gosudarstvennyi arkhiv noveishei istorii; hereafter, RGANI) f. 5, op. 43, d. 23, ll. 11–21.

9. "O razvitii zhilishchnogo stroitel'stva v SSSR," July 31, 1957, *Sobranie postanovlenii pravitel'stva SSSR*, no. 9 (1957) (hereafter, *SP SSSR*): 346.

10. By November 1957, the government lowered projections for furniture output (reported in rubles) in the RSFSR for 1957 from 3.556 billion rubles to 3.312 billion rubles. The production target for 1958 was downgraded from 4.491 billion rubles to 3.918 billion rubles. From 1956 to 1960, consumer demand in the RSFSR was projected to be 5 to 6 billion rubles annually and 27 to 30 billion rubles over the entire period. Since output already lagged behind demand in 1956 and 1957, the unsatisfied demand would carry over into 1958, raising the estimate for that year to approximately 8 to 9 billion rubles. The source was a report to the Central Committee from the Department of Administrative and Commercial and Financial Organs of the Central Committee of the RSFSR. State Archive of the Russian Federation (Gosudarstvennyi arkhiv Rossiiskoi Federatsii; hereafter, GARF), f. A-259, op. 42, d. 298, ll. 99–103.

11. GARF, f. A-259, op. 7, d. 9288, ll. 48–50.

12. Ibid., ll. 48–49.

13. Ibid., l. 49.

14. Ibid., ll. 49–50.

15. "Ob uvelichenii proizvodstva mebeli dlia prodazhi naseleniiu v 1958–1960 godakh i uluchshenii ee kachestva," March 19, 1958, *SP SSSR*, no. 5 (1958): 111–14. The Soviet of Ministers of the RSFSR implemented this decree with its own in April 1958. GARF, f. A-259, op. 1, d. 1039, ll. 190–95.

16. "Ob uvelichenii proizvodstva mebeli," 111–14; GARF, f. A-259, op. 1, d. 1039, ll. 190–95.

17. The categories of furniture remained constant throughout the editions of the sourcebook cited in the source note for table 6.1. Each edition reported its year as well as several other preceding years. The selection of preceding years varied from one edition to another. Some years were reported in several editions, whereas others were reported in only one edition. With the exceptions of 1951 and 1954, the data for each year from 1950 to 1970 have been located by examining these sourcebooks together. Table 6.1 is the result of compiling the data from these editions. In general, production figures were reported in the same amounts for years reported in more than one edition. However, there are some discrepancies. For cases in which one edition provides a more detailed number while another rounds up or rounds down the number, I have reported the more detailed number. For all other discrepancies, which cannot be attributed to rounding numbers up or down, I have used the data that appeared most accurate in my judgment of the evidence.

18. GARF, f. A-259, op. 1, d. 1494, ll. 207–14.

19. Ibid., ll. 207–14; GARF, f. A-259, op. 1, d. 1636, ll. 220–25; GARF, f. A-259, op. 1, d. 1789, ll. 89–94.

20. Svetlana Boym, "Everyday Culture," in *Russian Culture at the Crossroads: Paradoxes of Postcommunist Consciousness*, edited by Dmitri Shalin (Boulder, Colo.: Westview Press, 1996), 157–83; Buchli, "Khrushchev, Modernism"; Susan Reid, "Destalinization and Taste, 1953–1963," *Journal of Design History* 10, no. 2 (1997): 177–201.

21. Architects' Union, "O merakh po podniatniiu," 4–5.

22. L. Cherikover, *Tipy i gabarity mebeli* (Moscow: Gosudarstvennoe arkhitekturnoe izdatel'stvo Akademii arkhitektury SSSR, 1944), 3–4.

23. See also a resolution published by furniture manufacturers in the Ministry of Lumber and Paper Industry in *Reshenie soveshaniia rabotnikov mebel'noi promyshlennosti Ministerstva lesnoi i bumazhnoi promyshlennosti SSSR po voprosu uluchsheniia kachestva mebeli* (Moscow, 1949).

24. Bowlt, "Ideology of Furniture."

25. Bittner, *Many Lives of Khrushchev's Thaw*, 105–40.

26. For examples of architects and designers who drew from Soviet avant-garde designs, see Aleksandr Saltykov, *O khudozhestvennom vkuse v bytu* (Moscow: Gosudarstvennoe izdatel'stvo "Iskusstvo," 1959).

27. Greg Castillo, *Cold War on the Home Front: The Soft Power of Midcentury Design* (Minneapolis: University of Minnesota Press, 2010); Susan Reid, "Who Will Beat Whom? Soviet Popular Reception of the American National Exhibition in Moscow, 1959," *Kritika: Explorations in Russian and Eurasian History* 9, no. 4 (Fall 2008): 855–904; Steven Harris, *Two Lessons in Modernism: What the* Architectural Review *and America's Mass Media Taught Soviet Architects about the West*, Trondheim Studies on East European Cultures and Societies 31 (Trondheim: Norges Teknisk-Naturvitenskapelige Universitet, 2010).

28. Castillo, *Cold War*.

29. S. Alekseev et al., *Inter'er zhilogo doma* (Moscow: Gosudarstvennoe izdatel'stvo literatury po stroitel'stvu i arkhitekture, 1954), 20–23, 28, 99–100. The other contributors to this collection were O. Baiar, R. Blashkevich, M. Makotinskii, and L. Cherikover.

30. Alekseev et al., *Inter'er zhilogo doma*, 97–99, 102, 105.

31. L. Cherikover, *Mebel' dlia kvartir massovogo stroitel'stva* (Moscow: Akademiia stroitel'stva i arkhitektury SSSR, Nauchno-issledovatel'skii institut zhilishcha, 1957), 2.

32. N. Popov and M. Brener, *Al'bom mebeli* (Moscow: Tsentral'nyi institut nauchno-tekhnicheskoi informatsii bumazhnoi i derevoobrabatyvaiushchei promyshlennosti, 1962), 100; I. Gol'verk, *Novaia mebel' i oborudovanie dlia kvartir odnosemeinogo zaseleniia, Seriia: Derevoobrabatyvaiushchaia promyshlennost'*, vypuski 5–6 (Leningrad: Leningradskii dom nauchno-tekhnicheskoi propagandy, 1959), 6.

33. Gol'verk, *Novaia mebel'*, 5–6; Boris Merzhanov and Konstantin Sorokin, *Eto nuzhno novoselam* (Moscow: Ekonomika, 1966), 17; I. Serediuk, *Kul'tura vashei kvartiry* (Kiev: izdatel'stvo "Budivel'nik," 1970), 47–49.

34. Gol'verk, *Novaia mebel'*, 7, 11, 17–18; Serediuk, *Kul'tura vashei kvartiry*, 55.

35. Gol'verk, *Novaia mebel'*, 11–12; A. Cherepakhina, *Blagoustroistvo kvartiry* (Moscow: Izdatel'stvo Ministerstva kommunal'nogo khoziaistva RSFSR, 1961), 53–54; Merzhanov and Sorokin, *Eto nuzhno novoselam*, 17; Serediuk, *Kul'tura vashei kvartiry*, 51–52.

36. Popov and Brener, *Al'bom mebeli*, 165.

37. Gol'verk, *Novaia mebel'*, 20.

38. Ibid., 19–21; Cherepakhina, *Blagoustroistvo kvartiry*, 50, 55; Merzhanov and Sorokin, *Eto nuzhno novoselam*, 24–34.

39. Gol'verk, *Novaia mebel'*, 33–34; Merzhanov and Sorokin, *Eto nuzhno novoselam*, 79–84, 89–90; Serediuk, *Kul'tura vashei kvartiry*, 62–63.

40. On the tension between the consultative and didactic functions of exhibitions, see Susan Reid, "Khrushchev Modern: Agency and Modernization in the Soviet Home," *Cahiers du monde russe*, 47, nos. 1–2 (January–June 2006): 254–55.

41. "Ob uvelichenii proizvodstva mebeli"; N. Luppov, "O vsesoiuznom konkurse na luchshuiu mebel': Novye resheniia," *Dekorativnoe iskusstvo SSSR* no. 5 (1959): 3.

42. RGANI, f. 5, op. 41, d. 114, l. 32.

43. Luppov, "O vsesoiuznom konkurse," 3.

44. Ibid., 4–5.

45. N. Luppov, "Mebel' dlia kvartir novogo tipa," *Arkhitektura SSSR*, no. 5 (1959): 11–12; V. Kisin, "Konstruktsii mebeli," *Arkhitektura SSSR*, no. 5 (1959): 13–16; R. Blashkevich, "Obraztsy mebeli dlia kukhon'," *Arkhitektura SSSR*, no. 5 (1959): 17–20; Luppov, "O vsesoiuznom konkurse," 3–9; F. Varaksin, "V novye kvartiry—udobnuiu, krasivuiu i deshevuiu mebel'," *Arkhitektura SSSR*, no. 8 (1959): 7–8; I. Gol'verk and G. Mindlin, "Komplekty novykh obraztsov mebeli (iz praktiki Leningrada)," *Arkhitektura SSSR*, no. 8 (1959): 9–11.

46. Central State Archive of Literature and Art, Saint Petersburg (Tsentral'nyi gosudarstvennyi arkhiv literatury i iskusstva Sankt Peterburga; hereafter, TsGALI SPb), f. 341, op. 1, d. 547, ll. 17–18, 47–51, 60–61, 66.

47. TsGALI SPb, f. 341, op. 1, d. 547, ll. 17–18, 41.

48. Ibid., ll. 51, 54–55.

49. Alekseev et al., *Inter'er zhilogo doma*, 98.

50. TsGALI SPb, f. 341, op. 1, d. 547, ll. 20, 39.

51. S. Gurevich, "Psikhogigienicheskoe znachenie zhilishcha," *Gigiena i sanitariia*, no. 2 (1948): 14–15. I thank Benjamin Zajicek for bringing this article to my attention.

52. TsGALI SPb, f. 341, op. 1, d. 547, ll. 34–35, 38.

53. Buchli, "Khrushchev, Modernism"; Castillo, *Cold War*.

54. Boym, "Everyday Culture"; Reid, "Destalinization and Taste."

55. TsGALI SPb, f. 347, op. 2, d. 201, ll. 2–3.

56. Ibid., d. 194, ll. 1, 1a–1b.

57. For a description of how a family used old furniture in the 1950s to demarcate zones in a communal apartment room, see Joseph Brodsky, "In a Room and a Half," in *Less Than One: Selected Essays*, by Joseph Brodsky (New York: Farrar Straus & Giroux, 2000), 473–76.

58. V. Artem'ev and A. Bobrov, *Vasha mebel'* (Moscow: Izdatel'stvo "Ekonomika," 1964), 84; Merzhanov and Sorokin, *Eto nuzhno novoselam*, 19, 25.

59. James Holston, *The Modernist City: An Anthropological Critique of Brasília* (Chicago: University of Chicago Press, 1989), 31–58.

60. Merzhanov and Sorokin, *Eto nuzhno novoselam*, 6, 22–25, 28–29, 34; Cherepakhina, *Blagoustroistvo kvartiry*, 41; Artem'ev and Bobrov, *Vasha mebel'*, 83–84.

61. Merzhanov and Sorokin, *Eto nuzhno novoselam*, 61–62, 75, 82–83, 86–88; Cherepakhina, *Blagoustroistvo kvartiry*, 40; G. Kulebakin, *V pomoshch' vstupaiushchemu v zhilishchnyi kooperativ* (Moscow: Moskovskii rabochii, 1966), 84.

62. A. Strongin, *Mebel'* (Moscow: Tsentral'noe biuro tekhnicheskoi informatsii, 1958), 5, 12.

63. A. Cherepakhina and I. Shilova, *Detskaia mebel' v kvartire* (Moscow: Izdatel'stvo "Lesnaia promyshlennost'," 1964), 10–11; Merzhanov and Sorokin, *Eto nuzhno novoselam*, 50–51.

64. Merzhanov and Sorokin, *Eto nuzhno novoselam*, 32.

65. Ibid., 24–25, 46–53; Cherepakhina, *Blagoustroistvo kvartiry*, 45; Kulebakin, *V pomoshch'*, 105–6; Artem'ev and Bobrov, *Vasha mebel'*, 87–88.

66. On three-generation families and the presence of grandmothers, see L. Gordon and E. Klopov, *Man after Work*, translated by John Bushnell and Kristine Bushnell (Moscow: Progress Publishers, 1975), 75–77, 182–90; and Gail Lapidus, *Women in Soviet Society: Equality, Development, and Social Change* (Berkeley: University of California Press, 1978), 108.

67. Amir Weiner, *Making Sense of War: The Second World War and the Fate of the Bolshevik Revolution* (Princeton, N.J.: Princeton University Press, 2001); Miriam Dobson, *Khrushchev's Cold Summer: Gulag Returnees, Crime, and the Fate of Reform after Stalin* (Ithaca, N.Y.: Cornell University Press, 2009).

68. Monique Eleb and Anne Debarre, *L'Invention de l'habitation moderne: Paris 1880–1914* (Paris: Hazan, 1995).

69. E. Torshilova, "Byt i nekotorye sotsial'no-psikhologicheskie kharakteristiki sovremennogo zhilogo inter'era," *Sotsial'nye issledovaniia*, no. 7: *Metodologicheskie problemy issledovaniia byta* (Moscow: Izdatel'stvo "Nauka," 1971), 137, 141.

70. Kulebakin, *V pomoshch'*, 73–74.

71. I. Sharov and G. Poliachek, *Vkus nado vospityvat' (Besedy dlia molodezhi)* (Novosibirsk: Novosibirskoe knizhnoe izdatel'stvo, 1960), 73.

72. Torshilova, "Byt i nekotorye," 140–41.

73. Merzhanov and Sorokin, *Eto nuzhno novoselam*, 63–64, 68–69, 71–73; Cherepakhina, *Blagoustroistvo kvartiry*, 14, 25–26; Serediuk, *Kul'tura vashei kvartiry*, 97.

74. Susan Reid, "The Khrushchev Kitchen: Domesticating the Scientific-Technological Revolution," *Journal of Contemporary History* 40, no. 2 (2005): 289–316.

75. Merzhanov and Sorokin, *Eto nuzhno novoselam*, 63–65; Cherepakhina, *Blagoustroistvo kvartiry*, 12–15.

76. Merzhanov and Sorokin, *Eto nuzhno novoselam*, 66–71; Cherepakhina, *Blagoustroistvo kvartiry*, 14, 19–21.

77. Aleksandr Peremyslov, *Dom budushchego (Zametki arkhitektora)* (Moscow: Gosudarstvennoe izdatel'stvo politicheskoi literatury, 1962), 12–17.

78. Karel Teige, *The Minimum Dwelling*, translated by Eric Dluhosch (Cambridge, Mass.: MIT Press, 2002), 240–41.

79. Merzhanov and Sorokin, *Eto nuzhno novoselam*, 70; Cherepakhina, *Blagoustroistvo kvartiry*, 27, 30; Kulebakin, *V pomoshch'*, 93.

80. Cherepakhina, *Blagoustroistvo kvartiry*, 30; Serediuk, *Kul'tura vashei kvartiry*, 97–98.

81. GARF, f. A-259, op. 42, d. 9114, ll. 53–60.

82. Ibid., ll. 53–54.

83. Ibid., l. 53.

84. Ibid., l. 71.

85. Their data for this table did not include a separate line for construction workers.

86. GARF, f. A-259, op. 42, d. 9114, l. 52.

87. Ibid., l. 57.

Chapter 7

1. "Ob ustranenii izlishestv v proektirovanii i stroitel'stve," *Izvestiia*, November 10, 1955.

2. On this aspect of Khrushchev's populism, see Stephen Bittner, "Exploring Reform: De-Stalinization in Moscow's Arbat District, 1953–1968," (Ph.D. diss., University of Chicago, 2000), 38–100.

3. On the elevation of engineering and construction expertise over architecture during the mass housing campaign, see Stephen Bittner, "Remembering the Avant-Garde: Moscow Architects and the 'Rehabilitation' of Constructivism, 1961–1964," *Kritika* 2, no. 3 (2001): 553–76.

4. Anatolii Darinskii, *Nevskii krai: Sankt Peterburg i Leningradskaia oblast'* (Saint Petersburg: Firma "Glagol," 2000), 156–60.

5. Central State Archive of Literature and Art, Saint Petersburg (Tsentral'nyi gosudarstvennyi arkhiv literatury i iskusstva Sankt Peterburga; hereafter, TsGALI SPb), fond (f.) 341, opis' (op.) 1, delo (d.) 357, listy (ll.) 1, 13–16, 21, 24.

6. Ibid., ll. 1, 28–29.

7. TsGALI SPb, f. 341, op. 1, d. 386, ll. 28–29, 31, 35.

8. By "unpaid for space," Iakovlev meant auxiliary spaces. Residents paid rent according to the amount of living space per person; the amount of auxiliary spaces they had at their disposal did not factor into the calculation of rent. The basic legislation governing rental rates was the June 4, 1926, law "On Apartment Rent and Means for the Regulation of Using Housing in Urban Settlements." Izrail Mart-

kovich et al., *Zhilishchnoe zakonodatel'stvo v SSSR i RSFSR* (Moscow: Izdatel'stvo literatury po stroitel'stvu, 1965), 212–13. The law remained the basis of rental regulations throughout the Soviet period. Alfred DiMaio Jr., *Soviet Urban Housing: Problems and Policies* (New York: Praeger, 1974), 144–45; Gregory Andrusz, *Housing and Urban Development in the USSR* (Albany: State University of New York Press, 1984), 28.

9. TsGALI SPb, f. 341, op. 1, d. 357, ll. 30–31, 40–42.

10. TsGALI SPb, f. 341, op. 1, d. 386, ll. 20–21.

11. TsGALI SPb, f. 341, op. 1, d. 357, ll. 48–49. Drebezgov described auxiliary space as "vspomogatel'naia zhilaia ploshchad'." No such hybrid of auxiliary space and living space existed in housing space terminology. The terms for auxiliary space were "vspomogatel'naia ploshchad'" and "podsobnaia ploshchad'."

12. In the late Stalin years, Gintsberg was among a small number of architects developing designs for five-story panel housing to be built with modern building materials and technology. See Z. Kaplunov, "Zhiloi dom karkasno-panel'noi konstruktsii," *Arkhitektura i stroitel'stvo Leningrada*, no. 13 (1950): 17–22.

13. TsGALI SPb, f. 341, op. 1, d. 386, ll. 1–5.

14. A. Gintsberg and A. Liubosh, "Proektirovanie i stroitel'stvo zhilykh zdanii na osnove tipovykh sektsii," *Arkhitektura i stroitel'stvo Leningrada*, no. 12 (1950): 13–22.

15. TsGALI SPb, f. 341, op. 1, d. 386, ll. 14, 19–20.

16. TsGALI SPb, f. 341, op. 1, d. 357, l. 41.

17. TsGALI SPb, f. 341, op. 1, d. 386, ll. 14–15.

18. Ibid., l. 22.

19. Ibid., ll. 22–27.

20. Ibid., l. 24–28. For Khrushchev's speech at the meeting, see N. Khrushchev, *O shirokom vnedrenii industrial'nykh metodov* (Moscow: Gosudarstvennoe izdatel'stvo politicheskoi literatury, 1955).

21. Stephen Bittner, *The Many Lives of Khrushchev's Thaw: Experience and Memory in Moscow's Arbat* (Ithaca, N.Y.: Cornell University Press, 2008), 111-15.

22. Russian State Economic Archive (Rossiiskii gosudarstvennyi arkhiv ekonomiki; hereafter, RGAE), f. 339, op. 1, d. 1097, ll. 97–97ob.

23. Russian State Archive of Contemporary History (Rossiiskii gosudarstvennyi arkhiv noveishei istorii; hereafter, RGANI), f. 6, op. 6, d. 1776, ll. 91, 99.

24. RGANI, f. 6, op. 6, d. 1776, l. 92.

25. V. Ponomarenko, E. Tret'iakova, L. Mozhaeva, and P. Naumkin, "Vskore posle novosel'ia," *Pravda*, April 12, 1961.

26. I. Gainullin, G. Rakhmatullin, V. Nesterov, et al., "Stroit' bol'she, stroit' luchshe!" *Pravda*, May 28, 1961.

27. G. Arseev, "Sto ogorchenii v odnom dome," *Izvestiia*, April 12, 1960.

28. "Zhilishchnomu stroitel'stvu: Neoslabnoe vnimanie," *Izvestiia*, April 8, 1955, 1; Ia. Linetskii and A. Peremyslov, "Novyi dom," *Izvestiia*, June 26, 1955; V. Sokolov, "Za vysokuiu kul'turu stroitel'stva," *Leningradskaia pravda*, July 6, 1957; V. Ponomarenko, E. Tret'iakova, L. Mozhaeva, and P. Naumkin, "Vskore posle novosel'ia," *Pravda*, April 12, 1961.

29. V. Biriukov and Iu. Ponomarenko, "Sovetskoe stroitel'stvo: Neradivye khoziaeva goroda," *Izvestiia*, September 29, 1955.

30. A. Aleksandrov, "Doma: Novye, proschety—starye," *Trud*, August 21, 1965.

31. N. Milash and A. Zaitsev, "Plan formal'no vypolnen . . . Pokonchit's nedodelkami v zhilishchnom stroitel'stve," *Leningradskaia pravda*, February 14, 1961.

32. These problems were cited at a residents' meeting of a new house on Narymskii Prospekt in Leningrad in April 1957. Central State Archive of Saint Petersburg (Tsentral'nyi gosudarstvennyi arkhiv Sankt-Peterburga; hereafter, TsGA SPb), f. 103, op. 5, d. 464, ll. 23–24.

33. S. Britov, "Pis'ma v redaktsiiu: Nash schet stroiteliam," *Leningradskaia pravda*, June 12, 1957. The problem of nonfunctioning elevators in new housing was noted at the April 1957 residents' meeting cited above. TsGA SPb, f. 103, op. 5, d. 464, l. 23.

34. RGANI, f. 6, op. 6, d. 1776, l. 99.

35. S. Petrov, "Vnedrenie industrial'nykh metodov i snizhenie stoimosti stroitel'stva," *Pravda*, December 20, 1956; S. Verizhnikov, "Polnee ispol'zovat' rezervy v zhilishchnom stroitel'stve," *Leningradskaia pravda*, February 14, 1958; V. Butuzov, E. Smirnov, and N. Poriadkov, "Pust' zavody delaiut kvartiry," *Izvestiia*, October 26, 1960; V. Vlasovskii, "Komnata: Za 20 minut—novoe slovo stroitel'noi industrii," *Leningradskaia pravda*, November 15, 1960.

36. "Rozhdenie novoi ulitsy," *Leningradskaia pravda*, February 26, 1958; "Sobranie aktiva stroitelei Leningrada," *Leningradskaia pravda*, March 8, 1958; N. Mar'in, "XXII s"ezdu KPSS: Dostoinuiu vstrechu," *Leningradskaia pravda*, May 30, 1961.

37. V. Sokolov, "Za vysukuiu kul'turu stroitel'stva," *Leningradskaia pravda*, July 6, 1957; D. Zaporozhtsev, N. Kazakov, and G. Kireev, "Pis'ma v redaktsiiu: Tak li nado snabzhat' stroiku?" *Leningradskaia pravda*, July 26, 1957; "Zhilishchnoe stroitel'stvo: Pod kontrol' obshchestvennosti," *Pravda*, March 29, 1961; N. Chumakov, "Sto ogorchenii v odnom dome," *Izvestiia*, April 12, 1960.

38. "Zhilishchnomu stroitel'stvu"; "Za 700 tysiach kvadratnykh metrov novoi zhiloi ploshchadi," *Pravda*, March 26, 1958.

39. Aleksandrov, "Doma."

40. Zaporozhtsev, Kazakov, and Kireev, "Pis'ma v redaktsiiu."

41. "Zhilishchnomu stroitel'stvu."

42. On construction defects and delays in cooperatives, see a 1963 report from the Russian Republic branch of Stroibank of the USSR in State Archive of the Russian Federation (Gosudarstvennyi arkhiv Rossiiskoi Federatsii; hereafter, GARF), f. A-259, op. 45, d. 1086, ll. 74–81. See also a joint report from this agency, Gosplan of the RSFSR, and Gosstroi of the RSFSR in 1965 in GARF, f. A-259, op. 45, d. 1089, ll. 17–20. A November 1966 Soviet of Ministers of the RSFSR decree outlined cooperatives' construction problems and noted that both state and cooperative housing suffered from poor quality. GARF, f. A-259, op. 1, d. 2293, ll. 175–80.

43. I thank Susan Reid for informing me about the archived comment book records for the "Iskusstvo v byt" exhibition.

44. RGAE, f. 339, op. 3, d. 1108, l. 16.

45. Russian State Archive of Literature and Art (Rossiiskii gosudarstvennyi arkhiv literatury i iskusstva; hereafter, RGALI), f. 2329, op. 4, d. 1391, l. 82.

46. Ibid., l. 82.

47. RGAE, f. 339, op. 3, d. 1108, l. 8.

48. Ibid., l. 10.

49. RGALI, f. 2329, op. 4, d. 1391, l. 3.

50. Ibid., l. 16.

51. Ibid., l. 30.

52. Ibid., l. 70.

53. Ibid., l. 92.

54. Greg Castillo, *Cold War on the Home Front: The Soft Power of Midcentury Design* (Minneapolis: University of Minnesota Press, 2010).

55. RGALI, f. 2329, op. 4, d. 1391, l. 59.

56. Ibid., l. 30.

57. Castillo, *Cold War.*

58. RGALI, f. 2329, op. 4, d. 1391, l. 86.

59. Ibid., l. 33.

60. Ibid., l. 15.

61. Ibid., l. 51.

62. Ibid., l. 98.

63. Ibid., l. 31.

64. Ibid., l. 73.

65. Steven Harris, "'We Too Want to Live in Normal Apartments': Soviet Mass Housing and the Marginalization of the Elderly under Khrushchev and Brezhnev," *Soviet and Post-Soviet Review* 32, nos. 2–3 (2005): 143–74.

66. RGALI, f. 2329, op. 4, d. 1391, l. 11.

67. Ibid., l. 80.

68. "Ob ustranenii izlishestv v proektirovanii i stroitel'stve," *Izvestiia,* November 10, 1955.

69. Steven Harris, *Two Lessons in Modernism: What the* Architectural Review *and America's Mass Media Taught Soviet Architects about the West,* Trondheim Studies on East European Cultures and Societies 31 (Trondheim: Norges Teknisk-Naturvitenskapelige Universitet, 2010).

70. RGALI, f. 674, op. 3, d. 207, ll. 149-51. Emphasis in the original.

71. Ibid., ll. 31–32ob.

72. Steven Harris, "'I Know All the Secrets of My Neighbors': The Quest for Privacy in the Era of the Separate Apartment," in *Borders of Socialism: Private Spheres of Soviet Russia,* edited by Lewis Siegelbaum (New York: Palgrave Macmillan, 2006), 171–89.

73. See, for example, a group letter to the congress signed by 9 people. RGALI, f. 674, op. 3, d. 207, ll. 147-48.

74. RGALI, f. 674, op. 3, d. 209, l. 57–58.

75. Ibid., ll. 42–43ob, 60.

76. RGALI, f. 674, op. 3, d. 208, ll. 58–62.

77. Ibid., ll. 96–97.

78. See, e.g., the letter to the congress from a group of Muscovite residents complaining about construction defects. RGALI, f. 674, op. 3, d. 207, l. 61.

79. This resident sent his letter about the congress to an unspecified publication, not the congress itself. RGALI, f. 674, op. 3, d. 207, ll. 65–65ob.

80. RGALI, f. 674, op. 3, d. 209, ll. 17–17ob. Emphasis in the original.

81. RGALI, f. 674, op. 3, d. 208, ll. 27–27ob.

82. RGALI, f. 674, op. 3, d. 209, ll. 61–62.

83. RGALI, f. 674, op. 4, d. 10, ll. 27–28, 46–46ob. RGALI, f. 674, op. 4, d. 11, ll. 37, 95–98. RGALI, f. 674, op. 4, d. 12, ll. 29–30, 44.

84. RGALI, f. 674, op. 4, d. 10, l. 89.

85. For an example of this formulaic letter, see ibid., l. 43.

86. TsGA SPb, f. 103, op. 5, d. 464, ll. 23, 25–26.

87. Ibid., l. 26.

88. TsGA SPb, f. 103, op. 5, d. 495, ll. 62–64.

89. Ibid., ll. 48–50. UKS was the acronym for "Upravlenie kapital'nogo stroitel'stva," and ZhKO was the acronym for "Zhilishchno-kommunal'nyi otdel." See D. Alekseev et al., *Slovar' sokrashchenii russkogo iazyka: Okolo 17 700 sokrashchenii* (Moscow: "Russkii iazyk," 1983), 150, 368.

90. TsGA SPb, f. 103, op. 5, d. 495, ll. 49–50.

91. "Speaking Bolshevik" is the term Stephen Kotkin devised to denote the official discourses Soviet citizens learned in order to survive and navigate Stalinism in everyday life. According to Kotkin, such speech acts continued to be used in Magnitogorsk well into the Soviet Union's final decade. See Stephen Kotkin, *Magnetic Mountain: Stalinism as a Civilization* (Berkeley: University of California Press, 1995), 198–237.

92. A similar use of this language can be seen in Miriam Dobson's study of people's reactions to the release of Gulag prisoners. See Miriam Dobson, "'Show the Bandit-Enemies No Mercy!': Amnesty, Criminality and Public Response in 1953," in *The Dilemmas of De-Stalinization: Negotiating Cultural and Social Change in the Khrushchev Era*, edited by Polly Jones (London: Routledge, 2006), 21–40.

93. TsGA SPb, f. 6276, op. 273, d. 1270, ll. 1–79.

94. The possibility that meetings could devolve unexpectedly into a purge-like scenario had also existed in the Stalin period. See, e.g., Sheila Fitzpatrick and Yuri Slezkine, eds., *In the Shadow of Revolution: Life Stories of Russian Women from 1917 to the Second World War*, translated by Yuri Slezkine (Princeton, N.J.: Princeton University Press, 2000), 342–49.

95. TsGA SPb, f. 6276, op. 273, d. 1270, ll. 1, 3, 5–8, 65.

96. Ibid., ll. 41, 47–50, 58–59.

97. TsGA SPb, f. 6276, op. 273, d. 1270, ll. 60-61.

98. Ibid., ll. 61–63.

99. Ibid., ll. 3–4, 65, 71–74.

100. Ibid., l. 74. The word "ochkovtiratel'stvo" carries the general meaning of deception in English. Following the definition of the word in the dictionary below, I have translated the term to mean more specifically a form of whitewashing intended to convince people that certain conditions are better than they really are. See D. Ushakov, ed., *Tolkovyi slovar' russkogo iazyka* (Moscow: Astrel' AST, 2000), 2:1036.

101. TsGA SPb, f. 6276, op. 273, d. 1270, ll. 75–79.

102. Kotkin, *Magnetic Mountain*, 198–237.

Conclusion

1. One of the articles was published a month previously: A. Klushin, "Vash novyi dom . . . O nekotorykh problemakh kachestva stroitel'stva," *Leningradskaia pravda*, December 23, 1966.

2. Central State Archive of Saint Petersburg (Tsentral'nyi gosudarstvennyi arkhiv Sankt-Peterburga), fond 7384, opis' 42, delo 1634, listy (l.) 44, 48–52.

3. Ibid., ll. 48–49.

4. Ibid., ll. 48–49.

5. Ibid., l. 50.

Bibliography

Archival Sources

Central State Archive of Historical and Political Documents of Saint Petersburg (Tsentral'nyi gosudarstvennyi arkhiv istoriko-politicheskikh dokumentov Sankt-Peterburga, TsGAIPD SPb):
Fond 24: Leningrad Oblast Party Committee.
Fond 25: Leningrad City Party Committee.
Fond 415: Moscow District Party Committee.
Fond 1011: Party Committee of the Shoe Factory "Skorokhod."

Central State Archive of Literature and Art, Saint Petersburg (Tsentral'nyi gosudarstvennyi arkhiv literatury i iskusstva Sankt Peterburga, TsGALI SPb):
Fond 266: V. I. Mukhina Higher Artistic and Industrial School.
Fond 341: Leningrad Section of the Union of Architects of the USSR.
Fond 347: Leningrad Branch of the Academy of Construction and Architecture.

Central State Archive of Saint Petersburg (Tsentral'nyi gosudarstvennyi arkhiv Sankt-Peterburga, TsGA SPb):
Fond 103: Moscow District Soviet.
Fond 1008: Leningrad City Housing Administration.
Fond 1776: Shoe Factory "Skorokhod."
Fond 3343: Leningrad City Soviet Administration of the Inventory and Distribution of Living Space.
Fond 4965: Statistical Administration of Leningrad.
Fond 7384: Leningrad City Soviet.

Russian State Archive of Contemporary History (Rossiiskii gosudarstvennyi arkhiv noveishei istorii, RGANI):
Fond 1: Congresses of the Communist Party.
Fond 2: Plena of the Central Committee of the Communist Party.
Fond 5: Central Committee of the Communist Party.
Fond 6: Party Control Commission.
Fond 13: Central Committee Bureau for the Russian Republic.

Russian State Archive of Literature and Art (Rossiiskii gosudarstvennyi arkhiv literatury i iskusstva, RGALI):
Fond 674: Union of Architects of the USSR.
Fond 2329: Ministry of Culture of the USSR.
Fond 2466: Moscow Branch of the Union of Architects of the USSR.

Russian State Archive of Socio-Political History (Rossiiskii gosudarstvennyi arkhiv sotsial'no-politicheskoi istorii, RGASPI):
Fond 17: Central Committee of the Communist Party.
Fond 81: Personal Archival Collection of Lazar' M. Kaganovich.
Fond 82: Personal Archival Collection of Viacheslav M. Molotov.
Fond 586: Materials Related to the Third Party Program.

Russian State Economic Archive (Rossiiskii gosudarstvennyi arkhiv ekonomiki, RGAE):
Fond 5: Committee on Civil Construction and Architecture.
Fond 339: State Committee on Construction for the Council of Ministers of the USSR (Gosstroi SSSR).
Fond 355: State Planning Committee of the USSR.
Fond 1562: Central Statistical Administration of the USSR.
Fond 4372: State Planning Committee of the USSR.
Fond 8216: Ministry of Urban and Rural Construction of the USSR.
Fond 9432: Architectural Affairs Committee of the Council of Ministers of the USSR.

State Archive of the Russian Federation (Gosudarstvennyi arkhiv Rossiiskoi Federatsii, GARF):
Fond A-259: Council of Ministers of the Russian Soviet Federated Socialist Republic (RSFSR).
Fond A-314: Ministry of the Communal Economy of the RSFSR.
Fond A-339: State Control Commission of the RSFSR.
Fond A-374: Central Statistical Administration of the RSFSR.
Fond R-5446: Council of Ministers of the USSR.
Fond R-5451: All-Union Central Council of Professional Unions (VTsSPS).
Fond R-7523: Supreme Soviet of the USSR.
Fond R-9401: Ministry of Internal Affairs of the USSR.

Published Sources of Party, State, and Professional Bodies

Bukharin, Nikolai, and Evgenii Preobrazhenskii. *Azbuka kommunizma: Populiarnoe ob'iasnenie programmy Rossiiskoi kommunisticheskoi partii (bol'shevikov)*. Odessa: izdanie Politicheskogo otdela, 1919.
Chernenko, K. U., and M. S. Smirtiukov, eds. *Resheniia partii i pravitel'stva po khoziaistvennym voprosam, 1941–1952 gody*. Vol. 3. Moscow: Izdatel'stvo politicheskoi literatury, 1968.

Ermakova, T. S., and A. E. Mushkin, eds. *Resheniia Ispolkoma Lengorsoveta po zhilishchnym voprosam.* Leningrad, 1965.

———. *Resheniia Ispolkoma Lengorsoveta po zhilishchnym voprosam.* Leningrad: Lenizdat, 1967.

Grazhdanskii kodeks: Ofitsial'nyi tekst s ismeneniiami na 1 sentiabria 1947 g. i s prilozheniem postateino-sistematizirovannykh materialov. Moscow: Iuridicheskoe izdatel'stvo Ministerstva Iustitsii SSSR, 1948.

Grazhdanskii kodeks RSFSR. Leningrad: Izdatel'stvo "Rabochii Sud," 1925.

Grazhdanskii kodeks RSFSR i grazhdanskii protsessual'nyi kodeks RSFSR. Moscow: Izdatel'stvo "iuridicheskoi literatury," 1965.

Grazhdanskii kodeks RSFSR: Ofitsial'nyi tekst s ismeneniiami na 1 fevralia 1961 g. i s prilozheniem postateino-sistematizirovannykh materialov. Moscow: gosudarstvennoe izdatel'stvo iuridicheskoi literatury, 1961.

Grazhdanskii kodeks RSFSR: Ofitsial'nyi tekst s prilozheniem postateino-sistematizirovannykh materialov (izdanie vtoroe s matrits). Moscow: Izdatel'stvo "Iuridicheskaia literatura," 1968.

Kommunisticheskaia partiia Sovetskogo Soiuza v rezoliutsiiakh i resheniiakh s"ezdov, konferentsii i plenumov TsK. Vol. 1, 1898–1917. Moscow: Izdatel'stvo politicheskoi literatury, 1970.

———.Vol. 2, 1917–24. Moscow: Izdatel'stvo politicheskoi literatury, 1970.

———. Vol. 8, 1945–55. Moscow: Gosudarstvennoe izdatel'stvo politicheskoi literatury, 1985.

———. Vol. 9, 1956–60. Moscow: Gosudarstvennoe izdatel'stvo politicheskoi literatury, 1986.

———. Vol. 10, 1961–65. Moscow: Gosudarstvennoe izdatel'stvo politicheskoi literatury, 1986.

Konstitutsiia (osnovnoi zakon) Soiuza Sovetskikh Sotsialisticheskikh Respublik: Priniata na vneocherednoi sed'moi sessii Verkhovnogo Soveta SSSR deviatogo sozyva 7 oktiabria 1977 goda. Moscow: "Iuridicheskaia literatura," 1978.

Konstitutsiia (osnovnoi zakon) Soiuza Sovetskikh Sotsialisticheskikh Respublik: S izmeneniiami i dopolneniiami, priniatymi na piatoi sessii Verkhovnogo Soveta SSSR piatogo sozyva. Moscow: gosudarstvennoe izdatel'stvo iuridicheskoi literatury, 1960.

Osnovy grazhdanskogo zakonodatel'stva Soiuza SSR i soiuznykh respublik: Osnovy grazhdanskogo sudoproizvodstva Soiuza SSR i soiuznykh respublik. Moscow: Izdatel'stvo "Izvestiia Sovetov deputatov trudiashchikhsia SSSR," 1962.

Osnovy grazhdanskogo zakonodatel'stva Soiuza SSR i soiuznykh respublik. Moscow: Izdatel'stvo "Iuridicheskaia literatura," 1967.

Sbornik dekretov i vazhneishikh rasporiazhenii po zhilishchnomu voprosu: Vypusk vtoroi. Za period s oktiabria 1920 g. po oktiabria 1921 g. Moscow, 1921.

Sobranie postanovlennii pravitel'stva RSFSR.

Sobranie postanovlennii pravitel'stva SSSR.

Sobranie uzakonenii i rasporiazhenii rabochago i krest'ianskago pravitel'stva.

Sobranie zakonov i rasporiazhenii raboche-krest'ianskogo pravitel'stva Soiuza Sovetskikh Sotsialisticheskikh Respublik.

Sbornik zakonov SSSR i ukazov Prezidiuma Verkhovnogo Soveta SSSR, 1938–1956. Moscow: Gosudarstvennoe izdatel'stvo iuridicheskoi literatury, 1956.

Tretii vsesoiuznyi s"ezd sovetskikh arkhitektorov, 18–20 maia 1961 g. Sokrashchen-nyi stenograficheskii otchet. Moscow: Gosudarstvennoe izdatel'stvo literatury po stroitel'stvu, arkhitekture i stroitel'nym materialam, 1962.

XX s"ezd kommunisticheskoi partii sovetskogo soiuza, 14–25 fevralia 1956 goda: Stenograficheskii otchet. Vols. 1–2. Moscow: Gosudarstvennoe izdatel'stvo politicheskoi literatury, 1956.

XXII s"ezd kommunisticheskoi partii sovetskogo soiuza, 17–31 oktiabria 1961 goda: Stenograficheskii otchet. Vols. 1–3. Moscow: Gosudarstvennoe izdatel'stvo politicheskoi literatury, 1962.

XXIII s"ezd kommunisticheskoi partii sovetskogo soiuza, 29 marta—8 aprelia 1966 goda: Stenograficheskii otchet. Vols. 1–2. Moscow: Izdatel'stvo politicheskoi literatury, 1966.

Vedomosti Verkhovnogo Soveta SSSR.

Vneocherednoi XXI sezd kommunisticheskoi partii sovetskogo soiuza. 27 ianvaria–5 fevralia 1959 goda. Stenograficheskii otchet. Vols. 1–2. Moscow: Gosudarstven-noe izdatel'stvo politicheskoi literatury, 1959.

Voprosy zhilishchnoi arkhitektury: III plenum orgkomiteta soiuza sovetskikh arkhi-tektorov SSSR, 3–5 iiunia 1936 goda. Moscow: Izdatel'stvo vsesoiuznoi aka-demii arkhitektury, 1936.

Zakonodatel'stvo o zhilishchno-kommunal'nom khoziaistve. Vols. 1–2. Moscow: "Iuridicheskaia literatura," 1972–73.

Zhilishche: Voprosy proektirovaniia i stroitel'stva zhilykh zdanii—Materialy II ple-numa pravleniia Soiuza sovetskikh arkhitektorov SSSR, 23–27 dekabria 1937 goda. Moscow: Izdatel'stvo vsesoiuznoi akademii arkhitektury, 1938.

Zhilishchnyi kodeks RSFSR: Ofitsial'nyi tekst po sostoianiiu na 15 dekabria 1999 goda. Moscow: Izdatel'skaia gruppa NORMA-INFRA*M, 2000.

Newspapers

Gor'kovskii rabochii
Izvestiia
Komsomol'skaia pravda
Leningradskaia pravda
Leninskoe znamia (Lipetsk party obkom and oblispolkom newspaper)
Literaturnaia gazeta
Moskovskie novosti (post-Soviet newspaper)
Pravda
Trud
Vecherniaia Moskva
Vechernii Leningrad
Za industrializatsiiu

Journals, Magazines, and Encyclopedias

Arkhitektura i stroitel'stvo Leningrada
Arkhitektura i stroitel'stvo Moskvy

Arkhitektura SSSR
Biulleten' Mossoveta
Biulleten' po obmenu zhiloi ploshchadi (Moscow)
Bol'shaia sovetskaia entsiklopediia
Dekorativnoe iskusstvo SSSR
Finansovoe i khoziaistvennoe zakonodatel'stvo
Gigiena i sanitariia
Gorodskoe khoziaistvo Moskvy
Krokodil
Narodnoe khoziaistvo RSFSR
Narodnoe khoziaistvo SSSR
Neva
Novyi mir
Ogonek
Partiinoe stroitel'stvo
Sotsialisticheskaia zakonnost'
Sotsial'nye issledovaniia
Sovetskaia arkhitektura
Sovetskaia istoricheskaia entsiklopediia
Sovetskaia iustitsiia
Sovetskaia zhenshchina
Sovremennaia arkhitektura
Spravochnik partiinogo rabotnika
Spravochnik po obmenu zhilploshchadi (Leningrad)
Stroitel'naia promyshlennost'
Voprosy filosofii
Za rulem
Zhilishchnoe delo
Zhilishchnoe stroitel'stvo
Zhilishchno-kommunal'noe khoziaistvo
Zhiloi dom: arkhitektura i stroitel'stvo

Primary Sources

Books, Pamphlets, Dissertations, Dictionaries, and Articles

Aganbegian, Abel Gezevich, ed. *Akademgorodok bliz Novosibirska—element novoi sistemy rasseleniia.* Novosibirsk: Izdatel'stvo "Nauka," Sibirskoe otdelenie, 1968.

Alaverdian, Stepan K. *Zhilishchnyi vopros v Moskve.* Erevan: Izdatel'stvo AN Armianskoi SSR, 1961.

Alekseev, A. *Mebel': Ubranstvo zhilogo pomeshcheniia.* Leningrad: "Nauchnoe knigoizdatel'stvo," 1931.

Alekseev, D. I., I. G. Gozman, and G. V. Sakharov. *Slovar' sokrashchenii russkogo iazyka: Okolo 17,700 sokrashchenii.* Moscow: "Russkii iazyk," 1983.

Alekseev, S. S., et al. *Inter'er zhilogo doma.* Moscow: Gosudarstvennoe izdatel'stvo literatury po stroitel'stvu i arkhitekture, 1954.

Alekseev, Tikhon D. *Zhilishchnye l'goty grazhdan SSSR*. Moscow: Gosudarstven- noe izdatel'stvo iuridicheskoi literatury, 1962.

————, ed. *Zhilishchnye zakony: Sbornik vazhneishikh zakonov SSSR i RSFSR, postanovlenii, instruktsii i prikazov po zhilishchnomy khoziastvu: Po sostoianiiu na 1 noiabria 1957 goda*, 34th ed. Moscow: Izdatel'stvo Ministerstva kommu- nal'nogo khoziaistva RSFSR, 1958.

Artem'ev, Vladimir E., and Artur A. Bobrov. *Vasha mebel'*. Moscow: Izdatel'stvo "Ekonomika," 1964.

Artmanis, Bruno, and Aleksei Nikolaev. *Sovremennaia mebel' i kvartira*. Riga: Izdatel'stvo Akademii nauk Latviiskoi SSR, 1959.

Baiar, O. *Vstroennoe oborudovanie kvartir*. Moscow: Izdatel'stvo Akademii arkhi- tektury SSSR, 1945.

Baikova, V. G., A. C. Guchal, and A. A. Zemtsov. *Svobodnoe vremia i vsestoronnee razvitie lichnosti*. Moscow: Izdatel'stvo "Mysl'," 1965.

Balezin, V. P. *Pravovoi rezhim zemel' gorodskoi zastroiki*. Moscow: Gosudarstven- noe izdatel'stvo iuridicheskoi literatury, 1963.

Baranov, A. V. *O sotsial'noi modeli zhilishcha sotsialisticheskogo urbanizirovan- nogo obshchestva*. Moscow, 1970.

Barkhin, M. G. *Arkhitektura i gorod: problemy razvitiia sovetskogo zodchestva*. Moscow: Izdatel'stvo "Nauka," 1979.

Blokhin, P. N. *Maloetazhnyi zhiloi dom*. Moscow: Izdatel'stvo Akademii arkhitek- tury SSSR, 1944.

Bol'shoi tolkovyi slovar' russkogo iazyka. Saint Petersburg: Norint, 2000.

Broner, David L. *Kurs zhilishchnogo khoziaistva*. Moscow: Izdatel'stvo Minister- stva kommunal'nogo khoziaistva RSFSR, 1948.

————. *Zhilishchnoe stroitel'stvo i demograficheskie protsessy*. Moscow: "Statis- tika," 1980.

————. *Zhilishchnyi vopros i statistika*. Moscow: Izdatel'stvo "Statistika," 1966.

Bukharin, Nikolai, and Evgenii Preobrazhenskii. *Azbuka kommunizma: Populiar- noe ob"iasnenie programmy rossiiskoi kommunisticheskoi partii bol'shevikov*. Gomel': Gosudarstvennoe izdatel'stvo, 1921.

Cherepakhina, Anna N. *Blagoustroistvo kvartiry*. Moscow: Izdatel'stvo Minister- stva kommunal'nogo khoziaistva RSFSR, 1961.

Cherepakhina, A. N., and I. N. Shilova. *Detskaia mebel' v kvartire*. Moscow: Izdatel'stvo "Lesnaia promyshlennost,'" 1964.

Cherikover, Lazar' Z. *Mebel' dlia kvartir massovogo stroitel'stva*. Moscow: Aka- demiia stroitel'stva i arkhitektury SSSR, Nauchno-issledovatel'skii institut zhilishcha, 1957.

————. *Tipy i gabarity mebeli*. Moscow: Gosudarstvennoe arkhitekturnoe izda- tel'stvo Akademii Arkhitektury SSSR, 1944.

Cherneev, Petr M., and Aleksandr P. Torbin. *Svoimi silami*. Moscow: Izdatel'stvo VTsSPS Profizdat, 1957.

Chernenko, K. U., and M. S. Smirtiukov, eds. *Resheniia partii i pravitel'stva po khoziaistvennym voprosam*. Vol. 3, 1941–52. Moscow: Izdatel'stvo politicheskoi literatury, 1968.

Chulanov, Iu. G. *Izmeneniia v sostave i v urovne tvorcheskoi aktivnosti rabochego klassa SSSR. 1959-1970 gg.* Leningrad: Izdatel'stvo leningradskogo univer- siteta, 1974.

Darinskii, Anatolii V. *Nevskii krai.* Saint Petersburg: Firma "Glagol," 2000.

Dem'ianchuk, P. A., ed. *Po pochinu Gor'kovchan (iz opyta stroitel'stva zhilykh domov na Popasnianskom otdelenii).* Stalino: Professional'nyi soiuz rabochikh zheleznodorozhnogo transporta, 1958.

D'iakov, Iurii L. *Kapital'noe stoitel'stvo v SSSR. 1941–1945.* Moscow: "Nauka," 1988.

Dikanskii, M. G. *Kvartirnyi vopros i sotsial'nye opyty ego resheniia.* Saint Petersburg, 1908.

Dmitriev, Nikolai G. *Zhilishchnyi vopros: Dva mira—dva podkhoda.* Moscow: Moskovskii rabochii, 1973.

Filippov, Vitalii K. *Avtomobil'nyi transport SSSR (Khronologicheskii obzor).* Moscow: Avtotransizdat, 1957.

Gol'verk, Iosif V. *Novaia mebel' i oborudovanie dlia kvartir odnosemeinogo zaseleniia.* Seriia: *Derevoobrabatyvaiushchaia promyshlennost'.* Vypuski 5–6. Leningrad: Leningradskii dom nauchno-tekhnicheskoi propagandy, 1959.

Gorev, M. S. *O praktike massovogo stroitel'stva zhil'ia silami rabochikh na Gor'kovskom avtozavode (Doklad na plenarnom zasedanii konferentsii po massovomu stroitel'stvu zhilykh domov metodom narodnoi stroiki).* Gor'kii: Gor'kovskaia oblastnaia tipografiia, 1957.

Gorkin, Aleksandr F., Grigorii Z. Anashkin, and Valentin E. Paniugin. *100 otvetov na voprosy narodnykh zasedatelei : Posobie dlia slushatelei narodnykh universitetov.* Moscow: Izdatel'stvo "Znanie," 1970.

Grebtsov, I., ed. *My sebe khoroshii dom postroim.* Krasnoiarsk: Krasnoiarskoe knizhnoe izdatel'stvo, 1958.

Grigor'ev, N. *Zhilishchnaia problema budet reshena.* Moscow, 1963.

Iagodkin, V. N., ed. *Puti likvidatsii tekuchesti kadrov v promyshlennosti SSSR.* Moscow: Izdatel'stvo "Mysl'," 1965.

Iankova, Z. A. *Sem'ia, rodstvo, sosedstvo (k probleme formirovaniia lichnosti v bytu).* Moscow: Sovetskaia sotsiologicheskaia assotsiatsiia, 1970.

Isarov, G. Z. *Spravochnik nanimatel'ia zhilogo pomeshcheniia v voprosakh i otvetakh.* Moscow: Izdatel'stvo literatury po stroitel'stvu, 1966.

Iudel'son, K. S. *Polozhenie o tovarishcheskikh sudakh: prakticheskii kommentarii.* Moscow: Gosudarstvennoe izdatel'stvo iuridicheskoi literatury, 1962.

Kanaeva, I. *Perspektivy razvitiia sem'i i zhilishcha.* Moscow: Sovetskaia sotsiologicheskaia assotiatsiia, Institut konkretnykh sotsial'nykh issledovanii AN SSSR, 1972.

Kartasheva, K. *Sem'ia i zhilishche.* Moscow: Sovetskaia sotsiologicheskaia assotiatsiia, Institut konkretnykh sotsial'nykh issledovanii AN SSSR, 1972.

Katkovskii, Iu. B. *Zhilishchno-arendnye i zhilishchno-stroitel'nye kooperativy: Sbornik po zakonodatel'stvu v voprosakh i otvetakh.* Moscow: Gosudarstvennoe izdatel'stvo "Sovetskoe zakonodatel'stvo," 1936.

Kharchev, A. G., S. M. Verizhnikov, and V. L. Ruzhzhe, eds. *Sotsial'nye problemy zhilishcha: Sbornik nauchnykh soobshchenii.* Leningrad: LenZNIIEP, 1969.

Kheidmets, Mati Einovich. *Sotsial'nye-psikhologicheskie faktory formirovaniia prostrantsvennoi struktury zhiloi sredy.* Avtoreferat. Moscow: Akademiia nauk SSSR, Institut psikhologii, 1989.

Khrushchev, Nikita S. *O shirokom vnedrenii industrial'nykh metodov.* Moscow: Gosudarstvennoe izdatel'stvo politicheskoi literatury, 1955.

————. *Stroit' prochno, bystro, krasivo i deshevo: Rech' na soveshchanii po voprosam stroitel'stva v TsK VKP(b) 14–go dekabria 1935 g.*. Moscow: Moskovskii
rabochii, 1935.

Khudoleev, Vasilii M., and Ivan P. Piternov. *Moskovskii raion: Ot vyborov do vyborov (1962–1966): Materialy v pomoshch' propagandistam i agitatoram.* Leningrad: Lenizdat, 1966.

Klekovkin, Mikhail P. *Kukhnia (Planirovka i oborudovanie).* Kiev: Gosudarstvennoe izdatel'stvo literatury po stroitel'stvu i arkhitekture Ukrainskoi SSR, 1956.

Klimenko, G. P. *Metodom narodnoi stroiki (Iz opyta stroitel'stva zhilykh domov v
Cheliabinskoi oblasti).* Cheliabinsk: Cheliabinskoe knizhnoe izdatel'stvo, 1958.

Kolpakov, B. T., and V. D. Patrushev, eds. *Biudzhet vremeni gorodskogo naseleniia.* Moscow: "Statistika," 1971.

Komarov, B. K. *Prekrashchenie dogovora zhilishchnogo naima: Lektsiia dlia stu-
dentov iuridicheskikh fakul'tetov gosudarstvennykh universitetov.* Moscow:
Izdatel'stvo Moskovskogo Universiteta, 1963.

Konev, V. D. *Istochniki finansirovaniia narodnykh stroek i stoimost' rabot (Doklad
na sektsii "Formy organizatsii stroitel'stva i metody proizvodstva stroitel'nykh
rabot" konferentsii po massovomu stroitel'stvu zhilykh domov metodom narodnoi
stroiki).* Gor'kii: Gor'kovskaia oblastnaia tipografiia, 1957.

Kopeikin, Fedor F. *Kollektivnoe stroitel'stvo individual'nykh domov.* Leningrad:
Gosudarstvennoe izdatel'stvo literatury po stroitel'stvu, arkhitekture i stroitel'nym
materialam, 1958.

Kosmenkov, V. E. *O praktike massovogo stroitel'stva zhil'ia silami rabochikh
zavoda "Krasnyi Iakor'" (Doklad na plenarnom zasedanii konferentsii po massovomu stroitel'stvu zhilykh domov metodom narodnoi stroiki).* Gor'kii:
Gor'kovskaia oblastnaia tipografiia, 1957.

Krupianskaia, V. Iu., ed. *Etnograficheskoe izuchenie byta rabochikh: Po materialam otdel'nykh promyshlennykh raionov SSSR.* Moscow: Izdatel'stvo "Nauka,"
1968.

Kulebakin, Georgii I. *V pomoshch' vstupaiushchemu v zhilishchnyi kooperativ.*
Moscow: "Moskovskii rabochii," 1966.

Lebedev, S., ed. *Sila narodnogo pochina: Iz opyta stroitel'stva zhil'ia silami rabochikh kollektivov predpriiatii gor'kovskoi promyshlennosti i narodnoi stroiki
avtoguzhevykh dorog i tramvaino-trolleibusnykh putei.* Gor'kii: Gor'kovskaia
pravda, 1957.

Lenin, Vladimir I. *Gosudarstvo i revoliutsiia.* Moscow: Politizdat, 1975.

Lifanov, Mikhail I. *O byte pri kommunizme.* Moscow: Gosudarstvennoe izdatel'stvo
politicheskoi literatury, 1961.

————, ed. *Za kommunisticheskii byt.* Leningrad: Obshchestvo po rasprostraneniiu politicheskikh i nauchnykh znanii RSFSR, Leningradskoe otdelenie, 1963.

Littauer, Ia. and N. Sopikov. *Rabochii zhilishchnyi vopros.* Astrakhan, 1909.

Lunev, Vasilii S., and Vladimir V. Shilov. *Nevskii raion.* Leningrad: Lenizdat, 1966.

Maksimenko, V. D. *O praktike massovogo stroitel'stva zhil'ia silami rabochikh
zavoda (Doklad na plenarnom zasedanii konferentsii po massovomu stroitel'stvu
zhilykh domov metodom narodnoi stroiki).* Gor'kii: Gor'kovskaia oblastnaia
tipografiia, 1957.

Martkovich, Izrail B., and Vitalii R. Skripko. *Kvartirnaia plata.* Moscow: Izdatel'stvo
literatury po stroitel'stvu, 1965.

Martkovich, Izrail B., et al. *Zhilishchnoe zakonodatel'stvo v SSSR i RSFSR*. Moscow: Izdatel'stvo literatury po stroitel'stvu, 1965.

Marzeev, Aleksandr N. *Kommunal'naia gigiena*. Moscow: Gosudarstvennoe izdatel'stvo meditsinskoi literatury, 1951.

Medvedev, I. N. *Za 3 goda vmesto 12 let*. Khar'kov: Khar'kovskoe knizhnoe izdatel'stvo, 1959.

Merzhanov, Boris M., and Konstantin F. Sorokin. *Eto nuzhno novoselam*. Moscow: Ekonomika, 1966.

Mikhailovskaia, I. B. *Organizatsiia i deiatel'nost' tovarishcheskogo suda: Prakticheskii kommentarii k polozheniiu o tovarishcheskikh sudakh RSFSR*. Moscow: Izdatel'stvo "iuridicheskoi literatury," 1964.

Mineev, V. *Sankt-Peterburg*. Saint Petersburg: OAO "Ivan Fedorov," 1998.

Mulmanovskaia, Galina S. *Zhilishchno-bytovoe obsluzhivanie trudiashchikhsia i profsoiuzy*. Moscow, 1952.

Narodnoe khoziaistvo Kuibyshevskoi oblasti i goroda Kuibysheva: Statisticheskii sbornik. Kuibyshev: Kuibyshevskoe otdelenie Gosstatizdata, 1957.

Narodnoe khoziaistvo Kuibyshevskoi oblasti za 50 let: Statisticheskii sbornik. Kuibyshev: Kuibyshevskoe otdelenie izdatel'stva "Statistika," 1967.

Narodnoe khoziaistvo Voronezhskoi oblasti: Statisticheskii sbornik. Voronezh: Voronezhskoe otdelenie izdatel'stva "Statistika," 1972.

Nikolaev, A. I. *Zhilishchnoe stroitel'stvo v shestoi piatiletke*. Moscow: Gosudarstvennoe izdatel'stvo politicheskoi literatury, 1956.

O merakh po podniatiiu arkhitekturno-khudozhestvennogo kachestva massovoi mebeli: Rezoliutsiia soveshchaniia pri pravlenii Soiuza sovetskikh arkhitektorov SSSR, 15–17 aprelia 1941 g. Moscow: Pravlenie Soiuza sovetskikh arkhitektorov SSSR, 1941.

O peredache 10 protsentov zhiloi ploshchadi podriadnym stroitel'nym organizatsiiam i o zhiloi ploshchadi, peredavaemoi organizatsiiami i predpriiatiiami v rasporiazhenie isplokomov mestnykh sovetov (konsul'tatsiia po voprosam deistvuiushchego zakonodatel'stva). Moscow: Ministerstvo sel'skogo stroitel'stva RSFSR, Iuridicheskii otdel s arbitrazhem, 1968.

Osterman, N. A., and G. P. Pavlov. *9-i kvartal v Novykh Cheremushkakh*. Moscow: Gosstroiizdat, 1960.

"Otchet gruppy rabotnikov, komandirovannykh Len. gorkomom VKP(b) dlia oznakomleniia s zhilishchno-kommunal'nym khoziaistvom gorodov zapadnoi Evropy." Unpublished manuscript preserved in the National Library, Saint Petersburg.

Paushkin, N. A. *Formy organizatsii truda na narodnykh stroikakh v g. Gor'kom (Doklad na sektsii "Formy organizatsii stroitel'stva i metody proizvodstva stroitel'nykh rabot" konferentsii po massovomu stroitel'stvu zhilykh domov metodom narodnoi stroiki)*. Gor'kii: Gor'kovskaia oblastnaia tipografiia, 1957.

Peremyslov, Aleksandr S. *Dom budushchego (Zametki arkhitektora)*. Moscow: Gosudarstvennoe izdatel'stvo politicheskoi literatury, 1962.

Perepelov, Leonid A. *Stroim dlia sebia*. Moscow: Gosudarstvennoe izdatel'stvo politicheskoi literatury, 1958.

Poletaev, V. E., ed. *Rabochii klass SSSR (1951–1965 gg.)*. Moscow: Izdatel'stvo "Nauka," 1969.

Popov, N. V., and M. I. Brener. *Al'bom mebeli*. Moscow: Tsentral'nyi institut nauchno-tekhnicheskoi informatsii bumazhnoi i derevoobrabatyvaiushchei promyshlennosti, 1962.

Posobie dlia narodnykh zasedatelei. 2-e izdanie ispravlennoe i dopolnennoe. Moscow: Gosudarstvennoe izdatel'stvo iuridicheskoi literatury, 1950.

Posokhin, M. V., et al., eds. *Gradostroitel'stvo SSSR.* Moscow: Izdatel'stvo literatury po stroitel'stvu, 1967.

Potiukov, A. G. *Zhilishchnye spory v sudebnoi praktike.* Leningrad: Izdatel'stvo Leningradskogo Universiteta, 1962.

Reshenie soveshchaniia rabotnikov mebel'noi promyshlennosti Ministerstva lesnoi i bumazhnoi promyshlennosti SSSR po voprosu uluchsheniia kachestva mebeli. Moscow: Ministerstvo lesnoi i bymazhnoi promyshlennosti SSSR, 1949.

Rozantsev, S. *Sto otvetov na voprosy po zhilishchnomu zakonodatel'stvu.* Moscow: Izdatel'stvo VTsSPS Profizdat, 1965.

Rozhdestvenskaia, S. B. *Zhilishche rabochikh Gor'kovskoi oblasti (XIX–XX vv.): etnograficheskii ocherk.* Moscow: Izdatel'stvo "Nauka," 1972.

Repinetskii, Aleksandr I. *Demograficheskii sostav rabotnikov promyshlennosti Povolzh'ia, 1945–1965 gg.* Samara: Samarskii gosudarstvennyi pedagogicheskii institut, 1996.

Reshenie soveshaniia rabotnikov mebel'noi promyshlennosti Ministerstva lesnoi i bumazhnoi promyshlennosti SSSR po voprosu uluchsheniia kachestva mebeli. Moscow, 1949.

Saltykov, Aleksandr B. *O khudozhestvennom vkuse v bytu.* Moscow: Gosudarstvennoe izdatel'stvo "Iskusstvo," 1959.

Sarnov, Venedikt M. *Nash sovetskii novoiaz. Malen'kaia entsiklopediia real'nogo sotsializma.* Moscow: "Materik," 2002.

Sederevichus, V. *Opredelenie nomenklatury kvartir dlia gorodov Litovskoi SSR s uchetom izmenchivosti demograficheskogo sostava naseleniia i sostoianiia zhilishchnogo fonda.* avtoreferat. Vil'nius: Vil'niuskii inzhenerno-stroitel'nyi institut, 1972.

Serediuk, Igor I. *Kul'tura vashei kvartiry.* Kiev: Izdatel'stvo "Budivel'nik," 1970.

Sharov, Iurii V., and Galina G. Poliachek. *Vkus nado vospityvat' (Besedy dlia molodezhi).* Novosibirsk: Novosibirskoe knizhnoe izdatel'stvo, 1960.

Shneerson, Avraam I. *Chto takoe zhilishchnyi vopros.* Moscow: Izdatel'stvo VPSh i AON pri TsK KPSS, 1959.

Shuliakovskii, A. I., ed., *Zhilishchnyi spravochnik: Sbornik deistvuiushchikh zakonov i postanovlenii—Chast' I, Zhilye pomeshcheniia.* Moscow: Moskovskii rabochii, 1936.

Skripko, Vitalii R. *Poriadok obmena i razdela zhiloi ploshchadi.* Moscow: Gosudarstvennoe izdatel'stvo iuridicheskoi literatury, 1963.

Smekhov, G. M. *Vozvedenie zhil'ia metodom narodnoi stroiki.* Perm: TsVTI Soveta narodnogo khoziaistva Permskogo ekonomicheskogo administrativnogo raiona, 1959.

Sobolev, N. N. *Stili v mebeli.* Moscow: Izdatel'stvo Vsesoiuznoi Akademii Arkhitektury, 1939.

Sokolov, S. I. *Orientatsiia i dvizhenie cheloveka v mikroraione (na primere riada mikroraionov Leningrada).* Leningrad, 1970.

Soveshchanie po voprosam arkhitekturno-khudozhestvennogo kachestva mebeli i otdelochnykh materialov. Moscow, 1941.

Strongin, A. M. *Mebel'*, 3rd ed. Moscow: Tsentral'noe biuro tekhnicheskoi informatsii, 1958.

Sviatlovskii, V. V. *Kvartirnyi vopros.* Saint Petersburg: M. M. Stasiulevich, 1898.

———. *Zhilishchnyi vopros s ekonomicheskoi tochki zreniia: Vypusk II. Gorod i gosudarstvo.* Saint Petersburg, 1904.

Svoimi silami: iz opyta stroitel'stva zhil'ia khoziaistvennym sposobom na Orenburgskom uzle. Orenburg: Dorprofsozh i redaktsiia gazety "Orenburgskii zheleznodorozhnik," 1959.

Sysin, A. N., et al. *Sanitarnoe zakonodatel'stvo: Sbornik vazhneishikh zakonov i rasporiazhenii po voprosam sanitarno-profilakticheskogo dela.* Moscow, 1926.

Teige, Karel. *The Minimum Dwelling*, translated by Eric Dluhosch. Cambridge, Mass.: MIT Press, 2002.

Temerin, Sergei M. *Khudozhestvennoe oformlenie byta i vospitanie vkusa.* Moscow: Izdatel'stvo Akademii khudozhestv SSSR, 1962.

———, ed. *Prikladnoe iskusstvo i sovremennoe zhilishche.* Moscow: Izdatel'stvo Akademii khudozhestv, 1962.

Terent'ev, Mefodii I. *Milliony novykh kvartir.* Moscow: Izdatel'stvo VTsSPS Profizdat, 1958.

Tolstoi, Iu. K. *Zhilishchnye prava i obiazannosti grazhdan SSSR.* Moscow: Gosudarstvennoe izdatel'stvo iuridicheskoi literatury, 1960.

Velikanov, D. P., ed. *Voprosy razvitiia avtomobil'nogo transporta.* Moscow: Izdatel'stvo "Transport," 1971.

Volodin, P. A., et al. *Novye raiony Moskvy.* Moscow: Gosudarstvennoe izdatel'stvo literatury po stroitel'stvu, arkhitekture i stroitel'nym materialam, 1960.

Voprosy zhilishchnoi arkhitektury: III plenum orgkomiteta soiuza sovetskikh arkhitektorov SSSR, 3–5 iiunia 1936 goda. Moscow: Izdatel'stvo vsesoiuznoi akademii arkhitektury, 1936.

Vsesoiuznoe soveshchanie po gradostroitel'stvy, 7–10 iiunia 1960 g. Sokrashchennyi stenograficheskii otchet. Moscow: Gosudarstvennoe izdatel'stvo literatury po stroitel'stvu, arkhitekture i stroitel'nym materialam, 1960.

Zal'tsman, A. M. *Klassifikatsiia zhilykh domov*, no. 2, *Soobshcheniia Instituta massovykh sooruzhenii.* Moscow: Gosudarstvennoe arkhitekturnoe izdatel'stvo Akademii arkhitektury SSSR, 1943.

Zamiatin, Vasilii I., Gennadii P. Makarov, and Vitalii R. Skripko. *Zhilishchnye zakonodatel'stvo: Spravochnik dlia profaktiva.* Moscow: Profizdat, 1974.

Zazerskii, E. I., et al., eds. *Leningrad v period zaversheniia stroitel'stva sotsializma i postepennogo perekhoda k kommunizmu, 1946–1965 gg.* Vol. 6, *Ocherki Leningrada.* Leningrad: Izdatel'stvo "Nauka" Leningradskoe otdelenie, 1970.

Zezina, Mariia R. *Izmeneniia chislennosti i sostava intelligentsii soiuznykh respublik v usloviiakh razvitogo sotsializma.* Moscow, 1976.

Zhilishchnaia politika v SSSR. Moscow, 1965.

Zhilishchno-bytovaia rabota professional'nykh soiuzov. Moscow, 1953.

Zhilishchno-bytovaia rabota sovetskikh profsoiuzov. Moscow, 1954.

Zhilishchnoe stroitel'stvo za rubezhom. Gosstroiizdat (TsNIIEP—Tsentral'nyi nauchno-issledovatel'skii i proektno-eksperimental'nyi institut-industrial'nykh, zhilykh i massovykh kul'turno-bytovykh zdanii). Nos. 1–2. Moscow, 1962.

Zhilishchnyi fond RSFSR. Moscow, 1961.

Zhilishchnyi vopros" v" Moskve. Moscow, 1913.

Zhiloi dom: Sbornik nauchnykh trudov—Akademiia stroitel'stva i arkhitektury SSSR, Nauchno-issledovatel'skii institut zhilishcha. Moscow, 1960–64.
Zhukov, Konstantin V. *Rasskaz o nashem zhilishche.* Moscow: Stroiizdat, 1970.

Memoirs, Literature, Films, and Travel Accounts

Brodsky, Joseph. *Less Than One: Selected Essays.* New York: Farrar, Straus & Giroux, 1986.
Ehrenburg, Ilya. *Ottepel'.* Moscow: Sovetskii pisatel', 1954.
Ginzburg, Semen Z. *O proshlom: Dlia budushchego.* Moscow: Izdatel'stvo politicheskoi literatury, 1986.
Ironiia sud'by, ili s legkim parom. Moscow: Mosfil'm, 1977.
Kuhn, Delia, and Ferdinand. *Russia on Our Minds: Reflections on Another World.* Garden City, N.Y.: Doubleday, 1970.
Trifonov, Iurii V. *Izbrannoe: Povesti.* Moscow: Terra, 1997.
Voinovich, Vladimir N. *Antisovetskii Sovetskii Soiuz: Dokumental'naia fantasmagoriia v 4-kh chastakh.* Moscow: "Materik," 2002.
———. *Ivan'kiada ili rasskaz o vselenii pisatelia Voinovicha v novuiu kvartiru.* Ann Arbor, Michigan: Ardis, 1976.

Censuses

Boldyrev, Vladimir A. *Itogi perepisi naseleniia SSSR.* Moscow: "Statistika," 1974.
Chislennost' naseleniia SSSR, soiuznykh i avtonomnykh respublik, kraev i oblastei. Vol. 1, *Itogi Vsesoiuznoi perepisi naseleniia 1970 goda.* Moscow: "Statistika," 1972.
Chislennost', sostav i razmeshchenie naseleniia SSSR. Moscow: Gosstatizdat, 1961.
Itogi Vsesoiuznoi perepisi naseleniia 1959 goda. RSFSR. Moscow: Gosstatizdat, 1963.
Itogi Vsesoiuznoi perepisi naseleniia 1970 goda. Moscow: "Statistika," 1972.
Migratsiia naseleniia, chislo i sostav semei v SSSR, soiuznykh i avtonomnykh respublik, kraiakh i oblastiakh. Vol. 7, *Itogi Vsesoiuznoi perepisi naseleniia 1970 goda.* Moscow: "Statistika," 1974.
Natsional'nyi sostav naseleniia SSSR, soiuznykh i avtonomnykh respublik, kraev, oblastei i natsional'nykh okrugov. Vol. 4, *Itogi Vsesoiuznoi perepisi naseleniia 1970 goda.* Moscow: "Statistika," 1973.
O predvaritel'nykh itogakh Vsesoiuznoi perepisi naseleniia 1959 goda. Moscow: Gosstatizdat, 1960.
Pol, vozrast i sostoianie v brake naseleniia SSSR, soiuznykh i avtonomnykh respublik, kraev i oblastei. Vol. 2, *Itogi Vsesoiuznoi perepisi naseleniia 1970 goda.* Moscow: "Statistika," 1972.
Raspredelenie naseleniia SSSR, soiuznykh i avtonomnykh respublik, kraev i oblastei po obshchestvennym gruppam, istochnikam sredstv sushchestvovaniia i otrasliam narodnogo khoziaistva. Vol. 5, *Itogi Vsesoiuznoi perepisi naseleniia 1970 goda.* Moscow: "Statistika," 1973.
Raspredelenie naseleniia SSSR i soiuznykh respublik po zaniatiiam. Vol. 6, *Itogi Vsesoiuznoi perepisi naseleniia 1970 goda.* Moscow: "Statistika," 1973.

Zhilishchnye usloviia naseleniia Rossiiskoi federatsii: Po dannym perepisi naseleniia 1989 goda. Vols. 1–2. Moscow: Respublikanskii informatsionno-izdatel'skii tsentr, 1993.

Primary Sources outside Soviet History

Actes du Congrès international des habitations à bon marché tenu à Bruxelles (juillet 1897). Brussels: Hayez, imprimeur de l'Académie royale de Belgique, 1897.
America and the Mind of Europe. London: Hamish Hamilton, 1951.
Compte rendu et documents du Congrès international des habitations à bon marché tenu à Paris les 18, 19, 20 et 21 juin 1900. Paris: Secrétariat de la société française des habitations à bon marché, 1900.
Confidential U.S. State Department Central Files: The Soviet Union, 1955–1959, Internal Affairs.
Congrès international des habitations à bon marché. Paris: Imprimerie nationale, 1889.
Engels, Friedrich. *The Housing Question.* Moscow: Cooperative Publishing Society of Foreign Workers in the USSR, 1935.
International Housing and Town Planning Congress, Paris 1928. Paris: Imprimerie Chaix, 1928.
Papers Submitted to the 8th International Housing Congress, Held in London, August 1907. London: National Housing Reform Council, 1907.
Tucker, Robert C., ed. *The Marx-Engels Reader.* New York: W. W. Norton, 1978.
von Pettenkofer, Max. *The Value of Health to a City: Two Lectures Delivered in 1873*, translated by Henry E. Sigerist. Baltimore: Johns Hopkins Press, 1941.

Secondary Sources
Works on Soviet and Russian History

Aksiutin, Iurii. *Khrushchevskaia "Ottepel'" i obshchestvennye nastroeniia v SSSR v 1953–1964 gg.* Moscow: Rosspen, 2004.
Alexopoulos, Golfo. "Soviet Citizenship, More or Less: Rights, Emotions, and States of Civic Belonging." *Kritika: Explorations in Russian and Eurasian History* 7, no. 3 (2006): 487–528.
Aliev, Ismail. *Reabilitatsiia narodov i grazhdan, 1954–1994.* Moscow: Rossiiskaia Akademiia Nauk, Tsentr po izucheniiu mezhnatsional'nykh otnoshenii, 1994.
Anderson, Richard. "USA/USSR: Architecture and War," *Grey Room* 34 (Winter 2009): 80–103.
Andrusz, Gregory D. *Housing and Urban Development in the USSR.* Albany: State University of New York Press, 1984.
Attwood, Lynne. *Gender and Housing in Soviet Russia: Private Life in a Public Space.* Manchester: Manchester University Press, 2010.
Barnes, Steven. *Death and Redemption: The Gulag and the Shaping of Soviet Society.* Princeton, N.J.: Princeton University Press, 2011.

Barraclough, Geoffrey. "Late Socialist Housing: Prefabricated Housing in Leningrad from Khrushchev to Gorbachev." Ph.D. diss., University of California, Santa Barbara, 1997.

Berliner, Joseph S. *Factory and Manager in the USSR*. Cambridge, Mass.: Harvard University Press, 1957.

Bittner, Stephen V. "Exploring Reform: De-Stalinization in Moscow's Arbat District, 1953–68." Ph.D. diss., University of Chicago, 2000.

———. *The Many Lives of Khrushchev's Thaw: Experience and Memory in Moscow's Arbat*. Ithaca, N.Y.: Cornell University Press, 2008.

———. "Remembering the Avant-Garde: Moscow Architects and the 'Rehabilitation' of Constructivism, 1961–64." *Kritika: Explorations in Russian and Eurasian History* 2, no. 3 (2001): 553–76.

Bowlt, John E. "The Ideology of Furniture: The Soviet Chair in the 1920s." *Soviet Union/Union Sovietique* 7, pts. 1–2 (1980): 138–56.

Boym, Svetlana. *Common Places: Mythologies of Everyday Life in Russia*. Cambridge, Mass.: Harvard University Press, 1994.

Bradley, Joseph. *Muzhik and Muscovite: Urbanization in Late Imperial Russia*. Berkeley: University of California Press, 1985.

Brine, Jenny, Maureen Perrie, and Andrew Sutton, eds. *Home, School and Leisure in the Soviet Union*. London: George Allen & Unwin, 1980.

Brooks, Jeffrey. *Thank You, Comrade Stalin! Soviet Public Culture from Revolution to Cold War*. Princeton, N.J.: Princeton University Press, 2001.

Brown, Deming. *Soviet Russian Literature since Stalin*. Cambridge: Cambridge University Press, 1978.

Brumfield, William C. "Russian Perceptions of American Architecture, 1870–1917." In *Architecture and the New Urban Environment: Western Influences on Modernism in Russia and the USSR*, edited by Blair Ruble, Anatole Kopp, and William C. Brumfield. Washington, D.C.: Woodrow Wilson International Center for Scholars, 1988.

Brumfield, William Craft, and Blair A. Ruble, eds. *Russian Housing in the Modern Age: Design and Social History*. Cambridge: Cambridge University Press, 1993.

Buchli, Victor. "Khrushchev, Modernism, and the Fight against Petit-Bourgeois Consciousness in the Soviet Home." *Journal of Design History* 10, no. 2 (1997): 161–76.

Castillo, Greg. *Cold War on the Home Front: The Soft Power of Midcentury Design*. Minneapolis: University of Minnesota Press, 2010.

Chatterjee, Choi. *Celebrating Women: Gender, Festival Culture, and Bolshevik Ideology, 1910–1939*. Pittsburgh: University of Pittsburgh Press, 2002.

Churchward, L. G. "Continuity and Change in Soviet Local Government, 1947–1957." *Soviet Studies*, no. 3 (January 1958): 256–85.

Clark, Katerina. "Rethinking the Past and the Current Thaw: Introduction." *Studies in Comparative Communism* 21, nos. 3–4 (1988): 241–53.

Clements, Barbara Evans. *Daughters of Revolution: A History of Women in the U.S.S.R.* Arlington Heights, Ill.: Harlan Davidson, 1994.

Cohen, Stephen F., Alexander Rabinowitch, and Robert Sharlet, eds. *The Soviet Union since Stalin*. Bloomington: Indiana University Press, 1980.

Cohen, Yves. "Circulatory Localities: The Example of Stalinism in the 1930s."

Kritika: Explorations in Russian and Eurasian History 11, no. 1 (Winter 2010): 11–45.

Colton, Timothy J. *Moscow: Governing the Socialist Metropolis*. Cambridge, Mass.: Belknap Press, 1995.

Crowley, David, and Susan E. Reid, eds. *Socialist Spaces: Sites of Everyday Life in the Eastern Bloc*. Oxford: Berg, 2002.

Day, Andrew Elam. "Building Socialism: The Politics of the Soviet Cityscape in the Stalin Era." Ph.D. diss., Columbia University, 1998.

DiMaio, Alfred John, Jr. *Soviet Urban Housing: Problems and Policies*. New York: Praeger, 1974.

Dobson, Miriam. "Contesting the Paradigms of De-Stalinization: Readers' Responses to *One Day in the Life of Ivan Denisovich*." *Slavic Review* 64, no. 3 (2005): 580–600.

———. *Khrushchev's Cold Summer: Gulag Returnees, Crime, and the Fate of Reform after Stalin*. Ithaca, N.Y.: Cornell University Press, 2009.

Dodge, Norton T. *Women in the Soviet Economy: Their Role in Economic, Scientific, and Technical Development*. Baltimore: Johns Hopkins University Press, 1966.

Dunham, Vera S. *In Stalin's Time: Middle-Class Values in Soviet Fiction*, enlarged and updated ed. Durham, N.C.: Duke University Press, 1990.

Engelstein, Laura. *The Keys to Happiness: Sex and the Search for Modernity in Fin-de-Siècle Russia*. Ithaca, N.Y.: Cornell University Press, 1992.

Feifer, George. *Justice in Moscow*. New York: Simon & Schuster, 1964.

Field, Deborah Ann. "Communist Morality and Meanings of Private Life in Post-Stalinist Russia, 1953–1964." Ph.D. diss., University of Michigan, 1996.

———. *Private Life and Communist Morality in Khrushchev's Russia*. New York: Peter Lang, 2007.

Filtzer, Donald. *Soviet Workers and Late Stalinism: Labour and the Restoration of the Stalinist System after World War II*. Cambridge: Cambridge University Press, 2002.

———. *Soviet Workers and Stalinist Industrialization: The Formation of Modern Soviet Production Relations, 1928–1941*. Armonk, N.Y.: M. E. Sharpe, 1986.

Fitzpatrick, Sheila. "After NEP: The Fate of NEP Entrepreneurs, Small Traders, and Artisans in the 'Socialist Russia' of the 1930s." *Russian History* 13, nos. 2–3 (1986): 187–233.

———. "Ascribing Class: The Construction of Social Identity in Soviet Russia." *Journal of Modern History*, no. 65 (December 1993): 745–70.

———. *The Cultural Front: Power and Culture in Revolutionary Russia*. Ithaca, N.Y.: Cornell University Press, 1992.

———, ed. *Cultural Revolution in Russia, 1928–1931*. Bloomington: Indiana University Press, 1978; First Midland Books, 1984.

———. *Everyday Stalinism: Ordinary Life in Extraordinary Times—Soviet Russia in the 1930s*. New York: Oxford University Press, 1999.

———. *The Russian Revolution*. Oxford: Oxford University Press, 1994.

———. "Signals from Below: Soviet Letters of Denunciation of the 1930s." *Journal of Modern History* 68 (December 1996): 831–66.

———. *Education and Social Mobility in the Soviet Union, 1921–1934*. Cambridge: Cambridge University Press, 1979.

———. *Stalin's Peasants: Resistance and Survival in the Russian Village after Collectivization*. Oxford: Oxford University Press, 1994.

————. "Supplicants and Citizens: Public Letter-Writing in Soviet Russia in the 1930s." *Slavic Review* 55, no. 1 (1996): 78–105.

Fitzpatrick, Sheila, and Yuri Slezkine, eds. *In the Shadow of Revolution: Life Stories of Russian Women from 1917 to the Second World War*, translated by Yuri Slezkine. Princeton, N.J.: Princeton University Press, 2000.

Friedgut, Theodore H. *Political Participation in the USSR*. Princeton, N.J.: Princeton University Press, 1979.

Fürst, Juliane, ed. *Late Stalinist Russia: Society between Reconstruction and Reinvention*. London: Routledge, 2006.

Gerasimova, Katerina Iu. "Massovoe zhilishchnoe stroitel'stvo i izmeneniia v povsednevnoi zhizni gorozhan." *Sotsiologiia & Marketing*, no. 3 (1998): 23–31.

————. "Sovetskaia kommunal'naia kvartira." *Sotsiologicheskii zhurnal*, nos. 1–2 (1998): 224–43.

————. "Sovetskaia kommunal'naia kvartira kak sotsial'nyi institut: Istoriko-sotsiologicheskii analiz." Candidate diss., European University in Saint Petersburg, 2000.

————. "Zhil'e kak sotsial'nyi institut: Leningrad (1917–1941)." M.A. thesis, European University in Saint Petersburg, 1997.

Geiger, Kent H. *The Family in Soviet Russia*. Cambridge, Mass.: Harvard University Press, 1968.

Goldman, Wendy Z. *Women at the Gates: Gender and Industry in Stalin's Russia*. Cambridge: Cambridge University Press, 2002.

————. *Women, the State and Revolution: Soviet Family Policy and Social Life, 1917–1936*. Cambridge: Cambridge University Press, 1993.

Gordon, L., and E. Klopov. *Man after Work*, translated by John Bushnell and Kristine Bushnell. Moscow: Progress Publishers, 1975.

Groys, Boris. *The Total Art of Stalinism: Avant-Garde, Aesthetic Dictatorship, and Beyond*, translated by Charles Rougle. Princeton, N.J.: Princeton University Press, 1992.

Grushin, Boris A. *Chetyre zhizni Rossii v zerkale oprosov obshchestvennogo mneniia: Ocherki massovogo soznaniia rossiian vremen Khrushcheva, Brezhneva, Gorbacheva i El'tsina v 4-kh knigakh—Zhizn' 1-ia, Epokha Khrushcheva*. Moscow: "Progress-Traditsiia," 2001.

Gubin, Dmitrii, Lev Lur'e, and Igor' Poroshin. *Real'nyi Peterburg: O gorode s tochki zreniia nedvizhimosti i o nedvizhimosti s tochki zreniia istorii*. Saint Petersburg: Limbus Press, 1999.

Hamilton, Ellen Leith. "Social Areas under State Socialism: The Example of Moscow." Ph.D. diss., Columbia University, 1993.

Harris, Steven E. "'I Know All the Secrets of My Neighbors': The Quest for Privacy in the Era of the Separate Apartment." In *Borders of Socialism: Private Spheres of Soviet Russia*, edited by Lewis Siegelbaum. New York: Palgrave Macmillan, 2006.

————. "In Search of 'Ordinary' Russia: Everyday Life in the NEP, the Thaw, and the Communal Apartment." *Kritika: Explorations in Russian and Eurasian History* 6, no. 3 (Summer 2005): 583–614.

————. *Two Lessons in Modernism: What the* Architectural Review *and America's Mass Media Taught Soviet Architects about the West*. Trondheim Studies on East European Cultures and Societies 31. Trondheim: Norges Teknisk-Naturvitenskapelige Universitet, 2010.

———. "'We Too Want to Live in Normal Apartments': Soviet Mass Housing and the Marginalization of the Elderly under Khrushchev and Brezhnev." *Soviet and Post-Soviet Review* 32, nos. 2–3 (2005): 143–74.

Hayden, Carol Eubanks. "The Zhenotdel and the Bolshevik Party." *Russian History* 2 (1976): 150–73.

Hazard, John. *Soviet Housing Law*. New Haven, Conn.: Yale University Press, 1939.

Hessler, Julie M. "Culture of Shortages: A Social History of Soviet Trade." Ph.D. diss., University of Chicago, 1996.

———. *A Social History of Soviet Trade: Trade Policy, Retail Practices, and Consumption, 1917–1953*. Princeton, N.J.: Princeton University Press, 2004.

Hoffmann, David. *Stalinist Values: The Cultural Norms of Soviet Modernity, 1917–1941*. Ithaca, N.Y.: Cornell University Press, 2003.

Holquist, Peter. *Making War, Forging Revolution: Russia's Continuum of Crisis, 1914–1921*. Cambridge, Mass.: Harvard University Press, 2002.

Hudson, Hugh D., Jr. *Blueprints and Blood: The Stalinization of Soviet Architecture, 1917–1937*. Princeton, N.J.: Princeton University Press, 1994.

———. "'The Social Condenser of Our Epoch': The Association of Contemporary Architects and the Creation of a New Way of Life in Revolutionary Russia.'" *Jahrbücher für Geschichte Osteuropas* 34 (1986): 557–78.

Ilič, Melanie, Susan E. Reid, and Lynne Attwood, eds. *Women in the Khrushchev Era*. New York: Palgrave, 2004.

Ilič, Melanie, and Jeremy Smith, eds. *Soviet State and Society under Nikita Khrushchev*. London: Routledge, 2009.

Inkeles, Alex, and Raymond A. Bauer. *The Soviet Citizen: Daily Life in a Totalitarian Society*. Cambridge, Mass.: Harvard University Press, 1959.

Ivkin, V. I., ed. *Gosudarstvennaia vlast' SSSR: Vysshie organy vlasti i upravleniia i ikh rukovoditeli, 1923–1991 gg. Istoriko-biograficheskii spravochnik*. Moscow: Rosspen, 1999.

Jahn, Hubertus F. "The Housing Revolution in Petrograd, 1917–1920." *Jahrbücher für Geschichte Osteuropas* 38 (1990): 212–27.

Jones, Polly, ed. *The Dilemmas of De-Stalinization: Negotiating Cultural and Social Change in the Khrushchev Era*. London: Routledge, 2006.

Kornai, János. *Economics of Shortage*. Volumes A and B. Amsterdam: North-Holland, 1980.

———. *The Socialist System: The Political Economy of Communism*. Princeton, N.J.: Princeton University Press, 1992.

Kotkin, Stephen. *Magnetic Mountain: Stalinism as Civilization*. Berkeley: University of California Press, 1995.

Kotsonis, Yanni. "Ordinary People in Russian and Soviet History." *Kritika: Explorations in Russian and Eurasian History* 12, no. 3 (2011): 739–54.

Kozlov, Vladimir A. "Denunciation and Its Functions in Soviet Governance: A Study of Denunciations and Their Bureaucratic Handling from Soviet Police Archives, 1944–1940," translated by Christopher Burton, Matthew Lenoe, and Steven Richmond. *Journal of Modern History* 68 (December 1996): 867–98.

Kozlov, Vladimir A. *Massovye besporiadki v SSSR pri Khrushcheve i Brezhneve (1953–nachalo 1980-kh gg.)*. Novosibirsk: Sibirskii khronograf, 1999.

Krasil'shchikov, V. A. *Vdogonku za proshedshim vekom: Razvitie Rossii v XX veke s tochki zreniia mirovykh modernizatsii*. Moscow: Rosspen, 1998.

Kreis, Barbara. "The Idea of the Dom-Kommuna and the Dilemma of the Soviet Avant-Garde." *Oppositions: A Journal for Ideas and Criticism in Architecture* (Summer 1980): 52–77.

———. *Moskau 1917–1935: Vom Wohnungsbau zum Städtebau*. Berlin: Edition Marzona, 1985.

Krylova, Anna. "'Healers of Wounded Souls': The Crisis of Private Life in Soviet Literature, 1944–1946." *Journal of Modern History* 73 (June 2001): 307–31.

Lapidus, Gail Warshofsky. *Women in Soviet Society: Equality, Development, and Social Change*. Berkeley: University of California Press, 1978.

Latur, Alessandra. *Moskva, 1890–1991: Putevoditel' po sovremennoi arkhitekture*. Moscow: "Iskusstvo," 1997.

Lebina, Nataliia B. *Povsednevnaia zhizn' sovetskogo goroda: Normy i anomalii. 1920–1930 gody*. Saint Petersburg: Zhurnal Neva, Izdatel'sko-torgovyi dom Letnii Sad, 1999.

Lebina, Nataliia B., and Aleksandr N. Chistikov. *Obyvatel' i reformy: Kartiny povsednevnoi zhizni gorozhan v gody nepa i khrushchevskogo desiatiletiia*. Saint Petersburg: Izdatel'stvo "Dmitrii Bulanin," 2003.

Lih, Lars T. *Bread and Authority in Russia, 1914–1921*. Berkeley: University of California Press, 1990.

Linden, Carl A. *Khrushchev and the Soviet Leadership, 1957–1964*. Baltimore: Johns Hopkins University Press, 1966.

Linz, Susan J., ed. *The Impact of World War II on the Soviet Union*. Totowa, N.J.: Rowman & Allanheld, 1985.

Livschiz, Ann. "Growing Up Soviet: Childhood in the Soviet Union, 1918–1958." Ph.D. diss., Stanford University, 2007.

Medvedev, Roy A., and Zhores A. *Khrushchev: The Years in Power*, translated by Andrew R. Durkin. New York: W. W. Norton, 1978.

Meerovich, Mark G. *Biografiia professii: Ocherki istorii zhilishchnoi politiki v SSSR i ee realizatsii v arkhitekturnom proektirovanii (1917–1941 gg.)*. Irkutsk: Izdatel'stvo IrGTU, 2003.

Messana, Paola. *Kommunalka: Une histoire de l'Union Soviétique à travers l'appartement communautaire*. Paris: J.-C. Lattès, 1995.

McAuley, Mary. *Labour Disputes in Soviet Russia, 1957–1965*. Oxford: Clarendon Press, 1969.

———. *Soviet Politics, 1917–1991*. Oxford: Oxford University Press, 1992.

McCauley, Martin. *The Khrushchev Era, 1953–1964*. New York: Longman, 1995.

Millar, James R., ed. *Politics, Work, and Daily Life in the USSR: A Survey of Former Soviet Citizens*. Cambridge: Cambridge University Press, 1987.

Morton, Henry W. "Who Gets What, When and How? Housing in the Soviet Union." *Soviet Studies* 32 (April 1980): 235–59.

Müller-Dietz, Heinz. "Zur Tätigkeit des Hygienikers F. Erismann in Moskau" (Unveröffentlichte Dokumente und Briefe an M. V. Pettenkofer)." *Clio Medica* 4, no. 3 (1969): 203–10.

Nove, Alec. *An Economic History of the USSR, 1917–1991*. London: Penguin Books, 1992.

Obertreis, Iuliia [Julia]. "'Byvshee' i 'izlishnee'—izmenenie sotsial'nykh norm v zhilishchnom sfere v 1920–1930-e gody." In *Normy i tsennosti povsednevnoi zhizni: Stanovlenie sotsialisticheskogo obraza zhizni v Rossii, 1920–30-e gody*, edited by Timo Vikhavainen. Saint Petersburg: "Neva," 2000.

————. "The Changing Image of the 'Individual' Apartment in the 1920s and 1930s: Individualism versus the Collective in a Soviet Discourse on Housing." Paper presented at the National Convention of the American Association for the Advancement of Slavic Studies, Pittsburgh, 2002.

Osokina, Elena. A. *Ierarkhiia potrebleniia o zhizni liudei v usloviiakh stalinskogo snabzheniia, 1928–1953 gg.* Moscow: Izdatel'stvo MGOY, 1993.

Papernyi, Vladimir. *Architecture in the Age of Stalin: Culture Two*, translated by John Hill and Roann Barris in collaboration with the author. Cambridge: Cambridge University Press, 2002.

————. *Kul'tura Dva*. Moscow: "Novoe literaturnoe obozrenie," 1996.

Parkins, Maurice Frank. *City Planning in Soviet Russia*. Chicago: University of Chicago Press, 1953.

Péteri, György. "Nylon Curtain: Transnational and Transsystemic Tendencies in the Cultural Life of State-Socialist Russia and East-Central Europe." *Slavonica* 10, no. 2 (2004): 113–23.

Pikhoia, Rudolf G. *Sovetskii Soiuz: istoriia vlasti, 1945–1991*. Novosibirsk: Sibirskii khronograf, 2000.

Platz, Stephanie. "Past and Futures: Space, History, and Armenian Identity, 1988–1994." Ph.D. diss., University of Chicago, 1996.

Pyzhikov, Aleksandr. *Khrushchevskaia "Ottepel.'"* Moscow: Olma Press, 2002.

Qualls, Karl D. "Raised from Ruins: Restoring Popular Allegiance through City Planning in Sevastopol, 1943–1954." Ph.D. diss., Georgetown University, 1998.

Reid, Susan E. "Cold War in the Kitchen: Gender and the De-Stalinization of Consumer Taste in the Soviet Union under Khrushchev." *Slavic Review* 61, no. 2 (2002): 211–52.

————. "Destalinization and Taste, 1953–1963." *Journal of Design History* 10, no. 2 (1997): 177–201.

————. "The Khrushchev Kitchen: Domesticating the Scientific-Technological Revolution." *Journal of Contemporary History* 40, no. 2 (2005): 289–316.

————. "Khrushchev Modern: Agency and Modernization in the Soviet Home." *Cahiers du monde russe*, 47, nos. 1–2 (January–June 2006): 227–68.

————. "Who Will Beat Whom? Soviet Popular Reception of the American National Exhibition in Moscow, 1959." *Kritika: Explorations in Russian and Eurasian History* 9, no. 4 (Fall 2008): 855–904.

Reid, Susan E., and David Crowley, eds. *Style and Socialism: Modernity and Material Culture in Post-War Eastern Europe*. Oxford: Berg, 2000.

Rossi, Alice S. "Generational Differences in the Soviet Union." Mimeographed report of the Harvard Interview Project on the Soviet Social System. Cambridge, Mas., 1954. In revised form, unpublished dissertation, Columbia University, 1957.

Ruble, Blair A. "The Applicability of Corporatist Models to the Study of Soviet Politics: The Case of the Trade Unions." *Carl Beck Papers in Russian and East European Studies*, no. 303 (1983).

————. *Leningrad: Shaping a Soviet City*. Berkeley: University of California Press, 1990.

————. *Second Metropolis: Pragmatic Pluralism in Gilded Age Chicago, Silver Age Moscow, and Meiji Osaka*. Washington and New York: Woodrow Wilson Center Press and Cambridge University Press, 2001.

————. *Soviet Trade Unions: Their Development in the 1970s.* Cambridge: Cambridge University Press, 1981.

Schlapentokh, Vladimir. *Public and Private Lives of the Soviet People: Changing Values in Post-Stalin Russia.* New York: Oxford University Press, 1989.

Schultz, Kurt S. "Building the 'Soviet Detroit': The Construction of the Nizhnii-Novgorod Automobile Factory, 1927–1932." *Slavic Review* 49 (Summer 1990): 200–212.

Schwartz, Harry. *Russia's Soviet Economy.* New York, 1965.

Shalin, Dmitri N., ed. *Russian Culture at the Crossroads: Paradoxes of Postcommunist Consciousness.* Boulder, Colo.: Westview Press, 1996.

Shearer, David R. *Industry, State, and Society in Stalin's Russia, 1926–1934.* Ithaca, N.Y.: Cornell University Press, 1996.

Siegelbaum, Lewis H. *Cars for Comrades: The Life of the Soviet Automobile.* Ithaca, N.Y.: Cornell University Press, 2008.

————, ed. *Borders of Socialism: Private Spheres of Soviet Russia.* New York: Palgrave Macmillan, 2006.

Smith, Mark B. "Individual Forms of Ownership in the Urban Housing Fund of the USSR, 1944–64." *Slavonic & East European Review* 86, no. 2 (2008): 283–305.

————. *Property of Communists: The Urban Housing Program from Stalin to Khrushchev.* DeKalb: Northern Illinois University Press, 2010.

Sosnovy, Timothy. *The Housing Problem in the Soviet Union.* New York: Research Program on the USSR, 1954.

————. "The Soviet Housing Situation Today." *Soviet Studies* 11, no. 1 (1959): 1–21.

Stites, Richard. *Revolutionary Dreams: Utopian Vision and Experimental Life in the Russian Revolution.* New York: Oxford University Press, 1989.

————. *The Women's Liberation Movement in Russia: Feminism, Nihilism, and Bolshevism, 1860–1930.* Princeton, N.J.: Princeton University Press, 1990.

Torchinov, Valerii A., and Aleksei M. Leontiuk. *Vokrug Stalina: Istoriko-biograficheskii spravochnik.* Saint Petersburg: Filologicheskii fakyl'tet Sankt-Peterburgskogo gosudarstvennogo universiteta, 2000.

Trushchenko, O. E. *Prestizh tsentra: Gorodskaia sotsial'naia segregatsiia v Moskve.* Moscow: Socio-Logos, 1995.

Urbany, Charles George, Jr. "Accomodating the Masses: Housing Policy and Habitation Under Khrushchev." M.A. thesis, Michigan State University, 1994.

Utekhin, Il'ia. *Ocherki kommunal'nogo byta.* Moscow: OGI, 2001.

Vail, Petr, and Aleksandr Genis. *60-e: Mir sovetskogo cheloveka.* Moscow: Novoe literaturnoe obozrenie, 1998.

Varga-Harris, Christine. "Constructing the Soviet Hearth: Home, Citizenship and Socialism in Russia, 1956–1964." Ph.D. diss., University of Illinois at Urbana-Champaign, 2005.

————. "Homemaking and the Aesthetic and Moral Perimeters of the Soviet Home during the Khrushchev Era." *Journal of Social History* 41, no. 3 (2008): 561–89.

Weiner, Amir. "The Empires Pay a Visit: Gulag Returnees, East European Rebellions, and Soviet Frontier Politics." *Journal of Modern History* 78, no. 2 (2006): 333–76.

————. *Making Sense of War: The Second World War and the Fate of the Bolshevik Revolution*. Princeton, N.J.: Princeton University Press, 2001.

Wesson, Robert G. "Volunteers and Soviets." *Soviet Studies*, no. 3 (January 1964): 231–49.

Yanowitch, Murray. "Soviet Patterns of Time Use and Concepts of Leisure." *Soviet Studies* 15 (July 1963): 17–37.

Zezina, Mariia R. *Sovetskaia zhudozhestvennaia intelligentsiia i vlast' v 1950-e—60-e gody*. Moscow: Dialog-MGU, 1999.

Zubkova, Elena Iur'evna. *Obshchestvo i reformy, 1945–1964*. Moscow: Izdatel'stvo "Rossiia molodaia" tsentr, 1993.

Works outside Soviet History

Appadurai, Arjun, ed. *The Social Life of Things: Commodities in Cultural Perspective*. Cambridge: Cambridge University Press, 1988.

Auslander, Leora. *Taste and Power: Furnishing Modern France*. Berkeley: University of California Press, 1996.

Bauman, John F., Roger Biles, and Kristin M. Szylvian, eds. *From Tenements to the Taylor Homes: In Search of an Urban Housing Policy in Twentieth-Century America*. University Park: Pennsylvania State University Press, 2000.

Bullock, Nicholas. "First the Kitchen—then the Facade." *Journal of Design History* 1, nos. 3–4 (1988): 177–92.

Bullock, Nicholas, and James Read. *The Movement for Housing Reform in Germany and France, 1840–1914*. Cambridge: Cambridge University Press, 1985.

Burnett, John. *A Social History of Housing, 1815–1970*. London: David & Charles, 1978.

de Certeau, Michel. *The Practice of Everyday Life*, translated by Steven Rendall. Berkeley: University of California Press, 1988.

de Certeau, Michel, and Pierre Mayol, and Luce Giard, eds. *The Practice of Everyday Life, Volume 2: Living and Cooking*, translated by Timothy J. Tomasik. Minneapolis: University of Minnesota Press, 1998.

Ci, Jiwei. *Dialectic of the Chinese Revolution: From Utopianism to Hedonism*. Stanford, Calif.: Stanford University Press, 1994.

Desjeux, Dominique, Anne Monjaret, and Sophie Taponier. *Quand les Français déménagent: Circulation des objets domestiques et rituels de mobilité dans la vie quotidienne en France*. Paris: Presses Universitaires de France, 1998.

Eksteins, Modris. *Rites of Spring: The Great War and the Birth of the Modern Age*. New York: Anchor Books, 1990.

Eleb, Monique, and Anne Debarre. *L'Invention de l'habitation moderne: Paris 1880–1914*. Paris: Hazan, 1995.

Fehervary, Krisztina. "American Kitchens, Luxury Bathrooms and the Search for a 'Normal' Life in Postsocialist Hungary." *Ethnos* 67, no. 3 (2002): 369–400.

Geyer, Michael. "The Stigma of Violence, Nationalism, and War in Twentieth-Century Germany," *German Studies Review* 15 (Winter 1992): 75–110.

Guy, Roger. "Down Home: Perception and Reality among Southern White Migrants in Post–World War II Chicago." *Oral History Review* 24 (Winter 1997): 35–52.

Habermas, Jürgen. *The Structural Transformation of the Public Sphere: An Inquiry into a Category of Bourgeois Society*, translated by Thomas Burger and Frederick Lawrence. Cambridge, Mass.: MIT Press, 1996.

Hardy, Charles O., and Robert R. Kuczynski. *The Housing Program of the City of Vienna*. Washington, D.C.: Brookings Institution Press, 1934.

Healy, Maureen. *Vienna and the Fall of the Habsburg Empire: Total War and Everyday Life in World War I*. Cambridge: Cambridge University Press, 2004.

Hirsch, Arnold R. *Making the Second Ghetto: Race and Housing in Chicago, 1940–1960*. Chicago: University of Chicago Press, 1998.

Holston, James. *The Modernist City: An Anthropological Critique of Brasília*. Chicago: University of Chicago Press, 1989.

Lebas, Elizabeth, Susanna Magri, and Christian Topalov. "Reconstruction and Popular Housing after the First World War: A Comparative Study of France, Great Britain, Italy and the United States." *Planning Perspectives* 6, no. 3 (1991): 249–67.

Loyer, François. *Paris Nineteenth Century: Architecture and Urbanism*, translated by Charles Lynn Clark. New York: Abbeville Press, 1988.

Lüdtke, Alf, ed. *The History of Everyday Life: Reconstructing Historical Experience and Ways of Life*, translated by William Templer. Princeton, N.J.: Princeton University Press, 1995.

Poiger, Uta G. *Jazz, Rock, and Rebels: Cold War Politics and American Culture in a Divided Germany*. Berkeley: University of California Press, 2000.

Roth, Jack J., ed. *World War I: A Turning Point in Modern History*. New York: Alfred A. Knopf, 1967.

Scott, James. *Seeing Like a State: How Certain Schemes to Improve the Human Condition Have Failed*. New Haven, Conn.: Yale University Press, 1998.

Shapiro, Ann-Louise. *Housing the Poor of Paris, 1850–1902*. Madison: University of Wisconsin Press, 1985.

———. "Housing Reform in Paris: Social Space and Social Control." *French Historical Studies* 12, no. 4 (1982): 486–507.

Simmons, Dana J. "Minimal Frenchmen: Science and Standards of Living, 1840–1960." Ph.D. diss., University of Chicago, 2004.

Spain, Daphne. "Octavia Hill's Philosophy of Housing Reform: From British Roots to American Soil." *Journal of Planning History* 5, no. 2 (2006): 106–25.

Spensley, J. Calvert. "Urban Housing Problems." *Journal of the Royal Statistical Society* 81, no. 2 (1918): 161–228.

Stieber, Nancy. *Housing Design and Society in Amsterdam: Reconfiguring Urban Order and Identity, 1900–1920*. Chicago: University of Chicago Press, 1998.

Stovall, Tyler. "Sous les Toits de Paris: The Working Class and the Paris Housing Crisis, 1814–1924." *Proceedings of the Annual Meeting of the Western Society for French History* 14 (1987): 265–72.

Sutcliffe, Anthony, ed. *Metropolis, 1890–1940*. Chicago: University of Chicago Press, 1984.

Venkatesh, Sudhir Alladi. *American Project: The Rise and Fall of a Modern Ghetto*. Cambridge, Mass.: Harvard University Press, 2002.

Wall, Richard, and Jay Winter, eds. *The Upheaval of War: Family, Work and Welfare in Europe, 1914–1918*. Cambridge: Cambridge University Press, 1988.

Weintraub, Jeff, and Krishan Kumar, eds. *Public and Private in Thought and Prac-*

tice: Perspectives on a Grand Dichotomy. Chicago: University of Chicago Press, 1997.

Welch, Susan. "Sampling by Referral in a Dispersed Population." *Public Opinion Quarterly* 39 (Summer 1975): 237–45.

Research Aids

Aronov, L. G., et al. *Tsentral'nyi Gosudarstvennyi arkhiv Oktiabr'skoi Revoliutsii, vysshikh organov gosudarstvennoi vlasti i organov gosudarstvennogo upravleniia SSSR: Spravochnik*. Vol. 3. Moscow: Glavnoe arkhivnoe upravlenie pri Sovete Ministrov SSSR, 1990.

Frolic, B. Michael. *An Annotated Bibliography on Soviet Urban and Regional Planning and Administration*. Oakland: Council of Planning Libraries, 1963.

Koslov, Vladimir P., and Patricia K. Grimstead. *Arkhivy Rossii: Moskva i Sankt-Peterburg: spravochnik-obozrenie i bibliograficheskii ukazatel'*. Moscow: "Arkheograficheskii tsentr," 1997.

Mironenko, S. V., ed. *Fondy Gosudarstvennogo arkhiva Rossiiskoi Federatsii po istorii RSFSR: Putevoditel'*. Vol. 2. Moscow: Gosudartsvennyi arkhiv Rossiskoi Federatsii, 1996.

Woll, Stephanie, and Vladimir G. Treml. *Soviet Dissident Literature: A Critical Guide*. Boston: G. K. Hall & Co., 1983.

Index

377